Angel of
Vengeance

~

Angel of Vengeance

~

The "Girl Assassin," the
Governor of St. Petersburg,
and Russia's
Revolutionary World

~

Ana Siljak

ST. MARTIN'S PRESS ✖ NEW YORK

www.stmartins.com

Book design by Jonathan Bennett

Library of Congress Cataloging-in-Publication Data

Siljak, Ana, 1967–
    Angel of vengeance : the "girl assassin," the governor of St. Petersburg, and Russia's revolutionary world / Ana Siljak.—1st ed.
        p.   cm.
    ISBN-13: 978-0-312-36399-4
    ISBN-10: 0-312-36399-0
    1. Zasulich, Vera Ivanovna, 1849–1919.   2. Socialists—Russia—Biography.   3. Women revolutionaries—Russia—Biography.   4. Russia—History—1801–1917.   I. Title.

HX313.8.Z37S55 2008
947.08'1092—dc22
[B]   2007042758

First Edition: March 2008

10   9   8   7   6   5   4   3   2   1

For my parents,
Dragoslav and Dragana Siljak

Contents

Acknowledgments

~~~

I began work on this book in the depths of Harvard University's Widener Library, when I first sought to know more about the enigmatic Vera Zasulich and the incredible story of her now-forgotten trial. From there, my research took me to St. Petersburg and Moscow, and to the documents provided by the archivists of the Russian State Historical Archive, the Plekhanov House collection of the manuscript division of the Russian National Library, the State Archive of the Russian Federation, and the Russian State Archive of Socio-Political History. Later, the collections at Regenstein Library at the University of Chicago and the Hoover Institution Library and Archives at Stanford University proved essential. The staff of the Interlibrary Loan division at Queen's University in Ontario went the extra mile on countless occasions. And Queen's University generously provided assistance for the completion of the book in the form of the Fund for Scholarly and Professional Development.

At every step of this long project, I have been blessed with the support and advice of friends and colleagues. The Russian Studies Workshop at the University of Chicago provided a forum in which I could test my ideas, as did the Department of History Seminar Series at Queen's University. Richard Pipes, my graduate advisor at Harvard University, encouraged the project in its early stages. Leonid Trofimov was an invaluable research assistant. My literary agent, Henry Dunow, was enthusiastic from the beginning, and editors at St. Martin's—Michael Flamini, Vicki Lame, India Cooper, and Julie Gutin—saw the manuscript through to the end with their invaluable expertise. I am very grateful for the ideas, inspiration, and understanding that came from many, including: Jessie Cheney, Janelle Ciraulo, Jonathan Daly, Ben Frommer, Mark Kramer, Eric Lohr, Rebecca Manley, Tom Sanders, Jennifer Siegel, and Andrew Wachtel.

I owe my deepest debts to my family, for their inexhaustible reserves of love and patience. My husband, Jeffrey Collins, sacrificed countless hours in his tireless reading of the manuscript. My brother, Matija, believed I could do it. My children, Theodore and Natalia, endured as best they could for as long as they could remember. Finally, I must offer my profound gratitude to my parents for their unfailing faith and support. It is a great pleasure to dedicate this book to them.

NOTE ON TRANSLITERATION AND DATES

The transliteration of Russian words in the text mostly conforms to the Library of Congress system, with a few modifications. I have not included soft signs and diacritics, and I have retained English spellings for common names and names of well-known political and literary figures, such as Fyodor Dostoyevsky and Tsar Alexander II.

Except in chapter 12 and the epilogue, dates follow the Julian calendar, which was used in Russia until 1918 and is approximately thirteen days behind the Gregorian calendar.

Angel of
Vengeance

~

CHAPTER 1

Assassin

~⁓

Zasulich was not a terrorist. She was the angel of vengeance, and not of terror. She was a victim who voluntarily threw herself into the jaws of the monster in order to cleanse the honour of the party from a moral outrage. Yet this occurrence gave to the Terrorism a most powerful impulse. It illuminated it with its divine aureola, and gave to it the sanction of sacrifice and of public opinion.

—SERGEI KRAVCHINSKII, *UNDERGROUND RUSSIA*[1]

On the evening of January 23, 1878, a few close friends gathered spontaneously at Evtikhii Karpov's small, three-room flat on Rizhkii Street in St. Petersburg. Though sparsely furnished in the typical nomadic revolutionary style, with mismatched creaking chairs and a few wooden-plank beds, Karpov's apartment beckoned with its unending hospitality. On any given night, someone was visiting—taking tea, sharing news, or staying the night on the sitting room floor. The gas stove always had something cooking, and the samovar was always bubbling.

On that evening, however, gloom settled over the kitchen table. Gathered around their teacups, Karpov's guests found they had little to say. Vera Zasulich was particularly silent and withdrawn. Only Masha Kolenkina, in her usual irrepressible manner, occasionally made a joke or a comment, though no one responded. Finally, to dispel the gloom, Nikolai Shevyrev poured beer for everyone and proposed a toast to Vera and Masha, wishing them the best of luck. Without a word, everyone clinked glasses.

To break the silence, Vera asked Nikolai to sing "High Mountain," a mournful Ukrainian folk tune. Shevyrev obligingly began in his gentle tenor, "Yonder stands a mountain high . . . ," and was soon accompanied by Sergei Chubarov's melodious baritone. Vera laid her head on Masha's shoulder and closed her eyes. Around the room, many an eye was filled with tears.

Masha alone refused to submit to the general melancholy. To lift the spirits of her comrades, she asked that they all join in singing "She Lives On,

Our Ukraine," the patriotic Ukrainian tune that, for the group, evoked memories of days spent on the southern steppe lands, preaching revolution to the peasants. Her ploy worked. The conversation turned to reminiscences of those headier times, when Russia seemed poised on the brink of revolt. Soon enough, many began to laugh as Sergei Chubarov regaled the gathering with comical anecdotes about village life in Ukraine.

Not one person yet dared to mention what awaited them the next day, though the thought weighed heavily on all of them. On January 24, 1878, Vera and Masha planned to kill two government officials. For that, most likely, they would pay the ultimate price.[2]

The plot had been months in the making. Vera Zasulich would appear in the office of the governor of St. Petersburg, General Fedor Trepov, during the morning hours when petitioners were granted an audience. This was the best time: While the governor was "receiving," almost any person could walk in off the street and stand in line to present him with a request. And petitioners were invariably a timid, downtrodden lot. An anxious woman would arouse no suspicion in the midst of such company.

Her "petition" was simple. She would present herself as Elizaveta Kozlova, a prospective governess, and would carry a request for a certificate of conduct, a document required by those who sought to teach children. She bought a plain but respectable new dress and hat. In the seams of her clothes she carefully sewed the initials EK, so that they would be discovered during the police search. Most important, she purchased a voluminous gray shawl that was appropriate for the icy winter weather and large enough to conceal a gun. Through a comrade she obtained a six-chamber English Bulldog revolver—it was powerful, but easy to handle and small enough to be hidden in the folds of her clothing. She told her landlady that she was leaving for Moscow for good and gave instructions on where to send any remaining personal effects.[3]

Masha's plan was even simpler. She was to visit the prosecutor Vladislav Zhelekhovskii on the same day. Weeks of surveillance revealed that the prosecutor did not have regular receiving hours, so Masha had to bribe one of his servants to let her into his offices at the appointed time. Like Vera, she planned to hide a revolver under her coat, but she decided not to carry a petition with her. She planned to shoot Zhelekhovskii on sight.[4]

Two simultaneous gunshots, aimed at two government officials, would be fired on the same day. The women had no doubt: January 24, 1878, would be remembered in Russian history.

On the evening of January 23, after the festivities, Vera and Masha returned to Vera's tiny one-bedroom apartment and made their final arrangements in silence. Vera sat and carefully wrote her formal petition to the governor. Both women laid out their clothing for the next day. Then they went to bed.[5]

Up until the moment she laid her head on the pillow, Vera had been remarkably calm. This was no last-minute impulse but a long-deliberated decision, and she had no regrets. She was not afraid. She fully expected that the worst consequences would follow her act: imprisonment, exile, even death. Long before this night, she had mentally forsaken everything in her life. Her only desire was to pass through this "transitional state" so that she could embrace her fate.

But trepidation could not be delayed forever. Sleep eluded Vera that fateful night, as she struggled against a heavy spiritual weight that felt as if it were crushing her chest. Unbidden images flitted through her mind: The governor would approach her, perhaps look her right in the eyes. Mere feet would separate them. Then she would have to pull out the gun, point it at him, and pull the trigger. Despite her anger and hatred, despite her hard determination, that one act suddenly seemed "deathly difficult." It was as if she realized for the first time that she was about to kill a human being.

When she finally drifted into sleep, she was swept into a recurrent nightmare. She dreamed that she was lying in her bed, as if awake, fully conscious of losing her mind. In the dream, something pulled at her, dragged her into a dark corridor and compelled her to scream with all of her might; the urge was so relentless, she ran out of the room and began to scream and scream. Masha woke her up: Vera had cried out in her sleep. She closed her eyes again, but the dream reappeared, enveloping her, dragging her back into the corridor.

Relief only came with the first gray light of dawn. The women quickly got up and began to dress. Vera's thoughts and movements were now mechanical, as if previously rehearsed. She put on her old clothing, so that the new clothes would not arouse the curiosity of the landlady. The large gray shawl was particularly striking, and the landlady, who was up at all hours, would be sure to notice, and to remember when the newspaper accounts appeared. Masha accompanied Vera to the train station and helped her to change her clothes. The two women embraced briefly, and then Vera boarded the train to St. Petersburg. Masha would follow later. They did not know when they would see each other again, if ever.

Vera's thoughts were now silenced, except for the single observation that the streets of the city seemed empty, cold, and dark on that January morning in 1878.

Nineteenth-century travelers to St. Petersburg found a curious mix of the ordinary and the exotic. The city was born in the imagination of Tsar Peter the Great in the very early years of the eighteenth century, when that indomitable ruler decided to take a swamp and transform it into nothing less than a "window to Western Europe." Peter wanted his new city to be thoroughly European—he patterned its streets and canals on the city layout of Amsterdam—and the tsars that followed him remained faithful to his plan, importing architects and masons from Italy and other parts of Europe to design and build graceful mansions, palaces, and gardens. In 1712, when Peter unilaterally declared St. Petersburg the new capital of Russia and summarily ordered a thousand aristocrats to move there, it was widely considered a disease-ridden backwater. But by the end of the nineteenth century, visitors regularly compared St. Petersburg to Paris and London.[6]

By 1878, the city had become a first-rank European capital. Opportunity-seeking Russians and Europeans flocked to it in droves. The streets teemed with all classes and ethnic groups. Modest clerks mingled with aristocrats; high-ranking officials and destitute migrant workers often lived on different floors of the same building. From all over the growing Russian Empire, representatives from subject nationalities came to the capital to do business.[7]

Nevskii Prospekt, St. Petersburg's main thoroughfare, was appropriately grand and opulent, running in a straight line from the Aleksandr Nevskii Monastery at one end to the Admiralty building on the other. Even the most sophisticated of Europeans remarked on the street's "bejeweled" magnificence. Enormously wide, Nevskii was flanked on either side by rows of neatly constructed, pale stucco buildings. Gilded letters on azure or crimson backdrops adorned storefronts, and within the stores, discerning customers could find anything from costly jewels to Persian carpets, silver weapons from the Far East, leather boots, and European artwork. Food was imported from all over the world, and shops sought to tempt passersby with their exotic fruits and varieties of caviar heaped high in the windows.[8]

Nevskii was St. Petersburg's main promenade, the center of the city's social life. By noon on winter days it overflowed with humanity, as if everyone in the city had crowded onto one street. Elegant ladies rode in open carriages, their laps protected with piles of warm fur, while more modest sorts traveled in tiny one-horse cabs that recklessly careened through the crowds. Russian nannies in traditional red headdresses wheeled small carriages containing tightly wrapped babies. Boys in dusty street clothes sold rolls and pirogi from baskets on the sidewalks. Class, nationality, and rank were each marked by appropriate costume: gray coats for the guard officers, dark green for the civil servants, blue caftans for the merchants, glorious sable or black fox for the wealthy women, and plain cotton kerchiefs for the less well-born.[9]

But early on that January morning, when Vera ventured into the center of the city, Nevskii Prospekt was virtually deserted. In the heart of winter, when the nights were endless and bitter, the residents of St. Petersburg rose late. To compensate for the cold and dark, the city had a vibrant and colorful nightlife. Those who could afford it dined at restaurants and played cards at chandelier-lit clubs. Those who could not stayed outside to enjoy skating or sledding on enormous, man-made ice hills, accompanied by brass bands thumping out popular music. But since the winter sun did not rise until after 9:00 A.M., neither did the city. Foreigners complained that it was difficult to get so much as a newspaper before 11:00 in the morning.[10]

Dressed neatly in a new fur cap and thick gray cloak, Vera would have been an odd sight at that hour. Respectable women rarely ventured out so early, and they did not walk. But few were around to take notice. Yawning doormen swept snow off stoops, and *muzhiks*—servants wearing their characteristic high black boots and long shirts—carried pine baskets to the bakeries to fetch fresh bread for breakfast. In their tiny horse-drawn cabs, the *izvoshchiks* slumped over their reins, waiting for their first customers. Everyone else stayed sheltered behind frosted double-paned windows, sipping morning tea.[11]

The governor's apartments were situated directly across from the tall golden Admiralty spire that stood at the top of Nevskii Prospekt and marked the center of St. Petersburg. He lived and worked in the center of Russian officialdom, in close proximity to the Senate Building, the various ministry buildings, and the tsar's sprawling Winter Palace. This was a well-heeled neighborhood, home to the most elegant cafés and clubs. On sunny winter afternoons, the residents of the area strolled in all their finery—the men in gold-braided uniforms and the women in fox-trimmed velvet cloaks.[12]

When Vera appeared at the governor's door, the people who hovered in the entryway were a very different sort. A motley group of petitioners had gathered, a few poor clerks in threadbare overcoats, soldiers in faded military uniforms, and women hunched beneath tattered shawls. They were careful to be extremely punctual—the governor's receiving hours began precisely at 10:00 A.M.[13]

The plight of the petitioner in nineteenth-century Russia was almost medieval. Though bureaucratization had long ago introduced formal procedures for getting a document signed or a passport stamped, much was still done in the time-honored way: by personally presenting a request to an important person. Whether it was something relatively insignificant, like replacing a passport or finding an item of lost mail, or something of crucial importance, like resolving a property dispute or locating an imprisoned family member, formal bureaucratic channels were often useless. Thus did the routine of petitioning grind on as it had for centuries.

Receiving hours in an important official's home often played out like an elaborate court ceremony. As a petitioner, you might be forced to wait for hours until the official appeared. While you waited, it was advisable to carefully craft the wording of your petition, especially if it was a complicated request. Russian officials were known to cut off petitioners as they spoke, or take offense at minor mistakes in wording. And it was wise to speak in tones of the greatest humility, with bowed head and downcast eyes, since any hint of arrogance could inspire an official to reduce a petitioner to tears.[14] When later questioned by the police, the petitioners who waited in Trepov's office on January 24 remembered nothing about Vera Zasulich. One clerk recalled that he had not even looked at the other people in the room, so intently was he rehearsing his petition.[15]

Vera, however, was utterly calm. Quietly standing with the rest of the petitioners in the specially reserved waiting room, she felt confident enough to assist a fellow petitioner, a weepy and poor old woman, who asked Vera to read over a tear-stained document. Testing her nerves, Vera escorted the woman to the guard on duty, asking him to confirm that everything was in order. Her voice did not waver, and she gave no sign of agitation. Her confidence rose.[16]

After what seemed like a long time, an adjutant appeared from behind a door and ushered the petitioners into the governor's grand, wood-paneled reception room. The petitioners barely had time to line up against the back wall when the large, ornate double doors that led to Trepov's private office were flung open, and the governor strode in with his retinue of military officers. He was regally attired in a deep blue general's uniform. Among his array of medals was the Cross of St. Anne, hanging immediately under his chin. Trepov was known for a meticulously cultivated air of importance, constantly frowning as if in deep thought. Unfortunately, his portraits revealed a slightly comical appearance, with long, thick mustaches and a small round head perched on a thin neck.[17]

At that moment, a glitch nearly spoiled Vera's plans. She had intended to fire the gun when the governor approached the person in front of her, but she found herself first in line. For a moment, she was paralyzed. The attention of the officers and the governor was immediately upon her, and her hands held the petition. She did not know how she could reach into her shawl without attracting notice. She almost lost her nerve.[18]

With a deep breath, Vera calmed herself and improvised. She decided to hand the petition to the governor first and then wait until he turned to the next person. As soon as she made this decision, the governor stood directly in front of her, impatiently demanding, "What is your petition?" She quietly murmured, "It's about a certificate of conduct." Without a word, the governor took her formal request, marked it with a pencil, and turned to the next petitioner.

When his back was turned, Vera pulled the revolver out of the folds of her thick cloak. She pulled the trigger twice, then dropped the gun to the floor. A silent pause enveloped the room as everyone froze for a few brief seconds. Then, as the governor screamed and began to collapse to the ground, the room began to whirl with feverish activity. Two guards rushed over to Trepov, catching him in their arms as a dark stain spread on his uniform. The other petitioners fled. A few of Trepov's clerks ran to get the police and the doctor. One of the governor's guards charged toward Vera, enraged, and knocked her to the ground with a tremendous blow to the face. He continued to kick her as she lay motionless on the floor. "The gun, the gun, where is the gun?" someone shouted. It was some time before others finally pulled the guard off Vera and lifted her up.

"Everything happened as I expected" was all that Vera remembered about the scene. "But what was completely unexpected was the fact that I did not feel any pain."

Vera was led into a nearby room for interrogation. Witnesses were surprised at her extraordinary calm: She did not appear angry or deranged and did not attempt to flee or to justify her actions. She cooperated with the police and was invariably polite to the guards and the inspectors. She remained in constant command of herself, answering only the questions she wished to answer and otherwise maintaining an unyielding silence.

"And where did you learn to shoot like that?" one of the guards asked her.

"I just taught myself," she answered coolly. "It's not a great science."

The inspector who first appeared on the scene was Alexander Kabat. Vera would later remember that *he* seemed nervous—he approached her hesitantly and spoke quietly, as if fearing to disturb her. Pale and small, he had just recovered from an illness, and she noticed that his hands shook. He told Vera apologetically that she had to undergo a thorough search.

"You'll have to find a woman to do it," Vera told him.

Perplexed, Kabat remained silent for a moment. Vera directed him to use an official midwife; one could usually be found at the local police station. But the young inspector was still unsure. What if she had another weapon on her? What if she shot someone else in the meantime?

"If you are that afraid," Vera said dryly, "then perhaps you'd better tie me up."

The insolence of the remark was lost on Kabat. Again, he was merely baffled. A comical moment ensued; he wondered what he could tie her with, and she suggested an ordinary handkerchief.

As he rummaged through his pockets for a handkerchief, he managed to state his first question. "Why did you shoot him?" he asked abruptly. Vera spoke the only words of explanation that she would offer before her trial: "For Bogoliubov."

News of Vera's crime spread rapidly down Nevskii Prospekt, which was by now at the peak of its daily commotion. In front of the governor's residence a large crowd quickly gathered, necks craning to see past the guard each time the door opened. At the back of the building, a parade of elegant carriages rolled in as aristocrats and city officials arrived to pay their respects to the governor—and, of course, to get a glimpse of the young woman who had pulled a revolver out of a large gray shawl.

Military men and officials filled the reception hall of the residence. The public prosecutor and the minister of the interior arrived and could not resist peering, along with the others, into the adjacent room where Vera was being questioned. In the meantime, in Trepov's bedroom, the top surgeons in the city consulted grimly about his wounds. One bullet was lodged in the front of his left hip and would prove difficult to remove.[19]

Suddenly there was a commotion in the foyer. With effort, the crowds parted, and into the hall moved the entourage of the sovereign of the Russian Empire. Regally attired in full military dress, Tsar Alexander II nonetheless looked like a weary old man. Nearly twenty years before, he had assumed the throne accompanied by optimism and the cheers of the best and most intellectual classes of society. He had been anointed the "tsar-reformer," the man who had freed Russia's serfs and the author of liberalizing reforms in the military, the judiciary, and the educational system. But in recent years, he had become the target of the Russian intelligentsia's wrath. Revolutionary movements plagued his empire; uprisings had flared in Warsaw, Moscow, and St. Petersburg. He must have had a premonition that the shooting of Trepov was not a random crime. Observers recalled an empty, drained look in his eyes.[20]

Trepov, despite fearing for his life, could not resist the opportunity to curry favor with the sovereign. "This bullet might have been meant for you," Trepov gasped weakly, "and I was happy to take it for you." It is said that Alexander, greatly displeased with this melodrama, never visited Trepov again.[21]

Within a few days, every major Russian and European newspaper carried news of the shooting. In Moscow, St. Petersburg, New York, London, Berlin, and Paris, the story was followed with interest. Soon, the identity of the would-be assassin was revealed—she was the noblewoman Vera Zasulich, the daughter of the deceased Captain Ivan Zasulich. Her mysterious comment about her motive was also explained: Six months before the shooting, a cruel incident had taken place in the House of Preliminary Detention in St. Petersburg. General Trepov had ordered a young prisoner named Arkhip Bogoliubov to be flogged with birch rods for failing to doff his cap in the presence of the governor. Vera, it seemed, had sought to avenge Bogoliubov's humiliation.[22]

Initially a wave of shock and confusion swept through Russia, and the repercussions were felt abroad. The incident pointed to an as yet undefined Russian crisis. The *St. Petersburg Register* declared that the city was agitated by "the unusual and horrifying incident," which "emphasized domestic discontent." *The New York Times* found St. Petersburg "greatly excited" by the news, and *The Times* of London reported that the act was met with a "profound and most painful sensation" in Russia. The French *Le Temps* proclaimed that the incident was "as extraordinary as it was deplorable."[23]

Soon, however, decorous disapproval gave way to curiosity and fascination. The newspapers fueled an intense interest in the young woman who had gone to such great lengths to conceal her identity and had managed to hide a pistol under her shawl. And then there were the rumors that she had done it for another, unknown, man. In Russia, journalists spoke of Vera's ostensible long revolutionary career, of troubling anonymous threats sent through the mail, and of the police's intensive efforts to find all accomplices to the crime. Abroad, newspapers published speculations about this "young and educated woman" who was nonetheless an "emissary of a secret society" and, even more interesting, a "nihilist."[24]

Newspaper accounts only stimulated further gossip. In Russia, within the highest social circles, even Trepov's friends were morbidly intrigued by the young "villainess." The assassination attempt became the topic of the winter season. Around town, in the wealthiest homes, at brilliant dinner parties and balls, society men and women gossiped about the story that seemed to have all of the elements of the first installment of a serialized Dostoyevsky novel. Bogoliubov had to be Vera's lover, everyone assumed, and there had to be more to this tale of a prisoner's flogging and an angry woman's revenge. How did Vera come to this desperate act? Why was Bogoliubov imprisoned?

The Countess Palen, wife of Minister of Justice Konstantin Palen, took full advantage of her husband's access to the case files, to great effect. In the Palens' ballroom (recently renovated to the tune of eighteen thousand rubles), she caused a delicious stir by passing around copies of Vera's official police photograph, taken while Vera was still draped in her notorious shawl. Vera looked every bit the mysterious assassin. The photograph made the ball a tremendous success, guests later admitted.[25] At a dinner party held by the wealthy aristocrat Maria Shubina, conversation centered around Trepov and the rumors that he habitually tortured prisoners. To the shock and delight of the table, an old general declared that Vera Zasulich was nothing less than a model of feminine bravery and self-sacrifice.[26]

Among ordinary Russians, sympathy for Vera was still greater. Her youth and air of innocence charmed the Russian public. She became, in certain quarters, a heroine of the people. Her victim was nothing more than a government official, most likely a "thief" and a "bloodsucker." As one Russian in Geneva wrote to his friend in St. Petersburg, the assassination attempt was, perhaps, a vain gesture. After all, he declared, "Kill one idiot, and two take his place."[27]

As the story of Bogoliubov's flogging spread, the details were wildly exaggerated: that Bogoliubov had been flogged unconscious, that it was done publicly, in the prison courtyard, and that Trepov had personally slammed the birch rods onto Bogoliubov's back.[28] There were even a few popular verses composed in Vera's honor, one of which began:

The avenging shot was fired
God's whip came cracking down[29]

On the outskirts of St. Petersburg, where the pavement ended and the wide boulevards became muddy roads, was a world very different from the glittering center of the capital. Here resided the swelling horde of workers in St. Petersburg's mills and factories. Rows and rows of dilapidated wooden tenements recalled some of the most blighted slums of Dickensian England. Apartments and even single rooms were subdivided to accommodate several families, who often slept four or more to a bed. There was no running water; sewage ran through the courtyards and leaked into apartments on lower floors. Even amid such filth, rents were so expensive that twelve- to fifteen-hour workdays barely covered them. Some workers lived for weeks on nothing more than black bread, boiled cabbage soup, and whatever scraps of rotting meat they could find in the local markets.[30]

In late January, factory owners turned over to the Russian police leaflets they found on factory floors and in workers' dormitories. Bearing only the stamp of the outlawed "Free Russian Press," these anonymous tracts addressed the workers of the city, telling them of Vera Zasulich, who had fired the first shot in the battle for "human rights, and the establishment of peace and humanity on earth." By avenging the flogging of a prisoner, Vera had shown that "tyrants are not almighty." What other recourse did she have, the pamphlets asked, in a society "slavishly silent and oppressed?" Vera was not acting for one man; she was acting in the name of everyone who was poor and downtrodden. She was nothing less than a saint: "Your path will not be strewn with roses, oh fearless Russian heroine! Your path is one already sprinkled with the blood of martyrs."[31]

On the day of the assassination attempt, Evtikhii Karpov arrived at his apartment to find Masha Kolenkina weeping inconsolably in the arms of one of her comrades. It appeared that her bribe had failed to do its work, and she had been refused entrance into Zhelekhovskii's residence. When she arrived at precisely 11:00 A.M., the prosecutor's maidservant told Masha that he was not at home. Her assassination attempt had failed.[32]

Vera must have been distressed by the lack of news about her friend. She was now alone in the spotlight, Russia's first female assassin.

CHAPTER 2

Dreams of Martyrdom

~⁓

In the whole range of history it would be difficult, and, perhaps, impossible to find a name which, at a bound, has risen into such universal and undisputed celebrity. . . .

Who was this dazzling and mysterious being? her numerous admirers asked each other. And everyone painted her according to his fancy.

People of gentle and sentimental dispositions pictured her as a poetical young girl, sweet, ecstatic as a Christian martyr, all abnegation, and love.

Those who rather leaned towards Radicalism, pictured her as a Nemesis of modern days, with a revolver in one hand, the red flag in the other, and emphatic expressions in her mouth; terrible and haughty—the Revolution personified.

Both were profoundly mistaken.

—SERGEI KRAVCHINSKII, *UNDERGROUND RUSSIA*[1]

Vera Zasulich was not a conventional beauty. Her nose was slightly too large, her mouth too narrow. She was thin but broad-shouldered and lanky, like an adolescent girl. And she steadfastly refused to accentuate her most attractive features. Instead of tastefully arranging her hair to frame her face, as was common for women at the time, she let it hang loose around her shoulders or tucked it back behind her ears. Because she lacked the graceful movements of an ideal noblewoman, she was considered clumsy and awkward. Her clothing was notorious. She often received guests in a disheveled state, with uncombed hair, a stained dress, and scuffed workmen's boots. One admirer forever remembered her first encounter with Vera. The revolutionary heroine was dressed like a destitute vagrant, wearing what could only be described as "a length of fabric, with a hole cut in the center for the head, and two holes on each side for the sleeves."[2]

Nonetheless, all who met her found her surprisingly alluring. There was something fascinating about her elusive and enigmatic personality. On the one hand, she was modest, almost painfully shy. She avoided social events and public gatherings; she disliked ordinary conversations with strangers, and many found that she would not look them in the eye. Later in life, as one of the most famous women in Europe, she hid herself from public view, preferring to live a life of isolation where she could spend hours wandering the countryside or burying herself in dense socialist tomes. In the words of one friend, it appeared that she wished "to be as unnoticeable as possible."[3]

On the other hand, her large gray eyes were intelligent, dark, and almost mysterious, and some saw in them a deep warmth. Her friends and admirers were drawn to her precisely because her silence seemed to hide a passionate intensity and ineffable spiritual wisdom. Though she was not an eloquent woman—her voice was too shrill, her gestures too wild—her life experiences were so extraordinary that her stories held her audience rapt. After the shooting of Trepov, those who spoke with her experienced the thrill of being in the presence of a living paradox: a modest, gentle assassin.

The day after the shooting, Tsar Alexander II received a lengthy report on Vera's past. After reading of her long career of arrests, imprisonment, and exile, he too was puzzled by this biography of a quiet and modest noblewoman turned terrorist. In the margin of the police report, he scribbled just one, odd question: "What kind of woman is her mother?"[4]

Vera's life began in the quiet of the western Russian province of Smolensk, in one of the northeastern districts, near the city of Gzhatsk.[5] Even by the standards of the nineteenth century, the area was impoverished and backward. Gzhatsk had once been an important commercial city; its wharf on the Gzhat River was a center for the Russian river trade. But by 1860, all that remained of the region's former glory could be found in the ruins of the once elegant two- and three-story homes along the riverfront, their windows now shattered and their roofs rotted away. The city itself was tiny, and it appeared nearly abandoned, with wide streets that led to two small churches and a marketplace.[6] All of the splendor of the region was reserved for the surrounding countryside, which was mostly untouched and had a typical Russian beauty. The flat plain stretched infinitely into the horizon like a calm sea, with rare silvery patches of birch trees breaking up the limitless meadowland. Noble estates dotted the landscape, surrounded by villages arranged in neat little clusters of thatch-roofed dwellings.[7]

One hundred miles of post road stretched between Gzhatsk and Moscow. In nineteenth-century terms, these cities were like separate worlds. Even on the best winter days, when the roads were frozen and could be quickly traversed, twenty miles might consume a full day's travel. In the spring and summer months, when sudden rains created treacherous and foul-smelling torrents of water and mud, travel was impossible. Most decisively, Gzhatsk was part of the peaceful and slow-moving Russian countryside.[8]

Vera's maternal grandfather, Mikhail Alexandrov, had been a prosperous nobleman, owner of a sprawling and well-run estate. Her mother, Feoktista, was sheltered in the comfortable confines of a large Russian manor and spent her childhood mastering the refined pursuits of art, French poetry, and needlepoint. She needed no other skills. Her two older sisters were highly eligible young ladies, with handsome dowries, and Feoktista had every reason to expect the same.[9]

But catastrophe swept these expectations away. Mikhail Alexandrov died and, by Russian custom, his extensive lands were divided equally among his six sons. Feoktista and her younger sister inherited almost nothing, just a small plot of land and forty serfs. To support themselves, they had to build a modest cottage, hire a few servants, plant household gardens, and supervise the work of their peasants. The two privileged and sheltered women suddenly dropped into the lower stratum of the Russian noble world.[10] Poorer landowners labored relentlessly just to put food on the table: They rose at dawn to inspect the stables and then trudged across muddy fields to the peasant villages, where they progressed from hut to hut, hearing complaints, visiting the sick, and giving food and other goods to the impoverished. Some of the most destitute Russian noblemen were indistinguishable from peasants and harvested the grain side by side with the serfs. At the end of the day, they sat by candlelight to manage the family accounts and make careful lists of basic household needs. In their meager spare time, they took care of the darning and the washing of clothes and linens. In hard times, they were forced to forego the luxuries of sugar and white flour, or to sell homemade pastries, cakes, and handkerchiefs just for a little extra money.[11]

Feoktista's pampered childhood never prepared her for such grueling work. Some energetic single or widowed women were able to overcome barriers of gender and upbringing and assume independent responsibilities with zeal. But Feoktista lacked such willpower. One of her daughters remembered her as good, but "weak and characterless." When her sister died, Feoktista did not know where to turn. More than anything else, she wanted a husband to care for her.[12]

Hope, if not love, came in the form of Captain Ivan Zasulich, an army officer from a neighboring village. In Feoktista's younger days, Zasulich would have been an unfortunate match. He arrived in Gzhatsk with a clouded reputation, and few knew much about his past. He had once served in St. Petersburg, and he hinted of glorious military exploits and daring feats in unnamed battles. Later in life, Feoktista displayed his medals to her children, boasting of his bravery. But when Ivan arrived in Gzhatsk, he had already been demoted and was an ordinary guard on the post road that led through the city. Gossip blamed alcoholism. Still, Feoktista had little property and no dowry—Captain Zasulich was the best she could hope for. He was smart, energetic, and willing to take care of her. They were married.[13]

For a while, Feoktista was satisfied. Ivan Zasulich retired from the military and poured his energy into managing her estate. Feoktista devoted herself to raising a family, bearing four children in quick succession: one son and three daughters. But slowly Ivan's demons returned. He slid back into alcoholism and soon subjected the household to his terrible rages. Though he adored his son, he disliked his daughters, and beat his eldest daughter, Ekaterina, so frequently that Feoktista quietly sent her away to live with relatives. Marriage had been bought at a price.[14]

Even this fragile stability was not to last. As was so common in those days, Ivan caught an ordinary cold that soon became fatal. At the time of his death, Feoktista's four children ranged in age from three to nine, and she was pregnant with her fifth. If her life before Ivan had been difficult, it was now desperate. How could she manage an estate and feed her five children? She did the only thing she could: She begged her relatives to take her daughters, to care for them and give them a proper upbringing.[15]

Vera Zasulich, born in 1849, was only three years old when her father died, and she most likely had no memory of him. In 1853, she was taken to Biakolovo, an estate owned by her mother's cousins, some seven miles away. She would never live at home again. In Feoktista's mind, it was for the best, but Vera never forgave her mother. She would always feel that she had been abandoned into the care of those who had never loved her.[16]

~

In the gray, ramshackle house with a mezzanine and with rooms covered in dark blue wallpaper flecked with gold stars, everything reminded one of the French. There was a fissure on the drawing room door, which, according to legend, was made by a French officer's rifle butt in 1812, when a division of the enemy stopped here to rest on their march toward Moscow, "and," as was always added with indignation, "they used the sitting room as a stable." The furniture was also that old, though reupholstered, and French soldiers

probably sat on it as well. I always wanted to envisage that quiet, noble es-
tate with horses in the drawing room and French soldiers in the sitting
room, but I couldn't, I didn't have the imagination. In front of the house
there was a flower garden with lilacs, peonies, and roses. Then came a large
pond with geese and ducks, and along its banks lay the large post road to
Moscow, lined with two rows of leafy birch trees. Behind the house was a
garden so old and large that its fame spread throughout the whole region,
even though every estate had a large garden of its own. The endless rows of
linden trees were so thick that neither sun nor rain could penetrate them,
and the trees themselves were so large that one could rarely wrap one's arms
around them.

— VERA ZASULICH, "Masha"[17]

Among Vera's voluminous personal papers, among the impenetrable writings on socialist theory, illegible notes on Marx and Hegel, and prolific correspondence with leading Russian socialists, is found just one lengthy work of fiction. Simply entitled "Masha," it is an unfinished short story, most likely written in 1880, a few years after Vera's name became known throughout Europe. Strikingly, it tells the poignant tale of a young orphaned girl, raised by relatives on a provincial Russian estate. Dependent on the charity of others, Masha is condemned to a lowly existence in the haughty world of the Russian nobility. From passages in Vera's memoirs, and from the painful details in the tale itself, it is clear that the story closely follows Vera's own.

In "Masha" we most likely catch glimpses of Vera's adoptive home. It was a beautiful property, especially the carefully cultivated fruit gardens and wilder surrounding forests. Like so many provincial estates, the manor itself was slightly ramshackle; additions were added on almost as afterthoughts, and interiors were decorated haphazardly with worn furniture from the eighteenth century mixed with newer pieces bought recently in Moscow. Everything from the tall trees in the gardens to the clutter in the living rooms was meant to convey a sense of leisurely domesticity and casual comfort.[18]

Biakolovo was managed by two of Vera's distant relatives, women who were seen as pillars of good sense and wisdom. They understood it as their duty to welcome Vera into their home and to provide her with a proper upbringing. They were determined that Vera would never experience need and would never feel the anxiety of her mother's struggle for subsistence. She would become a respectable noblewoman, equipped with all of the proper refinements. She would be happy.

"Oh the happy, happy, never to be recalled days of childhood!" So runs the first sentence of Leo Tolstoy's novelistic memoir, *Childhood, Boyhood, Youth*. Toward the end of the nineteenth century, as the Russian country estate and its way of life were disappearing, noblemen remembered their childhoods with fondness and nostalgia. The Russian estate was recalled as a kind of lost paradise, a lovely world surrounded by the splendor of nature and filled with the warmth of familial love.[19]

Russia's provincial nobles did not live the extravagant, decadent lifestyles of the urban aristocracy. Theirs was not the world populated with hundreds of servants, where exotic meals were served on gold plates and guests were entertained with theatrical performances put together by serf actors. The provinces remained a more modest place, one in which gardens were smaller and wilder, manors had lower ceilings and fewer rooms, and servants lived as part of the family. Instead of elegance, the country estate strove for comfort. Rooms were furnished with old and well-worn chairs, stuffed with nut husks and covered in calico. Long rugs were spread over scuffed parquet floors, and rooms were filled with live plants and odd collections of knickknacks such as antique weapons, coins, crystal, and china figurines. Brick or tile stoves generated a cozy warmth, especially if servants diligently tended to the flames.[20]

Meals were remembered with particular fondness, as they were at the center of family life. Everyone was expected to gather around a table laden with homemade goods. Cheeses, breads, and meats were all produced on the estate, and the vast gardens usually boasted at least one well-kept orchard that grew apples, pears, and, in some latitudes, even oranges. Manors were often famed for producing a particular delicacy: pistachio nougat, honey cakes, or pickled plums.[21]

Noble children were, for the most part, openly spoiled. Nannies, servants, and parents either lavished affection on them or, at worst, left them alone to do as they pleased. Few tasks were required of the child of the manor, beyond the morning lessons given by a tutor or governess. Children were positively encouraged not to get underfoot. Memoirs recount hours of doing almost nothing—picnicking in fragrant meadows and lazily watching the butterflies, staring out of windows at the gathering piles of winter snow, playing hide-and-seek in spacious attics and winding corridors. Tolstoy remembered the long winter evenings of his youth, when he would curl up on a large chair in the sitting room and sit quietly until he drifted off to sleep, lulled by the murmuring sound of his mother's voice. Time seemed to stretch into infinity.[22]

Nobles who left the estate for school or business tended to carry with them the memories of this lost Eden. The rigid discipline of school, the bustle of city life, or the pressures of business were contrasted with the simplicity and calm of the estate. Often, a visit home would recapture the innocence of childhood. Toward the end of the nineteenth century, and in the beginning of the twentieth, noblemen like Vladimir Glinskii published lengthy memoirs filled with nostalgic recounting of times past. Glinskii remembered how a return home meant a washing away of all the concerns and anxieties of real life: "The country air dispersed all nightmares, healed all pains, and calmed the nerves." Meals, as usual, soothed the soul. "A welcoming murmur comes from the samovar, and rolls, butter and milk and other home-grown foods are tastefully arranged on the table. All feel a kind of satisfaction, a sense of country contentment, health and peace." In "Masha," Vera wrote of how coming home meant going back in time: "It seems to you as if you had left only yesterday . . . it seems that the years do not pass and instead one and the same long, idle, ordinary day extends from time immemorial into a future which has no end."[23]

The quiet, slow, and easygoing ways of provincial life were not for everyone. For some, this world was tedious, stuffy, and drearily conventional. The Russian gentry insisted on their proud role as guardians of the country's traditional values. The most self-righteous among them claimed to be pillars of provincial society and ran their estates as models of order and propriety. A well-to-do nobleman poured resources into his fields, gardens, and household, so that they might be seen as above reproach in the local community. Noble men and women were expected to perform their roles diligently: Men were the patriarchs and leaders of the household; women were the household managers and moral guides.[24]

Decorum was the foundation of gentry life and was rigidly observed. A proper nineteenth-century Russian lady commanded distinct social graces: She sat straight, with her head held high; she spoke politely and softly; she kept her collars and sleeves tidy, her hair neat, her fingernails clean. She could recite poetry and liberally pepper her conversation with French phrases. She was infallibly polite with everyone, but she was familiar only with her equals. If she was a wife and mother, she was gentle and caring toward her family and firm with her servants and maids.

It was a rigidly hierarchical world. Wealthier noble families looked down their noses at their poorer counterparts and felt free to treat them with disrespect. The poverty, dirt, and disorder of a declining noble home were condemned as a betrayal of class standards. Poorer nobles were castigated for failing to discipline their servants, neglecting to dust their furniture, ignoring the refinements of music and art, and, worst of all, posturing as the equals of their neighbors. "Nobles of the second level," wrote one noble-woman, ". . . although possibly good people, in terms of their spiritual attributes were not counted as society."[25]

In her adoptive home, Vera immediately felt her second-class status. Her mother was an impoverished widow who had married beneath her, and Vera was stigmatized as the product of this poor match. Vera's wealthy relatives took her in out of a sense of charity and even a sense that it was their duty to "rescue" the young girl from the scandal of noble poverty. They wished to turn this "wild" young girl into a proper lady. Vera captures this in her poignant short story: Masha is keenly aware of her position in her new home and of the expectation that she will be humble and grateful for the benevolence of her adoptive family.[26]

Almost from the day she arrived at her new home, Vera rebelled against these conventions. Like the fictional Masha, Vera seemed a cross between "a peasant girl and a tomboy." Invariably her dresses were torn or stained, and toys and dishes were broken or lost. Even elegant clothes hung shapelessly on her thin frame. And her thick, unmanageable brown hair stood on end no matter how many times she was reminded to tame it. She refused to do her French lessons; she ignored the finer points of etiquette. She even attempted to undermine the upbringing of her cousins, leading them into wild scrapes in the garden and encouraging them to rebel against their parents.[27]

The tranquillity of the estate was disrupted by this intransigent child who refused to become a proper lady. She was scolded; she was sent to bed without supper. Vera's aunts incessantly reminded her that her family was poor and that she could have no expectation of an income or a marriage to support her for life. For a girl in her position, proper etiquette was essential for her social survival. "I simply do not know what will become of her," one aunt laments in Vera's story, and one suspects that Vera heard those words much too often.[28]

Inevitably Vera became a bitter child. Her adopted family fed her, clothed her, and offered her an education, but it never made her feel welcome. She was expected to be grateful for her rescue from a life of poverty. She could not demand more. Estranged from her family, Vera developed a sullen demeanor, refused to look adults in the eye, and declined to speak unless spoken to. "The older I grew," she later recalled in her memoirs, "the more I became convinced that I was indeed an alien: I didn't belong. No one was ever affectionate toward me, no one kissed me or sat me on their lap, no one called me tender names."[29]

Throughout her childhood, Vera sought places of refuge where she could escape from the ceaseless nagging and cold disdain of her adoptive family. Her first love was the vast forested garden in the back of the estate. As soon as she was released from her daily lessons, Vera lived in the outdoors, and only the most severe weather could drive her inside. On all country estates, whether small or large, the endless gardens beckoned. Children skated and sledded in the depths of winter, swam and climbed trees in the summer. Particularly in warmer weather, Russian children would leave the house in the morning and return only in the evening, for supper.[30]

Vera's favorite season was the summer. For a few brief weeks every year, she would return to her mother's home. Vera's sister Alexandra remembered the joy of these reunions. The two sisters would do little but wander through the Gzhatsk countryside. Packing loaves of fresh bread in napkins, they set out early in the morning to explore the nearby woods, swim in the local ponds, or climb trees. If they got hungry, they ate the blackberries and raspberries that grew wild everywhere. From time to time they would return home with large bouquets of wildflowers plucked from the meadows.[31]

Roaming the countryside, noble children inevitably wandered into villages and spent hours playing with peasants. In a society of rigid social distinctions, an exception was made for the young. Noble parents rarely monitored the whereabouts of their children, and even if they did, they turned a blind eye to the wild games their children learned from their peasant counterparts. Often, it was the peasants who taught noble boys and girls how to climb trees, fish, swim, and forage for berries and mushrooms.

Vera felt far more at home with the rough, honest, but good-natured peasant boys than she did with her own cousins. Vera's young eyes saw village poverty as liberating—peasants seemed entirely freed from the conventions that governed upper-class life. The servants' children told her everything, gossiped about life on the estate, and treated her as a companion. Later, the memories of her peasant friends led to feelings of solidarity with their plight. "I always considered myself one of the poor," she would write in her memoirs, "at first against my will, with a feeling of deep resentment, and then, later, almost with pride."[32]

During these restless years of lonely roaming through the countryside and the peasant villages, Vera increasingly yearned for freedom from the monotony of provincial life. She chafed against the quiet and stability that so many of her class found comforting. She craved a more meaningful existence, one beyond the propriety of clean cuffs and starched collars. Unable to find her place within the Russian nobility, she believed she was destined for another fate, for a higher purpose.

~

I would see old men lying on the straw, friendless and famished, while all through the long summer days the entire population strong enough to work was in the fields, where they would toil until the night fell. The little children, dirty, emaciated, would be quarreling in the mud and dust, eating from the same dish with the dogs, and even the pigs. Every Sunday I would see the peasants going into our church, praying with fervor, pouring out their tears, and giving their last kopeck in the name of God, that there would be a better life in the next world, since that was their only hope of happiness."

—EKATERINA BRESHKO-BRESHKOVSKAIA,
"Memories of Prison and Later Life"[33]

When asked how a wealthy noblewoman could become a revolutionary, Ekaterina Breshko-Breshkovskaia, a Russian radical well known in the United States, explained that she simply could not endure the contrast between her life of comfort and that of the wretched peasant serfs who toiled on her family's estate. On one side was the carefree, easy world in which food was plentiful, houses were warm and clothing was luxurious, and hard work was unknown. On the other side was a world of grinding, ceaseless labor, of too many hungry mouths, of dirt and disease, and of tiny, smoky peasant huts into which whole families crowded for warmth.[34]

There was no doubt—the idyllic country estate was a parasite on the Russian peasant village. Before serfdom was abolished in 1861, Russian estates depended entirely on serf labor. Like plantation slaves of the American South, Russian serfs were property, bought and sold at will. Landowning wealth was partly measured in the number of "souls" a noble owned. Though American slave owners rarely owned more than nineteen slaves, Russian landowners of middle wealth had as many as five hundred serfs. Some of the most prosperous aristocrats boasted of owning nearly a hundred thousand souls.[35]

Whether bought, sold, or given as gifts, serfs either tilled the soil or served their masters in the household. In most regions, nondomestic serfs would work their masters' land and, in exchange, would be given land to farm for themselves. Usually serfs spent three days of each week on their master's land, followed by three days on their own. Luckier serfs would simply pay annual rent, in goods or cash.[36]

Serfdom also supplied the armies of servants that noblemen often maintained on their estates. Serfs were gardeners, cooks, maids, butlers, nursemaids, and nannies. The wealthiest families employed more than two hundred serfs as domestic servants. Most cooked and cleaned, but larger estates had serf choirs, orchestras, and even theaters. Young peasant children were tapped at a young age and then trained, sometimes by specially imported foreign teachers, in a particular art. Nikolai Sheremetev, one of Russia's wealthiest noblemen, was famed for his estate's theater, which boasted operatically trained soloists, set and costume designers, and even directors, all extracted from his extensive villages. Serf artisans and craftsmen were also common, and sometimes whole villages would be trained in woodworking, painting, gilding, sculpting, or metalworking. Estates proudly displayed paintings, vases, and tapestries by these artists.[37]

For the vast majority of serfs, however, life was a relentless struggle for existence. From an estate balcony one could often look out across the surrounding countryside at the clustered village huts where the peasants lived. It was an entirely different world. An ordinary peasant household (which typically numbered eight or nine people) often crowded into a single, thatch-roofed hut, a meager dwelling that had little more than a dirt floor, a table and a few stools, and straw mattresses for beds (if there were any beds at all). At the center of the hut stood the enormous wooden stove, for heating and cooking. Since most huts had no chimneys, smoke would fill the hut and blacken the walls; the only remedy was to open the door periodically to let some of the smoke out.

In the winter, life in the peasant hut was stifling. Bitter cold forced not only the entire household but also the family livestock inside for warmth. Cold muddy floors were covered in animal excrement, and the stench of animals and smoke was overpowering. Cockroaches filled the interior and were so common that some peasants even considered them good luck. Peasants' meals mostly consisted of porridge or bread, and the few vegetables grown in a kitchen garden. Meat was rarely eaten more than once a week. Daily toil was difficult and relentless, six days a week. In the summer months, peasants often worked from the first light of dawn to as late as nine or ten o'clock at night. During harvest times, serfs worked on Sundays as well.[38]

As with slavery in the United States, public horror at serfdom was stoked by tales of terrible abuse by sadistic landlords. Beatings were common, and serfs could legally be flogged for a number of offenses, including theft, flight, and mere laziness. Many landowners simply assumed that corporal punishment was the only language peasants understood. The lash was seen as the surest method of ensuring productivity.[39]

In fact, serfs did not necessarily oppose corporal punishment on principle. Particularly in cases of theft or assault, peasants were quite happy to have the perpetrators flogged, and flogging was a punishment much preferred to fines or imprisonment, which could ruin a serf's family. Serfs often were habituated to a certain brutality; the horror of corporal punishment was felt more keenly by the more humanitarian noblemen, who saw the beatings and floggings as a degradation of human dignity. Lev Obolenskii, an ordinary Russian liberal whose grandfather was a steward of a wealthy estate, remembered an incident in which his grandfather personally supervised the flogging of a serf. He never forgot the pleadings—"Have mercy, have mercy, I won't ever again!"—or the "animal-like screams" of the beaten man. Obolenskii's disgust was compounded by amazement, for his grandfather was a cultivated man who loved poetry and never once laid a hand on his own children. How could such a man treat the serfs like chattel?[40]

For most opponents of serfdom, by far the worst abuses were the rapes and sexual exploitation of the serf women. It is impossible to know how often serf women were abused, since the evidence is sparse. But the reports that did surface are appalling. One estate manager in Saratov, an Osip Vetvitskii, was, by his neighbor's accounts, a charming and well-bred young nobleman. He had taken a dilapidated estate and turned it into a productive enterprise, all without exploiting the peasants. The serfs, previously malnourished and clad in filthy rags, were now prospering under his new management. For his tireless efforts, Vetvitskii was rewarded with popularity and even the notice of authorities in St. Petersburg. Only much later, after the serfs were emancipated, was he accused of having seduced and raped well over two hundred of the women and girls on the estate. Former serfs charged that he had sent a high percentage of the men away to serve in the military, to give him easier access to their wives.[41] Stories of serf harems were also rampant. One wealthy landowner, P. A. Koshkarov, not only kept a personal harem of twelve to fifteen serf girls but also brought the girls out to entertain his male guests.[42]

Serfs did not always endure these abuses lightly. Riots and revolts occurred from time to time and often had to be put down with considerable force. Flight was also common, and sometimes whole villages would conspire to flee from a particular estate.[43] And, more rarely, some of the most abusive landlords became victims of violence or even murder. One landowner particularly prone to whipping her serfs was attacked while in her coach and severely beaten. In Saratov province, at least three landowners were murdered by their serfs in the 1840s, one by the brothers of a woman the landlord had seduced.[44]

But the outright physical abuses of serfdom should not be exaggerated. Unlike American slaves, serfs were often managed from a great distance. It was common for landowners to own two or more far-flung serf villages. Wealthier landowners, especially those who owned a hundred serfs or more, found it impossible to manage their estates without stewards to supervise the harvest and the transport of products to market, and the collection of dues. Many serfs thus lived lives that were relatively independent from their owner's control. In many ways, they lived like traditional peasants. They regularly attended church, got married, and had large families. Even when they were sold, most often they were sold as whole villages, with lands intact. They were often allowed latitude to manage their own affairs, resolve internal disputes, and distribute agricultural land.[45]

For the peasants, the poverty, hard work, and abuse were not, in and of themselves, the worst evils of serfdom. Far worse was the humiliation of living at the mercy of noblemen's whims. Even if they were treated well, they were always aware of the leash that held them fast. The yearning for freedom could be excruciating. As Alexander Nikitenko, a freed serf who eventually became a government official, remembered, "at times my craving for freedom and knowledge and for expanding the range of my activities possessed me to the point of physical pain."[46]

Revolutionaries like Ekaterina and Vera, who came from noble backgrounds, later felt tremendous guilt for indulging in the privileges of nobility. Those who remembered their childhoods with fondness could not reconcile their enchanted memories with the suffering they must have caused. For many, socialism became a means of personal expiation for the sins they committed as children. The plight of the peasant became their personal crusade.

Unlike Ekaterina, however, very few radicals made a decision to become revolutionaries *because* of their encounter with the peasants' plight. As young children, most nobles never truly understood the evils of serfdom or peasant inequality, even if their home estates had multitudes of peasants. They had fond memories of their cooks, maids, and nannies and loved playing with their serf playmates. Often, their parents were considerate landlords who did their best to feed, clothe, and even educate the serfs on their estates.[47] Vera herself was honest—she freely admitted that she did not become a socialist because of "sympathy toward the suffering masses." As a child, she simply was not conscious of the injustice of estate life. She knew of no instances of serfs being abused at Biakolovo. It took Vera years of education and deep immersion in socialist literature to understand the hidden harms of class inequality and the human suffering poverty caused.[48]

By her own admission, Vera's first impulse toward radical politics came from a seemingly unlikely source. Like so many nineteenth-century radicals, she did not seek to liberate the oppressed because of a personal understanding of economic or social injustice. Rather, Vera and her comrades sought to help the poor and liberate the captives because they were inspired to do so by the New Testament.[49]

～

Look at Christ, my friends, who suffered so much, who did not even know the joy of being fully understood by those around him, and yet he was happy, for he was the son of God, for his life was suffused with divinity, filled with self-denial, for he did everything for mankind and found all his satisfaction, his pleasure in the dissolution of his material I and in the salvation of all mankind.

—MIKHAIL BAKUNIN, letter to
Alexandra Beier, April 1836[50]

So wrote Mikhail Bakunin to a friend at the age of twenty-two, long before he became one of the world's most famous anarchists. Paradoxically, the man who would later condemn God as the main obstacle to revolution spent his early twenties immersed in Eastern Orthodox Christianity. As a youth in the 1830s, he believed it was his destiny to serve Christ. Europe's apostle of revolution began as his family's domestic prophet, creating a kind of monastery on their country estate. He sought complete control of their daily lives in order to lead them to the divine. "I feel God within me," he told his friends. "I sense paradise within me."[51]

Bakunin never did anything by halves. The composer Richard Wagner, no small figure himself, paid Bakunin the ultimate compliment: "Everything about him was colossal." His profound restlessness and his insatiable energy became legendary. He seemed to have been born, in the words of a contemporary, "not under an ordinary star, but under a comet." Yet Bakunin, like

Vera, spent the early years of his life in the quiet of the Russian provinces, on a beautiful, manicured estate, complete with lush gardens, a sprawling manor house, and a well-stocked library.[52]

There were no hints of rebellion in Bakunin's childhood. There was no reason for him to rebel. Bakunin's father embraced Rousseau's educational theories and was convinced that children needed full freedom to develop their personalities and talents. Bakunin never experienced the nagging insistence on decorum that characterized Vera's childhood. For the most part, the young Bakunin was indulged. Every opportunity was lavished upon him. Each child in the Bakunin family was taught a musical instrument, and a visitor often heard the sounds of impromptu concerts resounding through the manor. Bakunin also showed early talent in drawing and easily mastered several foreign languages, including the necessary German and French.[53]

More than anything else, the Bakunin family was drawn together through a deep commitment to the Orthodox faith. Provincial noble households often lived according to the meter of an almost medieval religious calendar. Fast days and feast days were scrupulously observed. Icons, whether painted or gilded, were displayed in prominent corners of the house, and families gathered around them to say their daily prayers. These icons often remained in families for generations and were reputed to have effected miracles in the past: healing the dying, protecting the family from fire, or, in one case, deflecting the knife of an assassin. Bakunin recalled that during Lent a mood of dark, somber reflection—"so quiet, so holy, so glorious"—encompassed the home. Faith gave his family life a harmonious, beautiful unity that was unspoken and yet deeply felt. Bakunin's father, who inclined toward the Romantic, encouraged his children to seek the transports of religious ecstasy.[54]

This passionate embrace of religion marked Bakunin for the remainder of his life. Daily existence, the petty concerns of ordinary Russians, could not hold his attention. "Dances, balls," he wrote, "these, the pinnacle of pleasure for our youth, the highest ideal they can imagine, bored me to death." Instead, he wanted far more; he longed for the otherworldly happiness he had experienced as a young child. As he grew older, these yearnings became so fervent that he found himself torn apart by deep passions. "Emotional forces seethe and demand nourishment," he lamented, "but all of this remains inactive, limited to dreams, which themselves cannot fill the emptiness of my heart."[55]

Bakunin was not alone. The most atheistic revolutionaries, who had nothing but contempt for religion, often came from keenly religious families and passed through periods of intense religious fervor. Some radicals affectionately remembered devout parents who fasted strictly, prayed daily, and set an example of self-abnegation for their children, even teaching them to follow the example of the Christian martyrs. Ekaterina Breshko-Breshkovskaia herself was raised in an atmosphere of piety, and she chose St. Barbara, who was persecuted for her faith, as her patron saint.[56] Jewish revolutionaries shared this trajectory. The radical Fanni Moreinis affectionately remembered her "fanatic" father, and the revolutionary socialist Genrieta Dubroskina held up her own father as a role model who romantically "dreamed of Jerusalem" and ended up dying in Palestine.[57]

Russian radicals did not deny their early religiosity. Quite the opposite—many were willing to admit that faith had taught them the value of loving, serving, and ultimately sacrificing for a higher good. Vera Figner, a key conspirator in the plot to kill Alexander II in 1881, declared that the New Testament ignited her revolutionary values. She once imagined herself as the Virgin Mother, stretching out her arms to the afflicted masses and offering them hope. Nadezhda Golovina went further, remembering that, as a child, she was sorry to learn that Christians were no longer martyred, and that thus she was deprived of the chance to die for the truth. "It did not occur to me at the time," she wrote, "that in ten years, I would die for another kind of 'truth.'"[58] Sacrifice, expansive devotion to others, martyrdom—the values of the fundamental Christian message infused themselves into young revolutionary hearts.

Above all, religion gave these early radicals a craving for a life of meaning; they yearned to break free from the paltry demands of everyday life and to live in a purer, more exalted world. At first, religion fulfilled their urges for a higher vocation, and many wished to become monks or nuns. Only later did revolutionary socialism beckon as a truer faith, more immediate than the one they would leave behind.[59]

Vera was no exception. In her childhood, the rhythms and rituals of Russian religion governed her daily life. She was taught to pray nightly and to wear a cross around her neck as a protection from demonic evil. But Vera's household, unlike Bakunin's, reduced religion to another emblem of propriety. Vera's relatives preserved the forms of piety: attending church, reciting prayers, observing fasts. Rituals were either routine and mechanical or rooted in superstition. Vera's governess, a cantankerous old woman, told her frightening tales of a spirit world, with God as its pitiless ruler, in order to terrify her into obedience. Vera saw traditional Orthodoxy as yet another set of rules for young ladies. None of it touched her heart. She was, at most, vaguely fond of the exotic Byzantine iconography and the incense, which rose up to the stained glass windows and "turned such pretty colors when the light fell on it."

But Vera, too, would experience the profound emotional turmoil of ecstatic religious experience. She was only a child, a mere eleven years of age, when she underwent a profound and shattering conversion. During Lent in 1860, Vera, as the oldest child, was given the solemn responsibility of reading aloud passages of the Gospel. With the family gathered in the sitting room every evening, enveloped by the warm glow of candlelight, Vera at first approached this task sullenly. After a few nights, however, she was drawn into the sublime beauty of the text. In time, Christ came to life for her, and Vera began to live with Him in her imagination. Years later, she remembered the experience vividly. "I lived with Him in my fantasies for several weeks," she wrote. "I imagined Him and whispered about Him when I was alone in my room."

As Christ's life unfolded before her, night after night, she felt herself increasingly attracted to Him—He was profoundly noble and yet real and human. He was perfect, beautiful, and yet kind and sympathetic. He loved children, the oppressed, the humiliated. By the final week of Lent, Vera found that she loved Christ with a "passionate love."

That year, during the Holy Week of Easter, Vera was torn apart by warring emotions of grief, awe, and joy. The treachery of Judas, the faithlessness of the disciples, the cruelty of the high priest—Vera felt of all of this with a painful intimacy. How could a man so good suffer such things? She imagined herself saving Christ, rectifying the injustice of his death, and proclaiming the true spirit of his message. In her bed, she dreamed of calling together the children of Jerusalem, rallying them to her cause. "Just listen to what they're going to do to Him!" she would address the crowd. "They're going to kill Him! And there is nobody better than Him on earth!" Ultimately, however, Vera was filled with a deep reverence for His willing death on the cross. She came to see His embrace of death as the perfection of His benevolence and the supreme act of His loving nature. Filled with wonder and adoration, she was no longer able to pray to Christ for His intercession; requesting things from Him would be petty and trivial. Only one thing mattered: "I wanted to serve Him, to save Him."

This was Vera's first encounter with the allure of martyrdom. The image of Christ on the cross remained with her forever. Like so many other nineteenth-century political radicals, Vera later became an atheist. But

"Christ remained with me," she later wrote, "engraved in my heart. In fact, it was as if I were more tied to Him than ever." As with Bakunin, the intensity of religious emotion inspired a yearning for passionate, unearthly experience. She began to dream of devotion, sacrifice, and martyrdom. "There is no greater love than this," the Gospel of John proclaims, "than a man who lays down his life for his friends." These words infused Vera's life with new meaning and an exalted sense of purpose.[60]

In the monotonous daily routine of Biakolovo, Vera was drawn to stories of heroism and self-sacrifice. On the shelves of the modest library of the manor, she found Romantic poems and revolutionary tales that fed her cravings. In her heart, Christ was soon supplemented by Kondratii Ryleev, Russia's first revolutionary, hanged for his participation in the aristocratic Decembrist uprising against the tsar in 1825. Ryleev, a romantic figure who courted death all his life, became known as the poet of the uprising. On the night before the revolt, Ryleev famously stood before his comrades and boldly declared that the conspirators were heading toward certain doom. But this, he told them, was their moment of glory. A deed could be heroic only if it ended in martyrdom. Long before the uprising he wrote these lines:

> *My coming doom I feel and know*
> *And bless the stroke which lays me low*
> *And, father, now with joy I meet*
> *My death, to me such end is sweet.*[61]

For Vera, the twin images of Christ on the cross and Ryleev on the gallows inspired the conviction that, in Ryleev's words, "there are whole ages when nothing is more desirable than a crown of thorns." Somehow she would follow in their footsteps, seeking out "heroism, struggle, and revolt," even if it led to suffering and death.[62]

By the tender age of seventeen, then, Vera had become a dedicated socialist. From the moment of her conversion until the day she died, she lived a life dedicated to liberating the oppressed masses and providing economic sustenance to the desperate. But the essence of her faith did not lie in the mere eradication of injustice. As she would write many years later, the true meaning of revolution lay in self-sacrifice. Above all else, her lifelong quest as a radical was, in her own words, "to join the ranks of the martyrs."[63]

In the meantime, however, life conspired against her dreams. Provincial ladies had few outlets for such yearnings, and poor provincial noblewomen had more pressing concerns. Her desire for heroism seemed destined to die in the suffocating world of the noble estate, unless she left home to find her own way.

～

Aunts, children, servants, and a whole crowd of servants' kids followed us to the main road; of embraces and tears there was no end. As long as Niko-laevka was visible, Masha did not take her eyes off of it, and cried bitterly. At the station, she took leave of the coachman several times, and even said good-bye to the horses. She told the coachman to kiss Lida and Vasia and all of the children, everyone, everyone.

— VERA ZASULICH, "Masha"[64]

Vera's aunts had determined what she would be from an early age: a governess. It was the respectable profession for impoverished daughters of the nobility. They offered to send her to an inexpensive finishing school, well suited for training future governesses and teachers. Vera's older sister Alexandra was already attending the school, and it seemed a perfectly respectable if modest establishment.

Everything within Vera rebelled against this dreary fate. Living forever as an attendant on some wealthy estate, caring for spoiled young children— "I could take anything but that!" she wrote. But more than anything else, she wanted to leave home. School would at least provide an escape from the oppressive "stagnant existence" of provincial life. Once she was in the wider world, she would make her own way and craft her own future. In 1866, at age seventeen, Vera left Gzhatsk for good.[65]

By the time she left Biakolovo, Vera had spent years of her life dreaming of freedom. "Life beckoned to me," she wrote later, "life in all its immensity." She was therefore unprepared for the sadness that overwhelmed her on the day she left. Vera, like so many others of her class, never escaped the nostalgia for her country childhood. At the age of sixty, she wrote in her memoirs, with some wonder: "I never thought that I would remember it all of my life, that I would never forget even one little bush in the front garden, one old cupboard in the corridor, and that the outline of the old trees, visible from the balcony, would appear to me in dreams in years to come."[66]

CHAPTER 3

Nihilists

~~~~~

On September 23, 1861, more than a thousand students at St. Petersburg University broke into a locked lecture hall and poured into the cavernous amphitheater. They were infuriated by a thin new booklet circulated by the university administration, one that was filled with restrictions on student activity. The university had decreed that all organizations and meetings must have official permission from the school authorities. To add insult to injury, students were required to sign the new books, indicating their consent, before they could register for classes.[1]

The crowd in the hall was seething with anger. Rebelliously sporting disheveled hair and overcoats worn askew, individual students marched to the podium to demand universal and open protest against this authoritarian assault on their rights. It was decided: No student was to obey the new rules, and anyone caught doing so would be shunned. Plans were even made to torch the booklets in a large, public bonfire.

In response, General G. I. Filipson, curator of the university, locked the doors to the main building and refused to open them on the day of registration. On that bright September day, students milled about in front of the buildings, unsure of what to do. Finally someone had the idea of marching across town to the curator's home and demanding that he open the university doors. The students spontaneously formed neat columns and began their march through the center of the city to his residence.

The warm weather lent the procession a jubilant quality, and crowds lined the streets and leaned out of windows to watch Russia's first student demonstration. Soon enough, the shiny helmets of the St. Petersburg gendarmerie appeared, but the police did little more than follow the line of students on horseback. When the demonstrators turned onto Nevskii Prospekt, the crowds were joined by French barbers who ran out of their shops and gamely shouted, "Revolution! Revolution!"

When the students reached Filipson's home, they aggressively broadcast their demands. To avert a confrontation, Filipson meekly agreed to open the university doors. The St. Petersburg residents then saw another astonishing sight: student protesters filing back through the city, led by Filipson himself, and followed closely by the ranks of police. When one professor approached the students and begged them not to harm "the cause of learning," one student answered: "What do we care for learning!"

That night several students were brought in for questioning. Others retaliated with further protests and demonstrations. When radicals began to harass students and professors who sought to attend lectures, officials in St. Petersburg decided to shut down the university indefinitely. It would not reopen for two years.

By then, however, what had started out as a student protest had become a revolutionary movement. By 1862, a new era of Russian radicalism had been born, populated by those who proudly called themselves *shestidesiat-niki,* or the "generation of the sixties."

Tsar Alexander II, who took the Russian throne in 1855, never understood why he had incurred the persistent, violent hatred of Russia's youth. He possessed none of the reactionary tendencies of his father, Nicholas I. Nicholas was a lover of everything military. He thought of his country as a military regiment and cast himself primarily as the national commander in chief. He was a firm believer in censorship and increased the reach of Russia's secret police. Dissent was naturally intolerable, but even overly vocal support for the state was discouraged. Nicholas's watchword was "one must obey and keep one's thoughts to oneself."[2]

Nicholas believed that Russia needed a strong hand to rule her. He went to great lengths to inculcate military habits into his son and heir. It was a strange irony that, in a land where most noble children were free to do as they pleased, the most powerful of Russia's children was subject to the most draconian of regimens. Alexander awoke at 6:00 A.M. and did not retire to bed again until 11:00 P.M. In between, he endured seven hours of schooling, including lessons in Russian and foreign languages, mathematics and the natural sciences, and athletics such as fencing and gymnastics. Almost every hour of his day was accounted for. Above all, his father's militarism governed his education. He was expected to review troops, excel at military studies, and learn to love a military uniform. As a boy of ten, Alexander was sent to the Cadet Corps for officer training.[3]

Unfortunately, as is often the case in such patriarchal households, the son proved a disappointment to the father. Alexander seemed curiously feminine, too ready to dissolve into tears. He was deeply attached to his mother, who was herself a sensitive and Romantic spirit. His soft-heartedness was also encouraged by his tutor, Vasilii Zhukovskii, a famous poet who shared the young boy's taste for melancholy and sentimentality. Nicholas once asked Alexander what he would have done to the rebels who had plotted against the tsar in the Decembrist rebellion of 1825. To Nicholas's disgust, Alexander replied: "I would have forgiven them!"[4]

In 1855, Tsar Nicholas died. Russian intellectuals heaved a collective sigh of relief, only because they believed that things could not get worse, not because Alexander gave them any hope. The crown prince gave no hints of reformist leanings. He made no bold declarations of renewal; he concealed his thoughts on Russia's political system, social order, and serf economy.

Indeed, it was hard to know whether Alexander was thinking at all. He promised to be the least talented and even the least intelligent of Russia's sovereigns. He was outwardly congenial, even charming—a handsome man with an erect carriage and fine blue eyes. But he was a cipher: He never voiced opinions, and he was almost physically averse to discussion and debate, whether from conservatives or reformers. "When the Emperor talks to an intellectual," one observer declared, "he has the appearance of someone with rheumatism who is standing in a draught."[5]

But Alexander intuited that the Russian Empire was on the brink of a crisis. Six months after his father's death, the Russian military suffered a historically humiliating defeat. British and French troops had besieged and then stormed the Crimean port city of Sevastopol. Russia was defeated on her own territory, a disgraceful end to the Crimean War, which had begun in 1853. In March 1856, Alexander conceded defeat in the Peace of Paris and was forced to destroy Russia's prized Black Sea fleet, the brainchild of Peter the Great. The humiliation galvanized public opinion, and far-sighted observers realized that the Crimean War had more than military significance. Slowly a consensus emerged that the real reason for the defeat was Russia's domestic disorder. From outside, Russia looked like a major European superpower. But inside, it was riddled with corruption, stagnation, and incompetence. Thirty years of reaction under Nicholas had taken their toll.[6]

Alexander, always ambivalent, always torturously slow, decided to experiment with a few ideas for reform. But the tsar's superficial caution sometimes masked an almost impulsive boldness. Because reform carried risks, Alexander decided, it should be considered from all angles. And what better way to test new ideas than to subject them to public debate? Defying predictions,

Alexander became the first tsar to court public opinion. This new approach soon received its name: *glasnost*.[7]

In 1858, Alexander signaled this departure from tradition with a highly symbolic act. One day, while he was taking his customary stroll through the palace gardens, Alexander was accosted by the fiery Nikolai Serno-Solovievich, whose restless energy would later lead him into revolutionary conspiracy. Before Alexander's guards could restrain him, Serno-Solovievich confronted the tsar and forced him to accept a rolled-up paper—a lengthy memorandum on the plight of Russia's serfs. Alexander, irritated, took the note without a word. The next day, Prince Aleksei Orlov, Chief of Gendarmes, summoned Serno-Solovievich for an interview. The young radical was certain that his free life was over. In a solemn voice, the chief intoned: "The Emperor Nicholas would have banished you to a place so remote that they would never even have found your bones." Then, to the speechless astonishment of Serno-Solovievich, he added: "But our present Sovereign is so kind that he has ordered me to kiss you. Here," he beckoned, "embrace me."[8]

There were other, less theatrical, signs of change and acts of clemency. Alexander granted amnesty to several political prisoners and declared that censorship was to be relaxed. Public debate cautiously emerged from the self-imposed shell created under Nicholas. "The Russian ear," Alexander Herzen later recalled, "unused to free speech, became reconciled to it, and looked eagerly for its masculine solidity, its fearless frankness."[9]

One issue dominated the civil debate: serfdom. Remarkably, Russian society all but unanimously acknowledged that serfdom had to go. The brute fact that nearly half of the Russian population was physically owned by the wealthy elite seemed increasingly untenable. While slavery had pushed the United States to the brink of one of the world's bloodiest civil wars, Russia's nobility had resigned itself to surrendering its prized privilege of owning others.[10] Strikingly, those landowners who campaigned against serfdom were the most vocal of all. One aristocrat bluntly stated the stinging truth: "The abolition of the right to dispose of people like objects or like cattle is as much our liberation as theirs."[11]

In 1856, Alexander hinted that serfdom was destined to be dismantled. In that year, he gave a speech that remarkably pronounced that "the existing system of serf owning cannot remain unchanged. It is better to begin abolishing serfdom from above than to wait for it to begin abolishing itself from below." Russia's fledgling press, emboldened by *glasnost*, began to beat the drum for emancipation. But Alexander refused to be rushed. For five years, a secret commission labored to fashion a form of liberation that would balance class interests by freeing the serfs, providing them land, and compensating their former owners.[12]

The eventual Emancipation Act reflected the difficulty of compromise. Running an astonishing 361 pages, it meticulously detailed every aspect of the emancipation process. Serfs would be freed but compelled to work temporarily on the land of their former owners while a purchase price for land was negotiated. The government would provide the peasants with a loan to be repaid over forty-nine years at 6 percent interest. It was a complicated arrangement.

Nevertheless, on February 19, 1861, forty-three million serfs were liberated from their bondage and were granted equal protection under Russian law. It was a momentous beginning to the tumultuous decade of the 1860s.[13]

The Russian government had issued the emancipation document with trepidation, fearing that it would raise the peasants' hopes, only to dash them as the meaning of the complicated text became widely known. As the document was distributed to the provinces and read out to groups of peasants in the villages, the military braced for violent peasant revolts and put soldiers on the alert in every Russian province. The Russian capital was heavily guarded—the streets were patrolled by armed soldiers, and Alexander II spent the night of February 19 at an undisclosed location.[14]

Revolts did occur. In Kazan province, in the village of Bezdna, a self-styled peasant prophet named Anton Petrov declared that the nobles were deceiving the people. The tsar had granted immediate, full freedom with land to all of the peasants, but the nobles were trying to disguise this in the impenetrable language of the emancipation decree. Entranced by his self-confidence, peasants gathered to hear Petrov's conspiratorial musings. Fearing rebellion, Kazan's provincial governor dispatched troops to the village. The soldiers fired directly at demonstrators armed only with pikes, killing forty-one people. Petrov himself was hanged. It seemed an ominous portent of things to come.[15]

But in the end, the government's anxiety proved overblown. After about a year of disturbances, dissatisfaction evaporated. Many peasants remained with their former owners and worked for a wage. Others benefited from the apathy of their former masters, as some nobles gave up, sold everything they had, and moved to the cities. Russia had avoided the kind of cataclysmic conflict that would soon engulf the United States over slavery.[16]

Sustained, vehement opposition to the Emancipation Act curiously came only from one quarter—the radical intelligentsia. Radicals heaped scorn upon the emancipation settlement, declaring it an elaborate fraud. Since the serfs should have been given their land and freedom outright, Alexander's 361 pages of complicated text amounted to a charade. The radical press agreed with the logic of Anton Petrov; as one angry editorial exclaimed in italicized print, *"The people have been deceived by the tsar."*

Many of the outraged voices came from among the university students. From them, the tsar got no credit, only relentless abuse. He was declared "incompetent," a liar, and a tyrant. Russia needed a new government, equal rights, and a redistribution of property. It needed revolution. It was time for the tsar to go. One student openly declared that he looked forward to the day when the tsar and his ministers could simply be killed, "without mercy."[17]

Alexander II was particularly baffled by the hostility of the students: One of his first reform projects was the Russian university system. He abolished the resented university uniform, allowed student publications to flourish, and, above all, opened up the university to a wider circle of Russians, including workers, Jews, and even women (as auditors). Professors had greater control over the curriculum and could teach a broader array of subjects.[18]

Rather than crediting Alexander for the reforms, the students used them as a springboard for further activism. They set up cafeterias to help feed the poorer students; they established impromptu libraries, where radical books, newspapers, and journals could be read for free. The burning political and social issues of the day were debated at the semispontaneous political assemblies known as *skhodki*. Whether they were held in cramped student apartments or in large banquet halls donated by progressive parents, *skhodki* often attracted hundreds. Whoever wished to speak would grab "the chair" (most often just an ordinary chair) and stand on it to make his speech.[19]

By the early 1860s, administrators feared that Russia's universities were spinning out of their control. Students were increasingly brazen: They refused to attend classes, protested teachers they deemed unworthy, and organized angry demonstrations at any hint of a supposed "infraction" of a student's rights. *Skhodki* were held every week, becoming unruly affairs where critics lashed out not just at the university but at the tsar himself. The minister of education decided to crack down. New regulations were promulgated. Some students were expelled; others were arrested.[20] But to no avail.

Alexander never understood the sixties generation. He was positively enraged by their ungrateful rebelliousness. He had done more to reform Russia than any other ruler, with the possible exception of Peter the Great. He had given Russia's youth greater opportunities to learn, to read, to write. Free expression flowed all around. And yet, perversely, the students seemed to hate Alexander more than his brutally authoritarian father.

Like others in his government, Alexander failed to realize that it was no longer a matter of what his regime did or did not do. The generation of the sixties had no interest in reforms and saw the Russian state as a mere obstacle to their dramatic plans. They wanted nothing less than to remake the world.

～

The boarding school is deserted again. Summer vacation has arrived, the fourth that Masha is spending all alone in the large, lonely rooms.

. . . She is living fairly well. She is the first in her class, everyone looks up to her, and they long ago stopped making irritating remarks on her manners, even though she made little effort to change. Now she is sitting alone in a large classroom bathed in sunlight and concentrating on finishing a longer strip of embroidery. The cleaning woman at the school promised that she would sell the embroidery. With that money, Masha would subscribe to a library and enjoy a more interesting summer break.

—VERA ZASULICH, "Masha"[21]

Those who traveled from the provinces to attend the various universities in St. Petersburg and other cities often brought little with them. Unable to work, and having no family income to rely on, these young men lived on almost nothing in the prohibitively expensive cities. Student aid often meant simply remission of tuition. To earn some money, students were forced to tutor children or do editing or proofreading on the side. It was, for those with little means, a dismal life. Constant work meant an inability to study, and only those with good grades were eligible for aid. They could not afford good food and were forced to live in tiny rented rooms, perpetually cold because they had no money for heat. They were easily visible because of their tattered coats and gloves—unable to afford better.[22]

The police were quick to blame this "half-educated proletariat" for the rebellious student atmosphere, since the poor presumably felt nothing but "hatred for the existing political and social order." Russian radicals heartily agreed, firmly believing that the fresh blood of the lower classes gave radicalism its powerful energy. But neither the police nor the students could admit the facts: Fully 64 percent of the Russian radicals in the years 1855–1869 were from the nobility. A mere 8 percent came from the lower middle class, the lower classes, and the peasantry combined. Poverty did not fuel activism, and poorer students mostly did what they could just to scrape by. Privilege alone gave young people the time and energy to devote to radical causes.[23]

Sixties radicalism was not born of oppression but was nurtured in privilege. It grew in places the Russian regime never suspected: in elite boarding schools and private high schools, in military academies and clerical seminaries. There, the sons and daughters of Russia's most elite citizens became passionate antistate activists, disdaining the very class that bred them.

For many of Russia's nobility, school proved an abrupt and painful transition into adulthood—the end of their leisured existence on the family estate. If Russian parents encouraged children to roam free, Russian schoolteachers were intensely disciplinarian. Rigid rules governed behavior, and punishments were physical and harsh. In the boarding schools, the curriculum was formal and required much memorization: Greek and Latin for the boys; often German, French, music, and dancing for the girls. The military academies were still worse, with their extreme physical demands and endless lessons in tedious military studies. Even the Orthodox seminaries seemed to thrive on rendering their students as mindless as possible, forcing future priests to read dull Protestant theological treatises in their original German. Everywhere, the emphasis was on good breeding, complete obedience, and rote learning. Few teachers made any effort to stimulate their students' intellects.[24]

For some, the transition to school triggered a deep spiritual crisis. Mikhail Bakunin left home for the military academy at the age of fourteen and experienced his new life as an endless nightmare. His free spirit felt confined by the regimentation and discipline of the academy, and his creative mind rebelled against the mechanized routine that prevailed. His fellow students seemed completely alien to him, interested only in cards, wine, and women. Bakunin realized that he could never join in these "dark, filthy, and vile" pursuits and was therefore unsuited to a normal life in polite society. He felt increasingly isolated: "Eternal silence, eternal sorrow, eternal anguish—these are the comrades of my seclusion!" He withdrew into himself and dreamed of a different world, which would fill him with the sweet ecstasy and harmony of his youth.[25]

If we take "Masha" as a guide, Vera felt similarly about her new school, located in an isolated suburb of Moscow. It was supposed to educate "noble girls," but, given the cheap tuition, it was mostly attended by the daughters of wealthy merchants and clergymen. It was run by two German women, who insisted that their charges speak only French or German; Russian was forbidden. For Vera, who spoke little French and less German, this meant mostly sitting in silence. Rules of behavior were equally strict: no running in the hallways, no skipping, no laughing, no loud conversations. Teachers punished their students by pulling their ears and hair or cuffing them on the head. The rigid atmosphere was complemented by an impossibly dry curriculum: languages, history, a smattering of music, and endless etiquette lessons.[26]

Within the confines of the school, Vera missed home. For all of its limitations, the estate allowed Vera to escape into the vast forested gardens and surrounding fields or into the hidden corners of the old manor house. In the school, there was no place of refuge. Like Bakunin, Vera had nothing but contempt for her fellow students; their interests revolved around petty love stories and dreams of being presented to the royal court. She stood aloof from her peers, refused to join in the gossip or good-natured pranks, and even skipped the mandatory dance lessons, defiantly dismissing them as "useless."[27]

For Vera, Bakunin, and so many others like them, school was tedious, tyrannical, and boring. However, it also contained a secret world: a world of ideas, of activity, of engagement—a world of books.

It was one of the most extraordinary periods in the history of Russian culture; at no other time did literature exercise such an explosive influence over the lives of so many. In Russia in the 1860s and 1870s, literature and life were indistinguishable. For Russia's sixties generation, a character in a story was often more influential than any living person, and living people were quickly transformed into literary characters. Life imitated literature, which in turn imitated life.

It all began at home. On the Russian country estates and in the Russian provinces, libraries were the sources of one of the only means of entertainment, and young nobles lived in the world of books, embracing authors and characters as friends, teachers, and role models. Tales of heroism and activism inspired many youths to seek a life of excitement and adventure.[28]

The trauma of school life not only inspired greater yearning for the extraordinary, it also brought together like-minded students, who sought to educate themselves beyond the dull school curriculum. Clandestine reading groups sprang up in every kind of educational establishment, and members passed illicit literature from hand to hand. Books and essays were surreptitiously exchanged in the school corridors and under school desks. Some stayed up late into the night, reading while everyone else was in bed; others spent their free time reading in the libraries, concealing one book behind another. A whole generation of students received a completely unauthorized education right inside school walls.

The readings were often complicated, sometimes foreign, and mostly revolutionary. They contained discussions of burning issues of the day— philosophy, politics, and socialism. And they promised a total transformation of society. Few radicals had ever experienced poverty or injustice. But they knew it existed because they had read about it in their books.[29]

For alienated and discontented students, this personal reading provided what they considered to be true learning. Radical literature spoke directly to those who yearned for something more than mundane careerism and social climbing. It called young people to think of those less privileged, who needed assistance, comfort, and, above all, knowledge. And it promised a life of meaning and purpose, a life lived for the future. While in school, ordinary Russian boys dreamed of military honors and lucrative positions in the bureaucracy, and ordinary Russian girls dreamed of elegant balls and eligible suitors. Completely entranced by their illicit reading, Vera and others like her dreamed of something far different. They yearned to become "nihilists."

～

"Hm!" Pavel Petrovich pulled at his mustaches. "Well, and this Monsieur Bazarov, what is he exactly?"

"What is Bazarov?" Arkady smiled. "Would you like me to tell you, uncle, what he is exactly?"

"Please do, nephew."

"He is a nihilist!"

"A what?" asked Nikolai Petrovich, while his brother lifted his knife in the air with a small piece of butter on the tip and remained motionless.

"He is a nihilist," repeated Arkady.

"A nihilist," said Nikolai Petrovich. "That comes from the Latin nihil— *nothing, I imagine; the term must signify a man who . . . who recognizes nothing?"*

"Say—who respects nothing," put in Pavel Petrovich, and set to work with the butter again.

"Who looks at everything critically," observed Arkady.

"Isn't that exactly the same thing?" asked Pavel Petrovich.

"No, it's not the same thing. A nihilist is a person who does not take any principle for granted, however much that principle may be revered."

"Well, and is that a good thing?" interrupted Pavel Petrovich.

"It depends on the individual, my dear uncle. It's good in some cases and very bad in others."

— IVAN TURGENEV, *Fathers and Sons*[30]

Without a trace of irony, Ivan Turgenev once naively confessed that the idea of writing about the new generation of Russian radicals came to him during summer vacation, while he was "sea-bathing" on the Isle of Wight, in August 1860. For some reason, the sun and the sea inspired a novel about an impoverished but well-educated rebel, whose ideology both inspires and frightens those around him. Thus was born *Fathers and Sons*, Turgenev's most famous work of literature.[31]

Turgenev was neither impoverished nor a radical, but throughout his life he was fascinated by those who were both. The heir of a wealthy aristocrat, Turgenev was raised on an extraordinary estate that threw sumptuous balls in a cavernous banquet hall and hosted concerts performed by a serf orchestra. His childhood was marred only by a domineering mother, whose bitter disposition was undoubtedly a reaction to the philandering of her cold and handsome husband.[32]

Ivan was well educated by his governesses and tutors, and he became an avid reader, with a particular taste for the nineteenth-century Romantics. To complete his upbringing, he was sent abroad in his early twenties. On tour, he encountered extraordinary Russian men and women, including Bakunin, and imbibed some of the most voguish of European ideas. When he returned to Russia at the age of twenty-five, he was an elegant, handsome, and extraordinarily refined man, the epitome of good breeding and elite fashion. If the caricature of him in Dostoyevsky's *The Devils* is to be believed, Turgenev was never seen in public without a starched collar, a perfectly adjusted cravat, and a delicately shaven and perfumed face.[33]

Turgenev was never a rebel by inclination—he desired public approval above all else. But destiny thwarted his taste for conventionality. On November 1, 1843, a day he remembered always, he first met the internationally famous singer Pauline Viardot. In that instant, with a passion he never thought possible, he fell desperately in love. Viardot was married but never discouraged Turgenev's attentions. For the rest of his life, Turgenev followed his beloved wherever she went. He never married and never loved another woman. This unrequited love compelled him to write and became a theme that threaded through all of his works.

This scandalous new lifestyle also partly contributed to Turgenev's brief stint as a social rebel. Turgenev's mother cut him off in 1849, and for two diffi-cult years, he struggled to get by. He regained his fortune when his mother died, but was then arrested and briefly confined to his estate for writings deemed sus-picious by the regime. Forever after, Turgenev loved the thrill of rebelling against convention. Or rather, he loved such unconventionality the way he loved his Mme. Viardot—safely, from a distance, in the life of his own mind.[34]

In so many ways, Turgenev was a man of his time, a member of a genera-tion that—in tribute to his most famous novel—would eventually be known as the generation of the "fathers." The fathers of the 1840s were Russian men of noble background, well educated and well traveled. They read the latest in Eu-ropean politics and philosophy, immersed themselves in the writings of Schelling and the poetry of Goethe, and felt at home in the universities and in-tellectual salons of Europe. They were filled with an almost intoxicating passion for ideas. They would spend hours, often well into the night, discussing difficult philosophical concepts. Alexander Herzen best captured the spirit of his age: "People who adored each other became estranged for entire weeks because they could not agree on a definition of 'transcendental spirit' or were personally offended by opinions about 'absolute personality' or 'being in itself.'"[35]

Herzen, one of Turgenev's lifelong friends, became the most famous man of his generation, a veritable archetype of the forties. Born the bastard son of a Russian nobleman, Herzen was always antagonistic to the class that had never fully accepted him. From an early age, he had heard stories of ex-traordinary abuses perpetrated by his fellow noblemen. His uncle was a de-bauched and violent man who was nearly murdered because he kept a serf harem, where young women were abused and saw their children heartlessly sold off to other landowners. Herzen's father was less abandoned but still a patriarchal despot. He never married Herzen's German-born mother and maintained her in a state of servitude. Herzen thus understood himself as the product of a corrupt and decadent caste that did nothing but inflict evil on others. He dedicated his life to transforming a social order that seemed to breed only decadence and oppression.[36]

For Herzen, Turgenev, and the rest of the fathers, Russia was a backward, despotic country. In their travels to the West, they were awed at the liberality of French and British society and were favorably impressed by cosmopolitan German life. At times, from a sense of wounded Russian pride, they lashed out at the bourgeois complacency of European culture. But they sought to preserve very little that was traditionally Russian, praising their native land merely for the fact that it was truly revolutionary because it had "nothing to lose." In essence, they wanted nothing more than for Russia to become more European than the Europeans themselves. In Russian parlance, the fathers were "Westernizers," who believed that Russia's salvation lay in adopting the "western" values of individualism, tolerance, and democracy.[37]

Their weapons were ideas. They took up their pens and wrote passionate articles on the need to introduce cultural enlightenment, to abolish censorship, and to eliminate the hated evil of serfdom. One of Turgenev's first literary efforts was a moving collection of essays that he innocently entitled *Sketches from a Hunter's Album.* The *Sketches* were, in fact, a series of vignettes about the plight of Russia's peasants. His humanization of Russia's serfs was said to be so eloquent that the future Alexander II was moved to abolish serfdom after reading Turgenev's book.[38]

Unfortunately, these reformist rhetoricians happened to live under one of Russia's most despotic regimes. During the 1840s, Nicholas I was at the zenith of his power, and his censors choked off all open criticism of the regime. The men of the forties were banished from Russian political life and were persecuted for their ideas. They dubbed themselves "superfluous men," men whose education and talents would have been recognized in any European society but who were rejected as rebels in Nicholas's Russia.[39]

But the life of a rebel was not so distasteful to Herzen and Turgenev, especially if they could be Romantic rebels—proud, lonely men, isolated geniuses, out of step with their times. Certainly, Herzen enjoyed playing the role of the scorned intellectual. In 1847, after years of persecution by the Russian regime, he fled abroad, never to return. From the safety of Europe, he became the scourge of tsarism, writing furious articles on serfdom, corporal punishment, censorship, and corruption. Intoxicated by his own indignation, he grew ever more extreme. He began to speak of "destruction"—the tearing apart of the entire "old world," including monarchical states, hierarchical societies, and moralizing churches. He sought a "revolutionary dictatorship, which must not invent new civil codes or create a new order, but must smash all monarchist relics."[40]

In the end, rebellion so addicted Herzen that he desired it for its own sake. What would happen after the old world was gone? Herzen did not know. "We do not build," he wrote to his son, "we destroy."[41]

Despite all of the violent rhetoric, Herzen and his generation never became true revolutionaries. They remained Romantics at heart and loved revolution as an elusive dream. When confronted with real revolutionaries, the men of the forties shuddered with antipathy. The refinement and gentility of the "superfluous men" could not tolerate the conspiratorial, narrow-minded, and even vulgar attitudes of true activists. Herzen was most satisfied when he was publicly acclaimed, even by his sworn enemies. The happiest period of his life was during the height of *glasnost,* when Russian government officials, perhaps even Tsar Alexander himself, were reading his articles.[42]

Herzen was aware of this ambivalence. He loathed the monarchism and feudalism of old Russia, but he was never at ease with socialism. In his writings, he often described the world in apocalyptic terms. He compared Europe to the dying Roman Empire, gutted by the barbarians and Christians. He knew the barbarians would win, but he could not join them. Instead, he cast himself and his friends as "the wisest of the Romans," who could neither defend the old world nor embrace the new, and who had disappeared "in the silent grandeur of their grief."[43]

Turgenev's description of his generation as "fathers" was apt. His passionate but passive cohort begat a far more radical generation. The literature of the fathers was read in the libraries of noble estates or in dormitories after lights-out. Energetic and enthusiastic young people devoured the works of Herzen and his contemporaries. They were entranced by the call to revolt, to take up arms, and to smash existing institutions. Destroying despotism, serfdom, and Russia's corrupt and decadent class system became the desire of idealistic young minds. Full of boundless energy, they sought action.

But no action followed. When it came time to act, the fathers retreated into their "personal dignity" and the "silent grandeur of their grief." Worse, they often acted like patriarchs, scolding their misbehaving children. Herzen sealed his own reputation by describing the younger generation as too single-minded, too angry. "Bilious men," he called them. It was the last straw. The sons dismissed their fathers as contemptible posers. Nikolai Dobroliubov, the revolutionary editor and prophet of the younger generation, mocked his predecessors: "If platonic love of a woman is ridiculous, a thousand times more ridiculous is platonic love of country, people, justice."[44]

Vera Zasulich later remembered that her generation respected the fathers for their education and their "rejection of traditional views." But the burning desire for practical activity made the sons unwilling to leave dangerous discussions "at the tea table." The fathers preferred to leave things in theory and were afraid of bringing their ideas into "living reality." The sons saw the world in categorical terms and wanted immediately to bring to life all of their fervent young ideas.[45]

In *Fathers and Sons,* Turgenev had the intellectual courage to parody the "superfluous men." He even mocked himself in the character of Pavel Kirsanov, a dainty aristocrat and quintessential westernized Russian noble-man. Pavel, like Turgenev, immaculately dresses in the latest European fash-ion and enjoys sprinkling his sentences with French and German phrases. The novel even describes Pavel's early love for a mysterious Princess R., a married woman who torments him and leads him to abandon society and a promising career. His failure in love, as in life, makes him impotent and "su-perfluous." He spends his days in the Russian provinces, doing little except reading the latest liberal European journals. He cherishes his "personal dig-nity" and leaves it at that.[46]

Like Herzen, Turgenev suffered from a deep ambivalence toward revo-lution and revolutionaries. He uncomfortably recognized his own passivity. But he feared the zeal and restless rage of youth. As a writer, he sought to capture the power of the new ideas sweeping through Russia: ideas that were bold, daring, and, to his mind, terrifying. He did this best in his most lifelike character, Evgenii Bazarov, the protagonist of *Fathers and Sons.*[47]

Bazarov is everything Turgenev was not: a poor, struggling, angry young student who resented the pampered and affected lifestyle of the Russian no-bility and rejected all of their pretensions. In Bazarov, Turgenev sketched the characteristics of the emerging sixties generation, the generation whom he christened the "sons." He later confessed that he was fascinated, and perhaps a bit frightened, by his own creation.

Bazarov first appears in the novel as a disheveled youth with long dark hair, dressed in a frayed black overcoat. He is intelligent, arrogant, at times re-freshingly unconventional, and often unnecessarily rude. He treats his elders with contempt and often mocks them. "Then we realized," Evgenii Bazarov tells Pavel Kirsanov, "that just to keep on and on talking about our social dis-eases was a waste of time, and merely led to a trivial doctrinaire attitude."[48]

Therein lies the core of Bazarov's rebellion—a comprehensive rejection of the complacent rhetoric of the 1840s. Beautiful ideas, Bazarov insists, are like beautiful dreams; they evaporate on contact with reality. Art, music, po-etry, journalism, and criticism, no matter how progressive, are mere amuse-ments for the idle rich. Philosophy is an obstacle to action. "You don't need logic, I suppose, to put a piece of bread in your mouth when you are hun-gry?" Bazarov asks Pavel rhetorically.

Turgenev's most fateful decision was to give Bazarov's ideology a name: nihilism, which Turgenev derived from the Latin *nihil,* or "nothing." Nihilism desired to destroy institutions and values in order to build something new. "At the present time," Bazarov explains, "condemnation is more useful than anything else, so we condemn." When he is asked what he will build after ceaseless negation, Bazarov answers: "That is not our affair. . . . The ground must be cleared first." It is an angry echo of Herzen's "we do not build, we destroy."

But Turgenev ultimately deceived his public with a poorly selected term. "Nihilism" implied an absence of belief, but, as Turgenev himself knew, the nihilists were, in truth, passionate believers. Herzen chose a better word. The new generation, Herzen wrote, were "apostles—men who combine faith, will, conviction and energy."[49]

～

For whilst religious tradition asserts man to be an exile from Paradise, and a degenerate descendant of his first father, created perfect by God, science, on the contrary, teaches that this Paradise is not behind, *but* before us, *and can only be reached by constant and slow advances amidst toil and labour; it farther teaches that we did not begin* great *and end* little, *but that we began* little, *to become greater and greater.*

—LUDWIG BÜCHNER, *Force and Matter*[50]

In a fraught moment in *Fathers and Sons,* Arkady removes a volume of Pushkin's poetry from his father's hands and gives him instead Ludwig Büchner's *Force and Matter.* After attempting to read this lumbering and repetitive German tome, Nikolai gives up, dejected. Much as he desires to keep up with the times, he cannot abandon Pushkin for German scientism. And yet, at the same time, hundreds of university students were doing just that. In the 1860s, *Force and Matter* was a wild bestseller.[51] For the nihilists, the book was more than just a treatise, it was a statement of new faith.

Force and Matter has a rather simple argument: The universe is made of matter, and matter alone. "God," "spirit," and "soul" are all meaningless words, because nothing exists outside of atoms and their interactions. Even human beings are nothing more than the sum of their chemical and biological processes. Inflexible natural laws govern the cosmos; even the most erudite of human thoughts is nothing more than a combination of physical impulses. As for consciousness and free will—these are nothing more than illusions, camouflaging the brute reality of biology.

Büchner was not afraid to state his conclusions directly: Philosophy and theology are nothing but vulgar frauds, reminiscent of alchemy, which deceive the gullible and poorly educated. Science is the sole path to truth.

As befits a prophet, Büchner's tone in *Force and Matter* is, by turns, angry and hopeful. He castigates heretics for clinging to the chimera of God, for refusing to face reality. Proof of the impotence of religion can be found everywhere: Thousands of years of religion and philosophy have failed to improve the human lot. Poverty and oppression are undiminished. Religion is a dangerous deception that keeps men ignorant.

But Büchner was confident that truth would set men free. He offered his followers a new hope—a new human destiny. Destroy the old God, Büchner exhorts, and a new, more powerful god will rise from the rubble: matter. Matter is eternal; matter is omnipotent; matter creates everything out of nothing. And science, the new theology, is in fact the "vehicle of all mental power, of all human and earthly greatness." Through an understanding of man and nature, science can feed the hungry, cure the sick, and free the oppressed. Overthrow conventional thinking, Büchner intones, and destroy the accumulated prejudices fostered by "a whole clique of pharisees, hypocrites, mystics, Jesuits, and pietists." Then possess ultimate knowledge.[52]

The Russian nihilists were entranced. Büchner's radical materialism appealed to their desire for rebellion, and they heeded his call to question all, dissolve all, and begin from the beginning. Captivated by this obscure German philosopher, they scorned Romantic dreams and all empty, idealistic words such as "principles," "values," "progress," "democracy," even "freedom." "All that matters is that two and two makes four," Bazarov tells Arkady, in a paraphrase of Büchner. "All of the rest is just trivial."[53]

In *Fathers and Sons,* Bazarov is obsessed with dissecting frogs, a potent metaphor for this desire of his generation to pull nature apart and lay bare its constituent parts. Art, music, and philosophy were replaced by the scalpel and the microscope. But the doctrine of destruction was not grounded in a love of chaos and disorder. Instead, it was based upon faith, the belief that if the old world was destroyed, a new one could be built on firmer, more scientific foundations. "Science," Büchner prophesied, "shall bring to man not only spiritual and moral, but likewise political and social deliverance."[54] In essence, the nihilists had faith in *Force and Matter.*

In *Fathers and Sons,* Turgenev sought to expose the shallow quality of this materialist belief system. Somewhat unfairly, Turgenev allowed Bazarov to meet his match not in a philosophy but in a woman: the cold, imperturbable Anna Odintsova. Bazarov, following Büchner, dismisses love as nothing more than a combination of biological reflexes. But after meeting Anna, he finds himself defenseless against an upsurge of irrational, passionate desire. Nihilism fails him, and he is forced to abandon his faith. Bazarov, like so many of Turgenev's characters, is undone by unrequited love. In the end, he dies, perhaps by his own hand, and his last words are a testimony to his loss of faith: "Now . . . darkness. . . ."[55]

By implication, Turgenev argued that nihilism was nothing more than empty rebellion, destined to die a quiet death. He could not have been more wrong.

～

The life of civilized people is full of little conventional lies. Persons who dislike each other, meeting in the street, make their faces radiant with a happy smile; the Nihilist remained unmoved, and smiled only for those whom he was really glad to meet. All those forms of outward politeness which are mere hypocrisy were equally repugnant to him, and he assumed a certain external roughness as a protest against the smooth amiability of his fathers. . . .

The Nihilist girl, compelled by her parents to be a doll in a doll's house, and to marry for property's sake, preferred to abandon her house and her silk dresses; she put on a black woolen dress of the plainest description, cut off her hair, and went to a high school, in order to win personal independence. . . .

Nihilism, with its affirmation of the rights of the individual and its negation of all hypocrisy, was but a first step toward a higher type of men and women, who are equally free, but live for a great cause.

— PETER KROPOTKIN, *Memoirs of a Revolutionist*[56]

In May 1862, shortly after the publication of *Fathers and Sons*, mysterious fires broke out in St. Petersburg. The city's buildings were mostly wood, so the flames spread rapidly from building to building, incinerating whole quarters of the central district. The most destructive of the fires swept through the enormous Apraksin market on Nevskii, where rickety shanties housed the sellers' wares. One eyewitness to the inferno was Peter Kropotkin, the future anarchist, who was at that time enrolled in the Imperial Corps of Pages, an aristocratic military school. He remembered the astonishing sight of clothing, books, furniture, and bedding succumbing to the whirling flames. "Like an immense snake," he wrote, "the fire threw itself in all directions, right and left, enveloped the shanties, and suddenly rose in a huge column, darting out its whistling tongues to lick up more shanties with their contents."[57]

The sudden eruption of the fires, and their unpredictable fury, led many to suspect arson. Conspiracy theories were plentiful; many were directed at the university students of St. Petersburg, whose protests and demonstrations seemed to indicate a general urge to incite disorder and mayhem. While the acrid smoke still wafted through the city, and workers were attempting to salvage goods from the smoldering wreckage, Turgenev strolled along Nevskii Prospekt. To his surprise, he was accosted by an excitable acquaintance, who immediately exclaimed, "Look at what your nihilists are doing! They are setting Petersburg on fire!"[58]

Suddenly, *Fathers and Sons* became the center of a swirl of controversy. The reaction to the novel was swift and astonishing. "Nihilism" was the word on everyone's lips, as Turgenev's characters seemingly sprang to life before everyone's eyes. The novel captured the generational disputes unfolding in the university hallways and on the streets of St. Petersburg. The irrepressible rebelliousness of Russia's youth had a handy new name.[59]

In the polemics between Russian conservatives and radicals, *Fathers and Sons* became a weapon. Conservatives eagerly adopted the new word, "nihilism," as a stick with which to beat all enemies of the government. Activists could now be branded as nothing more than irreverent, destructive "nihilists." For a time, the term was universally considered an insult. Only a few conservatives sensed that Bazarov was not so easily mocked. Mikhail Katkov, Turgenev's publisher, a prominent conservative and a friend of the Russian royal court, warned Turgenev in a letter that *Fathers and Sons* made Bazarov too seductive, too heroic. "There is concealed approval lurking here," he suggested.[60]

Initially, radicals were angered by what they took to be Turgenev's parody of their beliefs. Bazarov was far too crude and coarse to be a hero, and "nihilism" had such disparaging undertones. Turgenev was devastated by these criticisms. Like the "fathers" he parodied, he wanted nothing more than the approval of the younger generation. In letter after letter to his critics, he vainly tried to mend fences, pleading an earnest love for his character. "Many of my readers would be amazed," he lamented, "if I told them that I share almost all of Bazarov's convictions."[61]

Turgenev's progressive reputation was finally saved by Dmitrii Pisarev, one of Russia's leading left-wing polemicists. In a bold reversal, astonishing Russian conservatives and revolutionaries alike, Pisarev declared that *Fathers and Sons* was an accurate portrait of his generation. Pisarev was proud to call himself a nihilist.

In an 1862 review of *Fathers and Sons*, simply entitled "Bazarov," Pisarev pronounced Bazarov a hero. Bazarov's pride was mere honesty; his impolite behavior, mere transparency. He scorned false refinement, much like the "Americans" who, in Pisarev's words, "throw their legs over the backs of chairs and spit tobacco juice on the parquet floors of elegant hotels." Bazarov was a poor man, a man who had lived a hard life, and "from hard labor the hands coarsen, as do the manners and emotions." It was not a pretty sight, Pisarev acknowledged, but readers had to admit that Bazarov was straightforward, daring, and strong. "If Bazarovism is a disease," Pisarev insisted, "then it is a disease of our time."[62]

Pisarev's review swept through Russia's radical community and soon became as famous as the novel itself. The sixties generation was given full-throated permission to embrace nihilism. In an astonishing example of life imitating literary criticism, radicals became Bazarovs. Young men, though most often the sons of noblemen, deliberately dressed like workers, wearing grimy overalls or dirty, ill-fitting coats, as if they could not afford better. They allowed their hair to grow long and unkempt and wore dark, blue-tinted glasses. Young women cut their hair short and wore plain wool or cotton dresses that looked more like canvas bags, and they, too, often sported the tiny blue glasses that became all the rage. Clothing and behavior were invested with deep political significance: Gnarled wooden walking sticks, gnawed fingernails, and the particularly emblematic plaid shawl became the easily recognizable markers of nihilistic radical chic. Both sexes renounced the etiquette of the age: Men refused to stand when a woman walked into a room; women rested their feet on chairs or smoked in public. They refused to smile, to use conventional greetings, to act deferentially before parents and elders. They openly mocked religious beliefs and rituals, dismissed traditional art as Romantic nonsense, and scorned progressive opinions as mere talk. They conspicuously read Büchner's *Force and Matter* and declared that only science was worthy of study. Medicine became a popular subject at the universities; dissecting frogs, a popular pastime.

Turgenev's invented word had become a living concept. Alexander Herzen, thoroughly bemused, wrote, "This mutual interaction of people and books is a strange thing. . . . Real people take on the character of their literary shadows."[63]

In the gloomy confines of her boarding school, nihilism appeared to Vera as a ray of light. She sought out and eagerly devoured the illicit radical literature that so consumed her contemporaries. If "Masha" is any guide, she even spent her summer breaks in the school library, diligently studying radical books and journals. There was no doubt, nihilism perfectly suited Vera's rebellious temperament. Her tomboyish impulses and disregard for conventional etiquette made her an outcast among her noble peers. But nihilist literature convinced her that, somewhere, a whole cohort of young, energetic, passionate people would accept her for who she was, stained cuffs, torn skirts, unmanageable hair, and all. In Vera's story, Masha writes of the nihilists as a near obsession, occupying a primary place "in her internal world." They were "her secret, which she revealed to no one."[64]

Vera later explained that, for her cohort, nihilism simply meant liberation. The generation of the sixties wanted nothing less than the "merciless" destruction of the "stuffy, constricting" world of tradition and formality that held them fast. No longer content with the vacillations of their forties predecessors, the nihilists sought an uncompromising rejection of everything old. They wanted answers to the burning questions of the day—"all of them at once," in Vera's words, "without reservations and doubts."[65] And though she later lost some of the naive idealism of her youth, she never ceased to refer to herself as one of the *shestidesiatnitsy,* women of the sixties. Indeed, even as an old woman she dressed as a nihilist, wearing plain, poorly sewn dresses, oversized hats and shawls, and scuffed workmen's boots.

But in the end, for Vera and her compatriots, Bazarov's nihilism meant little more than posturing. It could inspire fashionable rebellion, but it could not satisfy deeper yearnings for meaningful belief and action. What would come of scruffy attire, brusque mannerisms, and amateur scientific experiments? After the ground had been cleared, what would be built in its place? The generation of the 1860s wanted a clearer statement of the faith. In 1863, an answer to their questions came in the form of another novel, whose title reflected the concerns of the age: *What Is to Be Done?*

CHAPTER 4

The New People

~~~

O n May 19, 1864, Nikolai Chernyshevskii was led to a specially constructed wooden scaffold in one of the central squares of St. Petersburg. Despite the persistent rain, a large crowd gathered to watch the
spectacle, including a number of students dressed in typical nihilist fashion.
Fearing demonstrations, the police closely guarded the scaffold and, by linking hands in a chain, did their best to keep the crowds back. A police carriage pulled up to the square, and Chernyshevskii was ushered out and led,
blinking through his rain-spattered glasses, to the center of the scaffold. A
sign around his neck read STATE CRIMINAL. Abruptly, he was ordered to
kneel. A gendarme took a wooden sword, held it over Chernyshevskii's head,
and then broke it in two. In this manner, Chernyshevskii was symbolically
"executed"—stripped of his civil rights and given over to the Russian penal
system.

As he was led away from the scaffold to begin his long journey to Siberian exile, flowers rained down upon Chernyshevskii's head, thrown from the
crowd by men, women, and even young girls. Spontaneously, with tears in
their eyes, his supporters cheered their hero. For them, the entire ceremony
marked not his humiliation but his martyrdom. Chernyshevskii was their savior, sacrificing all so that they might live.[1]

~

*No novel of Turgenev and no writings of Tolstoy or any other writer have
ever had such a wide and deep influence upon Russian society as this novel
had. It became the watchword of Young Russia, and the influence of the
ideas it propagated has never ceased to be apparent since.*
    —PETER KROPOTKIN, *Ideals and Realities in Russian Literature*[2]

In 1899, Nikolai Volskii, a Bolshevik and great friend of Vladimir Lenin,
was in the apartment of an old socialist, a man of Vera's generation. As the
old man consumed several glasses of vodka (with pickled mushrooms), he regaled Volskii with tales of his youthful political exploits. Toward the end of

the evening, the old socialist decided that Volskii was worthy of a special honor. Reverently, from a hiding place, the old man took out a copy of Nikolai Chernyshevskii's *What Is to Be Done?* Volskii was instructed to read the book carefully and to return it in perfect condition. Volskii did his best with the novel but found himself utterly bewildered: "I had never before read such a vapid, untalented and barbarously written book."

Volskii was determined to discover why Russia's old socialists so venerated this unexceptional novel. Five years later, after he befriended Vera Zasulich, he confronted her with the question—why was Chernyshevskii considered such an icon? Vera became nearly breathless with agitation. "You don't understand it," she stammered. "You just don't understand it." She claimed that Chernyshevskii wrote for socialists alone, and they alone recognized the deep profundity of his ideas. "Chernyshevskii was hampered by censorship and he had to write in allusions and hieroglyphs. We were able to decipher them, but you, the young people of the 1900s, don't have this knack. You read a passage in Chernyshevskii and find it dull and empty, but in fact there is a great revolutionary idea concealed in it."

Dissatisfied, Volskii later asked Lenin the same question. Lenin nearly exploded with rage when Volskii characterized *What Is to Be Done?* as "untalented, crude and, at the same time, pretentious." "I declare that it is impermissible to call *What Is to Be Done?* crude and untalented," Lenin fumed at Volskii. "Hundreds of people became revolutionaries under its influence. . . . I spent not days but several weeks reading it. Only then did I understand its depth. This novel provides inspiration for a lifetime." Volskii came to a startling realization: Much of what Russia and the world understood as "Leninism" was not derived from Marxism alone. Long before Lenin encountered Marx, he had been an ardent follower of Nikolai Chernyshevskii.[3]

Lovers of Russian literature will be astonished to learn what scholars have known for some time: In the second half of the nineteenth century—the age of Russian literature's most significant achievements—one of the most popular books was a barely readable political tract. Nothing written by Dostoyevsky or Tolstoy could rival the influence of *What Is to Be Done?* In an era when books were sacred, this book was the most sacred of all. The only comparable text—and it was a comparison the author would not have rejected—was the Bible itself.[4]

Young, educated Russians of the 1860s did not merely read this novel.

They reread it obsessively, memorized it, quoted passages from it like a cate-chism, and carried it around with them like a prayer book. "We read the novel almost like worshippers," one contemporary wrote, "with the kind of piety with which we read religious books." Its impact was immeasurable. All of Russia's most famous authors wrote about it, and commentaries on the novel can be discovered in *Anna Karenina* and *Crime and Punishment*. Every self-respecting Russian socialist, in particular, had to have an opinion of it.[5]

The author of this phenomenon knew he was no literary genius. He saw himself as something much greater: a revolutionary prophet.

It is perhaps unsurprising that Chernyshevskii was the son of a priest, born in 1828 in the provincial town of Saratov. Extremely devout as a child, Cherny-shevskii was expected to follow his father's vocation. He was sent to an Or-thodox seminary, where he flourished, mastering his studies with extraordinary ease. By the time he graduated, he had read most of the classics of world lit-erature, including all of the works that would later greatly influence his writing—Sand, Rousseau, and Dickens; he had also acquired a mastery of French, Italian, German, English, Latin, Greek, Old Slavonic, and even a bit of Persian.[6]

Convinced that a brilliant future awaited him, Chernyshevskii's parents and teachers eagerly encouraged him to study at the university, and so he was sent to St. Petersburg. At the young age of eighteen, flush with dreams of glory, Chernyshevskii boldly entered the city. In his heart, he knew that he was destined for greatness. In 1846, shortly before he left home, he wrote to his cousin: "To help work for the glory, not fleeting but eternal, of one's fa-therland and for the good of mankind—what can be higher and more desired than that?"[7]

Limitless dreams are inevitably disappointed. St. Petersburg, far from impressed at the arrival of this supreme talent, coldly ignored the arrival of another boy from the provinces. In Saratov, Chernyshevskii was sheltered and pampered, his confidence bolstered by constant praise. In St. Peters-burg, he was completely lost in the crowd.

In Russia's capital, a provincial son of the clergy was to know his place. Distinctions were rarely openly stated, but small things constantly marked social rank. Unlike his noble and wealthy counterparts, Chernyshevskii had poor French pronunciation, since he had never had a French nanny or tutor. He had no musical education and no talent for dancing. Finally, he had little money and could scarcely afford to heat his room, let alone buy a new, expensive overcoat. Humiliated by his obvious poverty and rustic manners, he began to avoid society.[8]

Chernyshevskii, like so many of his generation, thus experienced leaving home as a profound personal crisis. His appearance changed as a result—he became shy and awkward. Photographs show him squinting through his glasses, at times with his face hidden behind long, curly hair. Only his friends knew that behind the nervous, mouse-like manner, Chernyshevskii's brilliance persisted.[9]

He withdrew into himself, seeking solace in the life of his mind. Intensely self-analytical, he struggled to reconcile his deep ambition for greatness with his obvious social insignificance. The world grew increasingly alien to him. Soon, he was spinning into a vicious mental spiral: The more self-analytical he became, the more detached he was from reality; the more anti-social his attitudes, the more lacerating his inner life. For a time, he kept a diary, in which he recorded every detail of his outer life. He began to note absurd minutiae—the minutes it took him to walk from one place to another, the number of tears he shed when a friend died, the precise location of furniture at a party. He even drew elaborate diagrams of his movements during social events. It was a desperate attempt to break out of his isolation, but it failed. He began to complain of a coldness in his heart, of a lack of emotion. He might have descended into insanity.[10]

By this time, he had lost all faith in his father's God. The love of God seemed feeble, abstract, and distant. Salvation would come from somewhere else. For Chernyshevskii, as for so many Russians during that age, it was found on the road to socialism.

For the generation of the sixties, which had grown up steeped in religion, it proved impossible to merely cast aside what they had cherished for so long. Though they became convinced that religion, as an unscientific belief system, had to be discarded, they did not wish to relinquish their desire to believe in something far greater than themselves. Youthful religious dreams of martyrdom, self-abnegation, and faith in transcendence did not easily fade away.

Bazarovism, with its cynical, smirking attitude toward tradition, was fashionable for a time. But after a while, radicals turned to works of philosophy and literature with a yearning for flashes of insight and moments of transformation. Theirs was no cold, analytical attitude toward ideas. They were looking for living philosophies that could consume their souls with the power of faith.

In socialism, especially "utopian" socialism, the sixties generation found what it sought. Socialism was comfortably compatible with modern philosophical materialism. Like nihilism, it preached the destruction of the old: government, society, and God himself. It called for a scientific approach to equality and justice. But nineteenth-century socialism was rarely a mere political economy and promised far more than a mechanical redistribution of social goods and services. It was also a dream of human empowerment, a prophecy of universal enlightenment, and, above all, a tribute to the limitlessness of human possibility. If God was dead, many socialists suggested, what was to stop men from becoming gods?[11]

Mikhail Bakunin was among the first to capture the new spirit. Struggling against a mundane existence, he abandoned traditional Christianity and serially embraced, then rejected, the German philosophies of Fichte, Schelling, and Hegel. He did not "read" books—he was entirely consumed by them and allowed them to transform his views, his behavior, and his relationships. He craved more than mere insight; he sought an ideal to which he could devote his life.[12]

In 1842, his search finally ended. "My former faith and my strength," he wrote, "are gathering as for a resurrection." He spoke of having divorced his "wife," philosophy. His new bride? "Revolution." By 1843, his views were clear. "We are speaking of nothing less than a new religion, a religion of democracy, which began its struggle, its life and death struggle, under the banner of 'liberty, equality, fraternity.' "[13]

From faith to alienation to resurrection—for those who made the journey, socialism arrived as an epiphany. In their autobiographies, radicals recalled the books that placed them on the true path. Lavrov's *Historical Letters* "consumed" Osip Aptekman, "like the faithful are consumed by the Koran or the New Testament." Sofia Boreisho was tantalized by books which spoke of "another kind of life, so different from ours." Mikhail Drei spent a whole night reading a Pisarev article and remembered that "from that day, my life changed forever."[14]

"At that time, we did not see socialism as a science," wrote Alexander Pribylev, "but as an ethical system, like a faith or a religion." Nothing was more beautiful than dedicating one's life to the realization of mankind's deepest and most beautiful dreams—the creation of, in Bakunin's words, the "Kingdom of God on Earth."[15]

Chernyshevskii's trajectory was no different. Strangely, his quest for enlightenment began with *Principles of the Philosophy of the Future*, by Ludwig Feuerbach. Feuerbach was a German philosophical materialist who claimed, like Büchner, that the world was made of matter alone. Unlike Büchner, he infused his materialism with sensuality. To know what is real, Feuerbach wrote, one has to feel with all five senses, and feel with a fervent intensity. Above all, one must love. The *Principles* speak of the force of sensual love to reawaken and rehabilitate mankind. "Love," wrote Feuerbach, "is the ontological proof of the existence of an object apart from our mind; there is no other proof of being."[16]

For Chernyshevskii, Feuerbach's credo was a liberation. Love would recompose his inner turmoil. He began memorizing whole passages from Feuerbach's works. His reading came at a fortuitous time—he was falling deeply in love with a man who would change his life. Vasilii Lobodovskii, a university student and the son of a priest, was a fellow outcast from St. Petersburg society. A self-confident man of ferocious will, Lobodovsky urged Chernyshevskii not to suffer but to act. Together, they would rebuke society, not conform to it. The sheer power of his personality drew Chernyshevskii in. Soon, the two men shared their innermost thoughts, including dreams of a glorious future. "I love you, Vasilii Petrovich, I love you!" Chernyshevskii exclaimed in his diary.[17]

Chernyshevskii's love for his friend was strictly platonic, born out of a deep sense of gratitude. Nonetheless, it drew him out of his shell and into a world now made whole by that love. Inspired, Chernyshevskii was determined to create a new world, in which every man and woman could live in love fulfilled.[18]

Thus armed with a liberating philosophical materialism, Chernyshevskii was ready for the next step—the conversion to utopian socialism. He found what he sought in the works of the French socialist Charles Fourier. Fourier's utopian writings were so idiosyncratic that readers either dismissed them as lunatic or regarded them as revelation. For Chernyshevskii there was no doubt: Fourier's was the religion of the future.[19]

～

Finally you will see that passionate attraction, accused by your philosophers of depravity and corruption, is the wisest and most wonderful of all God's works. It alone, operating with no constraint and on no basis except the allurements of sensual pleasure, will establish universal unity across the globe and cause wars, revolutions, poverty and injustice to disappear. . . .

Alone, I have confounded twenty centuries of political imbecility, and it is to me alone that present and future generations will owe the initiation of their immense happiness.
— CHARLES FOURIER, *Theory of the Four Movements*[20]

Fourier, an ordinary merchant turned philosopher, apparently discovered the key to human happiness in the bowels of Paris's Bibliothèque Nationale. After emerging from piles of treatises, Fourier decided to write the single book that would end all writing, because it contained the key to "the most astounding, and happiest, event possible on this or any other globe, *the transition from social chaos to universal harmony.*" Caution was necessary, Fourier warned, for not every aspect of this marvelous discovery could be revealed. Some details would be so tantalizing that weak souls might be "struck dead by the force of their ecstasy."[21]

Lovers of science were reassured that Fourier had done precise, even mathematical, calculations. It was a scientific fact that history, philosophy, and theology had conspired to gravely mislead the human race. The past masters of these disciplines failed to recognize the supreme forces governing human destiny: the passions. For so many blighted years, ambition, lust, envy, and pride were derided as sins. A blind humanity had failed to recognize that these passions, in fact, propelled everything from planetary motion to climate change to social relations. Suppressing passions led to terrible human misery—poverty, crime, and tyranny. Even famines and earthquakes were nature's punishment, the natural world lashing humanity for failing to liberate human potential.[22]

The solution was simple. All existing human institutions, rooted in false premises, were to be ripped apart, root and branch: marriage, family, agriculture, industry. In their place, Fourier proposed a new society based on "associations" (also known as phalansteries, or communes). Associations would scientifically engineer human interactions according to the dictates of the passions. Marriage, the root of unhappiness, would make way for free love, thus releasing sexual passions. Children, who were in general "pretty intolerable," would be raised collectively. Ambition and pride would be properly harnessed and used as incitements to work long and hard: Work teams would be organized, adorned with uniforms, flags, and coats of arms. Teams would compete to construct buildings, harvest grain, and till the soil. Joining a particular industrial army would be even more tempting, Fourier thought, if each army were to publish a list of its own selected "virgins," whose favor could be won by a display of exceptional effort and enthusiasm.[23]

This proper arrangement of the passions would engender a new kingdom of "eternal bliss." Freed to achieve their full potential, Fourier declared, the human race would accomplish things unimaginable to previous generations. Sexual fulfillment would achieve new heights; aesthetic creations would astound (approximately thirty-seven million poets would be produced, all equal to Homer). Collectively prepared meals, designed by those whose passion was food, would taste better than anything found in the finest of old-world restaurants. And nature herself would bless this new order. The climate would become universally mild, and the sea would turn into a sweet, potable liquid much like lemonade.[24]

In Chernyshevskii's mind, Fourier's socialism melded perfectly with Feuerbach's philosophy of love. Fourier's had constructed an entire social order based on rationality and the proper ordering of the most essential human impulses, including love. Moreover, he promised nothing less than a harmonious, ecstasy-filled future order that seemed like heaven on earth. Chernyshevskii happily embraced Fourier's visions, and found his calling as a prophet of utopian socialism.

By the 1850s, then, Chernyshevskii had found his voice. As an editor of the radical journal *The Contemporary,* he penned article after article on aesthetics, art, literature, economics, and society. He tirelessly championed Russia's poor, especially the peasants. He was earnestly committed to the cause of women's emancipation and advocated full sexual and professional freedom for Russian women. But all of these causes—the emancipation of the serfs, the liberation of women, the foundation of a new economic order—were mere increments toward Chernyshevskii's ultimate utopian goal.

At first, Chernyshevskii collaborated with and admired the men of the forties—Herzen, Turgenev, and their devotees—believing them to be fellow travelers on the road to socialism. He was abashed to discover that they refused to accept him as an equal. His lower-class background drew their resilient snobbery to the surface. The most common term of derision hurled at Chernyshevskii was "seminarian." Tolstoy snidely remarked that he "smelled of bedbugs," and Herzen patronizingly dismissed Chernyshevskii and his cohort for having the manners of "court clerks, store assistants, and the servant's quarters of a landowner's house." The men of the forties revealed their true colors—as conventional noble snobs. As revolutionaries, they were elitist dilettantes.[25]

Chernyshevskii's disillusionment gradually became a fierce, abiding anger. Increasingly aggressive and polemical, he fashioned himself into a kind of literary Bazarov. He accused Turgenev and Herzen of lacking character and consistency. His rage at their hypocrisy grew to limitless proportions: "These are the people of whom the scriptures say they should be saved with iron. In literature we still need an iron dictatorship, to make them tremble."[26]

With wretched irony, Chernyshevskii himself would experience the "iron dictatorship" that he so fervently wished on others. His irate radicalism worried the tsarist regime. After the St. Petersburg fires, odd rumors began to circulate. Chernyshevskii was reportedly at the head of a monstrous revolutionary plot and was personally coordinating protests, demonstrations, and arson. It was said that he could halt a student demonstration with a stroke of his pen. He was arrested in 1862, almost entirely on manufactured evidence of subversive activity. He spent two long years under interrogation in St. Petersburg's notorious Peter and Paul Fortress.[27]

Only absurd incompetence prevented the regime from silencing this young firebrand. Chernyshevskii was allowed to continue writing and publishing from prison. The warden provided pens, ink, and carefully rationed sheets of paper. Since impassioned articles on the plight of peasants were obviously out of the question, Chernyshevskii decided to try his hand at writing a novel.

Long into the night, his fingers stiff with cold, he wrote *What Is to Be Done?* Despite his wretched circumstances, he found it an intensely liberating experience. He unleashed his pent-up creative urges and returned to his old dreams of realizing humanity's deepest yearnings. He poured all into this one text—Feuerbach's philosophy, Fourier's socialism, vitriolic criticism of Turgenev and Herzen, views on the woman question, and ruminations on love. Beneath it all was a single, breathtaking purpose: to inspire people to create a new world order.[28]

Serialized in *The Contemporary* in 1863, Chernyshevskii's novel was subtitled "Novel of the New People." To this day, it is a complete mystery why the Russian censors allowed the work to see the light of day. In his novel *The Gift*, Vladimir Nabokov maliciously speculated that the censor found Chernyshevskii's book so tedious, long-winded, and insufferable that he assumed it would only inspire mockery and disdain.[29]

Nabokov was right—by all imaginable critical standards, the novel is a disaster. The book's narrator is smug, and the characters are stiff, unlikable, and prone to bombastic speeches. The plot is so contrived as to defy belief. But *What Is to Be Done?* never aspired to literary style. Chernyshevskii did not care whether his readers enjoyed his novel. He wanted them to give up everything and follow him.

～

And, to begin with, I shall even tell you the outcome of the entire novel: it will end happily, amidst wine and song. There will be neither striking scenes nor embellishments. The author is in no mood for such things, dear public, because he keeps thinking about the confusion in your head, and about the useless, unnecessary suffering of each and every one of us that results from the absurd muddle in your thoughts. I find it both pitiful and amusing to look at you. You are so impotent and spiteful, all because of the extraordinary quantity of nonsense stuffed between your two ears. . . .

Yet there is among you, dear readers, a particular group of people—by now a fairly sizeable group—which I respect. I speak arrogantly to the vast majority of readers, but to them alone, and up to this point I have been speaking only to them. But with the particular group I just mentioned, I would have spoken humbly, even timidly. There is no need to offer them any explanation. I value their opinion, but I know in advance that they're on my side. Good, strong, honest, capable people—you have only just begun to appear among us; already there's a fair number of you and it's growing all the time."

—NIKOLAI CHERNYSHEVSKII, *What Is to Be Done?*[30]

Deceptively, the book begins as a conventional sentimental novel. The heroine, Vera Pavlovna, is forced by her family to accept the advances of a vulgar but wealthy young man whom she does not love. Like a true sentimental heroine, she finds it impossible to accept such a "vile, intolerable, and humiliating position." But Vera is not quite what she appears; even her most painful emotions seem calculated. At a critical moment in the novel, when Vera is in deepest despair, she contemplates suicide. Despair, however, is tempered by rather practical concerns:

And then what? Everyone will stare—the skull's split open, the face is smashed, bloodied, and muddied . . . No, if only you could spread some clean sand on the spot beforehand—but even the sand here is dirty. . . . No, I mean some of the cleanest, whitest sand: now that would be nice!

Fortunately, for lack of clean sand, Vera does not end her life.[31]

Instead, she is rescued, as young heroines must be, by a courageous hero

who braves all enemies to save her. He comes in the guise of an impoverished tutor, Dmitrii Lopukhov, who is a handsome but studious and extraordinarily serious young man. He immediately recognizes Vera's terrible
predicament and eventually comes to her rescue by marrying her. To the
shock of Vera's family, the two elope.[32]

Lopukhov then behaves quite unlike the standard love-struck protagonist. On his wedding night, he is tormented by a single thought: Will Vera erroneously believe that he is a noble person? He finally tells her the truth—his
motives were purely, utterly selfish. Vera, in turn, is by no means dismayed.
Instead, she is deeply impressed by his noble self-interest and his devotion to
a philosophy known as "rational egoism." Soon enough, Vera also begins to
dedicate her life, selfishly, to this principle.[33]

Lopukhov and Vera quickly arrange their lives in accordance with strict
rational-egoistic principles. They sleep in separate rooms, spend their lives in
separate pursuits, and meet only at predetermined times. Such formality is
intended to give each of them complete freedom of thought, movement, and
activity. Sex is out of the question—Lopukhov will not oppress Vera with his
masculine desires. Thus truly liberated, Vera is on her way to becoming a
fully independent and fulfilled human being.[34]

Chernyshevskii chose his main character's name wisely—in Russian, Vera
means "faith." Through faith, the path to wisdom is opened. Vera's road to rational egoism is fraught with difficulty, but she perseveres, drawing the
reader along with her. She is assisted along the way by those who share her
faith, men and women whom Chernyshevskii fatefully names "the new people." These are Russia's radicals, the restless generation of the sixties, who,
like Vera, are still searching for the new truth. They have embraced nihilism,
they emulate Bazarov, and their desires are noble. But they need to find a
better way.

Throughout the novel, Chernyshevskii continually references *Fathers
and Sons* as both inspiration and foil. Like Bazarov, the "new people" are
fascinated with medicine and science and scornful of tradition and social
conventions. They voraciously read materialist philosophy and dissect an
enormous quantity of frogs. Unlike Bazarov, however, they do not merely
reject—they act, decisively and with triumphant success, guided toward enlightenment by the utilitarian principles of rational egoism.[35]

As the novel didactically explains, a rational egoist acts only in accordance with his "advantage," asking one question of himself: "What is best for
me?" Seen in the proper light, the most noble acts of men are, in fact, but

"self-interest clearly understood." For Bazarov-like worshippers of science, this was a satisfying formula. Traditional philosophy and religious morality caused misery by demanding impossible restraint and sacrifice from men. Pursuing self-interest liberated "natural" impulses. In biological terms, outdated ethical systems like Christianity were "unhealthy." Health was achieved by following two simple maxims: Avoid pain, and seek pleasure.[36]

And what of those who found pleasure in deception, violence, and murder? They were ignorant and ill. They were victims of a society that failed to teach people where their true interest lay. *What Is to Be Done?* is full of stories of prostitutes, rakes, and corrupt souls deceived by whims and passing desires, blind to *rational* self-interest. That is, until they are healed. Chernyshevskii's was an entirely new theology, which abolished the concept of sin and replaced it with disease. Utilitarianism was the universal cure.[37]

Rational egoism was, in essence, the foundation upon which Russian socialism was built. A life lived in complete equality with others—equality of opportunity, equality of means, equality of pleasure—was only possible when people were guided by the proper ethical principles. But according to biology, people were motivated by selfish, material appetites. Thus the task of the socialist prophet was to create an ethics of self-interest, to explain how equality could become a natural, selfish aim. "Regarding the stupidity of people," Chernyshevskii wrote in his masterpiece, "a factor you consider to be an obstacle to the setting up of the new order, I am in complete agreement with you. But . . . people become smarter rather quickly when they realize that it's to their advantage to do so." This tautology influenced reformers for countless generations.[38]

Vera Pavlovna sees the beauty of this approach in her first challenge in the novel: constructing a worker's commune. She takes a group of uneducated but hardworking seamstresses and creates a sewing shop unlike any other in Russia—a communal enterprise that instructs, ennobles, and enriches its members.[39] In the book, the project consumes a few short pages: First, the seamstresses are given their share of the profits of the enterprise; then they willingly combine their profits to create a common expense fund; finally, in no time at all, they pool all of their resources to buy a communal apartment. Not only do the women enjoy the benefits of shared chores and shared expenses, but they even find the time for pure fun—communal outings to the theater, to balls, and to picnics. The project was, in Chernyshevskii's words, "very easy, simple, and natural." All Vera had to do was to explain, carefully, how each step benefited each woman individually. A blueprint for a socialist worker's commune, based on "rational" principles. It seemed a wonder that no one had thought of it before.

It was but a first step. For Vera, rational egoism had yet to prove its full worth. Soon, she faced a far more difficult challenge—she had to solve the problem of love.[40]

When reduced to its essentials, *What Is to Be Done?* is a novel about free love. This was no accident. As heir to Feuerbach and Fourier, Chernyshevskii deeply believed that love was the key to human enlightenment and the basis of the perfect social order. It made equality joyful and freedom productive. But for love to do its work in transforming men, it first had to be transformed. It needed to be liberated.

In no small part, Chernyshevskii blamed misconceptions about love for the tragedy of human society. Traditional beliefs about marriage played their part, but even progressive views of love were implicated. The lacerating Romanticism of the forties generation was just as dangerous as the stultifying morality of the traditional church. In a sense, Chernyshevskii wished to rescue would-be Bazarovs from their victimization at the hands of Romantic illusions.

No person was more at fault for perpetuating irrational views of love than the archetypical "father," Alexander Herzen. In his literary creations and his personal life, Herzen provided a perfect example of the damaging effects of Romanticism gone awry. Herzen's sole novelistic venture, *Who Is to Blame?* is a tale of a Romantic love triangle turned tragedy, where noble intellectuals are torn between traditional morality and transformative love. The consequences for the three embroiled characters are dire: despair, alcoholism, and death from grief. The love triangle, for Herzen, proved that human beings were destined for tragedy. And no one was to blame.[41]

Critically acclaimed, the novel eerily presaged Herzen's own life. In 1848, a year after its publication, Herzen's wife, Natalie, betrayed him with another man. Unlike the husband in his own novel, Herzen knew whom to blame, and responded with rage, defending his honor and demanding a duel. Confronted by her husband's fury, Natalie, a better Romantic, grew ill and died. The story became an international affair, followed by everyone from Richard Wagner to Karl Marx. Herzen launched a campaign to vindicate his own behavior, but the entire sordid tale confirmed his status as a quintessential forties man, whose enlightened posturing only masked an aristocratic traditionalism. His hypocrisy was further revealed when, six years later, he himself became the lover of his best friend's wife.[42]

For Chernyshevskii and his cohort, *Who Is to Blame?* and the tragicomedy of Herzen's personal life illustrated the sheer lunacy of traditional love. Exclusive love was an atavistic social convention. It was, additionally, a trap for women, limiting their possibilities and forbidding them from achieving full emotional satisfaction. Men had to free their wives to do as they pleased. Enforced love led to dishonesty and despair. Free love was true love.[43]

Chernyshevskii was determined to overturn convention, not just in word but in deed. In 1853, he happily married Olga Sokratovna, a carefree and flirtatious woman with no interest in radicalism or intellectual matters of any sort. She freely made dramatic claims about the men she seduced right under Chernyshevskii's nose. He knew everything but was determined to become the opposite of men like Herzen. "If my wife wants to live with another man," he once stated, with pride, "I will say to her, 'My friend, when you decide that it is better to come back, please do so without any embarrassment.'"[44] *What Is to be Done?* was the incarnation of this principle, redeeming the suffering of novels past. In *Fathers and Sons,* Bazarov abandons all that he believes because of a woman; in *Who Is to Blame?* love destroys the lives of three noble people. By contrast, in *What Is to Be Done?* Vera escapes the clutches of a literary love triangle and sets love free.

It was not an easy task. Enter Alexander Kirsanov, a biologist, nihilist, and "new man." Vera Pavlovna falls passionately in love with him, triggering a profound crisis in her soul. She deeply respects her husband and tries to love him, failing to understand that love cannot be forced. When Lopukhov proposes a "natural" solution to their triangular plight—living in a kind of "ménage à trois"—she recoils in horror. Clinging to social conventions, she is trapped.[45]

Lopukhov, on the other hand, knows just what to do. Adhering to the righteous principles of rational egoism, he quickly realizes that he can have no satisfaction in an unhappy marriage. It is "to his advantage" to let Vera go. Quite selfishly, he pretends to commit suicide and leaves the country. This act finally releases Vera's bonds, both physical and mental. She comprehends, with joy, that the solution to her own terrible conundrum is, quite simply, "self-interest clearly understood." Quickly, she repays Lopukhov's favor by thinking only of herself.[46] Vera and Kirsanov are married, and the love triangle is dissolved. Dreams of self-sacrifice had never accomplished half as much in the whole corpus of Romantic literature. Even the residue of tragedy was scientifically erased. "No spiritual travail can withstand a sufficient dose of morphine," Chernyshevskii explains. Lopukhov's pain, precisely calculated, only required two pills. "One pill would have been too little, and three would have been too much."[47]

Rational egoism was thus established as the ultimate theology. It built communal workshops, solved personal crises, brought people to self-understanding. But the new people were still condemned, in biblical terms, to "see through a glass darkly." Socialism was not a mere rearrangement of marriage and labor. It was, in fact, the full glorification of man, the Kingdom of Heaven on Earth. Only Vera is given the ultimate blessing—a vision of the world that is to come.

～

There stands a building, a large, enormous structure such as can be seen only in a few of the grandest capitals. No, now there's no other building like it! It stands amidst fields and meadows, orchards and groves. The fields grow grain, but they aren't like the ones we have now; rather, they're rich and abundant. . . .

But this building—what on earth is it? What style of architecture? There's nothing at all like it now. No, there is one building that hints at it— the palace at Sydenham: cast iron and crystal, crystal and cast iron— nothing else. . . .

The windows themselves are huge, wide, and stretch the entire height of each floor. The stone walls look like a row of pilasters that form a frame for these windows looking out onto the galleries. What sort of floors and ceilings are these? Of what material are these doors and window frames made? What is it? Silver? Platinum? Almost all the furniture is made the same way. . . . How elegant it all is! Aluminum and more aluminum. . . .

The groups working in the fields are almost all singing. What kind of labor are they doing? Oh, they're gathering in the grain. How quickly it progresses! Why shouldn't it? Why shouldn't they be singing? Machines are doing almost all the work for them—reaping, binding the sheaves, and carting them away. . . .

They enter the building. It's the same sort of enormous, majestic hall. The evening is well under way. It's already three hours after sunset, a time for merrymaking. How brightly the hall is lit, but how? There are neither candelabra nor chandeliers! Oh, that's it! In the dome there hangs a large pane of frosted glass through which light pours into the room. Of course, that's just how it ought to be: pale, soft, bright light, just like sunlight. Yes, indeed, it is electric light. . . .

It is an ordinary weekday evening. People dance like this and make merry every evening. But when have I ever seen such energy in merriment? . . .

Is it ever really possible to forget one's grief and need entirely? Don't the deserts cover everything with sand? Don't the marshy miasmas contaminate even a small amount of good land and air lying between desert and swamp? But there are no such memories here, no danger of grief or need, only the recollection of free and willing labor, of abundance, goodness, and enjoyment.

—NIKOLAI CHERNYSHEVSKII, *What Is to Be Done?*[48]

Vera dreams a dream. In that dream, a marvelous building appears, built of glass and steel. It is a copy of the Crystal Palace, which housed the Great Exhibition in Sydenham, England, in 1851. Streams of international visitors came to the palace in that year to be awed by this miracle of modern technology. The main hall was so cavernous that large trees were allowed to grow within it, their branches touching the roofs. Light poured in through the enormous panes of glass, and so thin did the girders seem in the vastness that they gave the impression of weightlessness. Chernyshevskii, upon visiting the Crystal Palace in 1854, saw it as a living monument to the power of technology and the liberation of man. It was a fitting place to keep his new world.[49]

In Vera's dream, the palace stands in magnificent opulence, surrounded by nature, a vision of natural and technological harmony. Inside, the palace is filled with all of modernity's comforts: exotic foods, luxurious clothing reminiscent of Greek togas, comfortable furniture made of aluminum, and ubiquitous, warm electric light. Surrounding the palace are hundreds of thousands of flowers, fields upon fields of wheat, and deserts turned into fertile gardens. The people who inhabit this palace follow Fourier's blueprint—they let their passions live free, and thus know nothing of the toil and sweat of labor that was the curse of Adam. They only do what they love.[50]

And love, of course, is at the core of this utopia. Free love reigns. Couples choose their partners at will, entering specially designed chambers, and then emerging with "glowing cheeks" and "sparkling eyes."[51] Freed from the shackles of traditional morality, from the dead weight of conventions past, the new people are reborn. Chernyshevskii never could rid himself of his early Christian upbringing, and so he envisioned the residents of his new Jerusalem as transfigured by free love. In her dream, Vera Pavlovna looks in a mirror and sees herself surrounded by a golden, radiant light, in the manner of a Christian saint. She has become a goddess.[52]

"And will everyone live like this?" Vera asks in the dream. "Everyone," comes the answer. "For everyone there will be eternal spring and summer and joy everlasting." The words were carefully chosen. They were the echo of heaven, as described in the Orthodox prayer for the dead: "A place of brightness, a place of verdure, a place of repose, whence all sickness and sorrow and sighing have fled away." Before she wakes, Vera is given one last task: to save others as she has been saved. "Tell everyone that the future will be radiant and beautiful." Having revealed the Kingdom, Chernyshevskii called for apostles to spread the good news, to toil until all can enjoy the fruits of their labor. "Come up out of your godforsaken underworld, my friends, come up!" he wrote. "Come out into the light of day, where life is good and the path is easy and inviting." It was a revision of Christ's "My yoke is easy and my burden is light."[53]

When *What Is to Be Done?* was published, it immediately drew the universal venom of the literary establishment. The fathers poured scorn on this latest outburst by the sons. Turgenev sneered at Chernyshevskii's masterpiece: "His manner arouses physical disgust in me, like wormseed." He added, "Chernyshevskii unwittingly appears to me a naked and toothless old man who lisps like an infant." Herzen could not have agreed more: "Good Lord, how basely it is written, how much affectation . . . what style! What a worthless generation whose aesthetics are satisfied by this." *What Is to Be Done?* seemed the living confirmation of all of the crass extremism of the younger generation.[54]

But among Chernyshevskii's peers, the novel succeeded beyond his wildest imaginings. If the older generation found *What Is to Be Done?* insufferable, the younger generation found it indispensable. Those who had spent their youth in religious fervor, who had dreamed of suffering for the truth, now found their new bible. Never before in Russia had a work of imaginative literature become an infallible guide to life. It was, in the words of one radical, "not only an encyclopedia, a reference book, but a codex for the application of the new word . . . a complete guide to the remaking of social relations." Another went still further: "Manna from heaven never brought so much joy to the starving as this novel brought to the young people who had previously been wandering aimlessly around Petersburg. It was just like a vision sent from on high." It was considered all but holy—a prized possession and the ultimate gift. After it was banned by the censors, some radicals took it upon themselves to copy the novel, word for word, by hand, so that others could have a version of their own.[55]

As with any sacred text, every sentence was meticulously scrutinized, and every word infused with both universal and intensely personal meaning. "Who has not read and reread this famous work?" asked George Plekhanov, who would later become known as the father of Russian Marxism. "Who has not become cleaner, better, braver, and bolder under its philanthropic influence?" Lenin agreed wholeheartedly, claiming that the novel had shown him "what a revolutionary must be like, what his principles must be, how he must approach his aim, and what methods he must use to achieve it."[56]

Extraordinary examples of life imitating art followed the publication of Chernyshevskii's novel. Men gallantly offered to marry young women to free them from oppressive domestic situations, and women trapped in patriarchal families yearned for a Lopukhov to rescue them. After the wedding ceremonies, couples arranged their lives according to the strictures of the novel, with separate rooms and separate lives. One of the most famous examples of such marital relations was that of Sofia Kovalevskaia, later a famous mathematician. Deeply stirred by Chernyshevskii's novel, Kovalevskaia yearned to live a life of independence. Fervently seeking a rescuer, she finally found Vladimir Kovalevskii willing to do the job. Once married, the spouses lived in separate rooms and tried not to consummate their marriage, succeeding for several years. In another instance, Sergei Sinegub inexcusably fell in love with his "fictitious wife" but refused to confess his feelings, lest he violate the principles of their marriage. He was later greatly relieved to discover that his wife had fallen in love with him as well.[57]

Dressmaking establishments began to spring up everywhere, organized according to Chernyshevskii's principles. Bookbinding, laundering, and translation cooperatives soon followed. Often, those who wished to establish a commune used *What Is to Be Done?* as an exact blueprint. They would advertise for expert seamstresses and laundresses, or they would offer positions to prostitutes, hoping to reform them through labor. Communes were often attached to these enterprises, housing men and women together in large apartments.[58]

The love triangle became a popular radical lifestyle. Sofia Kovalevskaia openly wished her husband was a Moslem, so that he could rescue her sister as well, and the three could live, as Chernyshevskii suggested, "à trois." Often, *What Is to Be Done?* would convince women of the emptiness of their marriages and rouse them to abandon their husbands, or even to bring their lovers into the household. In each instance, a generous acquiescence was expected of "enlightened" husbands. Bakunin obligingly raised all three of his wife's children, despite the fact that they were, in fact, the children of his good friend and financial benefactor. Lenin himself thought nothing of loving two women: his wife, Nadezhda Krupskaia, and his beautiful and intelligent mistress, Inessa Armand (herself a champion of free love). Communal living was always arranged in such a way that every person was free to live with whomever he or she wished, and to change partners when the impulse arose.[59]

Above all, however, radicals impatiently awaited the coming of the Kingdom. Careful readers of the text proclaimed that the new world would arrive as early as 1866. Wild dreams of revolution were common and were universally accepted as prophecies of the new age. The height of the sixties had arrived. It was a glorious time to be alive.[60]

What Is to Be Done? gave the radicals a deep faith in the transformative power of socialism. Vera Zasulich herself recalled how the sixties generation's belief in the coming revolution held them up "like faith in the coming apocalypse succored the first Christian martyrs." And well before 1917, Lenin had conceived of his own plans for a communist utopia, which was generously embellished with visions of verdant fields and lives transformed with electric light.[61]

Lenin himself summarized the Russian radical theology succinctly: Chernyshevskii was "the greatest and most talented representative of socialism before Marx."[62]

In 1867, Vera graduated from school and was finally free to find her own way. Still shy, and her tall, thin figure no less clumsy, Vera never quite lost her awkward, adolescent demeanor. For the rest of her life, Vera would give the impression of someone uncomfortable in her own skin. Nonetheless, an important transformation had occurred in Vera's boarding school years: She had finally chosen a way of life.

It must have seemed like fate that the heroine of Chernyshevskii's novel shared her name, Vera. Chernyshevskii's *What Is to Be Done?* provided her with a new hope. Vera was entranced by this description of the "new people." They had broken through traditional conventions, and they were entirely liberated from the stultifying expectations of society, especially when it came to conduct. Above all, they were achieving great things.[63]

Vera had always chafed against the restrictions Russian society placed on her sex. As a girl, and then later during school, her rebellion against her gender role confined itself to an as yet undefined aversion to the life of a governess. Even then, however, she felt that a boy in her position would have been more free. With luck and willpower, an eager young man could work hard at school, enter the university, and then apply for almost any profession. He would not be confined to a tedious life of teaching spoiled children. In Vera's day, women could not even formally attend university. Ambitious young Russian women had to travel to Europe to study subjects such as medicine and the sciences. Noblewomen with limited means, like Vera, were confined to the finishing schools, where they learned to be either teachers or moderately educated provincial wives.[64]

In the sixties, many young women rejoiced in radicalism, because it suddenly opened up a whole world of activity. One of the central tenets of nihilism was that women were equal to men—they were to be treated in the same manner and expected to behave in the same way. Radical men dispensed with the conventional tokens of courtesy bestowed upon the "gentler" sex and, in turn, assumed that women would hold their own, both intellectually and physically. Chernyshevskii was among the strongest proponents of women's equality: He fully believed that women needed to have unfettered access to the same educational and professional opportunities as men. Moreover, Chernyshevskii argued that women would never fully flourish without complete sexual liberation and exhorted men to sacrifice themselves for this greater idea.[65]

There was no better example than Vera Pavlovna in *What Is to Be Done?* Chernyshevskii fashioned his main character as a strong-willed, rational, and competent young woman fit to lead his new society. Unlike the stereotypical nineteenth-century Russian heroine, Vera Pavlovna is ambitious and decisive. She dictates to her husband the terms of their living arrangements, she competently runs a cooperative venture, and later she pursues studies in medicine as a means to self-fulfillment. Most important, Vera Pavlovna achieves a life of personal and sexual happiness. In the end, she becomes the new standard of womanhood. When Vera Pavlovna becomes a goddess in her dream, she has replaced the Virgin Mary and all of the Christian female saints as the new vision of female perfection.[66]

Educated Russian women were captivated by this new standard of womanhood. In imitation of Chernyshevskii's heroine, they abandoned parental homes and, in some cases, their husbands and children in the quest to become liberated women. They joined communes and cooperatives and refused to marry men who would not promise to preserve their full freedom. Most important, however, they felt free to dream of lives of activity, of professional endeavor, and, ultimately, of revolutionary action.[67]

Trapped in the suffocating confines of the estate and the finishing school, Vera Zasulich saw radicalism as the path to escape, the path to true personal fulfillment. Women of the sixties generation, Vera later wrote, achieved "the historically rare happiness of acting not as the wives or mothers or inspirers of men, but in the capacity of fully independent, equal social activists." Or, as she later phrased it in her memoirs: "And so it was that the distant specter of revolution made me equal to a boy."[68]

But Chernyshevskii gave Vera far more than a blueprint for liberation. Curiously, he validated her impulse toward self-sacrifice and martyrdom. Under the guise of rational egoism, Chernyshevskii had explained, it was natural to see that "work on behalf of the people is the highest joy on earth." Vera realized there were others like her, who knew that what normal people considered painful self-sacrifice, "the new people considered happiness."[69]

In Vera's short story, "Masha," the main character's conversion to socialism occurs, in truly Chernyshevskiian fashion, when she falls in love. Masha at first merely admires the elegant and stern radical, Alexandra Vasilevna, from afar, attracted to her "silent, almost sad seriousness." Then, one evening, Masha accidentally overhears a conversation between Alexandra and an earnest young student. "Suffering," Alexandra explains to her friend, "will be redeemed with the kind of happiness you cannot imagine." The revolutionary life, she adds, is thus a source of "joy that cannot be surpassed." The words are not meant for Masha, but she takes them to heart, and is immediately seized by a dizzy exaltation. For days afterward, Masha's heart is filled with a burning love for Alexandra, whom she now sees as a living icon of female radicalism. In an echo of the transfiguration of Vera Pavlovna in *What Is to Be Done?* Masha imagines Alexandra surrounded by a glowing halo. Consumed by this schoolgirl crush, Masha timidly asks Alexandra for books to read, and thus begins her own journey down the path to radicalism. For Vera, the model for this incident may have been Alexandra Ivanova, a devout follower of Chernyshevskii whom Zasulich met while in boarding school in 1866.[70]

In any case, it was Chernyshevskii and his vision of love that gave the generation of the sixties, in Vera's words, their "blind faith" in the "second coming." Intoxicated with his glorious, prophetic visions of happiness, they would do anything to bring people to this promised land.[71]

～

What is to be done with the millions of facts that bear witness that men, knowingly, that is, fully understanding their real advantages, have left them in the background and have rushed headlong on another path, to risk, to chance, compelled to this course by nobody and by nothing, but, as it were, precisely because they did not want the beaten track, and stubbornly, willfully went off on another difficult, absurd way of seeking it almost in the darkness. . . . Advantage! What is advantage? . . .

Is not reason mistaken about advantage? After all, perhaps man likes something besides prosperity? Perhaps he likes suffering just as much? Perhaps suffering is just as great an advantage to him as prosperity? Man is sometimes fearfully, passionately in love with suffering and that is a fact. There is no need to appeal to universal history to prove that; only ask yourself, if only you are a man and have lived at all. As far as my own personal opinion is concerned, to care only for prosperity seems to me somehow even ill-bred. Whether it's good or bad, it is sometimes very pleasant to smash things, too. . . .

—FYODOR DOSTOYEVSKY, *Notes from Underground*[72]

Of all of Russia's critics and literary figures, perhaps the only one to truly understand the power of *What Is to Be Done?* was Fyodor Dostoyevsky. The year after the novel appeared, Russia's greatest novelist felt compelled to write a response. What resulted was one of the most disturbing and powerful of Dostoyevsky's short works, *Notes from Underground.*[73]

Though this short novel is often viewed as the precursor to modern philosophical existentialism, it was born out of a passionate rejection of rational egoism and all attendant socialist fallacies. Even the title is a deliberate response to Chernyshevskii's call to come up from "the godforsaken underworld." The main character in the *Notes* pointedly refuses to do so, insisting on lobbing verbal sallies at Chernyshevskii's new men from underground, through a "crack in the floor." It deeply pleases the underground man to be the fly in Chernyshevskii's ointment: a man who rejects rationality, scorns his own personal advantage, and celebrates the absurd, the destructive, and the meaningless. The underground man is thus the antithesis of the new man. He is spiteful, dishonest, and weak. He admits that he is "diseased" but refuses to be cured. He tries to "save" a prostitute and ends up damning himself. In essence, the underground man is the true nihilist.[74]

Such a man cannot be healed by the preaching of the socialists. Dostoyevsky's antihero fears the Crystal Palace. Aluminum furniture and electric light, good food, and free love appear to him as the bait in a monstrous trap. The underground man contemptuously despises the socialist utopia as a "chicken coop" and "a block of buildings with apartments for the poor on a lease," as if casting a prophetic eye on the century to come. Men will not be deceived, he predicts, and human nature will not be constrained within this pleasant prison.[75]

Moreover, in *Notes from Underground,* Dostoyevsky had the uncanny prescience to foresee that socialists would discover that there were those who loved disorder and destruction for its own sake and found it "very pleasant to smash things, too." The great author merely did not realize just how soon he would be proven right.[76]

CHAPTER 5

Devils

~

O n the afternoon of April 4, 1866, Alexander II stepped into his open carriage after a walk through the St. Petersburg Summer Gardens. As customary, a crowd of spectators watched the tsar and his retinue as he prepared to depart. Suddenly, an emaciated and stringy-haired man rushed forward with a wild look in his eyes. As he approached the tsar, he fired a single shot from a pistol, missed, and then promptly turned to flee. Easily overtaken by the tsar's guards, he did little to struggle against them but kept one hand in his jacket. Alexander, his bravery matched by his curiosity, stepped over to his would-be assassin and calmly interrogated him. "What do you want?" he asked. "Nothing, nothing" was all that Dmitrii Karakozov would say, continually fingering something in his pocket. Later, investigators found that he was carrying morphine, strychnine, and prussic acid, items that he planned to use to first disfigure his face and then commit suicide.[1]

At first, the crime appeared to be a solitary act of a disturbed individual. Despite his noble origins, Karakozov had long ago developed an obsessive hatred of the aristocracy as a class, declaring that it did nothing but "suck the peasants' blood." He had halfheartedly participated in various radical organizations, had been expelled from two universities, and ultimately suffered from serious depression. As he grandiosely explained to anyone who would listen, the only thing that stopped him from putting a gun to his head was the thought that he had done nothing to help the suffering Russian people.

After a failed suicide attempt, he improbably retreated to the seclusion of a monastery. There, he apparently experienced a revelation: He would slay the tsar and then kill himself. Just before the attack, he wrote a manifesto and sent it to the governor of St. Petersburg. The tsar, Karakozov declared, was personally responsible for the evils inflicted on the poor and the downtrodden. For this, the tsar had to die. "I have decided to destroy the evil Tsar, and to die for my beloved people." It was a perfect marriage of suicide, terror, and martyrdom.

Thus did Karakozov become Russia's first terrorist.

〜

About a year before he vanished from St. Petersburg for the second and last time, Rakhmetov said to Kirsanov, "Give me a rather large amount of oint-ment for curing wounds inflicted by a sharp instrument." Kirsanov gave him a huge jar, assuming that Rakhmetov wanted to deliver it to some artel of carpenters or other workmen subject to frequent lacerations. The next morn-ing, Rakhmetov's landlady came running to fetch Kirsanov in great alarm: "Mr. Doctor, I don't know what's become of my tenant. He hasn't come out of his room for some time. The door's locked. I looked through the crack and saw him lying there covered with blood. I began yelling, but he called through the door, 'It's nothing, Agrafena Antonovna.'" . . .

Kirsanov ran off. Rakhmetov unlocked the door with a broad, grim smile and the visitor beheld a sight at which a person tougher than Agrafena Antonovna might have been aghast. The back and sides of Rakhmetov's under-clothes (that's all he was wearing) were soaked in blood; there was blood under the bed; the felt on which he slept was also covered with blood; in the felt were hundreds of little nails, heads down and points up, sticking out almost half a vershok. Rakhmetov had been lying on them all night. "What on earth is this, Rakhmetov?" cried Kirsanov in horror. "A trial," he replied. "It's necessary. Improbable, of course, but in any case necessary. Now I know I can do it."

—NIKOLAI CHERNYSHEVSKII, *What Is to Be Done?*[2]

By degrees, it emerged that Karakozov had not acted alone. Further in-vestigations revealed that his terrorist act had been carefully planned by an underground revolutionary group. The mastermind behind the assassination was, in fact, Karakozov's first cousin and childhood friend, a weirdly charis-matic firebrand named Nikolai Ishutin.

Born the son of a wealthy merchant in 1840, Ishutin was orphaned by the age of two. He, like Vera Zasulich, was adopted by his relations, the Karakozov family. Though treated well, he was a sickly, maladjusted child who had a very difficult time finishing school. But an iron will gave Ishutin the determination to make something of himself, and he left for Moscow in 1862 to "finish his studies." After auditing several courses at Moscow Univer-sity, Ishutin recognized that formal education did not suit his excitable tem-perament. He needed to find a new path to success.[3]

It was finally revealed to him the following year, in the pages of *What Is to Be Done?* One of Chernyshevskii's most devoted acolytes, Ishutin once de-clared: "There have been three great men in the world, Jesus Christ, Paul the

Apostle, and Chernyshevskii." Upon turning the last page of the novel, Ishutin solemnly vowed to dedicate his life to two goals. The first was to liberate Chernyshevskii from prison. The second was to follow Chernyshevskii's doctrines to the letter.[4]

Ishutin's first goal proved impossible and was quickly abandoned. To compensate, Ishutin did his utmost to render *What Is to Be Done?* a lived philosophy. He fervently sought out like-minded young men in the various student assemblies that blossomed around Moscow University. Such colleagues were not hard to find. In the heady days after the serialization of Chernyshevskii's novel, any self-proclaimed interpreter of the great man's words became an instant leader. Within months, Ishutin had a loyal, radical clique of devotees.[5]

Either because of a failure of imagination or to avoid the suspicion of the authorities, Ishutin's group called itself "the Organization." Superficially, its purpose was as bland as its title: to found a series of sewing and bookbinding cooperatives on the model of Vera Pavlovna's commune in *What Is to Be Done?* Soon, members of the Organization fanned out across Russia, leaving a string of half-baked cooperative efforts in their wake.[6]

Deep in his heart, Ishutin knew these activities would amount to little. Chernyshevskii himself had hinted that such efforts were mere exercises designed to train young radicals in rational egoism. Like the most careful of biblical interpreters, Ishutin read and reread *What Is to Be Done?* and discovered hidden truths embedded within the innocent tales of the "new people" and their adventures: hints of the cataclysm that would release the new world order from the realm of the imagination. Censorship prevented Chernyshevskii from detailing the revolution. But it was there, lurking between the lines, pointing the way to the Kingdom to come. A quiet suggestion lay in Vera Pavlovna's utopian dream. Immediately before the glorious description of the new world there was a missing passage in the text, indicated by a series of asterisks. A government censor might not understand it, but every radical knew that the missing passage was the story of the revolutionary apocalypse, where the old order ended and the new one emerged.[7] The task for readers of the novel, then, was to fill that blank passage with a narrative of their own.

In *What Is to Be Done?* the way to revolution was lit by one of the strangest characters in Russian fiction. Even by Chernyshevskii's standards, Rakhmetov stands out as truly extraordinary. In the novel, he appears as if sprung from the pages of a Russian folktale, more myth than man. Born into an old, rich noble family, Rakhmetov, in the Russian saintly tradition, sells all of his wealth to give to the poor. He then develops enormous physical strength through engaging in backbreaking labor, like hauling barges on the Volga River, and through consuming huge quantities of beef. One day, at the age of "sixteen and a half," he decides to acquaint himself with Russian radicalism. For three days and nights, without stopping to rest, he reads the classics of French and German socialism. On the fourth night, he collapses from exhaustion—but his task is accomplished. He has been born again into the revolutionary faith.

From then on, he becomes a monk of the revolution, denying himself every earthly pleasure: women, sugar, white bread. He eats only what the poor can afford. His mattress is a thin strip of felt, and out of extreme asceticism he refuses to "fold it double." His friends are in awe of him, and he is known as the "extraordinary man."[8]

Though his choices seem like mere personal quirks, they are, in fact, carefully calculated exercises in rational egoism. Rakhmetov is training himself to lead the revolution. When Rakhmetov is first introduced, he is reading Isaac Newton's *Observations on the Prophecies of Daniel and the Apocalypse of St. John.* In that eccentric book, the great scientist prophesied that the end of the world would come in 1866. Throughout the novel, Rakhmetov is ceaselessly involved in mysterious, intricate dealings and conspiratorial activities. He meets with shady characters and disappears for months at a time. No one knows his plans, but the author implies that Rakhmetov is carefully preparing for 1866, the year of the final cataclysm. Later readers would firmly believe that he was plotting acts of terror.[9]

For Ishutin's acolytes, Rakhmetov was the model revolutionary: the self-abnegating terrorist. The most extreme members of the Organization meticulously imitated Rakhmetov. They sold their possessions and gave everything to the cause. They dressed in rags and slept on bare floorboards (though none attempted the bed of nails). Furtively, behind the cover of the Organization, they established a small, tightly knit conspiracy designed to foment violent revolution. To distinguish themselves from the larger Organization, this inner circle assumed a new name, and this time, their imaginations did not fail them. They called their secret clique "Hell."[10]

Precise details about Hell are difficult to find, especially as Ishutin later testified that it was no more than a figment of his own fevered imagination. But it is clear that Hell was designed to be a terrorist organization. Convinced that the Russian order was propped up by nothing more than the rotten pillars of bureaucracy, Hell carefully plotted the simultaneous assassination of key figures in the Russian government. The most important target was the tsar himself.

Like Rakhmetov, members of Hell had devoted every thought and every action to the cause. Ishutin gave a chilling description of the personality of a terrorist:

> A member of Hell must live under a false name and break all family ties; he must not marry; he must give up his friends; and in general he must live with one single, exclusive aim: an infinite love and devotion for his country and its good. For his country he must give up all personal satisfaction and in exchange he must feel hatred for hatred, ill-will for ill-will, concentrating these emotions within himself.

Hell planned the assassination of the tsar down to the last detail. The assassin was to be chosen by lots. Once selected, he had to leave Hell and blend into ordinary society. His every action was to deflect suspicion from himself; he was even to denounce his comrades to the police if necessary. After the assassination, he was to first burn his face with acid until it was unrecognizable and then commit suicide by swallowing poison. After the tsar and his most important officials were killed, the Russian state would collapse, and society would melt into violent chaos.

And then? Then utopia could be built, just as Chernyshevskii so brilliantly prophesied. Throughout the confusion of the revolutionary violence, Hell would continue to direct events secretly, ensuring that all enemies of the new order were discovered and murdered. The ground would be cleared, the soil prepared. Then the Kingdom could come. Hell was the first Russian organization to believe that the path to universal love was paved with terror.

Despite the extremist rhetoric, it seemed that only Karakozov took these plans seriously. Some members of Hell even tried to dissuade him from the assassination attempt. After Karakozov was captured, these would-be assassins quickly lost their remaining nerve. Ishutin's followers were arrested, and more than half of them confessed everything to the investigators. Many eagerly agreed to testify in court. Their performance during their trial made their organization seem like nothing more than a youthful game gone terribly awry. While in prison, Karakozov converted to Orthodox Christianity and asked the tsar to spare his life. Despite clear evidence of mental derangement, he was hanged on October 3, 1866. Ishutin was exiled to Siberia and soon went insane.

Nonetheless, Hell was just the beginning. After Ishutin, generations of Russian radicals were convinced that only the complete and merciless destruction of the present kingdom of this world would bring about the glorious kingdom of the next. They did not repudiate the innocent pleasures of Chernyshevskii's perfectly ordered rational-egoistic life—the communes, the social events, the life of love. But as true disciples of socialism, Ishutin's imitators voluntarily sacrificed their own happiness to achieve a higher purpose. The evils of the present simply demanded a species of activism so different from that preached by Vera Pavlovna: single-minded, pure-hearted, ascetic terrorism.

~

She read a great deal, and with interest, but reading alone could not satisfy her; the only effect it had upon her was that her power of reasoning developed more than her other powers, and her intellectual requirements even began to outweigh her feelings. . . .

She wanted something greater, something loftier, but what it was she did not know; even if she did know she could not set to work at it. . . .

She is waiting, living on the eve of something. . . .

She becomes frightened, and the need for sympathy grows stronger, and she longs intensely and agitatedly for another soul that would understand her, that would respond to her innermost sentiments, that would help her and teach her what to do. A desire arises within her to surrender herself to somebody, to merge her being with somebody, and the lone independence in which she stands among those immediately around her becomes repugnant to her.

—NIKOLAI DOBROLIUBOV, "When Will the Real Day Come?"[11]

By 1868, Vera realized that a life of fulfillment was not easy to find, even among Russia's radicals. In Chernyshevskii's novel, it was all depicted so beautifully: the noble new men, whose selfishness led them to ever higher feats of courage; the new women, who found pure pleasure in helping others achieve equality and enlightenment; the life of pure self-sacrifice. But such people and such lives seemed few and far between.

Her hopes were first raised by a chance encounter in Moscow in the spring of 1868. There, entirely by accident, Vera ran into her sister Alexandra. The meeting was a joyous one—the sisters had lost touch with one another.

Vera had spent some time as a provincial court clerk but had to leave her post when the judge suddenly went insane. Alexandra, meanwhile, had spent a few years teaching at Vera's old boarding school but finally quit out of a restless hatred for the stuffy rules that restricted her. Both women were in the same position: They needed to find work, but they could not bear the thought of finding a traditional female job.[12]

Alexandra had welcome news: Ekaterina, their eldest sister, had devised a way to rescue all of them from their plight. The wildest of the three sisters, Ekaterina had long ago lived a bohemian life of radical activism. After experiencing her father's terrible temper in her early childhood, and then the spite and bitterness of a wealthy old aunt who took her in, Ekaterina grew up to be a fierce, restless young woman. After one brief year in a boarding school, she simply ran away and began living among a wild, radical set with ties to Ishutin's organization. While Alexandra was working as a teacher, Ekaterina continually wrote to her, tempting her with a life of freedom and rebellion. Alexandra finally succumbed and joined Ekaterina in St. Petersburg. There, the two women hatched the idea of renting a tiny two-room house on the outskirts of Moscow and, with the help of a sewing machine and a few seamstresses, setting up a sewing cooperative. It was the perfect way to make money and live a life of radical freedom. For Vera, the chance encounter with her sister proved a stroke of fate. She was thrilled—it was her first step into the pages of *What Is to Be Done?*

At first, it worked just as Chernyshevskii had promised. Alexandra had some experience in hand sewing and soon managed to line up a few wealthy customers in Moscow. She was also eager to learn from her professional seamstresses the techniques of working a sewing machine. For a few months, the cooperative flourished, earning money to support the workers and the three Zasulich sisters. And in spare moments, the sisters enjoyed the innocent pleasures described in *What Is to Be Done?* Friends came to visit from Moscow and would join them for picnics, hikes through the fields and nearby woods, and even boating on the local pond.

Nonetheless, something about the venture greatly disappointed Vera. Perhaps it was the monotony of the enterprise—in the end, it was tedious to sew for eight to ten hours a day. A kind of conventional business sense was also increasingly needed, as was a good head for accounting, neither of which Vera possessed. In the end, Vera was completely uninterested in conventional profit-making ventures. She wanted to transform the world. And after all of the garments were sewn, the money counted, and the accounts tallied, little time or energy was left for these ever-receding dreams. In her sisters' commune, Vera found a relatively interesting job. But it was not a life lived for the cause.

Years later, Vera would write with no little sarcasm about the fate of the sewing and bookbinding cooperatives. Radicals, it seemed, had forgotten that labor was laborious, that it required stamina, persistence, and attention to detail. For many radicals, especially those who came to radicalism in search of a kind of exalted, spiritual experience, sewing was a tedious business. It was no wonder, Vera later wrote, that the cooperatives became unprofitable, and that the best workers left for better wages elsewhere. Real-life seamstresses were intent on making a living and had very little interest in vindicating a utopian novelist. Often illiterate and ill educated, they had no patience for endless lectures on rational egoism. A lifestyle that Vera Pavlovna declared "easy, simple, and natural," Vera Zasulich found complicated and near impossible. Bitterness resulted on all sides. Vera recalled instances of the seamstresses leaving the cooperatives, taking the sewing machines with them. In court, they defended themselves by arguing that the radicals themselves had declared "the machine belongs to the laborer." As far as the seamstresses could tell, they were the only laborers. The radicals who ran the business "just kept talking."[13]

Vera and Ekaterina decided to continue their quest for true revolutionary activism. In August 1868, the two women headed to St. Petersburg.

To a young woman of the provinces, Vera later wrote, St. Petersburg beckoned as the glorious capital of nihilism. Eager provincial high school students and seminarians heard wonderful rumors of the energy of St. Petersburg's activist intelligentsia. Tales circulated of the St. Petersburg fires, the student demonstrations, and the experiments in communal living. Vera remembered the excitement she felt as she entered the city—it was, she believed, "the laboratory of ideas, the center of life, of movement, of activity."[14]

It was early September, and the male students of St. Petersburg University were just returning for the start of the school year. Vera and Ekaterina immediately sought contacts among student radicals. Ekaterina had many friends in the city, and soon the two women found themselves at the heart of the movement.

But by now, the heady days of the early sixties had passed. The repercussions of Karakozov's assassination attempt were still reverberating through the revolutionary ranks. Public support for the tsar was higher than it had been in years. The assassination attempt had shocked all but the most extreme in Russian society. A consensus emerged that the nihilists had gone too far. The Russian police, for their part, were no longer willing to tolerate even the most naive expressions of radical activity. Because so many of Ishutin's followers were university students, new codes were instituted at all institutions of higher learning: Students were subject to police surveillance, they could be searched at any time, and they were strictly forbidden to form any organizations, even the most innocuous. An ominous quiet descended upon the university—students feared imprisonment and exile.[15]

A few hardy radicals, still dressed in the plain, worn clothing of nihilists, did haunt the halls of the universities. But for the most part, the energy of the early communes and cooperatives had drained away. A kind of listlessness pervaded the movement. Vera Pavlovna's venture had proved a failed example, as had Rakhmetov's conspiracies. By 1868, Vera wrote, "the question—what is to be done?—caused depression and anxiety." Like the early Christians, who had so earnestly expected the end times to come within a few years, Russia's radicals despaired when the revolution did not arrive. The apocalypse was supposed to occur in 1866. Both Newton and Chernyshevskii had prophesied it. After 1866, the faithful soon lapsed into doubt and dissension.[16]

Left without a movement or a cause, Vera found herself lost in St. Petersburg. To earn money, she worked in a bookbinding cooperative. She took classes in pedagogy, in case she decided to become a teacher. But all of this was a matter of marking time, waiting for something to come along, something that would engage her spirit.[17]

It was then that Vera came across a short work of literary criticism by Chernyshevskii's friend and compatriot Nikolai Dobroliubov. It was a deceptively ordinary essay, a long review of one of Turgenev's lesser-known novels, *On the Eve*. Though it was published in 1860, it read like an epilogue to the 1860s, the sequel to *What Is to Be Done?*[18]

The heart of Dobroliubov's essay was an analysis of Turgenev's main character, Helena, a self-taught, energetic young woman who aspires to nothing less than an utterly consuming cause. Helena educates herself, reads important books, and seeks the right companions. Ready to act, to give her life for something larger than herself, she finds Russian society inhospitable to her dreams. Everywhere she turns, she sees weak men, dreamers, idealists— the same superfluous men of the previous generation.[19]

In Helena, Vera discovered herself. She shared Helena's deepest desires and most wrenching anxieties. Would she ever find an outlet for her yearnings? Dobroliubov's essay held out one slim hope: another character in the novel, a Bulgarian revolutionary named Insarov. Completely unlike others around him, Insarov is ruthless, driven, and at times filled with a cold anger. His whole life is consumed by one aim—the instigation of the Bulgarian revolution. To Helena, he is deeply attractive. In essence, he is her savior. He leads her out of her doubts and anxieties into a world of pure, bold activity. It is not surprising that Vera found this essay deeply compelling. She was not the only one who was breathlessly waiting for someone to come along and lead her into the life of her dreams.[20]

And then, in 1868, such a man appeared. His name was Sergei Nechaev.

～

1. The revolutionist is a person doomed. He has no personal interests, no business affairs, no emotions, no attachments, no property, and no name. Everything in him is wholly absorbed in the single thought and the single passion for revolution.

— SERGEI NECHAEV, *Catechism of a Revolutionary*[21]

All who knew Nechaev remembered his intense charisma, his almost hypnotic personality that led people either to love him or to fear him. Physically, he was unimpressive. He was very thin, and his face was narrow, with diabolically small, slanted eyes. Perusing his photographs, it is difficult to see his charm: In many portraits he appears much younger than his age, often dressed in ill-fitting suits that look as if they had been borrowed from someone else. Only one photograph captures something of his seductive power. Taken in 1865, when he was just eighteen, it shows a young man with rakishly slicked-back hair, light eyes with tiny, sharp pupils, and a slight, ironic smile. It provides only a hint of the essence of Nechaev's power: his devilish charm.

His control over others was almost supernatural. Many risked imprisonment and committed murder at his command. Later, they had difficulty explaining why. When asked to describe him, many of his former acquaintances seemed at a loss for words. He was "unpleasant," his former roommate declared, but also "seductive." One of Nechaev's comrades agreed: "A great power emanated from him but there was also something repellent and demagogic in him." He was terribly proud, argumentative, and resentful of anyone who had authority. One of the words people used most often to describe him was "despotic."[22]

But he demanded, and received, complete respect. All who knew him conceded that he was completely and fanatically devoted to his only cause: socialist revolution. He was determined to see the overthrow of the Russian monarchy, the abolition of social classes, and the redistribution of wealth. He permitted himself everything in the service of these goals. Hundreds of Russian radicals came to share his determination solely because they had faith in him.

His rapid rise to the top of the revolutionary movement was partly explained by his careful cultivation of his image. He wished to appear as if he had stepped out of the pages of Russian radical literature—a combination of Rakhmetov and Insarov—the archetype of the ruthless, dedicated, conspiratorial revolutionary. Sometimes he appeared with the latest revolutionary book under his arm; at other times, armed with a revolver. Like Rakhmetov, he disappeared for days at a time, always implying that secret business commanded him. He spoke of mysterious organizations no one else had heard of and intimated that he had contacts with the most important of European revolutionary movements. To the young, green student activists, eager for action, but unsure where to begin, he loomed as a battle-hardened veteran, who knew exactly how and when to take matters into his own hands.[23]

He never spoke about his background but slyly let others spread rumors and stories about his past. His closest comrades told fantastic and often contradictory tales about his life: that he was a former serf and was illiterate until the age of sixteen, that he was from a working-class background and had spent his childhood in grinding poverty and hunger. For so many of the radicals he encountered, especially the children of the nobility, this lower-class mystique enhanced his authority—he spoke of the sufferings of the poor and downtrodden as if from hard experience. In a radical world that was mostly inhabited by the children of privilege, he offered authenticity.[24]

The truth was, as ever, more tangled. Nechaev certainly had a more difficult childhood than that of his comrades. His family was considered lower middle class—urban shopkeepers who lived meagerly off their trade. His grandparents were all freed serfs who had moved to town in order to set up shop. Nechaev's parents lived with his grandparents, and the whole family contributed to the family business.[25]

Nechaev's hometown of Ivanovo was one of Russia's earliest industrial cities. Known as the Russian Manchester, it was later home to monstrous factories and winding streets littered with the poor, blackened wooden huts of the workers. But during Nechaev's childhood, Ivanovo was a small mill town. Approximately half of the proletariat that lived in the city were seasonal laborers. In essence, Ivanovo was something of a provincial backwater aspiring to be an industrial city. Real industrial development did not come to Ivanovo until long after Nechaev left. The town did not even have a railroad station until 1868.[26]

Nechaev's life was not easy. The family business was a small paint shop, and Nechaev's father worked several jobs, in the shop and as part-time waiter and caterer. His mother died when he was only eight, and his father was frequently absent, seeking work. Nechaev himself probably began to work at the age of eight, mostly assisting his father. By the time he turned ten, he had already learned how to paint signs, varnish floors, wait tables, and serve at large banquets. The family could only afford a small three-room flat, which was crammed with Nechaev and his parents, his grandparents, his two sisters, and, from time to time, the workers employed by his grandfather. Sergei helped raise his two younger sisters and later, when his father remarried, coped with the arrival of a stepmother and then two half brothers. There was no question, his life was a far cry from that of a typical provincial noble.[27]

But by the standards of nineteenth-century Russian life, Nechaev's childhood was reasonably comfortable. The family was relatively close, and real affection existed within it, especially between Nechaev and his younger sisters. Moreover, Nechaev, as the son of the family, was given every opportunity to better himself. When he decided to pursue an education, his family supported him—devoting their limited resources to hiring tutors for him.[28]

Nechaev may later have spread the rumors of a life of crushing poverty because the truth was infinitely more painful—he found his lower-middle-class background humiliating. Nechaev was sensitive to class differences at an early age. It was said that he hated working with his father as a caterer, because he disliked watching his father humiliate himself in front of his wealthy customers. When his father managed to secure him the position of errand boy in a factory, he was resentful: "I won't wipe the boots of those devils."[29]

Nechaev showed very early signs of a voracious intelligence. By the time he left Ivanovo at the age of seventeen, he had taught himself Russian history, world history, poetry and rhetoric, algebra, geometry, Latin, German, French, and a smattering of physics. His acute intellect soon made him the darling of the Ivanovo intelligentsia. The progressive elite of the town saw vast potential in the boy. He became such a local star that some began to prophesy great things for him. When he began to participate in amateur theater and displayed great talent as an actor, his tutors quickly discouraged him. They feared he would abandon his education for the stage and had bigger plans for him. He later found other uses for his dramatic talents.[30]

As he grew older, Nechaev grew increasingly bored and resentful. By virtue of his education, he felt endlessly superior to the wealthier but virtually illiterate factory owners that dominated Ivanovo society. He no longer wished to assist his father in menial jobs; it was beneath him to work as a caterer. But he could not simply sit around at home. It made him feel like a "parasite" to live on the family finances. Wherever he looked, Nechaev saw no outlet for his talents. Ivanovo, he wrote to one of his teachers, was nothing more than a "devil's swamp." In 1865 he left town.[31]

But it seemed that wherever he went, Nechaev could not escape the limits of his class status. When he was sixteen, his education was too scattered and informal for him to pass the Moscow gymnasium's entrance exam. A university education was forever barred to him. He turned to the only other option that seemed feasible—to pass the teacher's exam and become a primary school instructor. By 1866, he had completed his pedagogical studies and earned an appointment as a teacher of Bible studies at a St. Petersburg parochial school. It was a good job, but for a man of tremendous ambition, from whom so much had been expected, it was a setback. Life was conspiring to keep him in his place.[32]

In the summer of 1866, he received yet another crushing blow: His beloved sister Fiona had been forced to marry a friend of the family, mostly because the Nechaevs wished to avoid paying her dowry. The story was like a chapter out of Dostoyevsky's *Crime and Punishment:* For a long time, Fiona resisted her parents, always relying on Nechaev to back her up. But her parents deceived her, telling her that Nechaev had sent a letter approving of the match. When Nechaev returned home in the summer of 1866, Fiona greeted him holding her first child. Nechaev was enraged, reportedly crying out, "My God—Fotia, Fotia, what have you done?" It was yet more confirmation of the ties that bound him to his social position.[33]

In the fall of 1866, Nechaev returned to St. Petersburg to assume his teaching duties, filled with restless resentment. Over the next two years, no one could say precisely how he filled his days. He remained quiet and unobtrusive. He surrounded himself with books and pamphlets and was always seen reading or carrying a book. When he was not reading, he was engaged in other strange activities, studying practical crafts such as tailoring, shoemaking, and carpentry. When asked why, he replied with a laconic "It may come in handy," quoting Rakhmetov from *What Is to Be Done?*[34]

He was, in fact, increasingly consumed by Karakozov and his legacy. Throughout 1866 and 1867, Nechaev was fascinated by the details of the assassination attempt and the conspiracy. No one knows exactly how it happened, but Sergei came to St. Petersburg in 1866 as a resentful, ambitious young man and emerged in 1868 as a fierce radical. Along the way he had found his calling: to become the leader of the Russian revolution.

He assiduously studied the details of previous revolutionary organizations—not just the Organization and Hell but others, including various Polish and Italian secret societies, and the famous French "Conspiracy of Equals," led by the revolutionary Gracchus Babeuf in 1795. Nechaev took from each useful principles for future conspiratorial work: a secret hierarchy of cells, code names, passwords, secret seals, and coded messages.[35]

He was determined to build a new conspiratorial organization, peopled with Karakozovs. "There are many people to take Karakozov's place," he explained. And he knew exactly where to find them—among St. Petersburg's university students. When the university term began in September 1868, Nechaev enrolled as an auditor, which permitted him to attend lectures but not to receive a degree. He attended so regularly that many later swore that he was a fellow student—yet another rumor that Nechaev probably encouraged. But his real purpose in attending the lectures was to infiltrate the student movement and gather recruits for the radical cause.[36]

His tactics were brilliant. He made it a point to be at every potential radical gathering, including student meetings and reading groups. He would say little, but merely watch and wait. Inevitably, he would spot a potential recruit: someone who appeared more restless or eager or intelligent than the rest. After the meeting was over, he would quietly approach his target and suggest that they meet separately to discuss "true" revolutionary strategy. His intense charisma guaranteed that the most hotheaded and active of the St. Petersburg radicals soon fell under his control.[37]

In the late fall of 1868, Nechaev discovered Vera Zasulich. Their meeting would irrevocably alter her fate.

～

2. The revolutionist knows that in the very depths of his being, not only in words but also in deeds, he has broken all the bonds which tie him to the civil order and the civilized world with all its laws, moralities, and customs, and with all its generally accepted conventions. He is their implacable enemy, and if he continues to live with them it is only in order to destroy them more speedily.

— SERGEI NECHAEV, *Catechism of a Revolutionary*[38]

One day, Vera's instructor in pedagogy approached her after class and invited her to his apartment. Some colleagues were meeting there, he explained, to discuss what teachers should read to "prepare them for their work." Vera immediately realized that this was code—she was being invited to a radical reading group. She naturally agreed to come.[39]

The teacher's apartment was a small studio, and the people in the room were crushed around a tiny table and onto a bed in the corner. Perhaps because of the uncomfortable quarters, the meeting began as a tepid, awkward affair. The teachers were all young, and many were barely literate. When the time came to suggest books for the group, one naively suggested a book on pedagogy. Yet again, Vera was frustrated. The reading group seemed thoroughly unpromising—it was hard to see how these ignorant men and women could discuss the important radical ideas of the day.

Recognizing that she was the most knowledgeable person in the room, Vera overcame her shyness and began to dominate the meeting. She asked the teachers what they had read and suggested several books and articles. At one point, she told the group that they should read one of her favorite works, Dobroliubov's "When Will the Real Day Come?"

"And when will it come?" one of the teachers asked.

Vera boldly quoted Dobroliubov: "'When a whole generation has been raised in an atmosphere of hope and expectation.'"

A man who had been silently reclining on the bed in the corner now spoke up. "That means now," he stated with quiet authority. After the meeting, he pushed his way toward Vera and introduced himself. He was Sergei Nechaev.

With his usual acumen, Nechaev had sized up Vera instantly. "When Will the Real Day Come?" had betrayed her. He surmised that Vera was like Helena, a woman who had grown up yearning for an extraordinary life, a life of meaning and true fulfillment. Such a woman sought, amid all her acquaintances, a man who would share her desires and guide her into a life of action. She was, like Helena, waiting for an Insarov, someone who "irresistibly strove toward his goal and carried others with him."

He told Vera to stop by his school. "Why," she asked innocently, "are teachers meeting there as well?"

"No," he answered, "we need to talk."

In her memoirs, Vera later claimed that she initially had no intention of accepting this invitation. But by December 1868, she was entirely entranced. She told her sister of an extraordinary young man she had met, an intelligent and energetic person who had a particular genius for inspiring the students. Over the next year, she became entangled in Nechaev's web.[40]

With the sheer force of his charisma, Nechaev transformed a motley group of devoted young students into a conspiracy that had all the trappings of a cult. For a lost young generation, he provided an all-encompassing cause, and he expected nothing less than complete sacrifice. They, in turn, willingly believed him, captivated by his single-mindedness, his zeal.

His techniques borrowed from past conspiratorial movements, incorporating Masonic-style rituals. When he invited potential recruits to a meeting, he meticulously set the stage. At the designated apartment, he drew the curtains and lit a handful of candles. On the table, he placed portraits of two French Jacobins, Robespierre and St. Just. Once the meeting began, Nechaev would read to his acolytes of other revolutionary conspiracies, and they would debate the tactics of Gracchus Babeuf and others. He hinted that he was a member of a secret European revolutionary organization and had been sent to recruit only the best Russians for the cause.[41]

Nechaev seduced his followers with an exalted rhetoric, one that described the world in Manichean terms and rallied the faithful into battle. He circulated a radical manifesto, the "Program of Revolutionary Action," in which socialism was explained in the simplest of terms. The present world was one of poverty, subjection, and evil, where the poor wore "pitiful rags" and lived in "stinking cellars" while the rich enjoyed "every possible comfort and honor." Any man who looked impartially on these conditions would see Russian society as "the kingdom of the insane." Indeed, the whole social order would inevitably collapse under the very weight of its own injustices. The task of every honest revolutionary was to speed this inevitable collapse. "Thus, *the social revolution is our final goal and political revolution is the only means for achieving this goal.*" It was time for war.[42]

Nechaev and his followers dubbed themselves "the Revolutionary Committee." The date for revolution was set. On February 19, 1870, the ninth anniversary of the abolition of serfdom, Nechaev predicted, there would be widespread peasant unrest. Revolution would coincide with this date. The committee decided on a two-stage process. The first was to radicalize the Russian students, by encouraging them to stage protests and demonstrations. These radical students were then to fan out into the countryside, to distribute leaflets and mobilize the peasantry. Finally, precisely on February 19, a designated terrorist would murder the tsar. The rest of the organization, dressed as peasants, would stand on the street corners in St. Petersburg and Moscow, and shout, "The tsar has been killed, and they want to make everyone serfs." These words were meant to unleash a general conflagration, which would eventually consume all of Russia.[43]

What would happen after these paroxysms of violence? Nechaev had no need to explain. Devoted readers of Chernyshevskii knew that this was finally the path to the apocalypse according to *What Is to Be Done?* Nechaev, like Ishutin before him, was writing his version of the missing passage in the novel. First, the revolution: violence, bloodshed, merciless destruction. Then, utopia. As in the New Testament, the revolution would separate the wheat from the chaff.

Nechaev, then, appeared as the revolutionary version of the second coming of Christ. His followers were convinced that they had found a savior. "Read the New Testament, Luke, chapter 3, verses 9 and 17," Evlampii Ametistov, a devoted follower of Nechaev, wrote to a friend:

"And now also the axe is laid unto the root of the trees: every tree therefore which bringeth not forth good fruit is hewn down, and cast into the fire."

And: "Whose fan *is* in his hand, and he will thoroughly purge his floor, and will gather the wheat into his garner; but the chaff he will burn with fire unquenchable."[44]

～

6. Tyrannical toward himself, he must be tyrannical toward others. All the gentle and enervating sentiments of kinship, love, friendship, gratitude, and even honor, must be suppressed in him and give place to the cold and single-minded passion for revolution. For him, there exists only one pleasure, one consolation, one reward, one satisfaction—the success of the revolution. Night and day he must have but one thought, one aim—merciless destruction. Striving cold-bloodedly and indefatigably toward this end, he must be prepared to destroy himself and to destroy with his own hands everything that stands in the path of the revolution.

—SERGEI NECHAEV, *Catechism of a Revolutionary*[45]

In the winter of 1868–69, Nechaev and his followers began to execute the first stage of their plot. To radicalize the students of St. Petersburg, Nechaev subtly encouraged the revival of the old assemblies, the *skhodki* that had been so popular at the beginning of the sixties. Forbidden from meeting on university grounds, the students began to gather in private apartments throughout the city. Occasionally, assemblies were held in tiny one-bedroom apartments, and then the meetings would become awkward, as the large crowd had to separate into different rooms. But generous liberal benefactors or tolerant parents would at times allow the students to use their homes, and then glorious ballrooms lit with candles would be filled with hundreds of students, radicals, and mere curious onlookers.[46]

Though the student assemblies were technically illegal, they were hardly a secret. Often, they were advertised in newspapers, in lightly coded language. Sometimes, on the day of an assembly, students would go from door to door to rouse the lazy or reluctant. Police officers reportedly stood at the door of at least one of the meetings, counting the students as they filed in. But after the meeting was over, the officers quietly left, and no repercussions followed. The police seemed to have relaxed their grip on student activism.[47]

Vera, who attended many of these meetings, witnessed Nechaev's Machiavellian tactics at work. Nechaev rarely spoke at the assemblies and never sought to dominate discussion directly. Instead, his followers talked. The most radical of Nechaev's acolytes burned with evangelical zeal. Seizing the chair, these firebrands gave impassioned speeches. Rise up against the oppressive university apparatus and demand your rights! More moderate students called for calm, arguing that activism would needlessly antagonize the authorities. They were denounced and even shouted down as cowards. The most extreme of activists soon held the student movement in their grip.[48]

What the students did not know, and what even some of Nechaev's closest associates did not realize, was that Nechaev was engaging in an elaborate deception. Though he spoke eloquently about the imminent cataclysm, he knew this motley collection of radicals were not yet ready. They were still dreamers, entranced by visions of a future, harmonious utopia. They needed to cast aside their naïveté and become coldhearted revolutionaries.[49] They had to become angry. And there was only one way to awaken terrible, merciless anger in the students: the direct experience of the brutality of the Russian police.

Nechaev thus hatched his most pitiless plot. He would betray the students and his comrades to the authorities. He confided only in his most trusted friends, revealing his plan to encourage even the halfhearted student radicals to engage in protests and demonstrations. These students would be arrested, imprisoned, and exiled. This experience of regime persecution would harden them against the Russian regime, and they would carry this hatred with them into their places of exile throughout Russia. In effect, an army of bitter revolutionaries would fan out into the countryside, igniting revolt among Russia's peasants.[50]

On January 28, 1869, Nechaev, the consummate actor, took the stage at his last student assembly. Everyone grew quiet when Nechaev strode to the chair and stood upon it. Though he was small and thin, his eyes burned with terrible intensity. He told the hushed room that the time for discussion was over. The moment for action had come. On a table in front of him, there lay a petition, demanding that the university give the students the full right to hold their assemblies wherever they chose. Who was brave enough to sign it? "Those that do not fear for their own skin," Nechaev slyly intoned, "let them separate themselves from the rest; let them write their names on this petition."[51]

First, Nechaev's followers signed the petition; then the rest of the assembly swarmed over to the table. Swept away by the power of Nechaev's speech, they yearned to be part of this bold new movement. He managed to collect nearly a hundred signatures before a few doubters began to question the true purpose of the petition. His silence provoked fear. Murmurs in the crowd were heard that such a list could be dangerous, it could fall into the hands of the police. A few demanded that the petition be destroyed. But it was too late. The list of signatures was already in Nechaev's pocket, and Nechaev left the meeting with the fate of ninety-seven students in his hands.

On January 30, Nechaev was called into the police station for questioning. He probably gave the authorities the petition on that day.[52]

~

7. The nature of the true revolutionist excludes all sentimentality, romanticism, infatuation, and exaltation. All private hatred and revenge must also be excluded. Revolutionary passion, practiced at every moment of the day until it becomes a habit, is to be employed with cold calculation. At all times, and in all places, the revolutionist must obey not his personal impulses, but only those which serve the cause of the revolution.

— SERGEI NECHAEV, *Catechism of a Revolutionary*[53]

The next night, Nechaev visited Vera in the apartment she shared with another of his followers. Sitting in her small bedroom, Nechaev began his most earnest attempt to recruit Vera for his cause. He was going abroad, and he wanted Vera to join him. Although Vera could not recall their exact words, she long remembered how she felt that evening. She was intensely agitated and confused, held fast in the grip of this powerful personality. They engaged in a battle of the wills. He spoke to her of revolution, of a life of supreme dedication to the cause. He claimed that he knew what revolution was—he could guide her, teach her. He wanted her to follow him, to yield to him as her leader.[54]

Vera found her head spinning. What did he want from her? He was speaking of things that she had dreamed of for so long—it was as if he had looked inside her soul and seen all of her deepest yearnings. "Serving the revolution," she wrote later, "this was the supreme happiness, of which I could only dream." But doubts remained. Something held her back.

"At least you won't refuse to give me your address?" Nechaev finally said, trying to ease her doubts. She eagerly agreed, assuring him that she wanted to contribute to the cause. He seemed happy at this sign of surrender.

After Nechaev left the room, Vera paced back and forth. She could not rid herself of the confusion she had felt in his presence. Here was her first real discussion about revolution, her first steps toward living a life for the cause. How far was she prepared to go? Without warning, Nechaev reappeared. He resumed his seat and she nervously sat back down as well. Then came an unexpected declaration.

"I have fallen in love with you."

Vera leaped up again, as if stung. For a long time, she paced silently. Until this moment, Nechaev was a man she had admired from afar. Now, he seemed to have chosen her as his special disciple. Vera later claimed that his words elicited only "amazement" and concern about how to phrase her response. But her memoirs suggest that something about his declaration of love was deeply tempting. Could Nechaev become her Insarov? Could she, like Helena, finally say "that she has found the word her heart has been longing for"? If Vera were Helena, she would give everything up and follow him.

But something warned her against his proposition. After a long silence, she simply said, "I value your friendship, but I do not love you."

Much later, Vera wrote of the disquiet that had enveloped her during the night with Nechaev. She sensed that he was a man too encompassed with the revolution to honestly love anyone. Perhaps, in a practical sense, Vera could have been useful to him, providing cover for him in his travels abroad and assisting him with her working knowledge of French and German. But Nechaev was a man who required utter devotion, and his declaration of love was an effort to test her. It was not real feeling; it was a calculated strategy. Vera would not succumb.

Nechaev bowed and left. But he was by no means done with her.

A few days later, Vera played her role in the second act of Nechaev's drama. She received a letter in the mail, with no return address. Inside the envelope were two notes, one folded within the other. The anonymous outer letter told a creative story. "While walking today along Vasilevskii Island," the author wrote, "I encountered a carriage carrying a person under arrest. A hand appeared out of the carriage window and dropped a note on the ground. I heard a voice say 'If you are a student, take this to the designated address.'" Folded within this letter was a hastily scribbled note in Nechaev's hand. "They are taking me to prison," he wrote, "where, I don't know. Report this to the comrades. I hope to meet with them soon; let them continue our work."[55]

When Vera showed the letter to her friends, panic immediately swept through the ranks. Anna Nechaev, Nechaev's youngest sister, was devastated by the news. Beside herself with worry, she ran from prison to prison in St. Petersburg, searching for her brother. Police and prison officials denied all knowledge of his arrest. Perplexed and increasingly alarmed, university students occupied a large auditorium and demanded that the rector of the university explain Nechaev's incarceration. They were stunned to hear that no student named Nechaev had ever been enrolled at the university. It was assumed that the rector was lying. Rumors circulated that Nechaev had been secretly arrested and was kept in a concealed location. In his absence, his legend only grew, even among those who had never met him.[56]

Nechaev's theatrical performance completely entranced his audience. Of course, he had not been arrested. He had fled abroad, as he had long planned, to shake police surveillance. While in Europe, he sought exiled Russian revolutionaries and recruited them for the cause. He decided to concentrate his efforts on Mikhail Bakunin, who had, by now, become one of the most venerated European revolutionary figures. Nechaev had his charismatic arsenal well stocked. He knew just the trick to win Bakunin's favor. He would appear as Russia's long-awaited revolutionary savior.

~

I have here an example of these young fanatics, who have no doubts, no fears, and have decided that, however many of them are killed by the government, they will not rest until the people rise. They are charming, these young fanatics, believers with a god, and heroes without flowery rhetoric.

— MIKHAIL BAKUNIN, letter to James Guillaume, 1869[57]

By April 1869, Bakunin had already lived an extraordinary life. His boundless energy had led him into ever more dangerous exploits. Devoting his life to his revolutionary "bride," from 1843 on, Bakunin had attempted to join every revolutionary cause in Europe. In one single year, 1848, he managed to participate in each European revolt: In February he was demonstrating in Paris, by March he was arrested briefly in Berlin, and in May he joined the Slavic Congress in Prague. The failure of all of these enterprises did not deter him. By 1849, he was on the barricades in Dresden, exhorting wavering rebels to stand fast against Prussian troops—only to have the barricades crushed and find himself arrested, imprisoned, and extradited to Russia. He spent the next eight years in various prisons, and another five in Siberian exile. In 1861, Bakunin finally escaped and took an extraordinary journey from Nikolaevsk in Russia to Yokohama, San Francisco, New York, Boston, and finally London. From London, he began his revolutionary roaming all over again. He tried to participate in the Polish uprising against Russia in 1863; in 1864 he met Karl Marx.[58]

One single aim animated him all these years: He dreamed of the merciless destruction of the entire social and political world. Bakunin's dedication to universal harmony was oddly conjoined with his love of violence. Though he often spoke of the possibility of a new world, he more often spoke of smashing, tearing down, and annihilating. But for Bakunin, love and disorder were not opposites. One thing linked them, a concept that was, in Bakunin's mind, synonymous with revolution and destruction. That concept was freedom.

Bakunin, a wandering soul, viewed freedom as an intensely physical thing—it was the hammer that crushed the chains binding all mankind. He often spoke of the present world as "suffocating," preventing the indrawn, true breath of life. The state, with its police and military apparatus, was, of course, the primary force for servitude. But other institutions of the present order were implicated as well. Customs, conventions, religious beliefs, and the whole educational system conspired to keep men shackled to the corrupt, existing world.[59]

Destruction meant liberation—the smashing of prisons both mental and physical. Only after the present world was destroyed would men rise to their full potential, or, in Bakunin's terms, take their first real, full breath. Only then would love be possible—the love of powerful beings willing to give of themselves. The purpose of revolution, for Bakunin, was not parliamentary democracy, social welfare, the eight-hour day, or the work-free weekend. Nothing could be saved, and nothing could be reformed. To reform was to imprison man in softer shackles. The new world could only rise on the ashes of the old. "And therefore we call to our deluded brothers," he wrote in 1842: "Repent, repent, the Kingdom of the Lord is at hand!"[60]

By 1871, Bakunin, like so many revolutionaries before him, saw true liberation as human deification. The revolution would storm heaven itself and make men gods. "If God is, man is a slave," he wrote. "Now man can and must be free. . . . I reverse the phrase of Voltaire and say that if God really existed, it would be necessary to destroy him." Or, in the words that became his lifelong maxim: "The passion for destruction is also a creative passion."[61]

Destruction, then, became evangelism, the cry of the new faith.

The appearance of the young Nechaev thus seemed to Bakunin the advent of a new messiah. He literally fell in love with the austere young man, who seemed like a purer version of his younger self. Unencumbered by philosophical torments, single-mindedly devoted to the cause, Nechaev was the realization of the most raw revolutionary imagination. He lived a life devoted to merciless destruction and was thus a pure negative force. Bakunin was so devoted to Nechaev (he called him "my boy") that he was ready to give everything to this young "specimen" of the revolutionary Russian spirit. They lived together for four months, "in the same room," as Bakunin explained, "passing almost every night in conversations about all sorts of questions."[62]

Nechaev arrived in Geneva with his persona carefully crafted—and he made full use of his dramatic talents. He intimated that he was of peasant background and that his coarse manners were the result of his impoverished upbringing. He claimed, with feigned confidence, that Russia was on the brink of revolt and told fantastic tales of famines, uprisings, mass arrests, and general unrest. And he styled himself as the leader of a vast underground movement, which was on the verge of bringing the much dreamed-of revolution into being.[63]

Bakunin was filled with a new hope. Could this be the long-awaited cataclysm? Eager to assist, he gave Nechaev all he needed. Together they embarked on a relentless propaganda campaign, sending hundreds of leaflets into Russia to provoke a national uprising. It was time to abandon the universities, these pamphlets declared, as they were only corrupt institutions that deadened the mind with trivial knowledge. It was time to go to the people and fan the flames of hatred that the Russian government had for so long smothered.[64]

"The passion for destruction is also a creative passion." Nechaev echoed and amplified Bakunin's maxim, turning destruction into a holy and pure force, worth of all sacrifice. "Poison, dagger, noose, etc.!" he wrote in his leaflets. "The revolution sanctifies everything equally in this struggle. . . . It will be called terrorism!" No mercy should be given; no one should be spared. "It is much more humane to slash and strangle hundreds of hated persons than to partake . . . in the systematic legal murders, tortures and torments of millions of peasants."[65]

Certainly, this destruction would serve the purposes of a future world of humanity and justice. The new world, however, was not yet to be contemplated. Those who were now living were far too tainted with the filth of the existing world. But if "the abominations of the contemporary civilization" were razed to the ground, then a whole new generation would spring up, healthy and pure, to "build the structure of Paradise."[66]

"We do not build. We destroy." The genealogy from Herzen to Bazarov to Bakunin and Nechaev was clear. To destroy was to have faith in a new future. Like the most fervent of millenarians, Russian revolutionaries could confidently usher in apocalypse because only apocalypse would lead to a Kingdom of Heaven on Earth. Through Bakunin and Nechaev, radicals became convinced that Chernyshevskii's intoxicating vision of a world built on love could only be achieved after a period of relentless, ruthless terror. Love and terror became, for many, the Janus face of the revolution.

Alexander Herzen met Nechaev once and at once detested everything about him. In the eyes of the old man of the forties, Nechaev was crude, rabid, and cursed with an internal moral deformity. Herzen refused to see Nechaev as his intellectual heir. But Nechaev was to have the last laugh on his "father," in more ways than one.

～

8. The revolutionist can have no friendship or attachment, except for those who have proved by their actions, that they, like him, are dedicated to revolution. The degree of friendship, devotion and obligation toward such a

comrade is determined solely by the degree of his usefulness to the cause of
total revolutionary destruction.

— SERGEI NECHAEV, *Catechism of a Revolutionary*[67]

Except for Bakunin himself, few recognized just how far Nechaev was willing to go. In addition to instigating revolt in Russia, the leafleting campaign was intended to provoke an iron-fisted reaction from the Russian government. Nechaev predicted that the pamphlets, once discovered, would draw the police into a frenzy of persecution. Those caught with this extremist literature in their hands would soon feel the full, brute power of the Russian regime. Moderates, weak-minded radicals, and naive activists would soon realize what it meant to cross the Russian secret police.[68]

Nechaev therefore targeted his campaign carefully. Through diligent efforts, before he had left Russia, Nechaev had compiled a list of more than 380 names. His practice was immediately to elicit a name and address after meeting a person. In this manner, whether or not he saw the person again, he had him under his control. Now, the list served Nechaev well. Everyone named was sent a packet of leaflets. Sometimes, to further incriminate a person, Nechaev would write him a letter detailing revolutionary plans, as if assuming a full sympathy with Nechaev's methods. Dozens of such letters were recovered by the police, sometimes from shrewder individuals who surrendered them directly to the authorities.[69]

Each letter and pamphlet was a minor manifesto of exultant extremism. The rhetoric spoke of "dark forces," "enemies" in the "swamp of despotism" who must be "smashed so that the Russian peasant lands might breathe." Pure Nechaevite language in the leaflets was complemented by Bakunin's rhetoric in others, praising the urge to violence: "Many, many of your comrades have perished, but for every one of those lost, ten new warriors, enemies of the state, spring from the earth. It means the end of the state is approaching."[70]

All the while, as he firmly secured his place in the émigré radical community in Europe, Nechaev never forgot Vera. He insistently wrote to his former comrades, demanding information, money, and news about her. He urged that no effort be spared to send her to him. "I hear she is preparing to come abroad," he pressed them. "Let her come quickly!" Did this steel-willed revolutionary actually find himself in love with the only person who had ever refused him? Or did he still see her as a particularly useful instrument for his plans? It is impossible to tell.[71]

A third, more insidious possibility also suggests itself. The letters were composed in a kind of crude code, but the police had very little trouble deciphering it. Did Nechaev purposely write Vera's name, over and over, to ensure that she would be implicated in revolutionary activity? It might have been an elaborate act of revenge for the only rejection he had ever received.

Vera herself never discovered the truth. But intentionally or unintentionally, Nechaev's letters betrayed her to the police. Thanks to him, she spent five years in prison and exile, one of his many victims.

CHAPTER 6

The Fortress

~~~

In January 1867, in his émigré journal *The Bell*, Alexander Herzen published an exposé of the Russian secret police, entitled "White Terror." Anonymously authored, it purported to be the definitive account about the investigation of the Karakozov assassination attempt. The article painted an ominous picture of Russia's secret terror regime. Gendarmes, like wolves, hunted their suspects at night and grabbed whomever they could find—old women, nursing mothers, children. After subjecting them to humiliating strip searches and interrogations, the police unceremoniously thrust these innocents into the dark cells of the Peter and Paul Fortress. There they languished, for months on end, in abysmal cells reserved for the worst of political criminals. When released, the victims emerged from their ordeal emaciated, weak, and mentally scarred. The elderly barely survived.[1]

And these were the lucky ones. The most dangerous suspects were brutally tortured, often by the hand of the tsar's chief investigator, Mikhail Muraviev. To many of his victims, Muraviev was the devil incarnate: "He was fat and flaccid, and had an expression of animal-like ferocity on his face. Foaming at the mouth, his eyes filled with blood, disfigured with spite, he was repulsive as only a man who has lost every ounce of humanity can be." Animated with a hatred of all political radicals, Muraviev would order the gendarmes to beat them senseless for the slightest provocation, often until their faces were unrecognizable. Karakozov supposedly experienced the worst of Muraviev's techniques. He was kept in a padded cell for a week, forced to remain standing, and kept awake for several days on end. Then he was whipped every single day for eight days and subjected to other, nameless tortures devised by "medical experts."

Karakozov, according to this extraordinary article, exhibited limitless courage and iron willpower. He refused to answer questions, even when subjected to the most barbarous treatment; he even had the fearlessness to stand up to Muraviev, rattle his chains, and growl, "We'll see who will get whom."

Finally, Karakozov was so determined to resist a forced confession that he tried to commit suicide by biting through a vein in his arm.

These stories of evil crimes and uncommon heroism spread rapidly throughout the Russian radical community. They fit the infamy of Muraviev, who was known, even among his friends, as "the hangman" for his bloody suppression of the Polish revolt against Russian rule in 1863. Polite Russian society kept its distance from Muraviev, and even Alexander II, who appointed him to investigate the Karakozov affair, tried to avoid his company.[2]

There was but one problem with Herzen's anonymous story—it was largely fictional. Muraviev, despite his nickname, did not incarcerate people indiscriminately. Only fifty people were arrested, and only thirty-six were forced to stand trial. Moreover, Muraviev did not resort to torture—he did not have to. Almost everyone involved in Ishutin's conspiracy immediately and freely confessed participation. Karakozov, far from resisting tsarist oppression, was so consumed with remorse for what he had done that he found new faith in God and asked the tsar for forgiveness and clemency. The "hangman" succeeded in hanging only one man, Karakozov himself. Ishutin was also condemned to death but was reprieved at the last moment. Ten conspirators were sentenced to exile and hard labor, but even these men were released after a few years. The rest were simply acquitted.[3]

Nonetheless, with the publication of "White Terror," the Russian radical image of the tsarist state was set. Among radicals, Alexander was always seen as a closeted reactionary, a man who spoke grandiloquently about reform and liberalization but covertly sought every opportunity to keep his foot on the neck of the Russian people. Stories of "white terror" only served to confirm what radicals had suspected all along, that the slightest excuse would bring the whole apparatus of Russian tyranny down on the head of some unsuspecting victim. For the radicals, the Russian police was the sinister, secretive force that conspired to crush their dreams.

Those who longed to create a new community of love and equality, those who believed that the Kingdom was imminent, saw one enemy looming fiercely on the horizon—the Russian state. For radicals, the state, like Satan himself, feared nothing more than the promise of universal harmony and happiness. And so it sent its minions to harass, threaten, and ultimately kill all those who preached the good news. Within the radical belief system, there was no limit to the state's insatiable desire to torment and persecute socialists, anarchists, and nihilists.

Karakozov's bravery under torture became the model of revolutionary behavior. His failed assassination attempt was forgotten, and his martyr-like behavior idealized. Like his literary model, Rakhmetov, Karakozov was believed to have accustomed himself to torture. Generations of radicals believed that, in the end, they would suffer the same fate at the hands of the same devils. They aspired, like the Christian saints of antiquity, to bear witness by the manner of their death.[4]

When he assumed power in 1855, Alexander II inherited the state security apparatus devised by his father, whose paranoia about secret conspiracies was legendary. The Third Section of His Majesty's Secret Chancery—the convoluted name for Russia's nineteenth-century secret police—was infamous in Russian and foreign revolutionary circles. It became the icon of monarchical tyranny, the ugly face of Russian reaction, and the proof, if proof was needed, that the Russian regime had nothing but a deep hostility toward and fear of the Russian people.

Nicholas created the Third Section in 1826, after Russia's first failed political revolt in December 1825. Explicitly designed to repress further unrest within the empire, the Third Section kept watch on the Russian population—especially its most discontented members, the intellectuals—and sought to choke off the spread of subversive ideas and the organization of radical groups. Along with its subsidiary, militarized police force, the Corps of Gendarmes, it employed a variety of standard police methods, mostly borrowed from its European counterparts: censorship, interception of personal correspondence, and the collection of information from informants and spies. Everyone was a potential target: foreign visitors, students, writers, journalists, and bureaucrats. By the time Nicholas died in 1855, the Third Section was the most prominent symbol of his tyrannical tendencies, the institution designed to ensure that Russians obeyed and "kept their thoughts to themselves."[5]

In fact, the Third Section only fitfully earned its fearsome reputation. It was initially a small, meagerly staffed institution, smaller than western European police bureaus. For its first eighteen years it was headed by General Alexander Benckendorff, a man whose behavior often inspired amusement rather than fear. He was unfailingly polite, a proper gentleman, and apparently extraordinarily absentminded. Derisive rumors had it that he often forgot his own name and reminded himself by glancing at his visiting card. Most Russians had little reason to distrust the Third Section, and, as evidenced by the enormous quantity of petitions sent it during Nicholas's reign, many saw it as a watchdog against corrupt local administrators. Moreover, Russia's secret police was, for many years, scarcely "secret." A gendarme of the Third Section was strikingly dressed in a sky blue military-style uniform, complete with cumbersome sword.[6]

The Third Section's formidable reputation was chiefly generated by Russia's educated elite, who felt the sting of police persecution most often. The Third Section regularly censored whole passages from literary and poetic works, if it did not ban the publication of such works altogether. Moreover, to add insult to injury, Benckendorff took it as his personal duty to make sure that Russia's intelligentsia behaved well in almost every setting. Either out of some strange paternalistic impulse or because he had nothing better to do, Benckendorff pestered Russia's intellectuals with ceaseless nagging. He drove Alexander Pushkin, Russia's master poet, to near despair with his niggling criticisms. In letter after letter, Benckendorff harassed Pushkin, reporting that Tsar Nicholas wished Pushkin to rewrite one of his poems into a novel à la Walter Scott, chastising the poet for his informal attire at an ambassador's ball, and admonishing the young man to take special care of his "charming and attractive" fiancée.[7]

Even those subject to harsher punishments, such as exile, found that the regime was often surprisingly lax in dealing with its "political criminals." Alexander Herzen was exiled twice in the 1830s and 1840s, both times for minor political infractions. His places of exile, however, were major provincial cities. The cosmopolitan Herzen was certainly tormented with boredom, but he never suffered physical hardship. In 1841, he became an administrator in the local police bureaucracy in Novgorod, charged, incredibly, with supervising political exiles like himself. Turgenev was also exiled once, for a year, mostly confined to an easy life on his country estate.[8]

The Third Section could occasionally show its claws. By far the worst persecution was meted out to a relatively harmless reading group, organized by Mikhail Petrashevskii, Russia's most famous Fourierist. Petrashevskii's intellectual circle committed the crime of discussing socialist ideas in 1848, a year when all of Europe was feverish with revolution. A panicked Nicholas ordered the Third Section to root out all hints of dissident activity. In April 1848, Petrashevskii's followers were arrested, imprisoned in solitary confinement in the Peter and Paul Fortress, and, after eight months of interrogation, condemned to die. In December 1849, twenty-one men were marched out of prison to face the firing squad, robed entirely in white, according to Russian custom. Three of the men were blindfolded and led to the place of execution. Rifles were raised, and the order to shoot was about to be given, when an officer on horseback galloped in at the last minute, announcing the commutation of all sentences to exile and hard labor. Nicholas I had personally staged the ghoulish drama to put the fear of God into these potential subversives and to demonstrate his paternalistic mercy.[9]

For the men involved, it was a harrowing ordeal. One of the blindfolded men went mad shortly thereafter. Another, who was waiting his turn, remembered fixing his gaze on the horizon, on the beauty of St. Petersburg's gold cupolas, and wondering whether he was really facing his last moments on earth. That man was Fyodor Dostoyevsky.[10]

As part of his unofficial policy of *glasnost*, Alexander tried to shrink Russia's state security system. He began by issuing highly symbolic pardons of those who had participated in the 1825 revolt and the Petrashevskii circle. He relaxed censorship and introduced limits on the investigative powers of the secret police. The new head of the Third Section, Prince Vladimir Dolgorukov, tried to come up with innovative proposals for countering antistate activity. His most creative suggestion was to subject political subversives to a gentle lecture on the error of their ways. Tentatively, Alexander created a climate of relatively open political discussion, hoping to introduce a lively, if circumscribed, climate of debate within Russian society.[11]

The unremitting rise of radicalism in Russia thwarted these hopes. Russia's tsars had a history of distrusting any form of political dissent. It took little to provoke Alexander's fears. The St. Petersburg fires seemed to confirm the worst about Russian nihilism, and Alexander increasingly sought to crush radicalism in its cradle. On manufactured and exaggerated evidence, both Chernyshevskii and Pisarev were thrown into prison. Still, persecution was erratic. The Third Section did everything to place Chernyshevskii behind bars but did very little to prevent him from publishing *What Is to Be Done?* The young Leo Tolstoy found the police similarly unpredictable. In that same year, the Third Section, suspecting that Tolstoy was a radical agitator, tore apart his house trying to find subversive materials in the walls and floorboards. When they found nothing, they politely wrote a note to the chief of the Third Section clearing him of all suspicion, and never bothered him again.[12]

The year 1866 changed everything. Karakozov's pistol shot awakened in Alexander II equal measures of fear and wrath. His aspiration for a tolerant society, in which moderate, rhetorical opposition could be ignored or lightly reprimanded, receded. After 1866, Russia's radicals and the tsarist regime increasingly engaged in an open war, one that would ultimately become a war to the death.

Alexander's main end, after 1866, was to improve the police's intelligence-gathering capability. Karakozov's assassination attempt had exposed almost comical intelligence failures. Karakozov, bizarrely, had sent a note clearly expressing his intentions to the governor of St. Petersburg. The note got lost somewhere in the office, reaching neither the police nor the governor's desk. Alexander was determined not to get caught flat-footed again.[13]

Year by year, Russia's Third Section became a carefully constructed counter-terrorist institution, complete with spies, informers, security analysts, and interrogators. The appointment of Count Peter Shuvalov as the new head of the Third Section was a clear signal that things had changed. Shuvalov's power and prestige grew to such immense proportions that he was soon known as Tsar Peter the Fourth. Playing upon Alexander's fears after 1866, Shuvalov routinely reminded the tsar of the fate of France's Louis XVI. Under Shuvalov the reach of Russia's police administration greatly expanded. He broadly defined illegal activity to include mere participation in a secret organization. He created sixty new police stations throughout the empire, each with special investigators dedicated to the surveillance of the locals. To subdue student unrest, Shuvalov enlisted university administrators as informants and instructed them to report all suspicious activities to the police. The use of secret agents to infiltrate and report on revolutionary activity grew ever more widespread and sophisticated.[14]

In St. Petersburg, Alexander appointed a new governor and head of the city police, General Fedor Trepov. Again, it was a symbolic choice. Trepov had begun his career in the Russian cavalry, and he quickly scaled the ranks to become chief of police in Warsaw. There, in 1861, he first flourished his penchant for hard-line tactics when he ordered policemen to shoot into a crowd of peaceful Polish demonstrators. Though temporarily removed from his post for excessive use of force, he was reinstated in the aftermath of the Polish uprising of 1863, when he was allowed free reign to crush the rebellious Poles. Merciless, he supposedly fined Polish women for wearing mourning clothes for those who died in the uprising.[15]

As the police chief in the Russian capital, Trepov was second only to Shuvalov in the power he exercised over Alexander. Like Shuvalov, he carefully nourished the tsar's paranoid fear of the revolutionary movement in Russia. Rumor had it that if Trepov was late to his daily briefing, the tsar immediately panicked, thinking unrest had broken out in the city streets. Trepov used his authority to create a host of new security arrangements within the capital. He instituted Russia's first security detail dedicated solely to the protection of the tsar, and he created yet another police division, responsible only to him, tasked with the investigation of political crimes.[16]

The year 1866 began Russia's cycle of terror and counter-terror. The state and the radicals increasingly viewed each other with unflagging suspicion and loathing. Each fresh discovery of a conspiracy to overthrow the government, no matter how far-fetched, convinced Russian officials that tightened security was necessary. Each new security measure, in turn, guaranteed that innocent victims of state persecution became bitter enemies of the state. As the radical threat grew, so did the Russian police apparatus, until conspiracy and counter-conspiracy became an ever-escalating battle of covert tactics, deceptions, violence, and terror.

∽

Having escaped, through a stroke of good luck, from the freezing walls of the Peter-Paul Fortress, to the vexation of those dark forces which put me there, I send you, my dear friends, these lines from another country, where I have not ceased to labor in the name of the great cause which unites us. Let us continue more successfully what we have begun together. . . .

. . . Believe in deeds, my friends, and declare yourself with deeds and not with words, to gain the trust of those who made the bread that fed you, of those whose hands constructed the walls of your auditoria and printed your little books, of those who have yearned for freedom for so long. . . .

. . . During the operation, do not let vigilance and caution become a fear of danger that prevents action. Persecution is that evil which can be completely avoided when you firmly link hands. There has never been a true cause without sacrifices.

— SERGEI NECHAEV, "To the Students of the
University, Academy, and Technological
Institute in St. Petersburg"[17]

In April 1869, hundreds of letters began to inundate Russia, addressed mainly to students and political activists. Within the cryptically addressed envelopes, recipients found five to ten leaflets and instructions to distribute them. In just four months, from April through August 1869, some 560 packages of leaflets were sent to 387 people, all part of the campaign to incite revolution instigated by Bakunin and Nechaev. At first, the leaflets were sent to specific people, probably from Nechaev's list of addresses. When these ran out, Nechaev began to send the leaflets haphazardly—to factories, school libraries, even to military academies.[18]

Konstantin Filippeus, head of the investigative arm of the Third Section, was gravely alarmed. It was only three years after the Karakozov assassination, and here was evidence of another revolutionary conspiracy. The sheer number of pamphlets sent out, and their violent content, suggested a widespread antigovernment plot. Filippeus was new on the job and had to experiment with counter-conspiratorial techniques. He resolved that the Third Section should improve its investigative capacities and think creatively about attacking this new menace. He received some formal training in the latest European theories of investigation and detective work, and he used this knowledge to devise a multipronged attack on Nechaev's group.[19]

Sensing that Nechaev was sending leaflets to both hardened revolutionaries and those with only tenuous links to the cause, Filippeus tried to gain the trust of potential informers. He counseled his officers to wait a few days before investigating recipients of pamphlets. He wanted to make it clear that no one who cooperated with the police would be prosecuted. Full-blown investigations only followed in cases where suspects either kept the leaflets or distributed them. Soon, the Third Section was able to map, with precision, the pattern of leaflet distribution. By carefully scrutinizing the handwriting, the Third Section was also able to intercept all leaflets addressed by Nechaev himself. But the return addresses revealed little. The letters came from all over Europe: Finland, Germany, Switzerland.[20] Filippeus decided to concentrate on breaking up Nechaev's organization in Russia.

This he achieved with astonishing speed. One letter to a close associate, Elizaveta Tomilova, revealed the names of virtually all of Nechaev's inner circle. The letter, written in clumsy and easily decipherable code, was composed as if it were from a "wine merchant." In the letter, the Third Section read that "real wine without impurities is found only at Bakurskii's" and that casks were being "prepared for shipment." The author needed money, "a copy of the accounts," and information on "how much wine was being made." It was soon clear that Bakurskii was Bakunin, that the "casks" referred to leaflets, and that the "accounts" Nechaev wanted were names and addresses to which he could send his leaflets.[21]

Tomilova's apartment was raided on April 13, and she was arrested shortly thereafter. The Third Section found evidence incriminating the entire Nechaev organization, and they confiscated papers that bore the names of all of Nechaev's potential co-conspirators. Using this evidence, the police methodically gathered evidence against each suspect. During police interviews, investigators took careful notes, making sure to underline each name mentioned. The police then matched those names with the evidence confiscated from the apartments of other suspects. Finally, they went to the neighbors and acquaintances of the accused, asking them about each suspect's movements and activities.[22]

One of the prime suspects in the Nechaev conspiracy was Vera Zasulich. Nechaev's repeated mention of her name in various letters suggested that she was a person of extreme importance to him. Other suspects confirmed Vera's significance. Tomilova admitted that Vera often stayed with her in her apartment. One of Nechaev's closest associates revealed that he received Nechaev's letters through Vera. The daughters of Vera's landlady declared that Vera was involved in a secret society, where there was talk of establishing a republic in Russia and exiling the tsar to Siberia.[23] The evidence against her, though mostly circumstantial, accumulated.

Vera was brought in for questioning on April 15, when she claimed that she knew next to nothing about Nechaev or his organization. She suggested that her only connection to the Nechaev group was that she needed work and asked Tomilova to employ her to sew linens. Her apartment was searched the following day, but nothing was found. A casual comment by Vera's mother, however, increased police suspicions. When Vera was brought in for questioning, her mother let slip that she had always greatly feared that her daughter was "in for it."[24]

At the end of April, Vera's fate was sealed by the injudicious actions of a friend. Liudmilla Kolachevskaia, a young devotee of Nechaev's, fled St. Petersburg in mid-April to avoid the scrutiny of the police, taking a suitcase of illegal books and the typeface for a printing press with her. Arriving in Moscow on the train, she took a cab to the house of a relative. When she arrived at the house, she saw her cousin waving at her from a window. "The house is being searched," her cousin called to Liudmilla in French, hoping that the police would not understand. Liudmilla ran back to the cab and asked the driver to take her to Fili, the Moscow suburb where she had visited Alexandra Zasulich the summer before. Along the way, she asked the driver to stop, and she walked some way through the forest, lugging a heavy suitcase behind her. She hid the suitcase under some moss and leaves and returned to the cab. Then she asked the driver to take her back to Moscow, where she spent the night in a hotel.

The next morning, she went to visit Alexandra Zasulich, who was living in

Moscow at the time. Explaining the entire situation, Liudmilla asked for Alexandra's help. The two women decided to go back to the forest, recover the suitcase, and bury it in a carefully marked location. For this purpose they bought a large butcher knife (perhaps because it was easier to conceal than a shovel) and then hailed a cab to take them to the spot where Liudmilla had left her suitcase. Purporting to seek a summer home for rent, they stopped in a few villages along the way. And then they darted into the forest, found the suitcase, and buried it underground.

When the cab pulled up to Liudmilla's hotel, Liudmilla suddenly turned to Alexandra and whispered, "The police, quickly!" She pushed Alexandra out of the cab, and Alexandra ran. Only later that day did she learn that Liudmilla had been arrested. The cabdriver had reported her and her queer behavior to the police.[25]

Liudmilla's connection to the Zasulich sisters was soon exposed. Liudmilla was friends with Ekaterina and Vera, her brother had been questioned in early April about Nechaev, and he told the police about his friendship with the Zasulich sisters. Vera and her mother were arrested in Moscow on May 1, and incriminating documents and books were found on Vera. Ekaterina was arrested a few days later. Oddly, Alexandra was left alone.[26]

The final piece of evidence against Vera was discovered in Ekaterina's suitcase: It contained a list of addresses, some illegal books, and a passport. Ekaterina claimed that the objects belonged to several different acquaintances, and she was carrying them to return them to their owners. But the police were suspicious. It is likely that various puzzle pieces fit neatly together: Nechaev's importunate letters, asking Vera to come abroad and bring the addresses he required; Ekaterina's suitcase, filled with a passport and an address book; the fact that both sisters were traveling to Moscow from St. Petersburg. They must have suspected that someone was going abroad to meet Nechaev—and, given Nechaev's letters, it was most likely Vera herself.[27]

～

All of a sudden, unexpectedly, he found himself locked up without books and without friends, alone with himself. His agitated mind continued to spin day and night—he complained that from the very beginning he was plagued by insomnia—raising question after question without finding any answers. Rarely, an old journal would appear in his cell, filled with unfinished novels and gossip about odds and ends, or worse, with pages of surplus and unsubstantiated phrases about something that would not let him sleep. Soon, he completely stopped reading and only thought and thought, arriving

eventually at absolute skepticism. Nearly a year after his arrest the investi-
gation began. Until then, he knew nothing about the Nechaev affair, for
which he was investigated. Now, he learned a few fragmentary facts, which
seemed to him extremely pointless and inane. Under their influence, his low
spirits became bitter despair. Despair at himself, at those like him, at every-
thing without distinction.

— VERA ZASULICH, "Masha"[28]

"The Lithuanian Castle" was the extraordinary name of one of St. Petersburg's grimmest prisons. The name had vaguely Gothic overtones, although Russians had no history of European-style knighthood. The name
was derived from the building's original purpose as a barracks for the
Lithuanian Troop Regiment during the eighteenth century. The Castle became a prison only in 1823. Located near the outskirts of St. Petersburg, it
was an immense, ugly gray building, adorned solely with a statue of two angels holding a cross. It was a horrible place, described by one of its inmates
as "a graveyard for the living."[29]

Once brought through the towering prison gates, the inmate was led
through a series of courtyards, and then through a maze of corridors to the
tiny, dank cell that would confine him for months or years on end. Lev Nikiforov, a follower of Nechaev and later Vera's brother-in-law, remembered
how his heart sank when he first saw the sole window of his cell—a tiny, half-
circular plate of glass high above reach, covered, for good measure, by an
iron screen. The only thing visible from this window was a small patch of St.
Petersburg sky, and even during the brightest day, only a few thin rays of
light would penetrate the blackness of his cell. The prison was abhorrently
filthy: The sour stench of mildew penetrated the corridors, and the walls
were so damp that prisoners avoided touching them, lest they smear their
fingers with wet mold. The floorboards were nearly rotten, giving way under
the feet. Visitors reported finding the smell unbearable, even after a few
short hours.[30]

These wretched conditions were common throughout the Russian prison
system. In 1865, a commission established by Alexander II issued a devastating report on prisons throughout Russia. The report documented old and dilapidated buildings, rotten floorboards, collapsing roofs, and lack of basic
sanitation. Vera was, in fact, comparatively lucky, because she was given a cell
entirely to herself. In general, overcrowding was endemic, with several prisoners packed into each cell, causing the rapid spread of disease and death.[31]

Vera, like many prisoners, did not see her solitary confinement as a blessing but as a curse, the worst aspect of her prison life. Many prisoners were occasionally let out of their cells for periodic interrogations, something most of them welcomed as a chance for some meager contact with other human beings. But Vera was left entirely alone. Month after month she waited for some information on her plight, but she was neither questioned nor charged with a crime. She was permitted no visitors—Vera's mother complained to the authorities that she was allowed to see her daughters only once in an entire year.[32] The one thing that might have made her solitude bearable—reading material—was also unavailable. The prison kept a few old, yellowed issues of magazines and journals, and that was all. "Just imagine," wrote Lev Nikiforov, "you are in a narrow crypt, and everything around you is dead. . . . In your cell there is nothing, except yellow walls, to grab your attention. And in this merciless, grave-like silence you are walled up not just for a day or two, but for endlessly long months. The only things left to do are to pace from corner to corner, and to sleep, sleep without end."[33]

In her short story, "Masha," Vera provides insight into the private hell of her incarceration. A character in the story is imprisoned for his participation in Nechaev's conspiracy, much like Vera herself. When he is at last released, his mental health is shattered for good. His breakdown is neither physical, nor the result of torture, but the consequence of unremitting isolation, where he was left entirely to himself and his thoughts.[34]

The silence of solitary confinement, the panic of being buried alive, tormented prisoners more than any physical privations. Writing at a later date, the revolutionary Dmitrii Rogachev wrote that the most dire fear of prisoners was insanity. "From time to time," he wrote, "when I was sitting, I would begin to laugh hysterically or, more likely, to cry." "Many began to hallucinate," wrote another prisoner, "or to lose control of themselves. . . . From one cell or another you could hear violent, forcibly suppressed sobs and cries." One radical suggested that death, "for which he had long been prepared," was less terrifying to him than incipient madness brought about by months of solitary confinement.[35]

Vera may have dreamed of martyrdom for her cause, but this was not the sacrifice she imagined. After long years of searching, she had begun her life of radical activity. And perhaps just as she decided to finally join Nechaev, to become his assistant in his revolutionary endeavors, the Russian regime had foiled her dreams. Thrust suddenly into a tiny cell, she had endless hours to contemplate her decision and its outcome. She must have experienced long stretches of abject despair.

After thirteen months in the Castle, without any warning, the doors of Vera's cell opened and she saw the light of day for a brief moment. Without explanation, she was transferred to the Peter and Paul Fortress, known as the Russian Bastille.[36]

～

This was, then, the terrible fortress where so much of the true strength of Russia had perished during the last two centuries, and the very name of which is uttered in St. Petersburg in a hushed voice.

Here Peter I tortured his son Alexis and killed him with his own hand; here the Princess Tarakanova was kept in a cell which filled with water during an inundation—the rats climbing upon her to save themselves from drowning; here the terrible Minich tortured his enemies, and Catherine II buried alive those who objected to her having murdered her husband. And from the times of Peter I, for a hundred and seventy years, the annals of this mass of stone which rises from the Neva in front of the Winter Palace were annals of murder and torture, of men buried alive, condemned to a slow death, or driven to insanity in the loneliness of the dark and damp dungeon.

— PETER KROPOTKIN, *Memoirs of a Revolutionist*[37]

According to the legends that enveloped the Peter and Paul Fortress, it was more a torture chamber than a prison. Built in 1703 as a defense against a possible Swedish invasion from the north, the fortress was quickly rendered irrelevant with the construction of the Kronshtadt naval base. By 1721, it was used almost exclusively as a prison for the most dangerous of Russia's political prisoners.[38]

During its two-hundred-year existence, the fortress confined some of Russia's most famous figures: the poet of the Decembrist Revolution, Konstantin Ryleev, who penned one of his last lines on a metal plate in the prison; Fyodor Dostoyevsky, who awaited his mock execution within those walls; Mikhail Bakunin, who wrote his sycophantic "Letter to the Tsar" while awaiting his sentence there; and Dmitrii Karakozov, who was allegedly tortured by his captors and who converted to Orthodoxy just before he was hanged. The list could go on: Nikolai Chernyshevskii, Dmitrii Pisarev, and even Nechaev himself were all captives of the Peter and Paul Fortress.[39]

As with the Bastille itself, however, legend far outstripped fact. By the time Vera entered its gates, the "dark and damp dungeon" had become one of the first targets of Alexander's reform efforts. It was, by then, a reasonably bright, clean, and well-run prison. Many of the cells were large enough for two tall windows. The furniture was ordinary but serviceable. The food was praised by more than one prisoner: The tea, apparently, was exceptionally good, and from time to time, the cooks would insist that the prisoners taste some elegant new culinary concoction.[40]

For the more educated prisoners, the fortress had another enlightened accommodation: a well-stocked library. Moreover, family members were permitted to bring reading material to the inmates. While still behind bars, Kropotkin was granted a dispensation to complete research for the St. Petersburg Geographical Society and given access to the library of the Russian Academy of Sciences. According to his own testimony, his cell began to resemble a study, with mounds of books and papers surrounding his table. After the squalor of the Castle, the conditions in the fortress were so favorable that Lev Nikiforov, upon being transferred, declared that it was, "if not heaven, then at least purgatory."[41]

Vera was brought to the Peter and Paul Fortress in May 1870, on the eve of her twenty-first birthday, and was kept, along with other Nechaevites, in the Catherine Tower. Making up for lost time, she began to read ravenously, sometimes devouring several books per week. The anomalies of the Russian criminal system are revealed in Vera's prison records. Not only was she allowed to read, but her choice of reading material was uncensored. Surprisingly, political prisoners were permitted books of a decidedly radical character. While she was in prison, Vera kept up with the latest socialist literature, including Chernyshevskii's heavily annotated edition of John Stuart Mill's *The Principles of Political Economy*, a novel entitled *Two Generations* by the radical German author Friedrich Spielhagen, and two books by a Russian radical, *The Situation of the Working Class in Russia* and *The Proletariat in France*.[42]

Paradoxically, the better her conditions, the more irate Vera became. Suffering did not anger her half so much as the arbitrary, unpredictable, and incomprehensible treatment she received. She had not yet been informed of the charges against her. For all she knew, the regime had forgotten her. For how long could they possibly imprison her? Exacerbation came through a petition she addressed to the Third Section in May 1870. While most petitioners wrote their petitions in the most subservient language, Vera refused to beg for mercy. "I have been sitting in secret imprisonment for over a year," she wrote impatiently. "I have not been questioned since May 1869, and I do not know why I am imprisoned. I respectfully request a quick investigation into my case and my release."[43]

Vera did not know that, while she was behind bars, Nechaev had returned to Russia and launched a frenzied plot of terror and murder. Without ever leaving her cell, Vera had become implicated in "the Nechaev affair."

~

15. This filthy social order can be split up into several categories. The first category comprises those who must be condemned to death without delay. Comrades should compile a list of those to be condemned according to the relative gravity of their crimes; and the executions should be carried out according to the prepared order. . . .

17. The second group comprises those who will be spared for the time being in order that, by a series of monstrous acts, they may drive the people into inevitable revolt.

18. The third category consists of a great many brutes in high positions. . . . These must be exploited in every possible way; they must be implicated and embroiled in our affairs, their dirty secrets must be ferreted out. . . .

19. The fourth category comprises ambitious officeholders and liberals of various shades of opinion. The revolutionist must pretend to collaborate with them, blindly following them, while at the same time, prying out their secrets until they are completely in his power. . . .

20. The fifth category consists of those doctrinaires, conspirators, and revolutionists who cut a great figure on paper or in their circles. They must be constantly driven on to make compromising declarations: as a result, the majority of them will be destroyed, while a minority will become genuine revolutionists.

—SERGEI NECHAEV, *Catechism of a Revolutionary*[44]

Nechaev knew that his accomplices in Russia had been arrested. He knew that the police were watching him carefully as the one remaining target. These developments had no effect on Nechaev's plans. The arrests meant a loss of revolutionary capital, but many of those who fell into the hands of the police were probably weak radicals at best. Better, more ruthless individuals could certainly be found. Nechaev had little fear for himself—he was full of contempt for the Russian Third Section, since they were still amateurs.

An alias, a complicated route across the Russian border, and Nechaev would evade them.

In August 1869, Nechaev crossed back into Russia by traveling through Romania, under the comical alias of Ivan Petrovich Pavlov ("John Peter Paulson"). Incidentally, his detour through Romania would have extraordinary consequences for the Balkan peninsula. While there, he met with Bulgaria's most prominent revolutionary, Christo Botev. It is likely that Nechaev provided Botev with guidance on how to run a revolutionary organization. This tutelage was used to great effect in Bulgaria's uprising against the Turks in 1876.[45]

After nearly a month of traveling through the Balkans and the south of Russia, Nechaev arrived in Moscow. He appeared at the apartment of two of the remaining members of his old organization, who had somehow managed to escape arrest: Peter Uspenskii, who worked in a bookstore in downtown Moscow, and his wife, Alexandra, Vera's older sister. Alexandra remembered being impressed by this elegant, sophisticated man in a tailored European suit.

That very evening, over tea, Nechaev briefed the couple on his travels, his successes abroad, and his new plans for the revolution still to come. This time, there would be no halfhearted infiltration of student movements, no petitions, no lukewarm propaganda efforts. Alexandra listened, fascinated, as Nechaev sketched the blueprint of his new organization, developed after a long study of previous European conspiracies. The time had come, Nechaev explained, to create a terrorist group.[46]

Before he had crossed the border, Nechaev had carefully written, and then encoded, two documents that became the most extraordinary products of his long revolutionary career. Together, they were used to create a perfect terrorist organization—a cohort of fanatics bound together by a cult-like devotion to the cause.[47]

The first document was a mere four pages long. It later became known as *The Catechism of a Revolutionary*. Meticulously crafted with the help of Mikhail Bakunin, this document is one of the most extraordinary and most influential revolutionary pamphlets of all time. Describing, in near poetic terms, the characteristics of the true radical terrorist, the *Catechism* is a spellbinding account of the sheer dedication, ruthlessness, and fervor for violence that a "true" radical must achieve.[48]

"The revolutionist is a doomed man," the *Catechism* begins. "He has no personal interests, affairs, feelings, attachments, belongings, not even a name."

What follows is a mesmerizing call for purity, for self-abnegation, for the re-nunciation of everything extraneous to the cause. The *Catechism* demands that the revolutionary live his life as a weapon, mercilessly destroying every-thing that stands in the path of revolution. Nechaev had offered Russia its first glimpse into the mind of a terrorist.

A perfect child of Rakhmetov, and grandchild of Bazarov, Nechaev's rev-olutionary employed only one calculus: "utility." This new utility was purer, more refined—purged of all ethical or social considerations. Its aim was un-mitigated destruction. Everything useful for destruction was of great value; everything extraneous to the cause of total annihilation was to be discarded as useless. Even the cherished sciences, Chernyshevskii's tools for the creation of a new order, were now consecrated to terrorism. The revolutionary was to learn "mechanics, physics, chemistry, even medicine," but only with one aim, "the surest and quickest way of destroying this whole filthy order."

Nechaev, the consummate psychologist, knew that the *Catechism* was the perfect recruitment tool for the outcast and disaffected of Russian soci-ety. The heart of its appeal lay in its ruthlessness, its shocking amorality, even its promise of nothing but pain and death for the true revolutionary. The *Catechism* perversely implied that only a select few boasted the mental agility, stamina, and willpower to become true revolutionaries. Like early Christian ascetics, who sought to prove their faith through increasingly ex-traordinary feats of self-abnegation, the disciples of the *Catechism* wished only to submerge themselves into the personality of the revolutionary ter-rorist.

But Nechaev's diabolical brilliance was by no means exhausted by the *Catechism.* It equally shined in a document that is less well known but had worldwide effects that proved much more fateful. Colorlessly entitled *The General Rules of the Organization,* it described the perfectly constructed terrorist network.[49]

The basic building block of Nechaev's organization, and for virtually all effective terrorist organizations after him, was the cell. At the top, the cen-tral cell was the nucleus of the organization. Composed of five members, each known by number rather than by name, the central cell devised strat-egy for the organization and issued orders. Each member of the central cell was responsible for recruiting five additional members and organizing them into a subsidiary cell, itself bound together by loyalty and secrecy. No cell had sustained contact with any other. Each person unquestioningly obeyed orders that came from above and sent appropriate orders down the chain.

Reciprocally, each cell was required to send both intelligence and money through the proper cellular path up to the center.

Individual cells were given specific tasks: infiltrating police organizations, recruiting members from the criminal underworld, disseminating propaganda in the military, or extorting money from the wealthy. Except for those in the central cell, individuals in the organization were to remain ignorant of the overall structure or plans of the organization. They worked entirely in the dark.

Members were tapped only after a lengthy period of observation. They had to exhibit the proper combination of willpower and perfect obedience, loyalty and ruthlessness, love of the people and intense hatred for the state. After a trial period, the recruits swore an oath of secrecy and fealty. As the *Catechism* made clear, violation of such an oath was punishable by death. Even expressing the desire to quit the organization could get a member executed.

It was a brilliantly conceived conspiratorial structure. It was simultaneously hierarchical and flexible, easily able to transmit information to its members while preserving anonymity and secrecy. Most important, if any particular cell was exposed, no further damage to the organization would follow, as no one member could betray its nature and mission.

The ultimate goal of this organization was simply stated: to destroy all of the existing institutions of Russian government and society, and then to appropriate all private property and redistribute it among the workers and peasants. How this would happen and how a future society was to be ordered were matters left unclear. The *Catechism*, in fact, unequivocally declared revolutionaries free of any obligation to construct the new society. That would be "left to future generations." It was yet again the old idea, first pioneered by Herzen: "We do not build, we destroy."[50]

To most, Nechaev's was a frightening organization, filled with fanatics. For many revolutionaries, it was positively enticing, the key to a new life for all. As for Nechaev, whatever else he did, he never failed to follow his own *Catechism* to the letter.

Uspenskii and his wife were entranced. Alexandra, perhaps the least intelligent and most gullible of the three Zasulich sisters, fell particularly under Nechaev's spell. Willing to do anything for him, Alexandra was nonetheless limited in her capabilities—she was, at that time, in the last trimester of her pregnancy. In her memoirs, she recalled one emotion she felt around

Nechaev: shame. Because of her condition, she could do little for the cause. Somehow, her pregnancy was a public admission of her "private interests" and her inability to dedicate her life to the revolution.[51]

Peter Uspenskii, on the other hand, more than made up for his wife's incapacity. He became Nechaev's right-hand man, a loyal and efficient member of Nechaev's new organization, named the Society of the People's Revenge. It was structured according to the principles of the *Rules of the Organization* and immediately drew in some eighty members. They were a motley lot, including a former peasant who wrote a book entitled *A History of Pot-Houses* and whose research led him into crippling alcoholism; a young man, who, though a mere teenager, had managed to work, successively, as a prison advisor, a book peddler, and a carpenter; and an almost suicidal fanatic whose desire for violence sprang out of "bitterness, titanic bitterness." One thing all of these men and women had in common—an irrational, inexplicable devotion to Nechaev.[52]

At first, the tasks of the society were relatively benign. Members were asked to infiltrate peasant villages, student groups, and factories in order to gauge the general mood of the "people." One member even took on the task of scouting out the underworld, and thus spent innumerable evenings cavorting with the thieves, pickpockets, and prostitutes of Moscow.[53]

But eventually, the real purpose of Nechaev's society was revealed. It was to coordinate a series of assassinations—terrorist attacks on highly placed individuals in the government and in society. The wealthy and powerful who were spared death were to be exploited in other ways—implicated in conspiratorial activity, defrauded of money, or blackmailed into serving the organization. These coordinated actions would bring down Russian institutions, brick by brick. Then the apocalypse would begin.[54]

Nechaev carefully compiled a list of names of those slated for execution, in order of priority. They included government officials, noblemen, professors, and even students. Later, after his arrest, the full list was discovered on his person. It included nine hundred names.[55]

By November 1869, all seemed ready for the target date of February 19, 1870. The plan for revolution was set. But a small problem arose within the ranks—one of the faithful began to doubt. A sour-tempered and skeptical young man named Ivan Ivanov, known as Number Two in the society, resented Nechaev's cult-leader-like authority and began to voice doubts about his plans. Most dangerous, during meetings of the central cell, Ivanov took to openly laughing at Nechaev's comments. Finally, Ivanov told Nechaev that he had enough. He told others that he planned to leave the society and form his own separate organization.[56]

His unbelief was to seal his fate.

On November 20, 1869, Nechaev called a special meeting of the central cell. The only person absent was Ivanov. Nechaev claimed to have discovered some devastating information—Ivanov was a police informer. There was only one course of action, Nechaev solemnly proclaimed. To save the organization, Ivanov had to be killed. At first, those present began to voice doubts and objected with troubled mutterings. But Nechaev's logic seemed irrefutable. Late into the night, members of the cell made their plans.[57]

Deep in Petrovskii Park, in Moscow, there was a dark grotto, large enough to accommodate several people. Beside the grotto was a small pond, already covered in a thin sheet of ice. On the bitterly cold night of November 21, Nechaev and Uspenskii waited for the others to bring Ivanov there, under the pretext that revolutionary material was hidden in the grotto and needed to be dug up. As the two men waited, Uspenskii tied a couple of heavy stones to a rope. When he heard the footsteps of the others, Uspenskii began to shiver and leaned against the walls of the grotto.[58]

The moment Ivanov stepped past the threshold, the group attacked him. One of the conspirators grabbed his arms, another his legs. A strong, wiry man, Ivanov broke free for a moment and tried to run but was quickly tackled. At this point, Nechaev took control. Sitting on top of Ivanov, he began to beat his head on the ground and crush his throat. Ivanov screamed, "What did I do?" and tried to fight back, biting Nechaev's hands and arms. Finally, maddened by the struggle, Nechaev removed a revolver from his pocket and shot Ivanov in the head. The "traitor" was finally dead.

Quickly, almost thoughtlessly, the conspirators tried to cover their tracks. They weighed the body down with Uspenskii's rope and threw it into the pond, breaking through the ice with their feet. Then they fled. At the apartment of one of the conspirators, Nechaev changed his bloodied clothes and tried to wash the blood from his mangled hands. At the sight of so much blood, Ivan Pryzhov, one of the more reluctant conspirators, began to tremble. He picked up a decanter from the table in front of Nechaev and poured himself a stiff glass of vodka. Suddenly, a deafening shot exploded, and a bullet whizzed by Pryzhov's ear. He looked up in horror and saw Nechaev before him, holding the revolver. "Well," Nechaev said with eerie lightheartedness, "if we kill you, we can pin it all on you."[59]

The murder of Ivanov was Nechaev's first real terrorist act, but it would also be his last. It took the Third Section less than two weeks to unravel the mystery. Because the body was improperly weighted down, it was found in the pond a few days later. Ivanov's watch was also discovered; conveniently, it had stopped at the moment the body was dropped into the pond, thus establishing the precise time of the attack. Some receipts in Ivanov's coat pocket came from the bookstore where Uspenskii worked. Nechaev's hat had fallen next to the pond.[60]

In late November, Peter Uspenskii's apartment was scrupulously searched. Sofas were ripped apart; all drawers, closets, and crawl spaces were cleaned out. The police discovered everything pertaining to Nechaev's conspiracy: leaflets, the *Catechism*, minutes of meetings, and lists of assassination targets. Uspenskii was arrested and interrogated. He confessed everything in a torrent, almost with relief. For some time before his arrest he had been unable to leave his apartment. He was repeatedly plagued by visions of the grotto walls, splattered with blood, and everywhere he heard the final, strangled cries of Ivanov. Thanks to Uspenskii, by mid-December, all of Nechaev's accomplices were in prison.[61]

In late November, just before her husband's arrest, Nechaev approached Alexandra Uspenskaia and asked if she knew French and German. When she answered affirmatively, Nechaev asked her to flee abroad with him, to join Bakunin and other revolutionaries. Unlike her sister Vera, in identical circumstances, Alexandra was filled with unmitigated joy. "I could never dream of such happiness," she remembered years later. She immediately said yes. But then, after some thought, she realized it was impossible. For a moment, she had entirely forgotten that she was almost nine months pregnant.[62]

Nechaev, without hesitation, found another accomplice. He turned to Varvara Alexandrovskaia, a woman with a long revolutionary history. Though she was married and fifteen years his elder, Alexandrovskaia agreed to abandon her husband, lover, and child in order to follow Nechaev wherever he went.

On December 12, the Third Section began an earnest search for Nechaev, now suspected of murder and antigovernment conspiracy. Count Peter Shuvalov sent a directive to all of the heads of Russia's provinces, to keep a look out for a man "of small height, around 22 years old, young looking, with fuzz on his cheeks instead of a beard, chestnut hair, a dark face, his eyes dark brown, sharp and clever." He also added a curious detail: "sometimes wears women's dresses or engineer's uniforms."[63]

It was too late. On December 15, Nechaev and Alexandrovskaia boarded a train for Europe.

By January 1870, some 152 people were in custody for alleged complicity in the Nechaev affair. Included in this number were many arrested in December 1869, as well as those who, like Vera, had been incarcerated ever since the first arrests of Nechaev's conspirators. The tsarist government, desirous of a public victory over its potential enemies, planned public trials for the Nechaev conspirators and gave the entirety of the Nechaev files over to the Ministry of Justice. Konstantin Filippeus handed thousands of pages of depositions, denunciations, secret police reports, leaflets, and pamphlets to one man—Phillip Chemadurov, appointed the general prosecutor for the case. Somehow, Chemadurov had to wade through this mountain of material and put together a case against the Nechaevites.[64]

Chemadurov's investigation took more than a year to complete. He handled the case with extraordinary diligence, reinterviewing old suspects and asking the Third Section for further evidence against accused individuals. At first, the evidence against those such as Vera did seem incontrovertible. In May 1870, in response to Vera's petition for a reconsideration of her case, he wrote that, given the nature of the evidence presented by the Third Section, she should be kept incarcerated until the investigation was complete. But in later reports, his frustration at the Third Section often seeped through. His impatient requests for further evidence were met with unyielding resistance on the part of the police.[65]

In March 1871, Chemadurov decided that he had sufficient evidence to try only half of the suspects being held in connection with the Nechaev affair. So many of those incarcerated had been held without charges and without interrogations for over a year. Evidence that was originally circumstantial was now also outdated. His report to the minister of justice detailed reasons for allowing all charges to be dismissed against the remaining seventy-three of the accused. In the case of Vera Zasulich, Chemadurov concluded that her already lengthy incarceration mitigated against confirming the original evidence against her. Moreover, he wrote, almost with open irritation, it was impossible to build a serious case of revolutionary activity against Vera simply on a few bits of hearsay evidence. The charges against Vera should be dropped.[66]

Unceremoniously, without warning, the doors of the Peter and Paul prison opened. After two long years in semidarkness, Vera was allowed to go free, exonerated of all charges against her. Outside the prison gates, her mother waited, by now much aged by worry and grief. They both hoped that the family ordeal was over.

But this was only a spiteful trick of fate. Vera's freedom lasted all of ten days. On the tenth day came a knock on the door. A policeman stood at the doorway and announced that he had orders "to take her into custody again."[67]

～

It is now two hours since I arrived in Novgorod. I am only here temporarily, they are going to take me to some provincial town. I am sitting in a room in a hotel, and a guard is standing outside the door—he will stay there while I am here. The room isn't free. My dear, how hard it is, how heavily this lies on my soul! It is so hard that I cannot cope; in a few days I will certainly feel like I can manage and then I may even regret that I am writing this. I know that it is stupid and silly to complain, that this is not the way to endure such an ordinary thing, but you are so good, you will not laugh, and I just need to write. You see, even in the prison, even in the fortress I never felt this lonely (not even close!), as I do at this very minute. As if I am entirely alone in the world.

—VERA ZASULICH, letter to Alexandra Zasulich, April 1871[68]

Vera arrived at the St. Petersburg police headquarters wearing nothing more than a light dress and a thin scarf. She believed her rearrest was nothing more than a misunderstanding, one that could be easily cleared up. Vera's mother promised to go to Chemadurov and ask him to intervene. With increasing agitation, Vera waited for her release. She wrote a furious letter to Chemadurov, demanding that he investigate the reasons for her rearrest. "For my transgressions, if there were any, which is yet to be determined, I have already sat for 22 months in solitary confinement. Is this not enough?"[69]

The petition was too late. After five days, the doors of her cell opened. The guard announced that she was being taken to Kresttsy, a small town in the Novgorod province.

It was April, a cold month in the northern province of Novgorod. Vera was wrapped tightly in her shawl, but she was completely unprepared for the chilly weather and was lucky that one of her guards pitied her, giving her the coat off of his back. When they arrived in Kresttsy, the local police ordered her to report regularly, on Saturdays, and released her. Thus was Vera exiled to a tiny, alien town, with only one ruble in her pocket and the guard's coat on her back. She was homeless and penniless, a desolate victim of tsarist cruelty. The local church saved her. She was taken in by the sexton and his family. For three months, she lived there without hope of finding means to support herself, entirely dependent on the kindness of strangers.[70]

Vera was told nothing about her new punishment. Unbeknownst to her, she was the victim of a long-standing battle between the Ministry of Justice and the secret police. The trained prosecutors in the ministry, concerned with trials and convictions, often took a dim view of the methods of Russia's Third Section. Holding prisoners without charges, relying on the doubtful testimony of informers and on hearsay evidence—all of this was poor judicial practice, according to the prosecutors. It would never prevail in court. Often, prosecutors appointed by the Ministry of Justice examined particular cases and simply dismissed the charges against those arrested by the Third Section.[71]

Shuvalov's Third Section found such liberalism intolerable. It acted to break conspiracy rings and prevent acts of terrorism. Shuvalov took the arbitrary release of potentially dangerous suspects as a threat to Russian security. He convinced the tsar to take matters into his own hands. Alexander, increasingly fearful, agreed. He allowed the police to send those suspected of political crimes into exile without a trial or even a hearing. Vera was just one of the many prisoners released in the Nechaev affair who were subsequently subject to arbitrary "administrative" exile.[72]

When Chemadurov learned of Vera's plight, he was surely irate. In planning the prosecution of the Nechaevites, he had hoped to secure Vera's testimony. The antics of the Third Section thus jeopardized his case. Finally, in June 1871, after repeated petitions by Chemadurov and Vera's mother, Vera was allowed to return home.[73]

Vera testified in the St. Petersburg Court of Justice in June 1871. The trial of the Nechaevites was a sensation in the Russian press, and every detail was published in the newspapers. It had all the markings of a fantastic legal drama—a Svengali-like terrorist leader, his gullible, devoted followers, and a young student victim murdered for his willingness to doubt. The courtroom was packed, especially with students, who stood in line all night waiting to be admitted. The Third Section sent its informants as well—they noticed the preponderance of nihilist-style workers' clothing in the courtroom audience.[74]

Vera mostly kept quiet during the trial. She did not want to call attention to herself. When questioned as a witness, she provided short, terse replies, "I don't know" and "I don't remember." Chemadurov was frustrated; he had counted on her testimony to expose Nechaev's connections with the early St. Petersburg group. He accused her of contradicting her original deposition. Finally, the pent-up rage inside Vera burst out. "The statements I made during my deposition were erroneous," she snapped, "and it is little wonder that I said the wrong things. I was locked up for thirteen months in the Lithuanian Castle in solitary confinement without books . . . [and] my nerves were horribly agitated."[75]

The other suspects were far more loquacious. They attributed all of the deceptions, frauds, and violence to Nechaev. As for them, they were simply idealistic young people, who wanted nothing more than a good life for all Russians. Konstantin Filippeus watched the trial with a sinking heart. After all of his hard work capturing and incarcerating these terrorists and assassins, it seemed that the public, the judges, and the journalists would defend them and let them go free. They had proven too well spoken, too artful at depicting the evils of the Russian government and the supposed injustices of society. Their description of their communes, their Chernyshevskiian marriages, and their desires for a free and just society fascinated many spectators and journalists. They acted like "apostles of socialism" whose fate it was to accept "a martyr's crown for their faith."[76]

Filippeus wrote a mournful report to the tsar. The trial had exposed a deep rift between society and the tsarist government. The judges, heedless of the dangers of the Nechaev conspiracy, had handed down only a few harsh sentences. More than half of the defendants were acquitted. The newspapers refused to expose the seamy aspects of the terrorist group—they never saw fit to condemn the *Catechism* and other equally frightening documents. The trial had been turned upside down—with the government itself in the dock, charged with all manner of crimes with "the eloquence of a fanatical mind." If this continued, he concluded, the state would lose its war with revolution.[77]

Filippeus was overly dire. There was no doubt that many of Nechaev's co-conspirators were punished severely enough. Peter Uspenskii was sentenced to fifteen years of forced labor. His wife, Alexandra, followed him into exile with their young son. While incarcerated, Uspenskii met the fate he had meted out to Ivanov. Suspected of being a police informer, he was strangled in his cell.[78]

After the trial of the conspirators, Nechaev became Konstantin Filippeus's obsession. He persuaded the regime to exert every effort—judicial, investigative, and diplomatic—to arrest and extradite Nechaev. He was able to launch a special fund dedicated to the location and extradition of this arch-conspirator.

Nechaev himself was beginning to look indestructible. His second flight abroad proved more fantastic than the first. He became convinced that he possessed special charismatic powers, which exerted particular sway over women. He took Rousseau's *Confessions* with him wherever he went, as a kind of guide to the art of seduction. Having honed his skills on a variety of less important women (the list includes Vera, her sister Alexandra, Varvara Alexandrovskaia, and a host of others), he now set out to seduce the ultimate prize: Natalie Herzen, the eldest daughter of the lion of literary radicalism. Herzen was now deceased, and Nechaev wanted to become his heir. He set out to acquire Herzen's daughter, his money, and, more important, his journal, *The Bell*.[79]

Natalie, like Vera and Alexandra before her, was a woman of radical inclinations, who chafed against the decorum and propriety expected of her. She was also vacillating and easily led, and her relatives constantly shadowed her, fearing that she might fall into the clutches of someone like Nechaev. The only characteristic that made her a difficult catch was her prudishness—conventional seduction could not appeal to her.[80]

Nechaev proposed to her, as he did to Vera, and met with confused resistance. Natalie was, by turns, captivated and horrified by him. In one letter, she agreed to see him alone only if he promised not to try to kiss her. It seems that she alternately fell for his charms and was repulsed by his behavior. But the continual pressure of Nechaev's personality finally collapsed her defenses. In the spring of 1870, she finally agreed to hand over control of *The Bell*. It was the final victory of the sons over the fathers. Henceforth, *The Bell* became just another organ for the publication of Nechaevite propaganda.[81]

But Nechaev's deeds were finally beginning to catch up with him. News of the murder of Ivanov spread abroad, as did word of the arrests of Nechaev's co-conspirators. It became increasingly clear, even to Nechaev's friends, that he was a dangerous charlatan, a man who spoke of revolutionary deeds and terrorist acts but whose sole accomplishment was the murder of one of his own followers. Bakunin, in a plaintive letter written to Nechaev in June 1870, voiced horror at seeing the man he believed was a savior turned into a demon. But even Bakunin simply could not let Nechaev go. Nechaev's pure devotion to revolution elevated him to the status of a "saintly person." "I loved you deeply and still love you, Nechaev," Bakunin wrote.[82]

Filippeus dogged Nechaev's every step. He personally traveled abroad to recruit agents and informers to capture Nechaev. They trailed him all over Europe—to London, Paris, Geneva. Everywhere, however, just as the net came down, Nechaev would slip away again. For a time he posed as a Polish revolutionary, then as a Serbian exile. There were even rumors that he spent time in the United States.

In August 1872, he was betrayed by a fellow émigré and arrested. After long negotiations with the Swiss authorities, Nechaev was finally extradited to Russia. Tried in Moscow, he furiously raved against the court, denying its jurisdiction over his case. "I do not recognize the Emperor and the laws of this country," he bellowed at the judge. "Down with despotism!" This odd behavior turned the jury against him. After only twenty minutes of deliberations, Nechaev was found guilty and sentenced to twenty years' hard labor in Siberia.

But the Russian regime was too afraid of him to risk carrying out his sentence of exile. Instead, Nechaev followed his former comrades into the Peter and Paul Fortress. But even the walls of that ancient prison could not completely contain him. Soon enough, he would again begin to direct revolutionary activity, this time from the confines of his cell.[83]

~

Having devoted all my energies to the study of the social organization of the society of the future which is to replace our present one, I have come to the conclusion that all the inventors of social systems, from the ancient times to our present year, have been dreamers, storytellers, fools who contradicted themselves and had no idea of natural science or that strange animal called man. Plato, Rousseau, Fourier, aluminum pillars, all that is only good for sparrows, and not for human society. But as the future form of society is of the utmost importance now that we at last are all ready to act, I am submitting to you my own system of the world organization so as to make any further thinking unnecessary. . . .

I'm afraid I got rather muddled up in my own data, and my conclusion is in direct contradiction to the original idea with which I start. Starting from unlimited freedom, I arrived at unlimited despotism. I will add, how-ever, that there can be no other solution of the social formula other than mine.

— FYODOR DOSTOYEVSKY, *The Devils*[84]

When Fyodor Dostoyevsky published his novel about the Nechaev affair in 1871, radicals derided it as a caricature of the Russian revolutionary movement. To this day, the characters in *The Devils* seem like an odd assortment of erratic extremists, too extraordinary to be real. In fact, the plot of *The Devils* often seems a pale description of the true story of Nechaev and his antics. Peter Verkhovensky, the character whom Dostoevsky based on Nechaev, never quite reflects the merciless yet mesmerizing quality of Nechaev's personality. Stavrogin, the utterly unique protagonist in *The Devils,* is a far better approximation.[85]

The Devils, though a sometimes disjointed text, contains incisive commentary on the character of the Russian radical movement. In one extraordinary, and oft quoted, passage in the novel, one of the blander characters reveals the ultimate paradox of Russian radicalism: The desire for "unlimited freedom" had yielded, instead, "unlimited despotism." Moreover, human nature permitted "no other solution." Those who condemned the state as tyrannical created organizations that were, if anything, still more despotic. Those who believed in the free and equal society of the future unquestioningly obeyed an organization that was hierarchical, authoritarian, and brutal.[86]

But in the minds of the radicals, the ends justified the means. Fighting a powerful state required equal power and determination. The enemies of the state, to defeat the devil himself, had to become like him—diabolical, violent, and ruthless. If the state executed traitors, so would the antistate terrorists; if the state employed secret informers and agents, then the revolutionary organization would use infiltrators and spies. The future world justified all measures. In the words of the philosopher Albert Camus, "Nihilism, intimately involved with a frustrated religious movement, thus culminates in terrorism." This was Nechaev's legacy.[87]

Some have argued that, for all of Nechaev's seductions, threats, lies, and oaths, he accomplished nothing. The man who wished to assassinate nine hundred people ended up killing just one fellow revolutionary. After his comrades were arrested and his organization dissolved, the revolution seemed even further away than ever. The revolutionary messiah proved to be nothing more than a radical charlatan.

This was Vera's view. She never forgave Nechaev for his Machiavellianism. Long after she had become a famous revolutionary in her own right, she wrote with utmost condescension about Nechaev and his techniques. His influence on the revolutionary movement was negligible. He had succeeded only in demoralizing the younger generation through his endless lies. Once he disappeared from the scene, his influence evaporated.[88]

But as she wrote those words, Vera must have known they were false. Nechaev had pioneered the ultimate terrorist organization. Even those who were betrayed by him, and suffered because of him, remained his disciples. Bakunin, who derided Nechaev as a "Savonarola" and a "Jesuit," never relinquished his love for his demonic "boy." In 1872, when he formed his own revolutionary organization, the International Brotherhood, it was built on Nechaevite principles. The quintessential anarchist had no trouble building an organization on unquestioning obedience. For Bakunin, every revolutionary "vows himself irrevocably, body and soul, thought, will, passion, and action, with all his capacities, his energy, and his fortune to the service of the social revolution."[89]

No doubt, Vera could never forget or forgive the man who tried to ruthlessly use her and who allowed her to fall into the hands of the police. He had casually destroyed her naive young dreams of revolution before they could be realized. Nonetheless, like Bakunin and so many others, Vera became Nechaev's disciple. As Nechaev predicted, Vera's years in the clutches of the tsarist state transformed her from an idealistic young girl into a hardened revolutionary. Her lovely dreams of martyrdom were now twinned with a deep rage at the Russian state. It was the perfect raw material for Nechaev's ultimate creation: the revolutionary terrorist.

CHAPTER 7

To the People

~

O n a blazing June morning in 1875, Lev Deich began a daylong journey
from the quaintly named Ukrainian town of Goat's Ravine to the village
of Astrakhanka, some twenty miles down a straight, dusty road. By now, he
was used to wearing the clothes of a typical Russian peasant—the long white
cotton shirt covered, even in the heat of summer, with a thick, dark, fitted
linen coat. His hair was cut in rough, shaggy peasant style, and he was tall and
handsome, with strong dark brows, piercing brown eyes, and a powerful
manner.[1]

It was summer on the Ukrainian steppe. The sun beat mercilessly on the
parched road. Deich carried nothing but a walking stick and a shapeless linen
sack that held one change of clothes and some food for the journey. But the
day was blistering, and Deich had never walked twenty miles, much less in
flat shoes woven of birch bark strips. As the day wore on, he despairingly
searched the road ahead for any tree or bush that could shade him. All
around, as far as the eye could see, were waves and waves of dry mixed
grasses, Russia's equivalent of the American prairie. No shelter was in sight.
After some time, a passing peasant did point to a tiny little shepherd's hut a
few feet from the side of the road. It was not much, but Lev was relieved to
rest his feet on the freshly mown hay until the height of the day's heat had
passed.

His journey was to take him to the outskirts of Astrakhanka, where he had
heard that a small Christian sect known as the Molokans had set up a colony.
The Molokans were difficult to find, because they kept to themselves, fearing
the persecution of the tsarist authorities. Almost Protestant in their belief system, they rejected icons, relics, incense, and the rituals of baptism. Their very
name, Molokans, or Milk Drinkers, came from their refusal to fast from milk
and milk products on Wednesdays and Fridays, and during Lent. They were
rumored to have rejected the authority of the tsar and to live in communities
where absolute equality prevailed. Deich hoped to learn more about them by
simply appearing in their village, posing as a peasant seeking work.

Patient inquiries in Astrakhanka finally pointed him in the right direction. Not far from town, along the same forlorn highway, a prosperous-looking, shiny little village appeared on the horizon. Unlike most Ukrainians, the Molokans lived in stone homes with tile roofs, decorated with elaborate, colorful designs on the doors and shutters. Initially, they were suspicious of the shabby vagrant who wandered into their community. Repeatedly, when Deich inquired about lodgings, he was met with firm rejections. Finally, a kind older man took pity on him, offered him a place to stay, and invited him to dinner with his family.

That evening, Lev inquired about the customs of the Molokans, hoping to get more information about their beliefs. He observed that it was Friday, and yet the family was eating meat. Ivan, Deich's host, was eager to explain the Molokan faith. Molokans observed the scripture, Ivan argued, and the scripture clearly stated: "Not that which goes into the mouth defiles a man; but that which comes out of the mouth, this defiles a man." Deich mounted a defense of the traditional Orthodox understanding of the fasts. Their discussion became so heated that the meal was forgotten, and the two men debated Christian theology well into the night. Both went to bed happy: Ivan rejoiced to find a true "man of God," and Lev was content that he had been generously accepted into this strange, closed community.

The next day, as soon as the sun rose, Ivan woke Lev up. "Because of you, my boy, I didn't pitch the hay yesterday, so I'd like you to help me now." Lev reluctantly agreed. He could not refuse, but he feared the worst—never in his life had he held a pitchfork. As the two men stood on the hay cart, Lev realized just how foolish he looked. No matter how hard he tried to imitate Ivan, his effort was in vain. Either he grabbed too much hay on the fork, and then he could barely lift it, or he simply gathered too little. Finally, Ivan stopped work, looked at Lev, and began to laugh heartily. "What kind of a peasant doesn't know how to pitch hay?" he joked. By this time, the rest of the family had come to the barn and were doubled over with mirth at the sight of Lev's comical stabbings with the pitchfork.

The truth was, of course, that Lev Deich was no peasant. He was the son of a wealthy Jewish merchant, a university student, and a man who had spent his entire life in the crowded streets of Kiev. He had not come to Astrakhanka to become a Molokan; he had come to preach among them. His "gospel" was socialism, and he was convinced that the Molokans would eagerly hear his good news: A new world was just around the corner, and its credo was "to each according to his needs, from each according to his abilities."

～

Nothing similar had been seen before, nor since. It was a revelation, rather than propaganda. At first, the book, or the individual, could be traced out, that had impelled such or such a person to join the movement; but after some time this became impossible. It was a powerful cry which arose no one knew where, and summoned the ardent to the great work of the redemption of the country and of humanity. And the ardent, hearing this cry, arose, overflowing with sorrow and indignation for their past life, and abandoning home, wealth, honours, family, threw themselves into the movement with a joy, an enthusiasm, a faith, such as are experienced only once in a life, and when lost are never found again.

— SERGEI KRAVCHINSKII, *Underground Russia*[2]

For Russian radicals, the movement that would later be known by the awkward name "to the people" was remembered as the most innocent, most optimistic, and most beautiful phase in the history of the cause. Even as a "movement," it was hard to characterize, because it had no single leader, no formal organization, and no place of origin. It began more like a collective epiphany—suddenly, hundreds of very young Russians (most in their teens and early twenties) decided that they had had enough of radical theories, student demonstrations, and conspiracies. If socialism promised liberation for the people, then socialism should be preached to the people. If the beauty of the promised future order captivated the sons and daughters of Russia's nobility, it could not fail to entrance the impoverished, suffering masses. They decided to take their ideas directly to the people themselves—to the peasants and ordinary workers in Russia's cities, towns, and countryside.[3]

Like every other phase in the history of Russian radicalism, this populist impulse was sparked by a book. *Historical Letters* inspired the radicals of the seventies in the way that *What Is to Be Done?* transformed the sixties. The author, however, was a Russian professor of mathematics, and nothing like Chernyshevskii. Peter Lavrov had come to radicalism late in life—after he turned forty—and was thus, in the movement, generally considered an old man. Perhaps because of his age or because of his staid profession, he simply lacked rhetorical flair and untamed revolutionary passion. His most famous work was as dull as the title suggested.[4]

Historical Letters sought to be the sobering antidote to Nechaevism, leading the movement into a more ethical and patient activism. In effect, Lavrov's sixteen "letters" promoted a revision of socialist morality. But they were so poorly written, even by the standards of radical literature, that few readers could be bothered to decipher the whole thing. The ever impatient young Russian radicals found the passages that moved them, took them to heart, and ignored the rest.[5]

One oft-repeated declaration pierced their hearts: the call to repentance. Lavrov accused Russia's radicals of self-absorption in their own dreams. They played revolutionary games, complete with catechisms, conspiracies, and visions of the coming apocalypse. Meanwhile, Russia's peasants and workers toiled in the baking hot fields and dark factories. In essence, the children of privilege—radicals or not—lived like parasites on the backs of the poor. "Each of the material comforts I enjoy," Lavrov wrote, "each thought which I have had the leisure to acquire or develop, has been bought by the blood, suffering and toil of millions."[6]

There was only one solution—to give it back. "I shall relieve myself of responsibility for the bloody cost of my own development," Lavrov explained, "if I utilize this same development to diminish evil in the present and in the future." The vast sums of knowledge acquired by Russia's radicals—the ideas of Feuerbach, Fourier, and Chernyshevskii—were worthless unless they were shared with those who had neither the leisure nor ability to read them. Enlightenment was intoxicating, information was liberating—civilization depended on sharing progress with the poor.[7]

At first, such missionary work would not be easy, Lavrov warned. "Vigorous, fanatical men are needed," Lavrov declared, "who will risk everything and are prepared to sacrifice everything. Martyrs are needed, whose legend will far outgrow their worth and their actual service." But Lavrov knew his readers well. Such warnings would not deter but rather entice. Redemption through martyrdom was an intoxicating concept.[8]

Radicals rose to the challenge. They called themselves various names: Dolgushintsy or Chaikovtsy, as followers of different charismatic leaders. But their impulses were derived from the same source—the model of the early Christians, who wandered throughout the Mediterranean preaching their good news. Noble radicals renounced wealth and social status and forewent all the privileges permitted them. They abandoned expensive clothing, comfortable beds, carriages, and horses and went to live among ordinary people in peasant huts and tenement shacks, sharing their meals and working with them, side by side.

And then, in stolen hours, when they felt the time was right, they took out books, pamphlets, or even well-worn Bibles and spoke to their new companions of the truth that men were born equal and free and that a new world was coming, in which equality and freedom would reign, forever.

~

A small wooden house with three rooms and a kitchen. . . . Little furniture, spartan beds. A smell of leather. It is a workshop for cobblers. Three young students are working there with the greatest concentration. At the window is a young girl. She too is absorbed by her work. She is sewing shirts for her comrades who for days have been preparing to go to the people. Haste is essential. Their faces are young, serious, decided and clear. They talk little because there is no time. And what is there to talk about? Everything has been decided. Everything is as clear as day.
—OSIP APTEKMAN, *The "Land and Freedom" Society in the Seventies*[9]

According to some accounts, it began almost as a student prank. One day in 1873, without much preparation, two young radicals, Sergei Kravchinskii and Dmitrii Rogachev, donned peasant clothes, left Moscow on foot, and began wandering through the nearby villages. What they found surprised them. Everywhere, they were greeted with curiosity and interest. Peasants wanted to hear where they were from, where they were going, and what news they could share. In the evenings, in the small, smoky peasant huts, men, women, and children crowded around these new strangers and listened to their stories with fascination. Kravchinskii, who knew the New Testament by heart, would quote passages from the Bible to convince the peasants that it was their Christian duty to rise up against the state. The whole adventure abruptly ended with a brief stay in a local jail, but after plying the guards with beer, Sergei and Dmitrii managed to escape. They fled to Moscow and announced their success. Lavrov was right! The people were hungry for new ideas and the possibility of a new way of life.[10]

The story of this crazy venture spread through Russia's cities and towns. During the "mad summer" of 1874, students across the country abandoned their apartments and dormitories, their books and pamphlets. They traveled everywhere, throughout the vast Russian land, hoping to find revolutionaries in the most unlikely places. They went to factories in cities and small towns, to peasant villages and to migrant peasant communities. They reached out to every kind of Russian outcast: Christian sectarians, vagrants, ex-convicts.[11]

They bought or sewed peasant and worker clothing. For the men, long cotton shirts and linen coats were the norm; for the women, cotton kerchiefs and sarafans—sleeveless cotton dresses worn over embroidered shirts. They tried to hide their white skin and hands with dirt, grime, and sunburns. Praskovia Ivanovskaia, traveling by steamboat to a northern Russian village, remembered how her friend Galina "kept dropping her hands into the water as we moved along, bathing her face and offering her damp skin to the fiery rays of the southern sun in an effort to rid her complexion of its whiteness and delicacy." Those who worked in the factories donned tattered and faded overalls or coarse wool dresses. Peter Kropotkin, an aristocrat of the highest rank, boasted that he would often leave an elegant dinner party, change into a simple peasant sheepskin and boots, and wander into the St. Petersburg slums. Sometimes, the radicals were too eager to disguise themselves and dressed far more poorly than the average peasant. Vladimir Debagorii-Mokrievich was surprised that in his village peasants actually distrusted him because he looked too shabby. He and his companions, posing as painters, splotched paint so liberally on their clothes and faces that they had to suppress laughter whenever they looked at each other. "Everywhere we went we were met with suspicion," he wrote, "apparently for fear that we would steal something."[12]

In some cases, radicals prepared in advance by learning a trade like tanning, painting, or midwifery. In rented apartments, workshops were set up and ordinary workers were hired to teach students to become woodworkers or shoemakers. In other cases, students simply went to the villages and factories and did their best to learn hay mowing, sheep shearing, brick making, and weaving on the job. Some purchased huts in peasant villages or apartments in working-class districts and tried to live like their neighbors. Others stayed wherever they were offered lodgings, sleeping in foyers and on kitchen floors. They did their best to subsist on meager food—meatless soups, hard dumplings, black bread, salted pickles, and weak tea with little sugar.[13]

What they saw on their travels confirmed what they had long believed. More than a decade after the emancipation edict, Russia's poorest were no better off than they had been under serfdom. Their daily life was a relentless tale of poverty, dirt, and suffering. The tiny plots of land given the emancipated serfs could not sustain their existence. Poor soil and ancient farming techniques kept grain yields low; peasants rarely used fertilizer and could not afford mechanical farming tools. Peasants who could not produce enough on their farms were forced to migrate to the towns and cities, working twelve-hour days merely to afford tiny workers' shacks. Some were forced to move back and forth between city and country, earning a few rubles during the winter and then returning to their families during the planting and harvesting seasons.[14]

Ekaterina Breshko-Breshkovskaia vividly remembered the town of Smela, the first stop on her journey "to the people." The town was populated by worker-peasants, who supplemented crushing work in the local sugar factory with income scratched from sandy plots of land. The poorer inhabitants of the town lived in what could only be described as mud huts, which emerged, like burrows, out of the ground. They lived, Breshko-Breshkovskaia remembered, more like animals than people. An old man who lived in one of these dwellings offered Breshko-Breshkovskaia a place to stay, generously giving her his bed while he slept on the floor in the entry. He owned nothing, Breshko-Breshkovskaia recalled sadly, but a wooden bowl, a wooden spoon, and the clothes he wore. He could barely afford to feed himself. He had a tragic personal history. Fifteen years earlier, he had participated in a viciously repressed serf uprising and had been brutally punished: "One soldier stood on one arm, another on the other, and two on my legs. I was beaten, beaten until the earth was soaked with blood."[15]

Poverty and hunger were topped by disease. Vera Figner, later one of Russia's best-known terrorists, began her radical career as a medical assistant in a small town in Samara province. She was simply overwhelmed by the quantity of incurable illnesses she found there, "catarrhs of the stomach and intestines, wheezing chests heard from a distance, syphilis which spared no age, endless sores and wounds." She also wondered whether this could be considered a fully human life.[16]

The conditions of the urban proletariat were no better, and perhaps worse. The Russian working class, though still small in number compared to its European counterparts, suffered the same pitiful fate. Long workdays meant shuffling through the factory gates before dawn and then leaving well after dark. For many months of the year, workers never saw daylight. Praskovia Ivanovskaia began her adventure among the people in a rope factory and was shocked at the sheer filth of the place. Greasy, dust-covered rope was coiled everywhere. Her fellow laborers first twisted the resin-coated strands with bare hands, and then ate their meals and even napped on the sticky coils. The resin was so strong-smelling that it seeped into Ivanovskaia's hair and skin and permeated her tiny apartment. The frantic pace of labor on most factory floors was captured by another radical, Natalia

Iurgenson, who was amazed at the speed with which women in a tulle factory spun large rolls of fabric onto giant bobbins. They even ran when they went to drink their tea—swallowing it in hurried gulps before racing back to their stations. Overheated from their furious pace, they often stripped down to their short underskirts and sleeveless shirts. After a long day of such exertions, they ate their coarse bread and meatless soup, and then collapsed for a few hours on their cots until another day began.[17]

For those who had left everything behind to help the people, these tragic and often simply disgusting conditions were not repulsive. Quite the opposite, they were proof that radicals had finally found real people, whose sufferings, exhaustion, and oppression were tangible and larger than life. They had touched the true essence of socialism. "Imagine that you have known a woman for a long time, met her often, spent time in her company," wrote Vladimir Debagorii-Mokrievich allegorically about his experiences, "and she seemed to you an ordinary person. But one day it happened that something caught your attention; and that same smile, which earlier seemed ordinary, and which you had seen a hundred times on her face, now suddenly seemed beautiful." For Debagorii-Mokrievich, the "peasants" had always been a collective designation, an ideological abstraction. He and his fellow radicals had only vague notions about them—their lives, their desires, their dreams. During their wanderings through the Russian cities and villages, their hearts were finally touched by the physical presence of the ordinary poor. Misery and physical exhaustion gave ordinary Russians a kind of saintly quality— they were martyr-workers, toiling and suffering for the good of all. Debagorii-Mokrievich realized this with the shock of a sudden epiphany. It was like falling in love—"an ecstatic feeling began to overwhelm me, until it had completely conquered me."[18]

The hard labor required of those living among the people became holy work, an expiation for the sins of their formerly pampered lives. For those whose only previous work was done in the mind, the sheer physicality of working in the fields or in the factories seemed a kind of ritual exercise, designed to purify the whole being. And this was years before Leo Tolstoy made his own plea for the necessity of physical labor for the human soul.[19]

Populist radicals hoped that the peasants and workers would reciprocate these feelings. In working side by side with the people, radicals desired to earn the trust and faith necessary to win converts. They yearned to speak with the workers and peasants not as superiors, but as fellow sufferers and well-wishers. In the evenings and on weekends, during lunch breaks and after dinner, they did their best to raise questions of poverty and wealth, in-equality and injustice. They carried with them a few short socialist pamphlets, perhaps a book or two with underscored passages, or just a copy of the New Testament. Sometimes, they read aloud carefully written "folk tales," com-posed by radicals as socialist fables, with clever titles such as "About the Mar-tyr Nicholas, or How Man Should Live According to the Laws of Truth and Nature."[20]

In the factories, they spoke of emerging working-class movements abroad, strikes, and socialist political parties. In the countryside, they waxed eloquent about the topic most dear to the peasants—land, land enough to plow and harvest and feed their families. Every peasant dreamed of having more fields to work, and many believed that the day would come when all of the farmland in Russia would be appropriated by the tsar and redistributed, to each peasant according to his needs. "We demand," one socialist pamphlet told the peasants, "a general redistribution of all peasant, noble, and private land. It must be divided among everyone, according to justice, so that each receives as much as he needs."[21]

But these were no sober, dry lectures on the economics of labor ex-ploitation and land ownership. Despite Lavrov's exhortations, this socialism was far from "scientific." Not one of the eager young radicals of the move-ment believed they could sway peasants or workers with facts or concrete proposals for reform. They hoped not to convince but to convert. The injus-tice of the present order and the righteousness of the future world were described in religious, almost mystical terms.

In part, this was a tactical decision—revolutionaries understood the reli-giosity of ordinary Russians and hoped that religious rhetoric would appeal to them. Most poor Russians had read only one book, the Bible. Radicals who went to the people understood this and, like the pioneer of the movement, Sergei Kravchinskii, prepared by memorizing entire passages from the New Testament. Breshko-Breshkovskaia found this useful when, during a discus-sion in Smela, she was able to quote Christ's injunction to love one's neighbor. That kind of love, Breshko-Breshkovskaia told the peasants, demanded an end to injustice, and thus an uprising against the state. Needed were "people who not only glorified the Son of God by words, but would also follow his example in standing up for the truth in the face of the world."[22] Pamphlets produced by the "to the people" movement were liberally sprinkled with quasi-religious motifs and with quotations from the Bible. "Therefore all people are equal," one pamphlet explained, "thus taught our heavenly teacher, Jesus Christ." One populist was clever enough to manufacture a fake stamp, so that he could mark texts as "Approved by the Holy Synod."[23]

Religiosity, however, was only partly a strategy. It was also an expression of a deeply held faith in socialism. Many populists were entirely swept up in the mysticism of their own preaching. Alexander Dolgushin's peasant hut was decorated with religious symbols, including a cross that was inscribed with the words "in the name of Jesus Christ" and "liberty, equality, fraternity." Osip Aptekman was startled to see hardened atheists weeping as they read passages from the New Testament. Often, after long propaganda sessions in smoky peasant huts, someone would ask the participants to rise up and join in singing "revolutionary hymns." Moments like this, one radical reminisced, "brought to mind scenes of the first centuries of Christianity." Another openly proclaimed that it was "a form of crusade."[24]

Strikingly, this intensely Christianized socialist impulse was the first to draw a large number of Russian Jews into the radical fold. Young Jewish radicals were not repelled by this strongly Christian ethos but were often drawn to it. Like Deich, many Jews who had been raised in urban families, and had spent their young lives in Jewish communities, eagerly cast off their identities and donned the clothes and identities of Christian peasants. To blend more convincingly, they learned the unfamiliar New Testament. Once in local villages, they debated Orthodox theology and attended church. One or two even became baptized Christians to complete their transformation.[25]

They came from a variety of Jewish backgrounds. Some were born and raised in traditional, pious families and lived their early lives as deep believers. Such was the case of Aron Zundulevich, one of the earliest members of the "to the people" movement. His family was middle class, traditional, and intensely observant. As a young child, he believed his calling was to become a rabbi—and it was in the yeshiva that, paradoxically, he first encountered radical ideas.[26] An equal number of Jewish revolutionaries were raised in entirely secular homes and educated in the European manner. Deich was proud of his family's humanist tendencies and was grateful to his father for giving him what was then called a "Christian education." He read European philosophical and literary works at an early age, and when he was thirteen his older sisters introduced him to Chernyshevskii's *What Is to Be Done?* By his first year of high school, he was already a proud atheist. Once, caught eating sausages at lunch, he horrified his Jewish classmates by declaring earnestly that God did not exist and he would eat what he liked.[27]

Whatever their youthful attitudes toward religion, most Jewish radicals arrived at socialism via a Jewish form of the secular Enlightenment, known as Haskalah. Haskalah originated in the German states in the eighteenth century and militated for the Europeanization of Jewish life, emphasizing science, critical thinking, and, in effect, assimilation. By the 1840s, the Haskalah tradition had migrated to Russian Jewish communities, where it fostered the creation of a cohort of liberal, Europeanized intellectuals. These educated Jews played the same role as the wider Russian generation of the forties, criticizing what they considered to be the backwardness, ignorance, and suffocating patriarchy of traditional, Orthodox Jewish life.[28]

Perhaps predictably, these Haskalah "fathers" soon gave birth to a whole 1860s generation of Jewish nihilist "sons." Just as Russian Christian students found radicalism within the high schools, orthodox seminaries, and military academies, so young Jews encountered Chernyshevskii and Dobroliubov in rabbinical schools, yeshivas, and urban high schools. Jewish nihilism became as attractive and powerful as its Christian counterpart. At first, the two distinct groups of nihilists did not merge together, and Jews, for a time, remained aloof to more extreme forms of radicalism. Conspicuously, there were few Jews in Ishutin's Organization or in Nechaev's conspiracies.[29]

The year 1871 changed everything. On Easter Day of that year, the Russian Jewish community received a terrible shock—Russia's first major pogrom swept through the southern city of Odessa. In a pale foreshadowing of what was to come many years later, enraged mobs of ordinary Russians swept through the Jewish shops and homes of the city, vandalizing and destroying everything within them. Anyone who looked remotely Jewish was in mortal danger—all Jews, whether rich or poor, were the targets of random, brutal beatings. There was no loss of life, but it was an indication of the savagery of anti-Semitism.[30]

After the Odessa pogrom, Jewish liberals and radicals alike were forced to revisit the nature of Jewish identity. To the deep sorrow of many assimilationists, even the most earnest attempts to fully blend into Russian society had not averted anti-Semitic attacks. Jewishness could no longer be ignored, partly because others refused to ignore it. So for many Jews, a dilemma emerged. What did it mean to be a Europeanized, secular, antitraditional Jew?

For many of Russia's most radical Jews, returning to traditional cultural or religious Judaism was out of the question. They had spent years living a radical, Europeanized lifestyle and despised what they saw as the narrowmindedness of Jewish customs and traditions. Some, in a perverse attempt at self-defense, even blamed traditional, insular Judaism for the pogroms them-selves. Deich himself was startlingly harsh on his Jewish brethren, writing: "Our fellow tribesmen have given sufficient reasons for the hostile attitudes toward them, the main one being their preference for nonproductive and profitable occupations." Osip Aptekman openly declared in his memoirs that he believed his Jewishness to be a problem to resolve. "I was a Jew," he wrote, "and that circumstance gravely embarrassed me." But if Jewishness was not the way, what was?[31]

For some Russian Jews, the fervent, populist Russian socialism of the 1870s was the perfect escape from the dilemmas of identity. Formerly Chris-tian radicals had rejected tradition and Orthodoxy and had created an alter-nate world in which religious impulses could be satisfied in an all-embracing, nondenominational church of the present world. Jewish radicals were wel-comed into the movement with open arms. For revolutionaries, swept up in utopian dreams, there was, in the words of the New Testament, "neither Jew nor Greek." Pavel Axelrod remembered how he embraced the new socialism as the solution to his problems of identity: "There is only one question: the liberation of the working masses of all nations, including the Jewish," he wrote. "Together with the approaching triumph of socialism, the so-called Jewish question will be resolved as well."[32] Like Vera and other radical women, who saw radicalism as the hammer that would smash the bonds of gender, Jews saw socialism as a movement that sweep them in as equals. Many converted with ease.

The most extraordinary case of this kind of "born again" experience was that of Osip Aptekman. During his wanderings "to the people," Aptekman worked for a time as a doctor in a hospital run by the convent of St. Magda-lene. Awed by the ethereal benevolence of the nuns, he began to attend their services. One nun stood out—a young peasant woman known as Parasha. Soon, the two became friends. Aptekman, ever the earnest propagandist, began to teach Parasha the tenets of socialism. To counter his influence, she began to quote the New Testament. After long, quiet nights listening to pas-sages from the Bible, Aptekman, in a fit of exaltation, converted to Christian-ity. He went to St. Petersburg to be baptized. After entering the Russian Orthodox Church, Aptekman, though still an unwavering atheist, felt "re-newed." "I am going to the people," he told himself, "not as a Jew, but as a Christian. Now I can become one with the people!" He would later be grati-fied to learn that Parasha's influence on him was earnestly reciprocated. The young nun left the convent and became a dedicated socialist.[33]

For Jewish and Christian radicals alike, it was a heady time. The long-awaited socialist kingdom was at hand. In the initial phase of Russian populism, there were few concrete strategies for uprisings, battles, or attacks against the state. Instead there were inchoate dreams of blissful union with the peasantry, which was supposed to give birth to a kind of collective, mass conversion subsuming all of Russia. Dreams of universal transformation never seemed so close to realization.[34]

And reality never tasted so bitter.

～

"One day," he said, "I was walking along the road with a comrade when we were overtaken by a peasant in a sleigh. I began to tell the peasant that he must not pay taxes, that the functionaries plunder the people, and I tried to convince him by quotations from the Bible that they must revolt. The peasant whipped up his horse, but we followed rapidly; he made his horse trot, and we began to run behind him; all the time I continued to talk to him about taxes and revolt. Finally, he made his horse gallop; but the animal was not worth much—an underfed peasant pony—so my comrade and I did not fall behind, but kept up our propaganda until we were quite out of breath."
— SERGEI KRAVCHINSKII, quoted in Peter Kropotkin,
Memoirs of a Revolutionist[35]

The failures of the "to the people" movement came swiftly and continued mercilessly. The first, most painful shock came when the populists realized the true hardships of manual labor. There was a tremendous physical difference between those who had labored all of their lives and those who had never before operated factory machinery or held farm tools. It was romantic to dream of purifying oneself through hard work. It was quite another thing to work day after day, in the wet cold or in the scorching heat or on the greasy, stuffy factory floor. The meager diet, threadbare clothing, and lack of sleep often turned out to be more than many young radicals could bear.

Industrial and urban labor was perhaps the most difficult. Factories were filthy, full of noxious fumes, and an intense concentration was necessary to operate heavy machinery without suffering grievous injury. Deich spent some time in a railway yard, cleaning locomotives. The task proved so exhausting that his companion, a young man named Joseph, would collapse on his bed at the end of the day. Joseph soon became so thin and pale that Deich urged him to return home. Natalia Iurgenson remembered walking home from fourteen-hour days at a laundering facility, so dizzy from drying clothes on rotating spindles that "in my eyes, everything began to spin—the houses, the trees, even the lampposts."[36]

Field work often meant rising before dawn and then working through the afternoon under the blistering heat. After a long day, a farm hand might eat a meal of hard bread and olives or buckwheat groats and then sleep on felt bedding in the open air. Some young radicals, unable to keep up with peasant routine, took to rising late and joining the peasants after their morning break. The hardiest activists lasted a few months or, in rare cases, a year. Others gave up after a few weeks.[37]

It was this obvious lack of laboring experience that made the radicals aliens among the "people." The complete inability to perform the simplest chores mortified the radicals and made the peasants and workers suspicious. Soon, peasants took to deriding them as "weak kneed." And there were always other signs that the peasants-in-disguise were really nothing of the kind. One peasant woman exposed Deich's social origins by pointing to his hands. "They are white and small," she told him, "smaller than a girl's." When Debagorii-Mokrievich told one of his peasant hosts that he was a local, the peasant merely shouted, "Liar!" The local accent was missing from Debagorii-Mokrievich's genteel voice.[38]

But far more devastating than these embarrassments was the realization that those who needed socialism most were the least susceptible to its teachings. The oppressed seemed utterly unmoved by the news of their impending liberation. Certain that their vision of a new world order would open up a new hope for the poor, radicals were shocked to find peasants and workers at best mildly curious and at worst openly hostile.

Religion was perhaps the largest obstacle blocking the advance of socialism, despite the religious rhetoric of the radical propaganda. In essence, the socialist future order, however utopian, required human hands to construct it. Ordinary Russians, for the most part, believed that life's sufferings were to be redeemed by God alone, and were content to wait for divine providence. In the present time, the ways of the Lord remained inscrutable. When Deich confronted his Molokan host with the observation that, even among the Molokans, some were prosperous while others were poor, Ivan answered, "The Lord knows better than we do how much to give to whom." Aptekman was similarly disheartened after a lively meeting with a group of peasants in his village. After he gave a long, eloquent sermon on the injustices of a system where the laborers are poor and the idle are rich, after he had painted, in glorious colors, a picture of "the future order based on socialist principles," he stopped, breathless, inspired by the rapt attention of his audience. A single question shattered his hopes. An old peasant, in all earnestness, sought to compliment him on his efforts. "You are a smart man," he said, admiringly. "Tell us, what will it be like in the next world?"[39]

Among the peasants, the interest in socialism was also undermined by an unyielding faith in the tsar. Peasant mythology dictated that the "father-tsar" was kind, benevolent, and a loving parent to his faithful children. Evil bureaucrats, malicious noblemen, and scheming merchants all conspired to prey on the peasants. But the tsar remained on their side. "If the tsar only knew . . ." was one of the most common sayings in the Russian countryside. Someday, the tsar would prevail over his enemies and would order the repartition of all of Russia's land. Aptekman, drinking tea with a few peasant friends, carefully tried to explain socialism's theories about the peasantry. He used the history of England as his example, explaining how the peasants were persecuted through enclosure laws. The peasants nodded in sympathy. "We are so lucky to have a tsar," one of them solemnly concluded. "Better than living in those foreign countries, where the nobles have all the power."[40]

In the end, radicals and ordinary people simply inhabited different worlds. Radicals, given the leisure to contemplate a world of suffering, were prone to dream of change. The poor had no energy for such fantasies. Exhausted by their battles for daily bread, ordinary Russians were practical, cautious, and pessimistic.[41] They listened to these radical pilgrims, obviously from some foreign place of privilege, with the interest reserved for folk tales on a winter night. They sometimes smiled at the wild ideas of these eager young intellectuals. But socialism largely remained the pleasure of the well-to-do.

Deich distinctly remembered when the failures of populism first hit him. Some months after his arrival in the Molokan village, he decided that he would try to approach the younger Molokans with his socialist ideas, since the older ones were set in their ways. The perfect opportunity appeared when Deich was sent to the local market with Ivan's son, Vania. Deich asked Vania if he would like to hear a "tale," and Vania eagerly assented. Happy to find an avid listener, Deich soon became engrossed in telling "The Four Brothers," a story about four young men who lived in perfect harmony in a deep forest, only to emerge and find a shocking world of inequality and injustice. Suddenly, Deich was rudely interrupted by a blow to his shoulder. He failed to notice that his horse was straying off the path. "Tell your tales," Vania told him, "but watch your horse." It was almost like a peasant proverb.

Deich's pride was too wounded for him to appreciate the clever response of his companion. No matter how earnestly the boy insisted, Deich refused to finish the story. "It was obvious to me," he petulantly recalled, "that Vania's negligible practical concerns were dearer to him than any truths I could tell him." It was a thumbnail sketch of why the "to the people" movement failed.[42]

∿

The winter was bitter, and the tiny window of my room was half covered in snow. The other half was so thick with frost that even at midday it was dark as at dusk, and even if it, by chance, melted for an hour, one could see nothing, except an endless, snow-covered plain with black promontories on the horizon and black outlines of the village, just barely visible above the snow. It was a fitting place for a person finally deprived of a past and a future. . . . They only forgot to bury him.

—VERA ZASULICH, autobiographical fragment[43]

While her comrades were out in the fields and factories, enjoying this new springtime of radicalism, Vera must have felt that fate's invisible hand was continually pulling her away from her dreams. A taste of Nechaevism had led to years in a Russian prison. Then, after her testimony in the trial of the Nechaevites, she spent a brief year in Tver, a city outside of Moscow, in the custody of her mother. There, along with her sister Ekaterina and her brother-in-law Lev Nikiforov, she found herself once again tempted by the siren song of radicalism. The three set up a radical reading group in Tver's Orthodox seminary and began distributing illegal books. These were minor infractions, but committed by former Nechaevites. In no time, the local police brought the hammer down. In June 1872, Lev and Ekaterina were exiled to Soligalich, a pitiful town in the province of Kostroma. By the end of the month, Vera was forced to join them. She was an exile once more.[44]

Vera should have known that her police record would haunt her for years to come. Had she lived a modest, provincial life in Tver, the police would have forgotten her. But Vera's years of imprisonment had done nothing to temper her spite for ordinary life, especially the ordinary life of a Russian noblewoman. The years she suffered at the hands of the tsarist state scarred Vera for good. Ordinary people were now alien to her: They knew nothing of her suffering, of her months spent in cold solitude, with only her raw anxiety for company. In "Masha," Vera sketched the grim mental anguish of a released political prisoner. A minor character in the story, Volodia, was imprisoned for two years for his involvement in Nechaev's conspiratorial activities. While in prison, he became desperately depressed, caught between his hatred of the state that put him there and his anger at Nechaev, who had betrayed him. Once released, he found that his suffering completely alienated him from everyday routine. "Among people," Vera wrote, "Volodia tried to hide his emotions—to be like everyone else, but this became harder and harder, and he began to avoid all company." The character eventually kills himself. His psychological turmoil must have partly reflected Vera's own.[45]

But Vera was not suicidal. One thing remained undiminished within her—the memory of the heady excitement of her first steps in the revolutionary movement. Somehow, she would find her way back to her dreams.

Buried deep in the arctic Russian north, for a time she did little but try to survive exile. To this day, Soligalich remains a tiny city of only seven thousand residents. In the 1870s, it was little more than a desolate northern village, marooned on the banks of the Kostroma River. It boasted a few small churches and a lovely monastery, and that was all. The cold was relentless. In the winter, it was so bitter that the Nikiforovs slept in their fur hats, and winter began in late July. According to Lev, nothing grew there save a few birches and pines—even nature itself seemed to have deserted the godforsaken town. Just before Vera came to join them, Ekaterina sent her sister a letter full of complaints. "So, there they are, the bad aspects of Soligalich," she wrote. "I would like to tell you about the good aspects as well," she added, "but at present this is rather difficult, either because I haven't become acquainted with them, or perhaps because they don't exist."[46]

"Society," as the Nikiforovs called it, did not hold much promise. Ekaterina was perhaps exasperated when she harshly described it as divided between those "who drink without stopping and those who play cards without sleeping." No one liked Soligalich, Ekaterina added, "everyone complains: the old-timers, the merchants, the burghers, the nobles." Restless and rebellious, Vera never adapted to life in Soligalich. She soon earned the reputation of an eccentric town bohemian. Locals remembered her as the girl who wore rumpled dresses, down-at-heel boots, and an oilskin hat. She wore her hair cut short, in the nihilist fashion, which led the locals to give her the nickname "dock-tail." Sometimes, her strange appearance attracted curious young girls, who would follow her around town, gawking at her boots and hair.[47]

Rumors spread about her activities. Vera was said to have headed a conspiratorial revolutionary group, composed mostly of political exiles and operating right under the noses of the local police. One of the conspirators was supposedly arrested in Vera's apartment. A tantalizing story, but most likely untrue. Vera was under extremely tight surveillance. The local police constantly visited her apartment, and all of her letters were carefully scrutinized. According to the secret police, she did little to arouse any suspicions. Regarding her stay in Soligalich, the Third Section had only two remarks: "avoids all contact with society" and "political views undetectable."[48]

Vera's yearnings for radicalism most likely had to be satisfied as they had been during her years in the boarding school and in prison: through books. For most of the year, there was very little to do but read. Her mother sent her packages of books from St. Petersburg, and Vera read each page with relish. Endless, snowy, bleak winter days were spent in the company of books, where Vera could encounter imaginary comrades and their ideas of revolution. Even in the brief, warm summers, she was often seen lying in the meadows on the outskirts of town, reading. In the solitude of her Russian exile, Vera laboriously studied ideas that had successively swept through Russian socialism during its brief history. She immersed herself in Lavrov's writings, read about the situation of the Russian peasantry, and pondered the latest European theories. She was determined to shape her early, inchoate dreams of activism into something theoretically substantial.[49]

Of all of the authors she read, one man towered above the rest. She discovered Mikhail Bakunin.

It was not at all surprising that Bakunin's ideas touched Vera's heart. She and Bakunin had so much in common. Like Vera, Bakunin began his radical career with a fervent ambition to do something extraordinary in the world. Like Vera, he grew to love the profile of an outcast of battling for justice and to hate the fortress-like state institutions that stood in the way. They had both experienced the terrifying loneliness of prison and exile. Most striking, they had both been seduced by Nechaev and then betrayed by him. So when Vera encountered Bakunin's *Statism and Anarchy,* she immediately understood it, not just intellectually but emotionally.[50]

The purpose of *Statism and Anarchy* was to synthesize Bakunin's personal experiences and ideological proclivities into one coherent program. Written in the late summer of 1873, it was composed as a kind of last will and testament. On the surface, it was a multipronged attack on all of Bakunin's enemies: the Germans, Marx, Lavrov, and even Nechaev. Within its core was a single idea: destroy. The Germans were overly attached to their state, he wrote, and so was Marx, who could envision socialism as nothing more than a new dictatorship replacing an old one. Lavrov continually rode his professorial hobby horse of "enlightenment," and Nechaev was an obsessive conspirator. All missed the vital goal of socialism: the complete, earth-shattering razing to the ground of all political, economic, social, religious, and educational institutions. "Abolish all states," Bakunin wrote, "destroy bourgeois civilization, organize freely from below upward . . . organize the unshackled laboring hordes, the whole of liberated humanity, create a new world for all mankind."[51]

No complicated theories, elaborate conspiracies, or "scientific" rhetoric was necessary—only revolutionary cataclysm. The Russian people in particular were hungry for the energy of violence. "Their situation is so desperate," Bakunin optimistically argued, "that they find themselves ready to revolt in every village." After all, Russian history was replete with stories of brigands, famous peasant rebels who unleashed terrifying revolts, burned noble houses, and murdered government officials. The task of the modern revolutionary was to awaken this legacy of brigandage. Flee to the forests, Bakunin argued, with characteristically unquenchable enthusiasm. Hide with the rebels, stoke their anger. This time, the Kingdom of Heaven was sure to come.[52]

From her remote place of exile, Vera hearkened to Bakunin's call. Years of confinement and inactivity pressed intolerably on her heart. Bakunin's descriptions of a peasantry yearning for liberating violence captured the turbulent emotions pent up within her. He was summoning slaves to freedom—the freedom that would only arise from the rubble, when the state, the police, and the prisons collapsed into dust. Freedom was what Vera's anguished soul wanted now: freedom from the shackles of the state, freedom to join the people in suffering and in joy. When an acquaintance in Soligalich commented that Vera's life in prison must have been difficult, Vera dryly responded, "No worse than in Soligalich." She yearned to resume her old revolutionary life.[53]

Statism and Anarchy also sharpened another emotion within Vera: anger. When Bakunin spoke of the desire to smash the state institutions, to take revenge against state authority and its agents, from the tsar to the lowliest clerk, Vera rallied to these words. Love of the Russian people—the honest, good, beautiful Russian people—was little more than an inchoate emotion. The exiled Bakunin knew no more about the peasants than most radicals, Vera included. For Bakunin, and then for Vera, hatred of the state and its creatures was far more concrete, personal, and deeply felt. The state was, Bakunin raged, "a wicked stepmother, a pitiless robber, and a torturer," served by "the exploiters, destroyers, and enemies of the Russian people." It had to be smashed. In Vera's own words, this was the "essence" of her Bakuninist beliefs: "That a man might govern another was unjust; therefore, it was just to destroy."[54]

Bakuninism resolved Vera's discomposed doubts and ended her period of scholarly isolation. She, like millions of ordinary Russians, was a victim of the tsarist state. But she, like them, could be free if she smashed the official shackles that held her fast. By the end of 1873, Vera understood her destiny—she was to become a rebel.[55]

She immediately took practical steps to liberate herself from her exile. In December 1873, Vera took advantage of the complacency created by her year of impeccable conduct and applied to leave Soligalich. She declared her intention to study midwifery in Kharkov. The police saw no reason to object and granted her request, providing she report to the police when she arrived. By January 1874, Vera had left Soligalich for good. When she arrived in Kharkov, she dutifully enrolled in the Midwives' Institute and reported to the police. But Vera had no real intention of becoming a midwife. She moved to Kharkov because she had heard that the Russian South was teeming with energetic Bakuninists, ready to spark uprisings throughout the southern peasant villages.[56]

The failures of the initial phase of the "to the people" movement had been neatly explained in *Statism and Anarchy*. Peasants—starving, worked to the bone, crushed under the weight of the tsarist government—were not looking for solemn teachers intoning revolutionary theories. They needed practical insurrectionists who would inspire them to act. Under Bakunin's influence, by 1875, the enthusiastic preachers of socialism had become "Rebels."[57]

It took Vera a little over a year to find these new radicals. Her first contact was an unlikely one: Maria Kolenkina, one of Vera's fellow students in Kharkov. Maria, known to her friends as Masha, looked nothing like a "rebel"—she was thin and pretty, with wide blue eyes and cascading golden curls. She dressed impeccably in dresses fit for a noblewoman, even though she was born and raised in a decidedly middle-class family. Her most memorable characteristics were a boundless, irrepressible energy and an extroverted, almost brash manner. Unlike Vera, who could sit in one place and read a book for hours, Masha always seemed to be on the move.[58]

Masha had left home at the age of twenty, disgusted with her family life and enraged that her father refused to support her desire for more than an elementary education. By 1873, she was on the road to southern Ukraine in a peasant dress that she had sewn and dyed herself, ready to join the "to the people" movement. While Vera languished in exile, Masha was deeply frustrated by the failure of life among the peasants—she felt that radicalism demanded more.[59]

Vera instantly took to Masha, despite all their differences in appearance and demeanor. Just after they met, Masha enticed Vera with a proposition: They would head to Kiev and establish contact with the Bakuninist Rebels who had just set up a base of operations. For Vera, this was a long-awaited opportunity. Immediately, the two women purchased blank passports and falsified their identities, to avoid police surveillance. Vera was finally free. In 1876, the local police wrote their final report on her: "Escaped from Kharkov, destination unknown."[60]

~

> *I could already see it in my mind. Our detachment would appear in the villages, take the land away from the landlords, and immediately divide it among the peasants. At first, we would appear unexpectedly in one village or another, awakening and inciting the people, but after the uprising would gain strength, our movements would become more planned. In my mind, I already determined the path our detachment would take, and numbered the villages that lay along the route and that would therefore begin redistributing the land. Of course, at first we would evade battles with the army, attacking them only opportunistically, as partisan warfare is generally waged. We would destroy the railways and the telegraph lines, so that we could hinder the state's response and give the uprising time to gain strength. After conquering the cities, we would take whatever weapons were available and burn government buildings: offices, courtrooms, all kinds of archives. I even began to dream of how the uprising would grow and widen and how, in the end, a general conflagration would erupt, and the mutinous crowds would spill in terrible rivers throughout the whole land.*

> —VLADIMIR DEBAGORII-MOKRIEVICH, *Memoirs*[61]

In Kiev, on Tarasova Street, near the city's university, two small apartment buildings faced one another from either side of the street. One was owned by an old couple, the Debagorii-Mokrieviches, who lived there with their son. Vladimir thoroughly enjoyed living with his parents; though he was in his twenties, they doted on him as if he were a child. In addition, they were also fondly remembered by Vladimir's friends for their generous hospitality, accepting all newcomers and providing them with the comforts of home. It is unclear whether the elderly couple knew that their impromptu guests were revolutionaries plotting the downfall of the Russian government. They probably did not ask. Soon, the fame of this comfortable apartment spread throughout the radical movement, and it became the "headquarters" of the organization that was, by now, known as the Southern Rebels.

Across the street from the Debagorii-Mokrievich household was the so-called branch office of the Rebels, a tiny two-bedroom apartment that somehow managed to house more than ten people at a time. In the late fall of 1875, Lev Deich, who had finally abandoned his lone wanderings through the Russian countryside, heard about this new group and their base in Kiev. He decided to investigate. Without advance notice, he simply appeared at the apartment and knocked on the door. The person who admitted him was a quiet, pale, and somewhat sad-faced young woman, who shyly offered him some bread, cheese, and tea. Her name was Vera Zasulich. Lev remembered taking no particular notice of her. He had no inkling that the two of them would become friends and then lovers, in a relationship that would last over four decades.

Immediately, Deich remembered, he felt at home in the "branch office." The Rebels lived communally like characters in *What Is to Be Done?* Everything was shared: food, bedding, clothing. Defying all Russian social mores, men and women slept together in the same room, often on the same bed, simply lying down on whatever mattress was available and grabbing the first blanket that came to hand. Cooking and cleaning were all done in common. Anyone who dropped by was welcomed and was offered whatever food or drink was available.

Deich remembered that, in his first months with Vera, she impressed him as quiet and reclusive but content. Every Rebel had a nickname, and hers was Martha, probably meant as a satiric biblical allusion, since Vera was hardly "encumbered with much serving" and tended to avoid her share of cooking or cleaning. Even in this crowded place, she kept to herself and was often seen immersed in a book. Though a loner, she did not avoid company entirely and was loved by her comrades for her quiet sense of humor, her sincerity, and—above all—her devotion to others. In addition, she radiated a gentle serenity, and Deich was later surprised to learn that this quietly happy young woman had spent years in imprisonment and exile.[62]

Vera had finally found a group that accepted her as a member of the family. Her habitual daydreaming, her utter unconcern for making beds or sweeping floors, and, most of all, her disheveled hair, tattered clothes, and scuffed boots were nonchalantly accepted among the Rebels. They admired her intelligence and envied the immense knowledge of socialism she had gathered from years of intense reading.[63]

The Rebels were a happy, almost frivolous bunch. On many evenings, with a bottle of vodka and some bread and cheese, they sat around discussing the latest in revolutionary thought and then, with increasing merriment, told jokes and sang folk songs and revolutionary battle hymns. It was hard to believe that in this carefree atmosphere, plans were being hatched to knock out the pillars of the Russian state.[64]

Bakunin was their inspiration, but their encouragement came from abroad, from the Balkan provinces of the Ottoman Empire. As if to vindicate Bakunin, peasant revolts occurred immediately after the publication of *Statism and Anarchy* in the remote mountains of Bosnia-Herzegovina. Peasant Slavs, angered at the punishing taxes imposed by their Ottoman overlords, rose up. Soon, pitched guerrilla battles broke out in the forests and mountains of Bosnia. Some Russian revolutionaries, stirred by this sudden turn of events, rushed to Bosnia to join the rebellion. In the words of Anna Korba, who signed up as a nurse on the front lines, "I could not remain at peace from the very beginning of the war of the Slavic nations against the Turks. I wanted to be of even the slightest assistance for the freedom warriors." The Balkan peasants soon proved a disappointment. Expecting to find noble Bakuninist warriors, consumed with the desire to liberate the oppressed, Russian radicals found nationalistic, territorial warlords. "Religious fanaticism and love of looting" was the final verdict on the Bosnian revolt.[65]

But the lesson was not fully learned. Many still hoped that the Bosnian rebellion marked the dawn of a new age. The number of Rebels began to swell, as radicals grew increasingly convinced that Russia's peasantry was also eager for violence. In the end, violence against the state was considered an unquestionable good, no matter what the motives. Rebels would go to the villages and simply light the fuse. After the fires were burning, the rebellion could be turned in whatever direction the Rebels wished.

In the spring of 1876, the Southern Rebels abandoned their apartments on Tarasova Street. Their former occupants fanned out into the countryside. Dressed as peasants, they brought with them no books and no Bibles. They carried only revolvers.[66]

The strategy was simple. When they arrived at a village, they would not bother with socialist propaganda. Instead, they would offer the peasants weapons, men, and the backing of a large revolutionary organization. And they would spread word that the time had finally come to seize and redistribute all of the arable land in the southern Russian territories.[67] Inevitably, the conflagration would begin, as Bakunin had promised.

Many Rebels harbored fantastic dreams of the coming apocalypse—a Ukraine-wide revolt on a massive scale, men on horseback plowing through villages, seizing land, burning buildings, unleashing torrents of blood. The Rebels themselves would die—of this they were certain. But they would die as the martyrs of the vanguard. Mowed down in the field of battle, their eyes would close on the sight of legions of peasant soldiers finally breaking the chains of oppression and misery. No plans were made for the aftermath—they would not live to see it. And there was no need. As Debagorii-Mokrievich wrote: "Future generations would take care of themselves better than we could take care of them."[68] But there was no doubt—the future world would naturally compose itself on the cherished principles of liberty and equality and happiness for all.

Around Easter, Vera readied herself. She donned traditional peasant clothing—a sleeveless dress over a large cotton blouse—and tied her hair back in a kerchief. She switched her workman's boots for the high platform shoes worn by peasant women. Joined by Masha, she journeyed to the village of Tsibulevska to meet her "husband," a handsome and restless radical named Mikhail Frolenko. She rented a small peasant hut under the pretext of setting up a small tearoom. With great care, and no little irony, Vera and Mikhail ornamented their hut with icons, candles, and a large portrait of the tsar and his family. They fitfully tried to blend in with their neighbors, inviting them to tea and making sure to offer the men plenty of vodka.[69]

Unlike their "to the people" predecessors, the Rebels did not try very hard to imitate the peasants. They knew next to nothing about peasant cuisine and made rudimentary mistakes, such as making borscht with bacon during the Lenten fast or adding insufficient leavening to the Easter cakes. It quickly became clear that the tearoom was out of the question, since Vera and a few other women categorically refused to cook, and the others simply did not know how.

Vera was a particularly hopeless "peasant." Peasant dresses hung shapelessly on her thin, angular frame, and she refused to properly pin her hair. As she was already a rather clumsy woman, high peasant shoes made it nearly impossible for her to walk, so she stumbled around calling attention to herself. She refused to do housework, and her hut quickly became cluttered and dirty. And while the others did their best to make proper Easter kulich, she merely sat and watched, amused at their efforts.

In no time, the new "peasants" in Tsibulevka and their odd assortment of friends came under the suspicions of the local police. The peasant hut had to be abandoned, and the group dispersed. Vera and Masha were sent to another village, and Frolenko moved farther south, to Odessa. Just before they all scattered to their different villages, Frolenko caught sight of Vera one last time, this time wearing urban attire. He was stunned. His awkward, ugly "wife" had suddenly appeared attractive.

Vera and Masha grew increasingly discontented with their roles as village wives. When the action began, they wanted to join the men. They began to carry revolvers and practiced shooting daily. After Frolenko and the other Rebels began to speak of sending armed detachments into the villages on horseback, both women insisted that they would come along. They had no intention of standing on the sidelines.

Instead, by the early summer of 1876, they were sent to the village outside of the city of Krylov. For several months, Vera and Masha languished in a tiny peasant hut, accompanied by a teenage revolutionary who, because of his childish looks, was told to pose as Vera's nephew. Eager and naive, he followed Vera everywhere, engaging her in aimless arguments about revolutionary theory. Vera was at her wits' end. No word had come from anyone about a plan of action. She wondered how long she would be banished to the wilderness.[70]

Her frustration was shared by many. Despite the energy and enthusiasm of the Rebels, despite their thirst for violence, no action followed. In the end, Bakunin had misled his acolytes into thinking that it would require almost no effort to launch an uprising. Rebels went to the villages convinced that their presence would spark events. But nothing happened.

Detailed plans were never formulated. The Rebels had little money for weapons, and the peasants had only their pitchforks. Even the most enthusiastic of villagers were confused by the lack of foresight and planning. Who was to attack first, and what would they attack? How would they resist the inevitable contingents of soldiers that would be sent in? What would they do with landlords, hostile peasants, and priests? Peasants might have been oppressed, and many of them were unschooled. But they were no fools, and they knew a desperate venture when they saw one. They certainly had no intention of bearing the repercussions to follow. So the Rebels found little response to their calls for rebellion.[71]

Bakunin, like Lavrov before him, was proven flatly wrong. The oppressed were no more seduced by the siren song of violence than they had been by utopian visions of a better world. There was, no doubt, a long Russian tradition of peasant uprisings. Vladimir Debagorii-Mokrievich remembered how revolutionaries were heartened when they heard peasant songs about famous brigands like Emelian Pugachev and Stenka Razin. It was easy to be deceived, he wrote. The melodies were the clue: The peasant songs were not battle hymns but mournful ballads of battles lost. They were not meant to incite violence but to bring tears to the eyes.[72]

Despite the very real yearnings for land and freedom, peasants remained convinced they would get both when God and the tsar allowed it. Unlike the revolutionaries, they were willing to wait very patiently. Slowly, steadily, frustration began to permeate the Rebel group.

One day, Vera was overjoyed to hear familiar footsteps at her hut. It was Lev Deich. Covered in filth, exhausted by a journey of nearly twenty miles, Deich was equally relieved to see a friendly face. After Deich had cleaned himself up, he was treated to as nice a meal as Vera, no talented cook, was able to offer. They spent the afternoon and evening gossiping about events.[73]

They finally went to bed but conversed far into the night, lying next to each other on straw mattresses on the floor. The conversation turned to Nechaev. Vera never talked about him, and few of her friends knew anything about her experience with the infamous Russian terrorist. Deich was pleased that Vera trusted him enough to confide in him, and he eagerly tried to listen to her story. Unfortunately, what she told him is lost to history. Deich, exhausted, could not keep his eyes open. He barely heard her say, "Are you awake?" when he mumbled that he was tired and fell asleep.

In the morning, Deich told Vera to pack up and return to Elizavetgrad, the new Rebel headquarters. She was overjoyed to be released from her confinement in the village and hoped to find more action in the city. Plans would finally be made for a more concerted Rebel effort.

Plans were indeed made, but Deich left Vera out of them. He did not tell her that he was on his way to join a secret, conspiratorial mission. His questions about Nechaev may not have been innocent. He was about to join a plot that would have made the old terrorist proud.

The idea was entirely the brainchild of Iakov Stefanovich, a Rebel who had spent some time in the Chigirin district in southern Ukraine. There, Stefanovich heard extraordinary tales of a peasant named Foma Priadko, who created a stir in his native village of Sagunovka sometime in 1874. Priadko claimed that he had been to St. Petersburg and had met with the tsar himself. The tsar had taken pity on the plight of the Chigirin peasants and had written a decree ordering that the land in Chigirin be immediately redistributed according to need. Priadko even had a document, stamped with a special seal, to prove it.[74]

Many believed him. Here was the long-awaited moment—the tsar's order for the repartition of the land. Priadko himself quickly became surrounded by legend. He had an uncanny ability to escape the police, and some believed that he could actually walk through walls. One day, a peasant testified, Priadko's enemies surrounded his hut and, peering through the window, saw that he was reading the Bible inside. Thinking they had trapped him, they knocked on the door. But in that instant, the light in the hut went out, and when they entered, Priadko was gone.[75]

Emboldened by Priadko's manifesto from the tsar, the peasants refused to allow local officials to survey their land or levy taxes on it. They would remain firm in obeying their sovereign. It took the arrest of Priadko and the quartering of troops in the villages to convince the peasants to change their minds. By the end of 1875, things in the district had returned to normalcy.

Impressed with Priadko's cleverness, Stefanovich decided to imitate him, hoping to dupe the Chigirin peasants into revolt. He shared this idea with Debagorii-Mokrievich, who was instantly elated. Together, the two of them wrote to Bakunin of their brilliant new tactic and promised the old man that he would finally witness the uprising he had been waiting for. But Bakunin was curiously negative: "A lie is always sewn with white thread and is easily discovered" was his response. Most likely, Bakunin was disheartened by the failure of his original predictions and by the relentless allure of the Nechaevite revolutionary style.[76]

Stefanovich was chastened but not deterred. He merely decided that he would keep the whole thing a secret, except from his closest comrades. Only Deich, Debagorii-Mokrievich, and a few select others were brought into the plans.

The Chigirin plot was developed in Elizavetgrad in the summer of 1876. Stefanovich, Deich, and the others involved were tense. Widespread arrests were decimating the "to the people" movement, and there were stories of secret police informers spying on villages and infiltrating radical meetings. The old open, hospitable, and carefree environment of the Kiev "headquarters" was gone. A growing number of people were becoming "illegals," fleeing police arrest and changing their identities to hide from the authorities. Just in case, Rebels never referred to each other by their real names, using only predetermined nicknames. They hid in their apartments, making no effort to meet or blend in with the neighbors. It became common practice to carry a revolver at all times. All attempts at propagandizing workers or peasants were abandoned. The populism of the "to the people" movement was slowly dissipating. Radicalism was inexorably becoming, once again, a secret, elite phenomenon.[77]

The Chigirin conspirators had the double burden of avoiding arrest and keeping their plot a secret from their comrades. The strain particularly began to wear on Deich. Perhaps for this reason, the arrival in Elizavetgrad of a mysterious young man named Nikolai Gorinovich drove him to near distraction. Gorinovich had found the Rebels by asking about Deich, using his real name. Once Gorinovich found the Rebels, comrades observed that he was anxious, constantly looking over his shoulder, as if afraid of being followed.[78]

Gorinovich claimed that the police were after him, but few believed this story. Rumors spread that he had already been arrested in 1874 and then suspiciously released after only a few days. No one could prove it, but it was widely assumed he was a traitor. Fears about him grew. Was he a police spy? Would he help them locate the Rebel hideout? In every respect, Gorinovich seemed poised to betray all at any moment.[79]

So Lev Deich decided to kill him. It was an almost inexplicable decision—Deich had never killed a man before. Until that moment, he was known as a jovial, easygoing man, whose radicalism was generally benign. Many years later, Deich himself had difficulty explaining what had possessed him—to so coldly and deliberately plan the murder of a comrade. It was as if the spirit of Nechaev had suddenly taken hold of his soul.

Together with a fellow Rebel, Victor Malinka, Deich plotted the execution. Deich gained Gorinovich's trust and agreed to help the ever-nervous young man hide more completely from the police. Gorinovich would accompany Deich and Malinka on a train to Odessa, where they could more easily evade surveillance. Gorinovich agreed. On the way to Odessa, Malinka and Deich somehow lured Gorinovich off the train and into an abandoned freight station. Once there, Deich and Malinka suddenly knocked Gorinovich to the ground, bashed his head in with their bare hands, and then kept beating him until he was covered in blood. When he stopped moving, they poured acid on his face, to render it unrecognizable. Around his neck they hung a sign: THIS IS THE FATE OF ALL SPIES.[80]

The crime recalled the tragic murder of Ivan Ivanov in every respect but one. Gorinovich did not die. It might have been better if he had—the acid had made him permanently blind and melted away his nose and mouth. The ordeal left him with only his life and an unquenchable hatred of all radicals. He agreed to tell the police everything and, when the time came, to testify in court.

Even forty years later, the attack on Gorinovich filled Deich with deep shame. In his memoirs, he lamely justified his actions by claiming that he had been certain that Gorinovich would cause the movement deep harm. But even Deich must have realized by then that he had been wrong. Prior to the attack, Gorinovich had never been a police informer.

But at the time, consumed with the Chigirin plot, Deich had little time for remorse. Soon, it came time to act. In November 1876, Stefanovich appeared before a few peasants in one of the Chigirin villages and unrolled an enormous sheet of parchment paper, stamped carefully with an imperial seal. It was a charter from the tsar, and it told a remarkable tale.

In the year 1861, the charter stated, the Russian tsar had decreed that Russian land be equally divided among peasants and nobles alike. But through a variety of conspiracies and deceptions, the Russian nobles had schemed to prevent the tsar's wishes from being fulfilled. The tsar found himself hemmed in by malevolent advisors and sly courtiers. He found himself powerless to help his beloved peasants. The tsar therefore decreed that it was time for the peasants to take matters into their own hands. They were to band together into secret societies and carefully arm themselves for a general revolt. Even if the tsar himself were to die, the peasants were to continue the fight, until all of the Russian land was equally divided.[81]

In the forged charter, the tsar was very specific about the nature and organization of the secret society he wanted. Oddly enough, Alexander II turned out to be a keen disciple of his arch-enemy, Nechaev. A hierarchy of secret cells was to be established, with a commissar at the head of each cell. Members of the society were to swear an oath of absolute secrecy and loyalty and to obey orders from above without question. Every cell was to recruit new members wherever they could find them, pay dues of five kopecks every month, and stand ready at all times for the signal to begin the uprising.[82]

At first, this duplicity succeeded beyond Stefanovich's wildest dreams. As word of the "imperial decree" spread through the Chigirin district, nearly a thousand peasants joined the society in less than a year. There were reports of massive gatherings of men, in fields and in barns, eagerly waiting their turn to take the oath of loyalty decreed by the charter. Stefanovich and Deich at first rejoiced at their success, and it was all they could do to swear in new members.

Soon, however, this success evaporated. The sheer number of recruits exceeded Deich's and Stefanovich's control. Stefanovich actually sent an order down the chain of command to stop recruiting members and start planning tactics. But Stefanovich was ignored, and the organization spun out of his control. There were rumors that many peasants had been bribed or deceived into taking the oath, without ever learning what the society was about. Many believed that by taking the oath, a peasant was automatically granted participation in the eventual land distribution. Peasants started to take the oath not out of any desire for revolt but merely to get on the tsar's good side, once the eventual repartition was held.

Predictably, all caution was abandoned. Soon enough, two peasants were arrested with a copy of the manifesto on them, and in no time the entire organization unraveled. Peasants freely confessed their participation to the police, hoping for leniency from the authorities. The Chigirin revolt failed before it even began. The arrests in the Chigirin case, combined with Gorinovich's statements to the police, destroyed the Southern Rebels. One by one, the Rebels were arrested. By the summer of 1877, all three of the instigators of Chigirin were in a Kiev prison.[83]

The Chigirin conspiracy was the frantic last attempt to spark a mass popular revolt. After the conspiracy was uncovered, the embers of the "to the people" movement finally died out. Every possibility had been exhausted, and yet the Russian people remained mute in their lives of suffering and toil. All of the passionate energies of "the mad summer," all of the glorious visions of the coming conflagration, slowly faded into confusion and listlessness.

Those who had found all of their longings fulfilled in the bosom of this radical family were now near despair. Something daring and new had to be proposed, something that would break through the wall of incomprehension that separated the people from the radicals. At the end of the 1860s, just as nihilism was fading, Nechaev had appeared as a savior, destined to lead believers into the new kingdom. Who would be their savior now?

If, in 1877, you had posed this question to the radicals, not one would have believed it would be Vera Zasulich.

Just before he left for Chigirin, Deich led Vera to the train station in Elizavetgrad. The movement was disintegrating, he told her, and he wanted her to go somewhere to rest and gather her resources. He convinced her to visit her sister and brother-in-law in Penza, in the Volga region of Russia's southeast, to hide with them for a while. By now, Ekaterina and Lev had mostly abandoned their activism for a peaceful life in the countryside, tending to Lev's family estate and raising their children. Deich probably thought that Vera, with her abstract, bookish demeanor and her innocent view of the world, was not really cut out to be a true revolutionary. A kind of old-fashioned chivalry seems to have overtaken Deich, and masculine impulses prevailed. He did not want Vera or her friend Masha exposed to any danger. "We were convinced," he later wrote about his decision to exclude both women, "they would have served no function that would have justified the enormous risks they would have to face."[84]

Many people who knew Vera made the same mistake. No one, except perhaps Nechaev himself, had seen the steely, cold, determined side of her personality. And so no one predicted that she could single-handedly revitalize the movement and lead it into decades of virulent activism.

In the end, all it took was an occasion to impel Vera to show her mettle. It finally came on July 13, 1877, deep within the heart of Russia's most celebrated prison: the House of Preliminary Detention.

CHAPTER 8

The European Prison

~~~

A leksei Stefanovich Emelianov, best known by his alias, Arkhip Petrovich
Bogoliubov, seemed destined to be forgotten in the historical annals of
Russian radicalism. A large bull of a man, with Cossack blood in his veins, he
was paradoxically gentle, sensitive, and deeply concerned for the suffering of
others. At one time, his father hoped that he would become a Cossack soldier
in the tsar's army, and even outfitted Bogoliubov with an appropriate uniform. But Bogoliubov was, at heart, no soldier. A love for animals led him to
try veterinary studies, but he was expelled for political activism and in 1874
became one of the apostles of the "to the people" movement. After years of
wandering up and down the Don and Volga rivers, his socialist mission
achieved little, and he returned to St. Petersburg to try his luck with the city
workers.[1]

Then, by chance, he ended up on the wrong street at the wrong time.
That one accident was to set off a series of events that would bring Bogoliubov to unsought, worldwide fame.

The date was December 6, 1876, and the occasion was supposed to be Russia's first workers' demonstration. On that winter day, workers were called to
gather at the center of St. Petersburg to flaunt their newfound solidarity and
strength. Behind them, Russian socialists would array themselves, anxious to
prove to the world that Russia finally had developed its own authentic
working-class movement. The site was chosen for maximum effect: downtown, in the square before the imposing, pillared church of Our Lady of
Kazan, immediately in the center of the Nevskii Prospekt. The designated
time was equally significant: at noon, when every class in Russian society was
represented on the Nevskii, high-society ladies and gentlemen, shopkeepers,
market women, cabdrivers. On occasion, even the tsar and his family would
make an appearance. Russian society would confront, for the first time, the
swelling anger of the downtrodden in their midst.[2]

Radicals were convinced that the moment was ripe. In the factories, they sensed a new enthusiasm among the workers, a yearning to make their voices heard. This may well have been wishful thinking, born of desperation over the failures of the movement in the countryside. Organizers of the demonstration, with reckless optimism, predicted as many as two thousand workers would appear in Kazan Square.[3]

But on the morning of December 6, hopes were deflated. Bravely, protesters later insisted that some three hundred workers had shown up, but even this was optimistic. Undaunted, the "intellectuals," as they called themselves, used noise to cover over their meager numbers. They began to shout, cheer, and chant socialist slogans. At one point, a tall, thin young man mounted the church steps and briefly addressed the crowd. He was George Plekhanov, just embarking on his decades-long career in the radical cause. Later, he would make his name as the father of Russian Marxism and the mentor of Lenin. But in 1876, he was just one more radical bellowing, "Long live the social revolution!" After a speech that paid tribute to the patron saints of socialism, including Nikolai Chernyshevskii and Sergei Nechaev, he hoisted a young worker boy on his shoulders, who promptly unfurled a banner over Plekhanov's head. On the banner, a slogan read LAND AND FREEDOM. The protesters cheered.[4]

Until that moment, bystanders on the Nevskii had watched the protest with mere bemusement. But when the young worker boy appeared, a few were seized with apprehension, fearing he might get lost in the crowd. Hands reached out to grab the boy, and he was jostled by the confusion around him. Chaos ensued. The police were called, but their attempts to break up the protest were met with insults and shouts. Fists were raised, punches were thrown, and a general melee broke out. Reinforcements had to be called, and General Fedor Trepov himself appeared at the head of a contingent of mounted policemen. Some thirty-two demonstrators were violently dragged off into police carriages, arrested, and thrown into prison.[5]

The demonstrators had expected the police response, but they had not anticipated what happened next. Suddenly, a crowd of street merchants, store clerks, and cabdrivers ran up to the demonstrators and began swinging their fists. Angry at what they perceived to be the hooliganism of the "ladies and gentlemen in plaid," these solid representatives of the working class gave their ostensible champions a serious drubbing. One street merchant, asked why he attacked the demonstrators, shrugged his shoulders. "And what was I supposed to do? Suddenly, I see that [the demonstrators] are getting thrashed. Was it right to stand around and do nothing?"[6]

The demonstration was an embarrassing failure. In the Russian press, the antics of the radicals were mercilessly derided. A British journalist was no less vicious: "As an attempt at popular agitation, a more ridiculous exhibition could scarcely be imagined." Later, Plekhanov himself sheepishly confessed that the protest had been miserably organized and ill considered.[7]

"Land and Freedom" puzzled everyone. Urban workers asked Plekhanov what on earth that slogan had to do with their movement. Land was a peasant obsession, and serfdom was abolished in 1861. The banner seemed "fifteen years late." Even peasants were dismissive. One told Plekhanov that the tsar was absolutely right to criticize the protesters: "If you wait, you will have both land and freedom. But you needn't wander the streets shouting about it."[8]

The organizers of the event, perhaps hoping to shield the sensitive Bogoliubov from any unpleasantness, told him to stay away from the demonstration. He later claimed to have done just that and remembered going to target practice on the outskirts of the city. But curiosity must have gotten the best of him. Later in the afternoon, he decided to see how his comrades had fared. He was standing on Nevskii when someone wrongly accused him of participating in the demonstration. Arrested and found with a gun in his pocket, he was assumed to be a violent revolutionary. His luck began its downward slide—soon he was sentenced to fifteen years' hard labor in Siberia.[9]

But that was not the end of his story. By chance, he was one of the few convicted prisoners held in the new House of Preliminary Detention while awaiting transportation to Siberia. There he managed to become the victim in the most famous state crime of the decade.

On December 6, 1876, Russia's minister of justice, Count Konstantin Palen, summoned his assistants into his office in the district courthouse and shut the door. A man of phlegmatic, almost listless temperament, he earnestly desired nothing more than an untroubled atmosphere in the halls of the Ministry of Justice. He was at his best when soothing ruffled feathers, defusing conflict, and delaying any painful or momentous decisions. On this day, however, it was sharply clear that something serious needed to be done. He knew that the sight of brazen radicals sloganeering in the streets, however ridiculous, would raise the hackles of "those above him." The police had arrested the offenders, but Palen knew that this was not the end of the story. In his experience, arrests, imprisonment, and exile had no effect on the Russian radical movement, which was like the Hydra—growing multiple heads for each one severed.[10]

Six years before, Palen had openly wept in disappointment over the acquittals of Nechaev's conspirators. Since then, bad news relentlessly arrived on his desk from the offices of Russia's Third Section. The secret police had documented, in meticulous detail, the devious works of the "to the people" movement, the Southern Rebels, and the Chigirin affair. And now, it seemed that radicalism had spread its tentacles right into the center of the empire. Men like the Third Section's Count Shuvalov and St. Petersburg's Governor Trepov relished confrontations with radicalism. The specter of revolution augmented their influence over the tsar. For the less ambitious Palen, radicalism was a perpetual curse, destined to forever postpone the tranquillity he desired for his country and himself.[11]

In 1875, Palen must have finally had enough—his anxiety would be shared by the regime as a whole. To ruffle feathers, he composed a sweeping report, using evidence mostly provided by the Third Section. It was a deliberately inflammatory document: It spoke of radicals rippling out to thirty-seven Russian provinces, disseminating revolutionary propaganda in villages, cities, and sectarian communities. It warned that radicals were fanning the flames of hatred against the state, preaching revolt against the elite classes, government officials, and local police. Palen included quotations from Bakunin's *Statism and Anarchy,* the more vividly to expose how these young fanatics wanted to tear down the institutions of society, brick by brick.[12]

From a certain perspective, the report might have been paradoxically reassuring. The information gathered by the Russian police was nothing short of astonishing in its scope, evidence that the Third Section had at last developed a robust and pervasive intelligence-gathering network. In 1875, the Third Section's approach to surveillance was significantly broadened; all possible places of spreading revolutionary propaganda were now carefully watched, including schools, publishing houses, and meeting places. The new approach bore fruit almost immediately. Revolutionary agitators were listed by name in the provinces where they resided. Their class background and their upbringing were noted, where relevant. Most important, their pamphlets, books, and even speeches were carefully documented. Nothing about the radicals was beneath police notice.

The report also revealed that 770 people had been arrested and detained

on charges of disseminating revolutionary propaganda. Of these, 265 remained imprisoned. The rest were allowed to go free, but "other measures
were taken against them." It would seem that the tsarist state had its foot on
the neck of the revolutionary movement.[13]

By 1876, however, Palen knew that these arrests and detentions had not
decimated his enemies. Indeed, shortly after his report was written in 1875,
an émigré radical newspaper, *The Worker*, secured a copy and published the
contents, complete with commentary. The editors of the newspaper exulted
over the captured report, taunting Palen with the claim that he had yet to see
the worst that the revolutionaries had to offer. Russia's youth "do not fear
your courts, jails and labor camps," the editors informed Palen. "After a long,
desperate battle," *The Worker* triumphantly declared, "they have finally succeeded in constructing a menacing revolutionary force that has made you
shudder with fear."[14]

Soon enough, evidence arrived that the word "menacing" had not been
misapplied. In October 1876, a prosecutor in Odessa sent a desperate request
to Palen asking that he establish an extraordinary commission of inquiry regarding the attempted murder of Gorinovich. The horrific nature of the
crime, and the conspiratorial manner in which it had been committed, marked
a ruthless new phase for the revolutionary movement. Another similar incident in Odessa soon sparked fears that the murders were part of a pattern.[15]

And now, in 1876, the radicals had rioted in the center of the tsar's capital, in broad daylight. In his office, on December 6, Palen's assistants engaged
in a heated debate over counter-revolutionary tactics. Eduard Frisch, a cold,
angry reactionary, had one response to Palen's request for suggestions: He
calmly fixed his eyes on the men in the room, wrapped his hands around his
neck, and squeezed them tight. "Hang them?" exclaimed the liberal Anatolii
Koni, overwhelmed by the brutality of the suggestion. Palen looked at Koni
expectantly, waiting for his advice. Koni counseled patience and leniency.
There was no need to "blow the matter out of proportion."[16]

Indeed, Koni's advice was echoed by *The Times* of London, whose foreign correspondent shrugged off the Nevskii demonstration with bemusement. It would be a mistake to make "much ado about nothing," intoned a
voice of European wisdom. England often suffered through such demonstrations of "malcontents," with no serious consequences. Give these youthful
miscreants an extra dose of "physical training" in the universities, and that
would nicely serve to release pent-up frustrations.[17]

Palen could not afford to be so cavalier; he would look weak in the face of the new revolutionary threat. In the end, he had little choice but to add thirty-two new prisoners to the total number already held in St. Petersburg's jails.

The House of Preliminary Detention loomed over Palen's offices in the Justice Ministry on Liteinyi Prospekt. It served as a constant reminder to the minister of the hundreds of political prisoners who languished behind its walls, some awaiting trial for over two years. Palen knew that forty-three prisoners had died, twelve committed suicide, and thirty-eight had gone mad. Adding thirty-two more prisoners to an already explosive environment would merely add fuel to the fire. But Palen did not know what else to do.[18]

∼

It is not the long, arcade-like corridors, nor the opera-lobby-like series of doors, nor the lengthy balconies stretching along each gallery, nor the paddle-box-like bridges connecting the opposite sides of the arcade, that constitute the peculiar character of Pentonville prison. Its distinctive feature, on the contrary—the one that renders it utterly dissimilar from all other jails—is the extremely bright, and cheerful, and airy quality of the building; so that, with its long, light corridors, it strikes the mind, on first entering it, as a bit of the Crystal Palace, stripped of all its contents. There is none of the gloom, nor dungeon-like character of a jail appertaining to it; nor are there bolts and heavy locks to grate upon the ear at every turn. . . .

Moreover, so admirably is the ventilation of the building contrived and kept up, that there is not the least sense of closeness pervading it, for we feel, immediately we set foot in the place, how fresh and pure is the atmosphere there; and that, at least, in that prison, no wretched captive can sigh to breath the "free air of Heaven."

—HENRY MAYHEW AND JOHN BINNEY,
The Criminal Prisons of London[19]

The St. Petersburg House of Preliminary Detention, unveiled on August 1, 1875, was considered a masterpiece of modern penal technology. It was an enormous six-story structure designed to hold seven hundred prisoners, built on the corner of Shpalernaia and Zakharevskaia streets, near the center of the city. The regime spared no expense in construction—it hired an expert in prison architecture, Karl Maievskii, and spent seven hundred thousand rubles, over a thousand rubles per prisoner. It boasted all of the conveniences of the modern age: a complicated ventilation system providing fresh and heated air, plumbing for running water, and a flushable toilet for each cell. In addition, the prison had a well-stocked library, a school, a church, and a courtyard for daily exercise.[20]

The prison was the brainchild of Vladimir Sollogub, who had begun his career as a modest prison warden in Moscow and had become by 1872 an internationally renowned proponent of prison reform. He had traveled extensively, observing prison conditions throughout Russia, and his verdict was damning. Russian prisons were dirty, overcrowded, and governed by corrupt warders who did little to discipline their prisoners. Disease spread mercilessly through the damp, foul prison cells. Often, those prisoners who had no family were abandoned to hunger and ill health. In one prison, inmates had been wearing the same clothing for more than four years and were packed together on the first floor, even though the second floor was entirely empty. Elsewhere, a chaotic permissiveness prevailed, and warders allowed prisoners to drink, gamble, and engage in bribery and theft.[21]

Sollogub construed these terrible prison conditions in Russia as a tragic symptom of a much deeper problem. European criminals, Sollogub explained, did not have the added disadvantage of ingrained Russian cultural habits. Russian crime stemmed from an "oriental fatalism," which led to passivity, indolence, and a barbaric indifference to pain and death. Traditional methods of rehabilitation would never work under such circumstances. As a result, Sollogub made a curious suggestion: To reform a Russian prisoner, one first had to make him more European.[22]

It was never difficult to convince Alexander II to launch a new reform program. In the years following Sollogub's report, a number of new prisons were built. Each was designed to conform to the most contemporary European penal theory. One particular foreign prison served as a template: Pentonville, in England, known worldwide as Europe's "model prison."

The Pentonville prison's reputation preceded its opening in 1842. In that year, visitors flocked from all over Europe to marvel and to take notes. It was an awesome sight: a monstrous brick, iron, and glass construction with a facade more befitting a castle than a prison. Most dramatic was the cavernous central atrium, lit by vaulted glass ceilings, from which radial wings fanned out. Standing in the center of the atrium, a person could survey rows upon rows of neatly spaced, identical prison cells. Visitors were suitably impressed by the cleanliness of the interior, the symmetry of the cells, and the modern amenities, including intricate plumbing and ventilation systems. Order and discipline reigned: Regulations were posted in each cell, and each day was scheduled by the hour. Warders and prisoners knew their exact rights and responsibilities. The atmosphere was clinical and orderly. One observer noted that Pentonville was the penal version of the Crystal Palace—a monument to the triumph of technology over human adversity.[23]

The comparison was apt. Like the Crystal Palace, Pentonville was a statement of the transformative power of knowledge. Crime, like disease, could be eradicated and criminals cured. A shrewd application of scientific technology was the key. Pentonville declared itself a laboratory for the conversion of criminals into law-abiding, moral citizens.[24]

One of the guiding principles of the new model prison was cleanliness: Hundreds of convicts were to be housed in close quarters without permitting the spread of contagion. Modern washbasins and lavatories encouraged personal hygiene. The ventilation systems were built on the theory that foul air caused disease to circulate, and they worked hard to pump fresh air into each cell. In addition, every wall and floor of the prison was frequently and meticulously scrubbed.[25]

Like disease, crime itself was thought to be contagious. Evil thoughts and deeds could spread from prisoners through unhealthy congress. For this reason, traditional prisons were thought to be breeding grounds of crime, where the seriously ill infected the mildly sick. Isolation of the criminally contaminated was considered a must. Solitude thus became the cornerstone of the model prison.[26]

Supposedly, solitude also had an internal cleansing effect. In silence, away from the company of malevolent influences, a prisoner could examine his guilty conscience. Confronted with the fruits of his wickedness, a criminal would finally realize that crime did not pay. His clean, well-appointed cell would encourage a new calm, reflective order within his mind. Distractions were banished. Solitary confinement was thus the key to breaking even the most "hardened hearts."[27]

Pentonville utilized modern architectural design to enforce strict solitude. Acoustic science helped construct cell walls that no sound could penetrate; water and ventilation pipes were intertwined between cells to further prevent the transmission of sound. Windows let in light but were so small and heavily barred that they provided no view of the outside world. Cell doors were constructed of wood covered in sheet metal and had only two openings: one a spy hole for the prison warder, the other a trapdoor for food. Warders were shod in felt overshoes, so that they could not be heard making their rounds, and they communicated with prisoners through the cell doors in whispers. Some observers in the prison declared that the building was un-cannily silent—almost as if uninhabited.[28]

The model prison was copied in far-flung regions, from Germany to Canada.[29] Soon, it was adapted as the proper model for the reformed Russian prison, a place to tame the undisciplined Asiatic soul.

～

At 7:00 a.m. [the prisoners] wake up, wash, dress, make their beds, and
complete their morning prayers;

At 8:00 a.m. those held in general cells are transferred from their night
quarters into their day rooms, all are checked and given bread and boiling
water for tea;

From 8:30 until 10:00 those in individual cells take walks in the court-
yard, and from 10:00 until 12:00 those in general cells do the same;

From 12:00 until 1:30 p.m. all eat, then rest;

From 2:00 until dusk those in individual cells are allowed walks;

At 4:00 all receive boiling water for tea;

From 4:00 to 7:00 letters, petitions, and declarations are received from
the prisoners;

At 7:00 all eat dinner;

At 8:00 those in general cells are taken to their night chambers;

At 9:00 p.m., lights out.

— Daily Schedule, St. Petersburg House of Preliminary Detention[30]

The House of Preliminary Detention was the first Russian prison built entirely on the Pentonville model. It was a grand project, designed to demon-strate the enlightened character of modern Russia. Its location, right at the center of St. Petersburg, made the prison a showcase for domestic and for-eign visitors, and future Russian prisons were to use the Preliminary prison as a template. When the prison was unveiled in 1875, it was hailed in the press as another example of Russia's Europeanization. *The Voice* praised it as "an enormous and long-awaited step on the path of improving our system of incarceration." The *St. Petersburg Register* agreed—it was an example of "the humanism and civilization" that "in educated countries, transformed the outlook of society and the law on crime and the means for battling it."[31] Fi-nally, the Asiatic, listless, and corrupt Russian soul would be disciplined and enlightened.

The very idea of housing preliminary detainees in a separate prison was meant as a humanitarian gesture. Prison reformers had long argued that pretrial prisoners should be held apart from hardened criminals. This was partly a question of fairness but was also intended to prevent the worst offenders from contaminating potentially innocent souls.

Traces of the Pentonville model were found throughout the House of Preliminary Detention. Of the 380 cells in the prison, 317 were designed for solitary confinement. Individual cells were equal in size, and each contained exactly one window, a fold-up bed, a desk, a chair, a sink, and a flushing toilet. Heating and light were powered by gas, which was centrally controlled. Cell doors had slots, through which prisoners could be observed and through which mail could be passed.[32]

As with Pentonville, cleanliness, order, and discipline were the governing principles. From the moment a detainee entered the prison, he was expected to behave according to strict regulations regarding hygiene and behavior. Prisoners were first thoroughly searched and their possessions confiscated and itemized. Then, they were registered on two lists: one organized alphabetically and the other according to time of arrival. Some prisoners were photographed. After this, the prison doctor assessed the health of each new inmate and filed a report. Then, after a compulsory bath, prisoners were finally taken to their cells, where the rules of the prison were conspicuously posted on the wall. If a prisoner was illiterate, the regulations were read aloud.[33]

Each inmate's daily schedule was tightly constructed, and no hour was left unfilled. No one was permitted to sleep during the day, and singing, playing music, card games, loud conversations, and generally "disturbing the peace" were forbidden. Men were allowed to smoke, but women were not. Clothing and bedsheets were changed once a week, and prisoners bathed at least once every two weeks. Inmates were responsible for keeping their cells clean, and searches were conducted at least once a month to locate and confiscate forbidden items.[34]

As inducements to better their lives, prisoners were offered many opportunities for edifying and educational activities. The prison kept a reasonably sized library, stocked with literature, religious and historical texts, textbooks, and trade manuals. Books were distributed three times a week, and prisoners could even receive prescreened books from outside the prison. The prison school was compulsory for minors, but adults could attend if they were so inclined. Church services were held in the prison chapel; attendance was voluntary. Inmates were freely allowed to correspond with the outside world, although letters were screened and censored;

and they were permitted visitors at stipulated times and could receive small packages.[35]

Isolation in the House of Preliminary Detention was supposed to be strictly observed, especially for pretrial prisoners who might collude with their fellow accused on testimony.[36] Those in individual cells were confined within them for most of the day, and during those times away from their cells, they were prevented from all contact with other prisoners. Even church services were attended by entering narrow booths, into which tiny slits were cut for viewing the altar.[37]

According to modern penal theory, exercise space posed a particular architectural problem. Prison reformers insisted that prisoners must get fresh air and exercise daily, believing that inactivity produced a kind of mental and moral lassitude. But prisoners held in isolation needed to get exercise without coming into contact with anyone else. The solution was found in Pentonville: a specially constructed exercise yard. In the Russian House of Preliminary Detention, the yard was a circular enclosure, separated into several wedge-shaped cells by large concrete walls. At the center loomed a tower, from which a sentry could gaze into the roofless cells. At the narrow end of each cell was a door; and at the wide end, the cell was separated from the rest of the prison courtyard by a tall wire fence. Within each cell, an inmate could pace back and forth at will, unable to see or hear his fellow prisoners.[38]

Within a year of its opening, the House of Preliminary Detention was presented with a golden opportunity to prove its worth as a factory for order and discipline. Its subjects were more than 200 of the 265 people arrested for participating in the "to the people" movement. Soon, the majority of the inmates in solitary confinement were political prisoners.[39]

But initial results were not promising. Overwhelmed by the sheer number of arrests, the government had difficulty keeping track of the flood of cases. Prisoners sat in their cells for more than two years without knowing the accusations lodged against them.[40] They were restless, bored, and lonely. Despite the cleanliness of the prison, illness was stubbornly rampant. The ventilation system often failed, and the air became as miasmic as in any other, medieval Russian prison. Solitary confinement broke the weaker souls, causing terrible psychological torment, even insanity. None of this should have been surprising. Even Britain's model prison, Pentonville, had its dark side. According to official statistics, every year some five to fifteen Pentonville prisoners tipped into insanity.[41]

Very quickly, however, it became clear that excessive severity was not going to be the main problem in the House of Preliminary Detention. Russia's Pentonville, for the most part, did not conquer its inmates. In the Prelim, as it was less than affectionately known, the prisoners overturned the system.

One by one, the prized regulations of the prison crumbled in the face of concerted efforts by prisoners. Isolation went first. Prisoners devised increasingly ingenious means of communication. At first, they were content with the time-honored, international system of the "tapping code," in which each letter of the alphabet corresponded with a particular series of taps against the wall. Old inmates taught the code to newcomers by persistently repeated taps on the walls of their cells. Once learned, the code allowed for lightning-fast communication. Inmates communicated not only with those in adjacent cells but, by stamping their feet or tapping on the ceiling, with those above and below. Pipes were a particularly effective conduit of tapped signals. After a while, a "telegraph" system was improvised, so messages could be relayed along a chain to their intended targets.[42]

Other means of communication followed. The piping for the sinks and toilets was designed in a simple vertical drainage system, so a toilet on each floor was directly connected to the one beneath it. If a prisoner removed the toilet lid, he could communicate with those above and below him. Those connected by a particular drainage pipe formed a "club," which would organize discussion sessions on socialist literature, communicate the latest gossip, and even plan court testimony.[43]

Means were even devised for sharing books, food, messages, or warm clothing and shoes received from relatives outside the prison. Though the windows of each cell were designed to remain closed, prisoners found ways to remove the entire window frame, including the glass and the bars. Not only could prisoners shout down to each other through the open windows, but through a system of ropes and trays, they fashioned what they dubbed "horses," miniature dumbwaiters that could raise or lower objects between windows.[44]

Since the infirmary was the only place in which isolation was not observed, prisoners feigned illness in order to spend time openly conversing with friends. Dmitrii Gertsenshtein, a particularly lenient doctor who worked in the prison during the 1870s, often allowed perfectly healthy prisoners into the infirmary in order to facilitate their meetings.[45]

Nevskii Prospekt, a nineteenth-century view
Courtesy of Library of Congress, Prints and Photographs Division

Life on the Nevskii
Courtesy of Library of Congress, Prints and Photographs Division

The office and residence of Governor Trepov
Courtesy of the State Museum of Russian
Political History, St. Petersburg

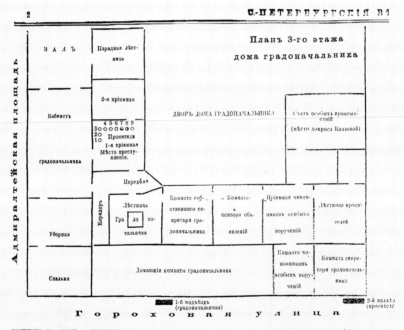

Diagram of the scene of the assassination attempt
Sankt-Peterburgskie vedomosti (January 25, 1878)

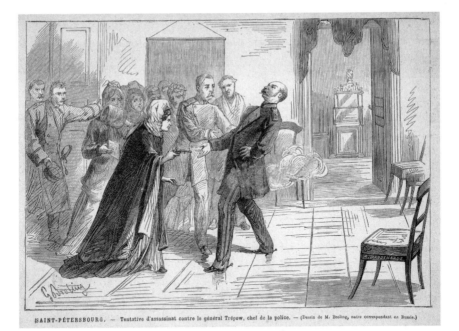

SAINT-PÉTERSBOURG. — Tentative d'assassinat contre le général Trépow, chef de la police. — (Dessin de M. Broling, notre correspondant en Russie.)

The attempt on the life of Fedor Trepov, as represented
to French readers of *Le Monde Illustré* (March 9, 1878)

Vera Zasulich in 1871, age twenty-two
L. G. Deich, ed., *Gruppa "Osvobozhdenie truda,"* no. 2
(Moscow: Gosudarstvennoe izdatelstvo, 1924)

Fedor Trepov, governor of St. Petersburg
Photography Collection, Miriam and Ira D. Wallach
Division of Art, Prints and Photographs, the New York
Public Library, Astor, Lenox and Tilden Foundations

Alexander II, the Reformer Tsar Courtesy of Library
of Congress, Prints and Photographs Division

TOP LEFT: Alexandra Zasulich, sister of Vera Courtesy of Library of Congress, Prints and Photographs Division

TOP RIGHT: Nikolai Chernyshevskii, radical author of *What Is to Be Done?*

BOTTOM LEFT: Sergei Nechaev, Theorist of Terror I. G. Pryzhov, *Ocherki, stati, pisma* (Moscow: Akademia, 1934)

BOTTOM CENTER: Lev Deich, longtime radical and Vera's closest companion Leo Deutsch, *Sixteen Years in Siberia: Some Experiences of a Russian Revolutionist* (London: John Murray, 1903), frontispiece

BOTTOM RIGHT: Sergei Kravchinskii, terrorist and author of *Underground Russia* Courtesy of Library of Congress, Prints and Photographs Division

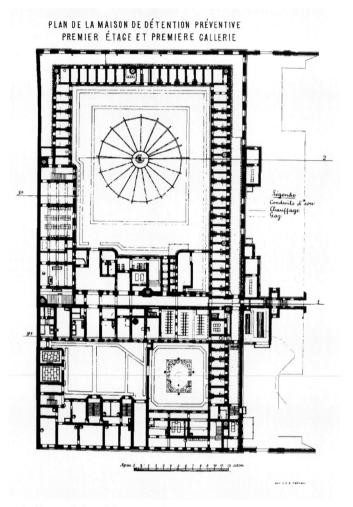

PLAN DE LA MAISON DE DÉTENTION PRÉVENTIVE
PREMIER ÉTAGE ET PREMIERE GALLERIE

Architectural plan of the House of Preliminary Detention, with sketch of circular exercise yards Glavnoe tiuremnoe upravlenie, *Sbornik proektov vyrabotannykh glavnym tiuremnym upravleniem dlia tiuremnykh zdanii v Rossii* (St. Petersburg: Tip. Sankt-Peterburgskoi tiurmy, ca. 1890)

Prosecutors of the St. Petersburg District Court: Konstantin Kessel (back row, seventh from the left) and Vladislav Zhelekhovskii (front row, eighth from the left) A. F. Koni, *Otsy i deti sudebnoi reformy* (Moscow: Izdanie T-va I. D. Sytina, 1914)

Anatolii Koni, chief judge during Vera's trial
A. F. Koni, *Otsy i deti sudebnoi reformy*
(Moscow: Izdanie T-va I. D. Sytina, 1914)

Konstantin Palen, minister of justice during Vera's trial Slavic and Baltic Division, the New York Public Library, Astor, Lenox and Tilden Foundations

St. Petersburg Courthouse, main entrance A. F. Koni, *Otsy i deti sudebnoi reformy* (Moscow: Izdanie T-va I. D. Sytina, 1914)

The riot after the trial of Vera Zasulich *Le Monde Illustré* (May 4, 1878)

As for the prison exercise yard, this too was soon vanquished. The wire fence along the outer edge of the "pens" was easily scaled, so a plot was hatched: At an appointed time, several detainees planned to climb out of the pens and simultaneously escape into the open courtyard. The first such incident was met with force: The malefactors were immediately apprehended and punished. For a time, all outdoor exercise was curtailed. But the plot was repeated, and the prisoners pleaded for the warden to look the other way. The defeated prison administration soon allowed the inmates to amble freely within the outer courtyard.[46]

This halfhearted observance of prison regulations became a pattern. Guards tried to forbid tapping on the pipes, punished those who communicated through the toilets, and tried to reinforce the window bars. They cut the ropes that held the "horses" together and confiscated items sent from one cell to another. But the administration, over time, lost the will to battle the prisoners and their ingenious tricks. By 1877, the Prelim's political prisoners had simply designed a parallel way of life within the prison, one that allowed them to communicate, converse, and exchange goods and services. A truce developed between the administrations and the prisoners: As long as no major disturbances or infractions occurred, minor deviations would be tolerated. In the women's section of the prison, it seemed that the guards all but encouraged violations of the rules. One guard even asked prisoners if they wished to "join a club" and provided swabs with which to clean the toilets before speaking into them.[47]

By the summer of 1877, for many, the House of Preliminary Detention began to feel like a kind of home. On cold days, the whole prison was filled with the racket of tapping on walls, pipes, and floors, as political debates were scheduled through the "clubs." On warm days, prisoners would remove the prison bars and sit in the windows, enjoying fresh air. One prisoner remembered fondly that "in the open windows we could listen to the singing—and we had many talented singers." High spirits led to extraordinary pranks, as on July 4, 1876, when one of the prisoners unfurled an enormous U.S. flag out of a window, in honor of the centennial of the "great transatlantic republic."[48]

~

I grabbed the heavy bars that had stood in the window (I have no idea where I got the strength) and began to pound them against the metal door. I cannot recall why I did this. It was simply necessary to find some outlet for the fury that took hold of me and I wanted to exhaust myself physically at

least. If I hadn't had the window frame in my hands and had not been able
to tear the metal bed or table from the wall, I would have, most probably,
started to beat my head against the floor or walls. This, I learned later, was
exactly what happened in some of the neighboring cells.

— SERGEI GLAGOL, "The Trial of Russia's
First Female Terrorist"[49]

July 13, 1877, was a warm, sunny day. All along the vast rectangular
courtyard, men and women dangled their feet in the summer sun. Some conversed with inmates across the yard; others were simply lost in thought, observing the prisoners walking below. Those who were in the courtyard had
just scaled the pens and were walking in quiet groups, stretching their legs. It
was around eleven in the morning, and a general calm pervaded the prison
atmosphere.[50]

Suddenly, a commotion erupted among the guards. The news quickly
spread through the prison: The governor of St. Petersburg had arrived for a
surprise inspection. All of those still in their cells rushed to the windows.
This was an event not to be missed—such a minor bit of drama rarely interrupted the daily monotony of prison life.[51]

When General Trepov marched into the courtyard, he was shocked at
what he saw. Violations of prison regulations greeted him at every turn. Prisoners leaned out of open windows, conversed with one another, and ambled
in the courtyard. The last prisoner had jumped the pen just as Trepov arrived. Not a single inmate acted contrite, or even startled. Indeed, when Trepov approached a group of prisoners walking together in the courtyard, they
merely greeted him politely and then shamelessly continued their stroll.

Trepov's rage grew by the minute. He stormed over to the guards standing watch in the courtyard and demanded an explanation for the infractions,
but the guards merely offered that the prison warden was away. The officer
on duty tried, unsuccessfully, to come up with some plausible response, but
Trepov would not listen. He returned in a fury back to the group of inmates
ambling in the courtyard. They ignored him, engrossed in their conversation.
This was the final straw.

Trepov chose a victim at random. The hapless Bogoliubov yet again found
himself in the wrong place at the wrong time. As he casually stood at one end
of the courtyard with his friends, Trepov approached him and roared, "How
dare you stand in front of me with your hat on!" Before Bogoliubov could answer, Trepov knocked the cap from his head. "Hat off!" he screeched.

By now, the courtyard had transformed itself into a theater, with the audience filling the rows of prison windows. Everyone was engrossed by the conflict unfolding below. Bogoliubov had probably merely flinched as the cap was knocked off his head, but to many of the prisoners, it looked as if he had been struck. Accustomed as they were to the lenient regime of the prison, the blow came as a shock, and the reaction was instant. From the windows, prisoners rained abuse down on Trepov: "Butcher! Bastard! Get out of here, you wretch!"

Trepov raised his eyes and surveyed the rows of inmates above, momentarily surprised by the defiance and outrage. And then he took his revenge. According to some accounts, he waited until everyone had quieted, then pointed to Bogoliubov and ordered: "Take him away and flog him!" Two guards dragged Bogoliubov out by the arms.

The pronouncement achieved the desired effect. For a moment, a stunned silence descended. The punishment—arbitrary and cruel—was entirely unexpected. Then, as helpless rage grew, a fierce riot exploded. From within their cells, prisoners grabbed whatever they could find and began to smash and destroy. Those who were strong enough ripped the beds and tables from the walls. Eyewitnesses and participants later recalled it as a terrifying group insanity.[52]

In the women's section, inmates broke down into wild screaming and sobbing. Prison staff found themselves completely overwhelmed and made no effort to quell the violence. The prison doctor, appalled by the crazed shouts and screaming, tried to enter the prison corridors to calm the prisoners. He was physically restrained by the staff, who warned him that he would not be recognized by the prisoners: "They might beat your brains out."[53] Twenty-four hours later, after over more than a hundred policemen were called to the scene, the worst of the violence finally stopped.

But the controversy had just begun.

~

Sentences of five hundred, a thousand or even fifteen hundred strokes were normally taken in one go; but if the sentence called for two or three thousand, its execution would be divided into two or even three parts. Those men who, once their backs had healed after the first part of their sentence, left hospital in order to receive its second part, were usually morose, sullen and unsociable on the day of their discharge. They would display a kind of stupefaction, a weird absent-mindedness. Such men would not enter into conversation and normally never uttered a word; what was most interesting of all was that not even the convicts themselves would ever speak or try to speak to such a man about what was in store for him. Not a word was wasted; there was no attempt to console; as a general rule the convicts even tried to pay as little attention as possible to such a man. This was of course better for him.

— FYODOR DOSTOYEVSKY, *The House of the Dead*[54]

Corporal punishment had a long, powerful history in Russia. As in other premodern societies, before the advent of imprisonment as a preferred form of crime control, beatings and whippings were the chief tools of justice throughout the Russian Empire. Physical punishments were most commonly meted out to serfs, who could be beaten or whipped for virtually any reason at all by their owners. But even high-ranking noblemen were only exempted from corporal punishment by Catherine the Great in the late eighteenth century. Those in the military suffered the worst: They could be forced to run a gauntlet where they would be beaten by their fellow soldiers, sometimes enduring a thousand strokes with birch rods or sticks. Ordinary criminals were subject to hundreds of lashes, depending on the severity of their crimes.[55]

After Alexander II abolished serfdom, liberal reformers pressured him to treat all Russians equally, and thus abolish corporal punishment. In 1861, bowing to liberal pressure, as he always did, Alexander formed a committee to investigate the practice and to study the possible effects of abolishing it altogether. He did not flinch when the committee came back with sweeping recommendations. Corporal punishment was uncivilized, the committee opined, leftover from a backward age. In the modern, civilized state, physical abuse was a violation of every humane and Christian principle. It "brutalized and demoralized" its victims. It was an "evil," a "remnant from times of rough ignorance."[56]

In 1863, Alexander did as the committee recommended and abolished almost all forms of corporal punishment in Russia. He reserved the practice for a few isolated categories of people, such as soldiers and sailors, and even in those cases markedly reduced the severity. Convicts en route to their places of exile could only be flogged if they committed additional crimes, and only the birch rod could be used. The number of strokes was strictly limited.[57]

In an instant, corporal punishment became a thing of the past, not just in law but in social attitudes. For most Russians, enlightenment dictated a new approach to crime, one that eschewed mere punishment and sought reform instead. The transformation of prisons and the building of preliminary detention centers marked a new approach to crime and criminals. The reform of 1863 was seen as a fitting counterpart to the abolition of serfdom, a monument to human rights and human dignity.[58]

Bogoliubov's punishment, then, was so shocking because it had become so rare. To subject anyone to violence seemed unacceptable, and Bogoliubov was an educated man. Only a retrograde, hardened, and ultimately bloodthirsty regime would have the audacity to subject an intelligent and sensitive young man to a kind of torture reminiscent of serfdom.

Palen, upon first hearing of the riots in the prison, was unexpectedly and perversely pleased. He must have known that Trepov's order would have serious repercussions. The tsar would soon demand an explanation for the disorders taking place in the prison. There would be investigations to conduct and reports to write. Palen, as a man of considerable laziness, understood that this would all require much annoying busywork. And yet he took a moment to savor this open confrontation with the student radicals.[59]

These "degenerates" had it coming, he once explained to Koni. They had openly declared war on Russia—planning to arm peasant bandits, occupy cities, and destroy government buildings. They had bandied about phrases like "rivers of blood" to describe their nefarious ends. Nonetheless, despite the flagrant illegality of their revolutionary actions, they were imprisoned in relatively comfortable conditions, and their fate would be decided in open trials. To make matters worse, these hooligans who had so openly rooted for the destruction of all of Russia's most cherished institutions now demanded that those institutions treat them with respect. They insisted on their "rights."[60]

Trepov himself appeared in Palen's office on that day. He told Palen of his decision to flog Bogoliubov. With the prison engulfed in a riot, Trepov, whose moods often vacillated, suffered pangs of conscience. Should he carry out the sentence impulsively handed down in a fit of rage? Palen was not merely supportive of Trepov's order to flog Bogoliubov, he was positively enthused. Even Trepov was taken aback by Palen's reaction. Finally, Palen rejoiced, someone would show these miscreants who was in charge.[61] Later, he would have much leisure to repent this decision.

An investigation was undertaken immediately after the riot was crushed. The prosecutor of the St. Petersburg Court of Appeals sent his assistant responsible for the supervision of prisons to investigate the disturbances, as well as complaints lodged by the prisoners about beatings and abuse. Stepan Platonov performed this task diligently, interviewing alleged victims and witnesses individually. For the most part, his report was ambivalent. Some evidence of police brutality was found, but the wildest stories remained mostly uncorroborated. Few prisoners had visible bruises or wounds.[62]

However, the report did contain one scandalous revelation. The Prelim had a dark secret: "refractory cells" hidden deep in its bowels, a form of punishment for prisoners who willfully and repeatedly committed infractions against prison rules. In these cells, prisoners could be kept in total isolation and darkness for up to six days. If they were particularly hard to control, the only additional punishment allowed was to keep them on bread and water.[63] The rules governing the use of the cells were strict: A doctor had to monitor the mental and physical health of every prisoner kept in the cell, and under no circumstances was a prisoner to be kept there for more than the prescribed limit. It was meant to be a humane punishment, keeping physical suffering to a minimum while, at the same time, providing some threat to the most recalcitrant of prisoners. In fact, it turned out to be a form of torture.[64]

The ghastly condition of the cells was first discovered by the prison doctor, Dmitrii Gertsenstein, during the riots. The day after the rioting began, he demanded to be allowed to visit the prisoners held in refractory confinement, to make sure that they were not suffering unduly. The warden of the prison obliged and led the doctor down innumerable steps underground into a dark, narrow corridor. A guard unlocked a cell door and admitted him.[65] The cell was pitch-black; even the lantern they carried was at first insufficient to pierce the darkness. Gertsenstein's first impressions were only of a wall of sauna-like heat and an overpowering, fetid smell that wrenched at his gut.

Then Gertsenstein heard a thin cry from a corner of the cell. "Look, look!"

"Who are you?" the doctor asked.

"Dicheskul," the voice replied, and then repeated, in terror, "Look, look!"

The lantern was brought deeper into the cell. Barely visible, a thin, tattered, disheveled figure rose from the bare asphalt floor. Once more, like a specter, he pointed to the walls around him. "Look, look!" he exclaimed once more. "Here! And here! Maggots, live maggots!"

A morbid horror seized the doctor, as he tried to shake off the sensation that this was a dream. He brought the lantern closer to the floor and found it was covered in clumps of human excrement. On top of these fetid piles, tiny white maggots were crawling and wiggling. The walls were spotted with human filth, and thus, in the flickering light, it seemed as if the entire cell were crawling, alive. To clean his cell, the prisoner, in pitch-blackness, had opened the tiny slot of his cell door and with his bare hands thrown some of the excrement, maggots and all, into the corridors. The doctor quickly realized that his coat was smeared with the fruits of the prisoner's labors.

Shockingly, Dicheskul had been in the cell for several days. Gertsenstein immediately used his power as the prison doctor to have Dicheskul sent to the infirmary. Nevertheless, the impression stayed with him for the rest of his life. It was, he remembered, "a real-life corner of hell, which still awaits its Dante."

Platonov was similarly appalled by what his investigation discovered. The refractory cells, he wrote, were positioned next to the heating pipes in the basement, and thus the temperature within them sometimes rose to a suffocating 100 degrees Fahrenheit. The baking heat, combined with the smell of excrement and human sweat, was unbearable. While Platonov visited the cells, he had to lean on the wall several times, and finally decided to interview the prisoners in the corridor of the basement, to avoid the worst of the stench. His condemnation of conditions was succinct: "This was not punishment, it was torture."[66]

For the regime's critics, the refractory cells were the perfect metaphor for Russia under Alexander II. On the surface, all was modern, humane, enlightened. But just beneath the surface, the old, Asiatic, Russian barbarity raged. Reforms were merely a facade, designed to dazzle the West. Visitors could come and marvel at Russia's version of the model prison, but the real Russia remained hidden below.

The truth was, of course, more complicated. Refractory cells were, in fact, a European invention. Pentonville itself had several in its basement, and visitors were allowed to experience the remorseless blackness of the confinement for themselves. The stifling heat in the Russian Prelim was possibly accidental, a result of poor architectural design. Before the riots, the cells were mostly unused and were never cleaned.[67]

Nonetheless, the imagery of barbarity wrapped in superficial enlightenment proved too compelling to shake. In England, Gertsenstein wrote with assurance, a man like Dicheskul would have been a member of Parliament. In Russia, he was thrust into conditions that no civilized person could endure. This became the perfect frame in which to set the story of Bogoliubov's flogging.[68]

Within a few very short days, Palen was swept into the whirlwind he had created. Along with Platonov's report, letters from officials in other ministries flooded Palen's office, officially demanding an accounting for the events of July 13. Suggestions were made for preventing future riots: Prisoners should no longer be allowed their daily exercise; prisoners sentenced to exile needed to be processed faster; the overcrowding in prisons needed to be addressed. There was widespread recognition that the political prisoners kept in the House of Preliminary Detention were an enormous liability, a perpetual powder keg waiting to be set off.[69] But all of these discussions came far too late. The flogging of Bogoliubov had set off a chain of reactions that were now impossible to contain.

Even after the riots were crushed and the prison returned to a semblance of normalcy, anger simmered among the Prelim inmates. Trepov's flogging of Bogoliubov was seen as a spiteful, deliberate show of power. Plans were made to lure Trepov to the prison on a pretext and then "mangle his face." The blind wrath of the radical prisoners soon spilled outside the prison walls into the wider radical community, and swelled as it spread. "One had to see the fury on everyone's face," wrote one radical, "hear their expressions of indignation and anger, and hear their oaths to stand up for the honor and human dignity, so horribly desecrated in the case of Bogoliubov."[70]

Oddly, the hypocrisy of the radicals on corporal punishment matched that of the regime. Those who had declared war against a state for its innumerable crimes, and so happily dreamed of going to their deaths in the wild flames of the coming revolutionary apocalypse, now complained that their "dignity" had been violated. Those who had wanted to become peasant brigands now demanded to be treated like sensitive noblemen. They were angered by a punishment—twenty-five strokes with birch rods—that most ordinary Russian peasants had endured for generations.

Within the radical community, July 13, 1877, resounded as a call to arms. The regime had removed its gloves—now the radicals would do the same. With one stroke, the new revolutionary path was revealed. The indifference of the peasants, the hostility of the workers, the failed uprisings and ineffective protests mattered no longer. All that mattered was to punish the tyrannical agents of the much despised Russian state.

The year 1877 found Vera Zasulich once again caught in the centrifugal force of fate, forced away from the scene of revolutionary action. While her comrades were fomenting uprisings in Chigirin or rioting in the prisons, Vera was once again in the provinces, with little to do. Lonely, she languished on her brother-in-law's estate. Her sister Ekaterina, who had been a firebrand in her youth, now had children to raise. Ekaterina's husband, Lev, was becoming a Tolstoyan, working the land alongside his peasants. Most likely, they looked upon Vera with pity, for refusing to abandon her naive radical dreams.

Vera must have despaired that the true revolutionary life would forever elude her. She had only experienced a few months of the "rebellion," and then only as a clumsy peasant wife. She had been poised to saddle her horse and ride through the countryside on horseback, revolver in hand. But the rebellion collapsed, and ordinary life resumed once more. Her friends were either in prison or in hiding. She was safe but had no regard for safety. She wanted to act.

In late July, she read an article on the Bogoliubov affair in *The Voice*. It was a short chronicle of the events of July 13, just a bare sketch of the flogging and the riot. But Vera's restless mind fixated on the story until it became an obsession. It was not difficult for her to put herself in the place of her imprisoned comrades. She knew very well the feelings of isolation and desperate boredom. It was not so long ago that she had been in the same position.

She fully understood why her comrades were so enraged by Trepov's order to flog Bogoliubov. At first blush, it was but one act of cruelty in the history of the Russian state. One prisoner was flogged. But the act was seen as a deliberate, provocative declaration of war against radicalism. Trepov had desired to show the radicals that he was untouchable, that he could do what he wished, on a whim. Russian radicals could protest, petition, and demonstrate, but they were ultimately powerless against the agents of the state. The subsequent riot was not a carefully considered statement of defiance but the impulsive cry of souls trapped in the loneliness and darkness of solitary confinement.

Though she was far away from St. Petersburg, in the warm sun of the Penza summer, the tsar's state must have loomed before her like some monstrous dark force, devouring her youth, her friends, and her most cherished aspirations. The state had thrust her into prison with no possibility of appeal and had exiled her for no reason at all. It had hounded her comrades and scattered the radical movement to the far corners of Russia. It had allowed revolutionaries to rot for years in the solitude of prison cells. And then, just to show them how brutal and arbitrary it could be, it chose a comrade at random and flogged him for no reason at all. Vera's despair overcame her. She once more yearned to burst the shackles of isolation and impotence.[71]

Though she did not know it yet, Vera was not alone. Others shared her yearnings. Throughout Russia, a new radicalism slowly rose out of the ashes of the "to the people" movement. The members gave it the name Land and Freedom. In 1876 and 1877, it was a nebulous group, and many revolutionaries had no idea it existed until the slogan "Land and Freedom" appeared on Plekhanov's red banner during the demonstrations in St. Petersburg on December 6, 1876. Different members of the organization believed very different things about its membership, principles, and organization.[72]

Nonetheless, the direction of the new revolutionary wave was clear. In the wake of mass arrests and imprisonment, beatings, and other forms of humiliation, the revolutionaries focused on one target: the Russian state. The state was a monster—a large, armed, violent dark force that conspired against the radicals at every turn. It was to blame for the peasants' blind faith in the tsar; it was to blame for the arrests of the radicals; it was to blame simply because it stood as a seemingly insurmountable obstacle to the perfect future world. The logic of this argument was soon taken to its conclusion: The masses were now of secondary importance—revolutionaries had to attack the state first. Ekaterina Breshko-Breshkovskaia summed up the general mood: "The state of things in Russia indicated clearly that without a life-and-death fight with the government, political problems would not be solved."[73]

It was the perfect strategy for the scattered and confused ranks of the revolutionaries. Their numbers had dwindled; their resources were few. It was time to openly embrace tactics that they had resisted for so long. At first, these tactics went under various names: armed resistance to arrest, defensive measures against tyranny, disorganization, and self-defense. Vague plans were formed against the police, prison wardens, and other government officials. But the turning point came with the flogging of Bogoliubov. After the events of July 13, many revolutionaries decided, spontaneously, that Trepov had to die. In time, they would accept a single name for their new strategy: terrorism.[74]

Vera never joined Land and Freedom. But after she read *The Voice*, her anger converged on a single, dark thought: She wanted Trepov dead. With a renewed urgency, she left Penza and blindly rushed to St. Petersburg. Her despair faded in the face of a newly discovered murderous purpose. Inevitably, it led her directly into the ranks of the terrorists.

CHAPTER 9

Justice

~~~~~

No one could exasperate Count Palen quite like his assistant minister Anatolii Fedorovich Koni. Koni was the thorn in Palen's side. The arch-reactionary minister was forced to listen endlessly to the opinions of one of Russia's most liberal intellectuals. Aside from Koni's long-winded speeches—which seemed to begin without provocation and end only when every philosophical point had been thoroughly exhausted—his main fault, in Palen's eyes, was his adamant adherence to abstract principle no matter what the circumstance. The most casual aside from Palen would result in a complicated, tedious, and thoroughly pompous sermon about the necessity of following procedure, of respecting due process, or of honoring *the law*. Koni could be especially indignant on the subject of political criminals. He had the temerity to argue that the Russian legal system's habit of handing down lenient sentences should be encouraged still further. Apparently, those who wandered throughout Russia preaching violence should be set free with a mere warning to never do so again.[1]

July 13, 1877, was no exception. On that afternoon, Palen was still feeling a lingering pleasure from the events of the day when Koni appeared and at once shattered his mood. Obviously agitated, Koni entered the office and loudly bemoaned the "horrible news." Palen felt that another protracted lecture was imminent. In normal circumstances, Palen would politely listen, stifling the violent urge to yawn. But on this day, he was in no mood to be harangued by a subordinate. Looking Koni straight in the eyes, he deliberately provoked him, announcing that he had personally and happily approved the flogging of Bogoliubov. "Those swindlers should be dealt with like this!" he said, as he smacked his fist into his hand.

Koni, momentarily taken aback, soon recovered. "But are you aware of what is taking place in the prison now?" he asked accusingly.

Palen's rage grew. "And so what? We should send over a fire hose and douse those girls with cold water. And if the riots continue, then we should shoot all that trash!"

After he had spoken these words, Palen immediately regretted them. A man of generally phlegmatic temper, he dreaded open conflict of any kind. And the inevitable, long speech came just as expected. In an angry tone, Koni sermonized: Palen had no idea what he had instigated; the repercussions of the incident would now spread far and wide. Trepov's flogging of Bogoliubov was not just illegal; it was a mistake of tragic proportions, or, as Koni put it in French: *"C'est plus qu'un crime, c'est une faute."*

This was unbearable. Palen's patience reached an end. Recently, Koni had petitioned for a new post—as a district court judge. Palen now resolved to give Koni's petition his heartfelt recommendation.

Anatolii Koni left Palen's office despondent. He was a man of some intelligence and education. He had patiently worked his way through the ranks of the Russian legal system and had been tapped by Palen himself to serve as assistant to the minister of justice. But as he became increasingly successful, Koni found himself increasingly disregarded. He was supposed to advise the minister and offer his opinions, but over the years, he found that Palen had no interest in his advice, and still less in his opinions.[2]

Koni saw himself as a devoted public servant, solemnly obliged to work tirelessly for the liberalization of Russia. In one letter to a friend, he declared, in all seriousness, "My whole life has been spent in the service of the legal and moral interests of the Russian people, and no personal or pecuniary interests ever deflected me from this chosen path."[3]

Outwardly, Koni was a modest, plain-looking man. In his portraits, he often wore simple suits and a neatly trimmed beard and had a contemplative, faraway look in his eyes. His blond hair was thinning in the front, and he was short and slightly stooped. When he walked around town he could have passed for an ordinary student. Young admirers recalled, however, that when he was in court in his judicial uniform, with its gold stitching around the collar and cuffs, his demeanor was transformed. He was soft-spoken but eloquent, and his voice had a compelling effect. Many of his young acolytes saw him as a defender of "pure and fearless truth."[4]

For Koni, the law was not a mere career, it was the path to Russian progress. Koni was a staunch defender of the Russian legal reforms promulgated in 1864. Independent judges, private lawyers, trials by jury—together they promised Russian liberalization and Europeanization. Throughout the 1860s and 1870s, idealistic young men flocked to legal careers, determined to expand the judicial reforms and defend the rule of law. Among this new generation of lawyers, Koni was a hero.[5]

But among the reactionaries of Russian officialdom, Koni was dismissed as a naive liberal. In vain did Koni suggest that political criminals were merely misguided youths who could be gently reproved for the error of their ways. If they were treated fairly by the legal system, he tried to explain, then they would gradually see that their best interests lay in supporting the state. But if they were abused, their rebellion would harden into deep, implacable enmity toward authority. For Koni's superiors, such trust in the malleability of the radicals was absurd. They had to be handled with force, with fire hoses if necessary.[6]

In truth, Koni himself was torn. Much as he despised the reactionaries for their intransigence, he feared the revolutionaries for their extremism. Though he hoped a liberal state would tempt radicals into public service, he feared that they would reject it as a half measure and hold out for the utopia of their dreams. At times, Koni felt trapped between the two extremes of Russian society. "A person of moderate political views," he once wrote to a friend, "cannot find himself a place in Russia." Liberals could do little but "look with inexpressible disgust at both our retrogrades and our radicals," each "equally dishonest in their methods, shortsighted in their goals, and improper and horrible in their means." He ended his letter on an almost paranoid note: "There is no one we can lean on, and sometimes one becomes despondent."[7]

As a moderate, Koni tried to temper fanaticism wherever he found it. He saw the tragic events of July 13 as, in part, his failure. On that very day, Koni had permitted himself a small indiscretion: He uncharacteristically took part of the day off. The night before, he had dined in Peterhof, a suburb of St. Petersburg. He had planned to catch the early ferry back to the city but found himself seduced by the warm weather, and he casually strolled the Lower Gardens of Peterhof Palace, immersed in conversation with a close friend. Koni finally reached his office late in the afternoon, long after the prison riot had begun.[8]

While he was away, Trepov had been to see him twice. Koni suspected that the governor had come to ask his advice on the decision to flog Bogoliubov, perhaps even to seek a reason to retreat from his initial overreaction. If Koni had only arrived a few hours earlier, Bogoliubov might not have been flogged and the riots might have subsided of themselves.

The very next day, Trepov appeared in Koni's office and, as if to confirm Koni's suspicions, had a meek, almost boyishly contrite look on his face. Koni never failed to marvel at the erratic moods of St. Petersburg's most powerful city official. He was ill-tempered and imperious one day, then sweetly ingratiating the next. His capriciousness was legendary.

Without consideration for Trepov's position of power, Koni brazenly upbraided the general for his impetuous decision to flog a prisoner. He gave him the same tongue-lashing he had inflicted on Palen. Trepov made no attempt to defend himself. "What could I do?" he merely pleaded. Knowing Koni to be a man of reason, Trepov had sought his advice diligently but could not find him. There was nothing to do but to approach Palen. Trepov leaped from his seat and theatrically crossed himself. "I swear to you that if Palen had told me half of what you tell me now, I would have changed my mind."

After a short pause, Trepov continued to ingratiate himself: "I transferred Bogoliubov to the Lithuanian Castle. He is healthy and at ease. I don't have anything against him, but an example was necessary. I sent him tea with sugar."

Then, abruptly, Trepov emphatically declared, "My situation is difficult, you know. I have to defend the capital!"

Koni merely shook his head, dejected. A man was flogged, then given tea with sugar. Faced with the obstacles of reaction, radicalism, and sheer irrationality, Russian liberal reform stood little chance.

～

One of Our first desires, expressed publicly in the Manifesto of March 19, 1856, upon Our accession to the throne of Our ancestors, was: "Let truth and mercy reign in the law courts." . . .

After having examined these drafts, We find that they correspond entirely to Our desire to establish in Russia fast, just and merciful courts, equal for all Our subjects; to increase judicial power, to give it the necessary independence and, in general, to strengthen in Our people the respect for law without which public prosperity is impossible, and which must serve as a permanent guide for the actions of all and everybody, from the person of the highest to that of the lowest rank.

— TSAR ALEXANDER II, Imperial decree, November 20, 1864[9]

The transformation of the Russian legal system in 1864 was by far the most liberal of Alexander II's reforms. Implemented in careful imitation of Western judicial theory and practice, the reforms gave Russia its first regular, predictable, and procedural system for adjudicating criminal and civil matters.[10]

The authors of this remarkable and sudden transformation had carefully studied European and U.S. legal systems and were particularly enamored by the respect for "legality" in Western society. Indeed, the Russian word for legality, *zakonnost,* soon became a necessary companion for *glasnost,* Alexander's policy of openness. Without legality, reformers argued, openness was impossible, and without openness, a true respect for the rule of law would never take root. Independence and impartiality were the new watchwords.[11]

In true Western fashion, Russian legal reformers insisted on the independence of Russia's judicial branch from the Russian bureaucracy, especially from the tsar and his police. Judges were appointed for life, removable only if they were convicted of a crime. Defense attorneys were also free from government control, answerable only to a council made up of senior attorneys. The Russian bar became a guild, jealous of its prerogatives. Trials were conducted in public, except in certain limited cases, such as those that involved grave breaches of public morality. Publicity was instituted not only to ensure the fairness of procedure but to increase public faith in the new institutions and to encourage the "feeling of legality and respect for the law."[12]

But by far the most momentous of the new reforms was the institution of the trial by jury. Reformers believed nothing would instill a respect for legal procedure like participation in the formality and deliberation of a jury trial. In such trials, public opinion would be given legal expression, and society be forced to judge the actions of its own members.[13]

The structure and function of the Russian jury were modeled on the European and American systems. Each case was decided by twelve jurors (with two alternates), and these were chosen from an initial list of thirty. The prosecution could peremptorily challenge six jurors, and the defense could eliminate as many as twelve. The jurors had the right to ask questions throughout the trial. After the presentation of the case from both sides, the judge provided the jury with a list of questions designed to aid them in their deliberations. A mere majority was sufficient to render a verdict valid. In one important respect, Russian jurors had more leeway than their counterparts in Britain and America. They could decide a case entirely according to their conscience, even if it meant a departure from the facts presented at trial. As was the case in much of continental Europe, a jury could render a verdict of "not guilty" even in cases when the accused confessed to the crime.[14]

Alexander's legal reformers hoped that, as models of legality and openness, the newly established courts would be a bridge between the tsarist government and Russian society, cultivating a "notion of justice and law, without which there can be no prosperity and order in society." Faced with the objection that Russia was not ready for the new courts, the reformers argued that it was precisely participation in a fair and just judicial process that would educate the people. Even the semiliterate and ill educated would benefit greatly from their encounters with the court system.[15]

The most liberal of Russia's elite viewed the reforms as a harbinger of Russian Europeanization. The new openness and accountability would give the Russian people faith in the power of a liberal, ordered world. And this would, in turn, become the essential precursor to bigger things—a movement toward representational government and constitutionalism. Men like Anatolii Koni did their best to preserve the reforms of 1864, not just in law but in principle.

The key principle in the new reforms was procedural justice. If the strict protocols were adhered to, then the outcome of each individual trial mattered little. Trust would develop when regularity was respected. A just legal system was one in which every person, regardless of class, position, or ideological perspective, received the same treatment.[16]

But it was precisely the inflexibility of these procedures that most provoked the enemies of the new reforms. Russia's hardened reactionaries, like Count Palen, were exasperated by the formalities of the new system. Reams of evidence, rules of testimony, the rights of defendants—all were obstacles to the smooth functioning of the government bureaucracy. Russia needed a firm hand to guide her, and liberals who restrained that hand were courting disaster.[17]

Paradoxically, the reactionaries found unexpected allies against the new courts on the far left of the political spectrum. For Russian revolutionaries, the new judicial reforms were nothing of consequence, mere cosmetic reforms of a corrupt society. The complicated rules of jury selection and judicial independence were merely designed to throw sand in the eyes of the Russian public. Justice could not be found in the courtroom—it had to be established by revolution. For these reasons, the revolutionaries were as pleased as their reactionary enemies to undermine the new judicial system at every turn.[18]

The opposite extremes of the Russian political spectrum did, however, find the new court system promising in one respect: It had the potential to become a stage for political theater. The adversarial system, with its witness testimony, cross-examinations, and summations, held out the possibility for crafting a thrilling plot and satisfying outcome. Courtroom architecture only enhanced the effect: Actors could take the stand and use it as a stage, playing their roles in front of the jury and a fascinated public. The courtroom provided space for a theatrical contest, in which competing ideas could wrestle for the hearts and minds of the audience. If one wished to wage a propaganda war in nineteenth-century Russia, whether from the left or from the right, there was no better place than the courtroom.[19]

Throughout 1877 and 1878, the trials of Russia's radicals became battlefields, on which was waged a war of words. Reactionary prosecutors declaimed against the forces of imminent revolution, and defendants declared their benevolent desires to save Russia from the evils of reaction. The intended audience was the Russian public. The result was justice as theater.

~

One of the main reasons for the grievous indifference felt by well-meaning elements in society toward the widespread propaganda of destructive ideas is the general lack of awareness which prevails not only among most of the general public, but also among government officials (including among the majority of the Committee of Ministers). The Committee believes that, in view of this ignorance, society cannot be blamed for failing to mount serious opposition to these false doctrines. . . .

For the most part, ignorance leads to frivolous reproaches against the government for measures taken to investigate or arrest these malefactors, measures which are often condemned as tyrannical and which arouse sympathy for the arrested and investigated individuals. . . .

They openly say that torrents, rivers, a deluge of blood are necessary for them to achieve their ideals. The Committee is deeply convinced that such ravings of a fanatical imagination cannot arouse sympathy. But in order for public opinion to reject those who teach such doctrines, such teachings must not remain in the dark. . . .

The Committee finds that the only true and direct path toward such beneficial publicity is the court. The legal proceedings will expose the full noxiousness of these doctrines and the degree of danger they pose.

— COMMITTEE OF MINISTERS, report on the
meetings of March 18 and 25, 1875[20]

It was an extraordinary sight. On October 20, 1877, with meticulous precision, the doors of the solitary cells within the House of Preliminary Detention were opened, one after the other. The inmates were marched slowly along the winding corridors of the prison into the long, narrow central hall. There, over a hundred prisoners were separated into two long columns. On the right-hand side was a long line of men standing shoulder to shoulder with a line of gendarmes, their swords unsheathed. On the left-hand side was a shorter line of women, with female gendarmes interspersed among them, also with their swords unsheathed. After the columns were arrayed, a gendarme officer read the prisoners a short, menacing order: All prisoners were to remain in their columns. Anyone attempting to flee would be stopped by any means necessary. Then the group was marched through a series of underground tunnels into the main courtroom of the St. Petersburg District Court. The "Trial of the 193," or the "Monster Trial," as it would later be known, was set to begin.[21]

The Monster Trial was the culmination of a strategy first developed in 1875, at the height of the "to the people" movement. In the highest ranks of Alexander II's regime, Palen's report on the scope of the Russian revolutionary movement caused a sensation. The ministers of interior and justice felt overwhelmed by the sheer numbers of radicals threatening to overcome the Russian countryside. Police measures, arrests, and interrogations had done little to stem the tide of students flooding into the villages and factories.[22]

There was some talk of reviving the policies of Nicholas I, who had summarily exiled to Siberia any and all subjects suspected of participating in antiregime activities. As tempting as this option was, the clock could not be turned back. Russia was now self-consciously reformed, and the Russian public, emboldened by years of *glasnost,* had made its voice heard. The mere arrests and detentions of suspected political criminals had been met with indignant cries of persecution in some quarters. Summary exile would only confirm that despotism had not loosened its grip on Russian society.[23]

In late March 1875, Alexander II's highest ministers met in committee to discuss the tactics of counter-revolution. In a moment of collective lucidity, even the most reactionary ministers recognized that the war against Russian radicalism could only be won with broad public support. The public needed to know that the Russian government was not arresting hundreds of radicals out of some perverse tyrannical impulse but rather to protect society from imminent danger. The intelligence previously reserved for high-ranking officials had to be widely shared with Russian society. The rhetoric, propaganda, and activities of the radicals had to be exposed.[24]

The promise of the new court system beckoned. Try the radicals in open court, some ministers argued, and thus demonstrate to the public that hundreds of Russian young people were fanning out to the villages and the factories and preaching murder, mayhem, and violent, bloody revolution. Everyone would hear, firsthand, the radical ideas about the destruction of the family, the redistribution of property, and the creation of a utopia based on free love and communal labor.[25]

It was not entirely a new strategy: The same tactics had been used in the trial of the Nechaevites. At that time, Palen had been certain that the revelation of a murderous conspiracy would rock the Russian public. That trial, of course, had ended in disaster when half of the defendants were acquitted. Alexander II himself had declared it an "absolute embarrassment."

But in 1875, the moment seemed ripe for another try. No longer were the radicals a tiny group of extremists; rather, they were a movement of thousands. Moreover, the regime had an ace up its sleeve. In the aftermath of the Nechaev trials, the Russian government had created an exception to the reforms of 1864. Political trials were removed from the general legal system. They were henceforth given over to the highest court in the Russian land, the Senate. In so-called special sessions of the Senate, hand-picked judges adjudicated cases in which antiregime activity was suspected. These sessions were restricted to those granted special passes, allowing the regime to control the number of "nihilists" in the audience. In many cases, news on the proceedings of the trials was confined to edited transcripts published in the regime's journal, the *Government Messenger*.[26]

Trials designed to denounce political enemies were thus conducted before special tribunals, with limited publicity, for a political purpose. In a later era, such proceedings would be known as "show trials," trials designed not to provide due process for the accused but to convict them in the eyes of society. The germ of just such an idea was sown in 1875.

Compared with their Soviet successors, however, Russian imperial officials were naive. Trials conducted in the special sessions still adhered, quite strictly, to the procedures that prevailed in other Russian courtrooms. Defendants could hire independent attorneys, cross-examine witnesses, and testify on their own behalf. Relatives of the accused were permitted in the courtroom. Prosecutors had to present credible cases and rebut countervailing evidence. The judges, appointed to their positions for life, had latitude to rule entirely according to conscience.[27]

These would-be show trials were thus laxly controlled. As Soviet leaders would later understand, a truly effective propaganda trial is carefully scripted, with no one allowed to deviate from the prescribed plot line. Otherwise, the defendants, lawyers, and judges are free to change the narrative, and even twist it back against the state. But Palen, in charge of planning and executing the trials against the radicals in 1877, simply did not have the malevolent intensity that his Soviet successors would have. As usual, a kind of helpless indifference overcame him. In the end, he threw the trials into the laps of the prosecutors and let them handle the matter as best they could. There was no script, no choreography, and, as would soon become evident, not even a well-considered plan of action. The result would be a disaster. One historian later observed: "The regime did not understand its opponents."[28]

~

> *The type of the propagandist of the first luster of the last decade was religious rather than revolutionary. His faith was Socialism. His god the people. Notwithstanding all the evidence to the contrary, he firmly believed that, from one day to the other, the revolution was about to break out; as in the Middle Ages people believed at certain periods in the approach of the day of judgment. . . .*
>
> *After the first disenchantment he no longer saw any hope in victory, and longed for the crown of thorns rather than that of laurel. He went forth to martyrdom with the serenity of a Christian of the early ages, and he suffered it with a calmness of mind—nay, with a certain rapture, for he knew he was suffering for his faith. He was full of love, and had no hatred for anyone, not even his executioners.*
>
> —SERGEI KRAVCHINSKII, *Underground Russia*[29]

In February and March 1877, the first experiment in the regime's new strategy was tried. In the so-called Trial of the Fifty, all fifty defendants were tried in one courtroom, mostly to drive home to the judges and the public the scope of the conspiracy against the Russian state. The indictments against the accused were meant to be terrifying: "rejecting religion, the family, and private property" and attempting to destroy "all classes of society by assaulting all of those who live above the level of the simple and poor peasant." The regime prepared for an all-out propaganda assault against revolution.

But Russia's revolutionaries had not been idle during their years in prison. Indeed, they had developed a nimble courtroom strategy of their own. Far better than their opponents, the radical defendants understood that if the courtroom was a stage, stagecraft would determine the outcome. The

Fifty defendants, by collective agreement, decided mostly to suppress their defiant, nihilist attitudes. Instead of wearing their traditional nihilist "plaids," they appeared in court in fashionable, elegant attire. They were clean, well groomed, polite, and respectable. They were all under thirty and often looked even younger. They spoke softly, in measured tones, without anger or violent rhetoric.

The carefully selected judges in the trial, expecting raving fanatics, were mystified. The defendants appeared to be innocent youth swept up in idealism, earnestly desiring nothing more than to help ordinary Russians in their daily lives. They had toiled alongside workers and peasants, had shared their grief and their hunger. And now they were persecuted for the sole crime of doing their Christian duty. They were not violent revolutionaries but martyrs for the Russian people.[30]

This operatic courtroom strategy was first devised, oddly, by the tepid Peter Lavrov. Lavrov dismissed the impending grand trials of "propagandists" as nothing more than kangaroo courts wrapped in a coat of liberalism. Comrades on trial should harbor no illusions—they would be convicted and exiled. Justice would be denied. Only one task remained for the accused: to use their last free breath to confess the socialist faith and thus dramatize their martyrdom. Above all, Lavrov movingly wrote, radicals should not fear. "You can act forcefully, even if passively, through the means of your suffering, and for this you will become one of the martyrs of Russian socialism." He added, "Your martyrdom is, perhaps, your final weapon."[31]

It was a beautiful image. But the radicals had no need for Lavrov to paint it for them. They had gone among the people first as preachers of the gospel, then as prophets of the apocalypse. Just as in ancient Rome, these new "Christians" would now test their faith in the fire of persecution.

In consultation with their fellow inmates, the defendants in the Trial of the Fifty spent long hours writing and rewriting their court statements. The key to effective propaganda lay in tempering some of the more angry revolutionary rhetoric. Instead, the witness stand would be used to denounce Russia's present order, to expose the flagrant abuses of the Russian state, and to show that activism was merely a means of helping the downtrodden.[32]

The resulting testimonies were, in many cases, masterpieces of eloquence. Sofia Bardina cleverly characterized the charges against her as the fabrications of a state desperate to hide its own crimes. She did not oppose private property—quite the opposite. She insisted that every person must be "the full owner of his labor and its product." She was not an enemy of the traditional family; its greatest enemy was the current socio-economic system, which positively encouraged women "to abandon their families and seek pittance wages in the factories" or allowed them to "throw themselves into prostitution." Finally, she sweetly assured the judges, she had never preached against religion but always remained true to "those basic principles, in their purest form, as preached by the very founder of Christianity."

In triumphant conclusion, she declared that she was not out to destroy the state: The state was destroying itself. "If a particular state keeps its people in political, economic, and mental slavery," she told her judges, "and subjects them to poverty, illness and crime—then certainly, I say, such a government brings about its own downfall."[33]

Bardina's speech was later considered a classic, but the testimony of the laborer Peter Alekseev stole the show. He carefully chose his outfit for the trial: a white shirt and a colorful peasant belt that not only signaled his belonging to the "people" but also beautifully accentuated his tall, lean figure. As he stood to speak, he looked every bit a man of solid Russian common sense. With the help of his comrades in prison, he had spent many hours crafting and practicing his delivery. The result was electric.

With eyes flashing and head high, he told the judges that his whole life had been one of suffering and toil. "We, the millions of workers," he began, "as soon as we are able to stand on our feet, are thrown by our mothers and fathers to the tyranny of fate, never receiving any education, because of the lack of schools and time, because of the back-breaking toil and its poor remuneration." He had worked seventeen-hour days to earn a crust of bread; he knew the condition of the working class. Enslaved by the capitalists, beaten by the police, the workers were abandoned at every turn. Saviors had come in the form of the brave Russian youths who extended a hand to the downtrodden workers, helping them to their feet.[34]

As Alekseev's voice rose in defense of the radicals, the presiding judge became increasingly angered by the bombastic rhetoric, fueled by indignation. Repeatedly, the judge tried to interrupt Alekseev's testimony and rebut his assertions. Alekseev continued unperturbed. Heedless of the impression he was creating, the judge finally lost his temper and barked for Alekseev to sit down. The effect was precisely what Alekseev desired. Just as Alekseev spoke the words "And they alone will accompany us until the muscular arm of millions of workers is raised . . . ," the justice shouted: "Quiet! Quiet!"

Undeterred, Alekseev triumphantly shouted over the din, ". . . and the yoke of despotism, defended with soldier's batons, collapses into dust!" With a flourish, he raised his fist into the air.[35]

The theatrics were brilliant. Radicalism had triumphed over the anger of reaction. Later, during a break in the trial, Alekseev's comrades asked him to repeat the performance in one of the corridors of the courthouse. They were just as delighted by the effect the second time around.[36]

Behind the judges' bench, in rows of red armchairs, high-ranking Russian officials observed the proceedings. They were eager to take a closer look at the radicals on trial, especially the attractive young women among them. Many found themselves spellbound. One of the tsar's adjutants went so far as to offer ten thousand rubles to assist in the "rescue" of any of the female defendants in the trial. Another officer promised Lidia Figner, a particularly beautiful defendant, anything she desired. Vera Figner, Lidia's sister, received nine hundred rubles through her lawyer from an anonymous donor.[37]

The judges were similarly captivated. With the exception of the presiding judge, they ultimately found little harm in the naive young idealists, who seemed so charmingly ready to suffer for the sake of their beliefs. It was particularly difficult to convict the women, who seemed merely misguided. Certainly, few deserved harsh punishment. In the end, however, only nine men and six women were convicted of harmful propaganda activities, and even these later successfully appealed their sentences. The sentences of all six of the women were eventually reduced to time served. Sergei Kravchinskii later claimed that some spectators at the Trial of the Fifty declared, "The age of the apostles has returned."[38]

For the Ministry of Justice, it was an appalling precedent for the upcoming Monster Trial of the 193 defendants in October of 1877. And as the trial date loomed closer, further events made the plan look like a disaster. By September 1877, Russia had a completely different, and more important, problem to attend to. It was losing a war.

～

And never has an alliance with Russia been more valued in Europe than now; never before could she have more joyfully congratulated herself that she is not the Old Europe but the New; that she, in herself, is a separate and powerful world whose moment has just now arrived.

— FYODOR DOSTOYEVSKY, *Diary of a Writer*[39]

In the summer of 1875, with ominous understatement, the Russian foreign ministry dismissed the revolt in the Ottoman province of Bosnia-Herzegovina as "one of the usual boundary incidents." Unfortunately, this particular incident escalated, despite the efforts of Russian and Austro-Hungarian diplomacy, and in June 1876, Serbia and Montenegro declared war on the Ottoman Empire. Throughout 1876, the tsar and his ministers endlessly negotiated with Istanbul and Europe, trying to secure greater protections for the Christian Slavs in the Ottoman state. But diplomacy continually failed, and negotiated cease-fires refused to hold. The regime was dragged toward war.[40]

Alexander II and his court were initially extremely reluctant to intervene in the Balkans. Russia could hardly afford to wage a war. The reforms of the 1860s had created a national debt of enormous proportions. The tight financial times had resulted in budget cuts for the army and consequent fears of insufficient military preparedness. Russia's finance minister was unequivocal: "The war would ruin Russia in the long run even if she should win."[41]

However, it was soon impressed upon Alexander that the decision was not his alone. Throughout 1876 and 1877, *glasnost* came back to haunt him. In the case of the abolition of serfdom, Alexander had managed the press and public opinion to his advantage. Now, the press and public opinion sought to influence him. And this time, the pressure came from an entirely unexpected quarter: Russia's most conservative, patriotic intellectuals.

The uprisings in the Balkans had generated a tide of sympathy in Russia. When Bulgaria followed Bosnia and mutinied against the Ottomans later in 1876, Ottoman troops tried to crush the uprising with ferocious brutality. Reports of hideous violence, both true and exaggerated, spread furiously throughout Europe: men mutilated; thousands of women raped; infants crushed under boulders, impaled on bayonets, and ripped from their mothers' wombs. Scandalized reporters spared no details of the atrocities of the Ottoman "Bashi-Bouzouks." Russia's conservative nationalists pointed out that the victims of Turkish atrocities were Orthodox Christian Slavs, just like their Russian brethren. Thus was the suffering of the Balkans cast as a civilizational struggle. Russia needed to act.[42]

During the nineteenth century, Russian nationalism was still in its cradle. Only a minority held fast to a vision of Russia as deeply Christian in religion, Slavic in character, and, most important, militantly non-European. But these men compensated for their numbers by their vocal, eloquent exposition of their beliefs. As a result, many enjoyed the patronage of members of the royal court. After the Balkan uprisings began, the nationalists took their cause to the public, writing furious pamphlets in support of Russian militarism abroad.[43]

Strikingly, in the nationalist press, the war against the Ottoman Empire was predominantly framed not as a war against Turks, nor as a war against Muslims, but rather as a war against Europe. Nationalists feared Europe as Russia's most cunning enemy. A century of great-power politics had supposedly twisted Europe into a Machiavellian clique obsessed with mere stability—especially the stability of its imperial conquests. Russia, for Europe, threatened this precarious balance of power. Nowhere was this more evident than in the case of the decaying Ottoman state. Russian nationalists believed that Europe knew full well that the "sick man" was drawing his last breath. But Europeans cynically propped up the dying state to check growing Russian might. European statesmen would ignore brutality on their doorstep merely to preserve their present order.[44]

In Russia, nationalist anti-Europeanism was not merely an attitude toward foreign policy; it was also a statement against prevailing domestic opinion. Within the Russian intelligentsia, a Europeanized liberalism prevailed. Russia's intellectuals—men such as Alexander Herzen, Ivan Turgenev, and Anatolii Koni—were enamored of all that was European and embarrassed of anything with a taint of Russianness. In the eyes of the nationalists, they were responsible for their progeny—a whole generation of nihilists, radicals, and anti-Russian revolutionaries. For men like Fyodor Dostoyevsky, the domestic confusion and unrest of the 1860s and 1870s betrayed a mortal illness in the Russian soul, one that could only be cured by rediscovering Russian national values.[45]

Nationalists thus greeted the Balkan revolts of 1875–76 as a godsend. A war against the Ottoman Empire in the name of the Balkan Slavs would contrast Russian idealism against European cynicism, it would school Europe in the power of the new Russia, and it would, in turn, unify the Russians in a common cause. Europeanism, at home and abroad, would fall before the advance of "Russianness." Nihilism, ersatz liberalism, and revolution would finally collapse. Dostoyevsky, in his widely read journal, *Diary of a Writer,* warned that inaction would cause Russians once again to repeat "mechanical phrases about European greatness."[46]

The mainstream Russian press was, for a time, infatuated with this narrative. The most reactionary of the journals, the *Moscow Gazette,* incessantly beat the drum for war, denouncing Russia's European rivals and promising that war would mean victory over that "deep inner evil," revolution.[47] The

New Times went still further. When the megalomaniacal and rebellious General Mikhail Cherniaev resigned his army post and fled to the Balkans to lead the Serbs, Alexander II was beside himself with fury. But the *New Times* praised the general for his bravery and chronicled his numerous military exploits. The paper also called for Russian volunteers to join Cherniaev on the side of their Slavic brethren.[48]

Liberal papers like *The Voice* sought to undermine Russian war fever. To avoid conflict with Europe, they counseled moderation. They countered pro-Cherniaev propaganda by publishing reports from disillusioned volunteers on Cherniaev's corruption, egotism, and general incompetence.[49] But *The Voice* was drowned out by public enthusiasm. Some five thousand volunteers flocked to the Balkan front: men to fight and women to serve as nurses. Those who stayed home collected funds and sent supplies to the troops. The Moscow Slavic Benevolent Committee alone was able to gather three million rubles for the war effort.[50]

Alexander knew that a war against the Ottomans would be costly and bloody. His ministers counseled patience and diplomacy. The entire regime, paradoxically, was infuriated at the supposedly patriotic Russian nationalists, who were embarrassing the tsar's efforts to enter the European concert of powers. Alexander's rage flared out erratically. Encountering one decorated officer, returning from a campaign in the Balkans, the tsar denounced him: "You are a deserter! You left my army without my permission!" The officer was thrown into prison. Russia's ministers of defense and internal affairs both nervously recorded in their diaries the tsar's anguish and indecision when faced with public pressure.[51]

Finally, in April 1877, Alexander II acceded to the public clamor and declared war on the Ottoman Empire. The streets of St. Petersburg and Moscow filled with jubilant crowds, all praising their glorious Russian tsar. Even those elites with little patience for foreign adventures joined the chorus supporting aggression against Turkey. The liberal newspaper *Messenger of Europe,* strictly pacifist until the declaration of war, "embraced" the cause because "there was never a deeper and more universal conviction that Russia should wage war."[52]

For a time, the nationalists were vindicated—Russia was united, patriotic, and rejoicing. Fyodor Dostoyevsky crowed that Europe would now encounter Russian mettle: "People will believe in us and discover us for the first time, as Europe once discovered America." Russian military successes were astonishingly swift: In no time, victorious Russian armies crossed the Danube River and were on their way to southern Bulgaria and apparently ready to take Istanbul. To the delight of the Russian public, Alexander II arrived at the front in his full military regalia, accompanied by trainloads of resplendently decorated horses and elegant carriages.[53]

Then, with equal suddenness, Russian military fortunes declined. The supposedly demoralized Ottoman armies rallied around the ancient Bulgarian fortress of Plevna. The late summer of 1877 turned into early fall, and nearly ten thousand Russian soldiers died in repeated, failed attempts to conquer the fortress. The Russian advance ground to a halt.[54]

Alexander was about to receive a second, still more painful lesson about public opinion—it was extremely fickle. Early war enthusiasm melted as the prospect of victory receded. Rejoicing gave way to harsh recriminations. Newspapers that had celebrated the war now denounced the tsar as a warmonger. Reports of incompetence and mismanagement arrived from the front: Insufficiently supplied soldiers were freezing in the cold of the high Balkan mountains. Russia's declining relations with Europe were lamented, and it was feared that European statesmen would now try to isolate Russia. Even administration officials complained of a lack of leadership at the highest levels. The tsar's decision to accompany the troops to the battlefield, at first seen as an act of bravery, was now derided as nothing more than militaristic showmanship.[55]

It was at this very moment, at the pinnacle of the Plevna debacle, that the Trial of the 193 was scheduled to begin. Worse timing could hardly be imagined. The Grand Duke Konstantin Nikolaevich, Alexander's brother, was so disturbed at the prospect of a large public trial of the regime's enemies that he petitioned the Ministry of Justice for a full cancellation of the trial and release of all prisoners. Konstantin Pobedonostsev, the arch-reactionary tutor to Alexander's son and heir, stated succinctly: "Only a completely blind or a completely unthinking or incompetent administration would hold such a trial at such a time."[56]

But what could be done? It was unimaginable that hundreds of dangerous revolutionaries be released, unpunished, to continue their dangerous activities against the state. And postponement was impossible, since the prisoners could not reasonably be held without trial any longer—their very presence had taken a serious toll on the prison system. No, the trial would go forward, come what may.[57]

∾

And so they can torture us, make us suffer, but we are not only forbidden to seek justice—naturally, I am not so naive that I expect justice from this court or from the authorities—we are even deprived of the opportunity to reveal to society, that in Russia, political prisoners are treated worse than the Christians under the Turks!

— Testimony of Ippolit Myshkin, Trial of the 193[58]

It was an inauspicious beginning. As the 193 prisoners filed into the large courtroom of the St. Petersburg District Court, an immediate problem arose: There were not enough seats for all the defendants. A scramble ensued as those who entered the courtroom took up every available space: on the defendants' benches, in the seats reserved for the defense attorneys, in the galleries. Some had to remain standing along the walls. Then thirty-five defense attorneys proceeded in and looked around in confusion—their chairs were occupied. A makeshift table was positioned in the center of the courtroom, and the attorneys crowded around it. The judges, overwhelmed by the chaos, did not even try to sound their bells for order in the court.[59]

The defendants, sensing the power of their numbers, were swept up in a mood of festive rebellion, and thus abandoned initial plans for exhibiting the genteel decorum of the Fifty defendants. Amid the chaos, the trial became a grand game. Joyous cries pierced the general din, as old comrades from the "to the people" movement recognized one another after years of incarceration. Others found themselves embracing friends they made in prison but had never seen face-to-face. Soon, everyone began talking at once, engrossed in reminiscences, news, and gossip. No one paid any attention to the proceedings.[60]

The indictment in the case of the 193, initially intended as a shocking tale of "anarchism," "violent revolution," and plans for "the extermination of the upper classes," ended up as an interminably long, tedious history of the "to the people" movement. The prosecutor, the rather bloodless Feliks Zhelekhovskii, droned on and on in a characteristic monotone. But it did not matter, because no one was listening. Some of the radicals openly wandered the room, trying to enlist support for a general protest against the proceedings. A majority of the defendants had already decided that the trial was a charade. They were looking for any excuse to boycott.[61]

Finally, one defendant sounded the call to arms. Standing up, he declared that the number of the defendants in the courtroom meant that the public was excluded from the galleries. This violated his right to an open trial. He did not wish to defend himself, he said, and asked to leave the court-room. The presiding judge, happy to have at least one defendant leave the courtroom, politely acceded. All of a sudden, a barrage of shouts assailed the judge: "Let us all go! We do not recognize the court!" Without waiting for permission, a number of defendants massed toward the exit but were blocked by the gendarmes. Defeated by the chaos, the judge shouted, "The court is adjourned. Clear the courtroom!"[62]

On the second day, the presiding judge announced that, in order to alle-viate the confusion in the courtroom and allow selected members of the pub-lic to attend the proceedings, the defendants would be divided into seventeen groups, each of which would face trial separately. Immediately, cries arose from the accused, as many stood up, hurling insults at the judges and at the prosecutor. The court was again unceremoniously cleared.[63]

In protest, 150 defendants decided never to appear in court again, dub-bing themselves the "Protestants." At first, the judges resisted this tactic and ordered that defendants be forcibly dragged into the courtroom to testify. By prearranged plan, the accused allowed themselves to be escorted to the court by gendarmes and then declared: "I do not recognize this court and I refuse to defend myself. I wish to leave." Some began to shout that they were treated "like a herd of beasts," that the whole process was an "insult," and that the verdicts were "decided in advance." The spectacle was too much for the judges, and from that day on, the "Protestants" were left alone.[64]

By November, the trials had settled into a dull monotony—a hollow vic-tory for the state. The judges, the witnesses, the public were all present, but only to observe the wrath of the state rain down on one or two "Catholic" de-fendants. As show trials, these were limp affairs—empty courtrooms where dangerous accusations were hurled at nobody in particular.[65]

Even this was not to last. One of the "Protestants," Ippolit Myshkin, de-cided that silent defiance was insufficient. He had to make one final stand against the state. To the delight of his comrades, he planned a spectacular speech that would be sure to cause a stir within the courtroom. Without warn-ing, he appeared in the courtroom one November day and told the surprised judges that he was prepared to testify. Myshkin took his place on "Golgotha," the nickname the radicals gave the defendants' bench. After the presiding judge asked, "How do you plead?" Myshkin stood up, raised his handsome head high, and delivered a "terrifying oration against the enemies of the people."[66]

Myshkin pleaded no contest to the charge of being a "social revolutionary."

"I will not plead guilty," he added, "because I considered it my responsibility, indeed my duty, to join the ranks of the social-revolutionary party." He was forced into radicalism by the Russian state and the Russian capitalist system, which brought ordinary working people into "desperately poor circumstances, to unheard-of chronic hunger." Suffering Russians had lost their faith in the tsar and in Russian society. As a radical, Myshkin merely wished to voice popular anger against the Russian regime.[67]

For this, he and his fellow revolutionaries had to suffer all of the brutality of the Russian police. To the astonishment of the judges, he declared himself a victim of torture. To be sure, his list of abuses was less than convincing: For a time, he was shackled without socks; he was denied tea and even boiling water; he was forced to sit alone in his cell; and he was provided with neither books nor newspapers. Myshkin brazenly declared this to be evidence that while the tsarist regime was fighting the Turks abroad, it was behaving worse than the Turks at home.[68]

As a result, Myshkin concluded, the Trial of the 193 was a sham. Indeed, he intoned, "this is not a trial, but a simple comedy, or even something worse, something more disgusting, more shameful. . . ."

By this point, the presiding judge had repeatedly asked Myshkin to finish his statement and take his seat. As Myshkin began to pronounce his final indictment, the judge finally had enough and shouted, "Take him away!" A guard approached the defendant's bench and reached for Myshkin. When two other defendants tried to block the guard's path, they were knocked aside. Finally, the guard grabbed Myshkin by the arm and tried to place his hand over Myshkin's mouth.

But Myshkin was able to shout his final words: ". . . more shameful than a house of prostitution—there women sell themselves out of need, but here the senators, out of vileness and servility, out of a desire for rank and high salaries, sell everything that is valuable to humanity!"[69]

More gendarmes arrived. A melee erupted on the courtroom floor. The public in the galleries began to scream and cry out, thinking that Myshkin was being beaten. A few women fainted. In the ensuing confusion, the judges and the prosecutor hastily fled the room. Before he ducked out, Zhelekhovskii shouted, "This is revolution!" Only a few minutes later did a clerk of the court remembered to rush back into the room to announce "The court is adjourned!" before running out again. Ekaterina Breshko-Breshkovskaia fondly remembered that Myshkin declared "pitiless and fearless warfare on a strong foe . . . in a voice like that of the Archangel Michael."[70]

The regime's intended "show trial" had officially degenerated into a farce.

On January 23, 1878, the verdicts were finally handed down, to the great relief of the Russian regime. The outcome, from the state's perspective, was embarrassing. After all of the dramatics in the courtroom, and the open, brazen defiance of authority, most of the defendants received little more than a slap on the wrist. Ninety of them were acquitted of all charges, sixty-one sentenced to time served, and twenty-two sentenced to house arrest. Of the twenty-eight sentenced to hard labor and exile, only thirteen actually served their time. The others were shown leniency on appeal for various reasons: They were under twenty-one, they were "sorry for their actions," or, like the suffering Gorinovich, they were victims of revolutionary violence. It looked as though the radicals had successfully intimidated the Russian state.[71]

By 1878, however, officials such as Konstantin Palen wanted nothing more than to put the year 1877 behind them. The trials had become a publicly acknowledged disaster. Because journalists were not allowed to attend the trials, the public heard only wild reports spread by those who had witnessed the proceedings. Revolutionary groups had used illegal presses to publish and disseminate the texts of the defendants' speeches, which cast the revolutionaries in a flattering light.[72] The sufferings and travails of the political prisoners became widely known. Paradoxically, the lenient verdicts only heightened the criticism of the state. If so many of the defendants were innocent, why had they languished in prison for so long?

Still, the charade was over, and the prisons were partially emptied. Even the news from abroad was good: Plevna had finally fallen on November 28, 1877, and the Russian army resumed the march toward Istanbul. By January 19, 1878, the Ottoman Empire had sued for peace. The regime entertained hopes that that the new year might be a good one.

~

Upon the horizon there appeared a gloomy form, illuminated by a light as of hell, who, with lofty bearing, and a look breathing forth hatred and defiance, made his way through the terrified crowd to enter with a firm step upon the scene of history.

It was the Terrorist.

—SERGEI KRAVCHINSKII, *Underground Russia*[73]

Apartment No. 5 on English Street in St. Petersburg was little more than a tiny, dingy three-room flat with a cramped, dark kitchen. Nonetheless, in the fall of 1877, Vera rejoiced to call it home. Shared with Masha and two other women, the apartment quickly became known as the English Commune, as it often hosted more than one guest on its floorboards, bare of all furniture. Almost every night, radicals of every stripe, students, and even a few workers would stop by, and in no time guests would be arguing violently over the latest revolutionary theories or, after a few drinks, singing songs, dancing, and making merry.

Vera remained her usual reticent self. By now, she stood out in a crowd— sitting quietly in her usual black dress and black hat, surrounded by a cloud of smoke from her habitual cigarette, lost in thought even during the most rowdy of gatherings. Her silence hid a quiet contentment. Once again she was at the heart of the movement. She would, by now, do anything for these people that she considered her true family.[74]

The carefree, bohemian lifestyle of the English Commune masked a deeper anxiety. The arrests, the trials, the failed street demonstrations had taken their toll. The revolutionary movement was besieged on every front. On one side, a cruel tyranny used all of the crushing might at its disposal. A scattered, lightly armed movement had no chance against a police force, an army, a chain of prisons, and an array of labor camps. On the other side, the peasants and workers remained mute, almost uninterested in the plight of their would-be saviors. Circumstances suggested one inexorable truth: Radicalism was dead.[75] But young idealists, who had sacrificed wealth, careers, and families for the cause, refused to concede defeat. They had devoted too much to their vision of a beautiful future order, where all of the poverty and suffering of the present world would melt away. If anything, the fragility of the dream increased its seeming purity.

Among the guests of the English Commune, many began to debate the new trend of "disorganization" and "defensive measures" in the Land and Freedom movement. One of the most vocal was Masha. With burning eyes, she urged immediate and decisive action against the government. Police officials, military men, prosecutors—these were nothing more than the tsar's lackeys, oppressing ordinary people beyond endurance. They needed to be taught a lesson.[76]

Her vehemence proved instantly infectious. Out of the failed "to the people" movement, a new narrative was born, a fable like that of David and Goliath. The mighty Russian state strode like a behemoth over the land, crushing enemies underfoot. Ordinary Russians were not indifferent; they were merely cowed into silence, mute with fear. But a few brave men and women would courageously take up their weapons on behalf of the silent many. And perhaps, like the legendary David, they could fell the Russian state with a single shot. Terrorism tempted the revolutionaries not just as an act of revenge but as a statement of a deep, burning faith, cherished through the valley of darkness. All it would take was a man or a woman, armed with confidence in the imminent victory of a new world order—and a gun. The shock of assassination would topple the pillars of the Russian autocracy, and the Russian masses, suddenly released from their bondage, would pour into the streets, filled with revolutionary fervor.[77]

Vera said next to nothing. Few knew what she thought of these new plans. Visible on her face was merely a grim determination to act.

News from the south soon made the decision for Masha and Vera deeply personal. Their beloved friends Lev Deich and Iakov Stefanovich were in prison in Kiev, arrested for participating in the Chigirin plot. Vera, in particular, was devastated; she was already profoundly attached to Deich as a man who accepted her for who she was. Borrowing money from her sister, she sent it to Kiev, where plans were being made for a spectacular escape.[78]

The women's concern, however, was mixed with a crushing feeling of betrayal. The men had gone to great lengths to conceal the plot from their female comrades. Deich and Stefanovich knew that both Vera and Masha had eagerly awaited some plan of action and yet had deliberately sought to keep them in the dark. If Vera recalled the night spent in conversation with Deich on the floor of her peasant hut, and his happy farewell at the train station, she also now realized that he had not fully trusted her. He had treated her like a traditional woman, a woman unable to handle the most difficult, the most conspiratorial, and the most violent aspects of revolution. Nechaev, for all his faults, had never insulted her in this manner.[79]

In truth, Deich and Stefanovich had left many out of their conspiracy, concerned that their fellow revolutionaries would disapprove of their efforts to deceive the peasants. But Vera and Masha suspected something else, something that they had long feared: The men simply did not see women as true revolutionaries. Despite the movement's commitment to equality, despite the shared apartments and peasant huts, when it came to violence, the men preferred to leave the women out.

In the end, this betrayal was paradoxically liberating. Vera and Masha no longer needed the movement to direct them. They would formulate plans of their own. In time, they would vindicate the revolutionary credentials of their sex. Masha wrote of the decision to a friend: "We decided to turn to terror, and our decision, once made, was irrevocable."[80]

By December 1877, a number of different groups had laid plans to kill Trepov. A few former Southern Rebels, including Vera's ex-"husband," Mikhail Frolenko, conspired to assassinate the governor. They had rented an apartment across the street from the governor's offices and were carefully following Trepov's movements. One day, Vera, who had heard rumors about the plot, asked Frolenko about the progress of his plans. He was under strict instructions not to talk, so he only gave her a vague answer: A strategy was currently under consideration. Frolenko thought Vera seemed satisfied by his answer.[81]

But Vera and Masha quickly laid plans of their own. They selected another target for assassination, so that both women could commit a terrorist act on the same day. Masha chose the prosecutor in the Trial of the 193, Zhelekhovskii, because his indictment had publicly sown "lies" about the revolutionary movement. Vera's early conspiratorial training stood them in good stead. As Nechaev had explained, the key to the perfect terrorist plot was for the terrorists to appear as ordinary people. The women soon discovered that their sex provided the perfect cover, especially if they dressed and acted like society ladies. No one would suspect them, they surmised, if they each posed as an ordinary female petitioner seeking an audience with a powerful man. Each woman, through careful surveillance, attempted to discover the precise times that each official was receiving. Vera prepared her fake petition, and Masha bribed Zhelekhovskii's servant. Both bought large cloaks and shawls to conceal their weapons.

Neither woman made a plan of escape; neither had any intention of fleeing the scene. In their eyes, their acts of just terror would inevitably lead to a glorious end: martyrdom.[82]

Vera's long-awaited dream was about to be realized. Previously, in her years of imprisonment and exile, she had been a passive victim of fate, suffering injustice in obscurity. But now, she deliberately and willingly courted punishment, believing that through her suffering, her actions would be redeemed, even hallowed. Trepov's death would be a powerful statement against the repression of the tsarist regime. It would reverberate through society and show that the behemoth was not invincible. Ordinary people would be freed from their crushing fear. And then—martyrdom would crown her triumph. Through Vera's suffering and possible death, Russians would be moved by the spectacle of her heroism. Terror and martyrdom would be joined in one perfect, enduring act of violence.[83]

Karakozov was her model. Two years after her attempt on Trepov, she wrote of her predecessor in assassination as an inspiration: "Oh Karakozov! If the Russian people ever achieve a humane life, if freedom and justice have not been murdered forever on Russian soil . . . they will erect a monument to you, to you above all, in the forum of the new age!"[84]

On January 23, the verdicts in the Trial of the 193 were handed down. The comrades on trial were now safe from any possible retribution that might be meted out in the wake of a terrorist act. On January 24, the two women struck.

On January 23, Mikhail Popov, a member of Land and Freedom, had been given a mysterious task for the following day. He was told to fill out a form to report a lost passport, and to appear at the governor's office between 11:00 A.M. and noon. He did as he was told. When he arrived at the appointed place on the following morning, he was surprised to see a large crowd gathering at the entrance. After pushing his way through the throng, he approached a guard and asked to see the governor. At first, the guard simply ignored him, and then, after Popov grew persistent, he irritably answered, "Now is not the time. Come back later." Frustrated, Popov turned to leave.

Just then, a carriage pulled up right to the steps, and a man rushed through the crowd. Popov recognized him—St. Petersburg's most famous surgeon. A minute later, he overheard the guard say, "Some lady came with a revolver under her shawl, said she wished to present a petition to Trepov. Then, it turned out, she shot him with her revolver."

When Popov heard this, he quietly slipped back through the crowd. He knew why he had been sent: to witness this new weapon in the battle against the Russian state. He hurried back to the designated meeting place to spread the news to the rest of his comrades. The revolutionary movement was now in a new phase. The turn to terror had begun.[85]

CHAPTER 10

The Trial

~~

By perverse chance, on January 24, 1878, Anatolii Koni formally assumed his duties as the newly appointed chief justice of the St. Petersburg Circuit Court. Though he tried to preserve some modesty with colleagues, he could not hide his elation. He had been dreaming of this moment for years. Raised from relative obscurity, he would now become an important figure in the city. His mind was filled with elaborate plans for the future. He would exploit his position not merely to adjudicate but to educate Russian citizens in the true meaning of the law. He would insist on impartiality, order, and justice. Reactionary sentiments, corrupt practices, and institutional inertia would be banished from his offices. The St. Petersburg Circuit Court would become a beacon of the Russian legal reforms, shepherding the citizens of St. Petersburg into liberalism and westernization. Finally, he could live a life dedicated to the cause of Russian progress.

He could not, as yet, foresee the furor that would arise over the first case tried in front of him.[1] Indeed, Koni had just finished a long speech to his new subordinates on the importance of impeccable personal conduct for building public trust in the legal system when a colleague entered his office and gave him the news: Fedor Trepov had been shot.

By the time Koni made it across town and had pushed through the mob surrounding the entrance of the governor's residence, he found Trepov's wood-paneled reception room densely packed with guards, policemen, and doctors, all speaking in hushed tones. And there, behind a set of doors, in the adjoining room, sat the assassin. Koni remembered that her pale, almost gray face was so thin as to look sickly, and that her sharp chin was held high, in defiance of the interrogator across from her. She was still refusing to give evidence regarding her crime.

As he stood watching Vera, Koni's eyes caught sight of his former superior, Count Palen, in deep discussion with Alexander Lopukhin, Koni's predecessor as chief justice and now the chief prosecutor of the St. Petersburg Court of Appeals. Palen caught Koni's glance and suddenly said to Lopukhin in a louder voice, "Oh, yes, Anatolii Fedorovich will handle this trial beautifully."

Suspicious, Koni turned to the two men. "Is the case already so clear?"

"Indeed," answered the prosecutor, "very simple: It is a case of personal revenge, and the jury will convict her in no time." Palen nodded in agreement.

Koni was uneasy. He was already chosen to preside over Vera's trial, and was expected to do so "beautifully." A conviction was apparently a foregone conclusion. Koni's blissful feelings of freedom evaporated. The year had not begun as well as he had hoped.

∿

All at once, a single, muted shot, fired by Vera Zasulich, muffled the thunderous guns of Plevna.

— OLGA LIUBATOVICH, "Far and Near"[2]

The investigation took scarcely a month, and plans for a jury trial were immediately announced in the papers. The Russian public was delighted; it was, in most respects, Russia's first real celebrity trial. In the short fourteen years of press freedom in Russia, a number of cases had passed through the spotlight: women accused of murdering their lovers, parents accused of blood-curdling child abuse. But nothing could top the tale of a mysterious female assassin.[3]

The Russian press was perfectly poised to make the Zasulich case into a national sensation. The newspapers had already cut their teeth on the Russo-Turkish War. The Bulgarian atrocities, the stalemates on the front lines, and the cynical diplomatic wrangling had filled reams and reams of paper. Russian editors had at last found their voice as opinion-makers, guiding the public and the politicians alike into the proper frame of mind. In no time, the Russian press had begun to serve its function as a debating forum, as liberal, radical, and conservative papers vied against each other for allegiance of ordinary Russians.

The public devoured it all. Intelligent, educated Russians now discussed— in drawing rooms, dining rooms, letters to the editor, and letters to one another—Russia's military conduct, its leaders, and its place in the world. "The voice of the people" became something to divine, to court, and to sway, if at all possible. The tsar's reluctant declaration of war against the Ottomans dramatically confirmed the power of the press.[4]

By the time Vera's shot rang out in the governor's office, the Russian press was already a well-oiled machine, primed for turning such an event into a cause célèbre. By 1878, the war was a stale subject. Though Plevna had fallen, and the victorious Russian armies had reached the gates of Istanbul, doubts about the war failed to dissipate. Even after the Ottomans signed an armistice with Russia and accepted the loss of their Balkan territories, the chances that Russia would hold on to its new possessions seemed slim. Britain and Austria vocally demanded a revision of Russia's new Balkan map and ominously threatened war, a war the Russian military simply could not fight. The costs of empire-building in southern Europe proved exorbitant. The entire effort was beginning to look like a waste of lives and treasure.[5]

The tsar, in particular, came in for vicious criticism. He was accused of fighting the war out of personal vanity, and it was whispered that he had long planned the invasion of the Balkans to compensate for his father's defeat in the Crimean War of 1856. Before the war, an attack on the Ottomans was widely urged as a just response to the "Bulgarian atrocities." Now, in the eyes of many Russians, the Turks were "brave fighters," and the Balkan rebels were barbarian cowards, unworthy of Russian support. Anatolii Koni remembered the mood distinctly. "Skepticism appeared," he wrote, "the kind of skepticism to which our nation is particularly inclined." Even those who had greeted the declaration of war with sanguinary zeal now repeated one word like a mantra: "mistake."[6]

For those tired of the endless articles on corruption in the military and Machiavellianism in Europe, the Zasulich assassination attempt provided a perverse relief. The mystery of the "girl" assassin provided just the kind of dramatic detail to satisfy the public's craving for escapism. Throughout the country, newspapers allowed Russian readers to relive every moment of the crime. The *St. Petersburg Register* published an extraordinary minute-by-minute account, complete with a diagram of the interior of Trepov's apartment, showing the position of the various petitioners and the location of the exact spot where the gun was fired. Other papers echoed and reechoed the dramatic elements of the crime: Trepov's groan, "I am wounded," as he fell, the feverish rushing about of the guards, and the grim faces of the city's most famous surgeons, as they repeatedly failed to extract the bullet. In the days that followed the event, Trepov's health was recorded down to the hour: The public could carefully monitor his body temperature, his level of consciousness, and even the precise time he was allowed to take his first cup of tea. Vera was described in detail: She was "a young girl" with "clear brown eyes, a large sharp nose, and a sickly pale face." Tantalizing speculations about her state of mind were revealed: her insistence on concealing her real identity, even to the point of sewing false initials in her cloak; her near paralysis after the shot was fired; her "extraordinary cold-bloodedness" during questioning. The public reaction to this new scandal was also noted. Newspapers described the noble and royal visitors that graced Trepov's apartment, as well as the outpourings of concern from the crowds that surrounded his building and from those who sent letters of condolence.[7]

In the days after the event, the newspapers continued to follow the investigation into Vera's motives and background. Many accounts divulged her involvement in the Nechaev affair, and one article claimed that Vera had first met Nechaev when she was a girl of fifteen. The *New Times* revealed that Vera's gun was a six-chamber English Bulldog and that all six chambers were loaded with large-caliber bullets. In time, the link to Bogoliubov's flogging was explained. A few newspapers editorialized on the assassination attempt, decrying it as an act of vigilante justice. But most were content to simply report on the story as it unfolded.[8]

In the weeks and months that followed, rumors filled in where the newspapers left off. According to some stories, Vera was brutally tortured by the Russian regime. According to others, she was visited by the tsar and was commended for telling him the truth about Russian abuses. Some had heard that Vera was Bogoliubov's lover; others heard that she was part of a vast, revolutionary terrorist plot.[9]

For a time, Trepov's health was also obsessively covered by the press. His wound was analyzed in excruciating detail—its size, its location, and the amount of bleeding from the opening. The bullet was not lodged near any internal organs, but in the age before antibiotics, any major flesh wound could rapidly become fatally infected. Newpapers daily reported Trepov's body temperature and general state of consciousness as signs of whether he was developing such an infection. As the days passed and no fever developed, Trepov was considered in the clear. He had survived the attack.[10]

If he had died, Trepov might have become a much lamented victim of a vicious terrorist attack. Because he lived, he became the center of a public firestorm. In no time at all, the man who had been the victim in the story quickly became Russia's most notorious public villain.

Trepov had never been a popular man. After his appointment as governor in 1866, he had greatly consolidated and expanded his control over the police functions of the city. In the aftermath of the Karakozov assassination, his chief task was to combat political unrest and prevent further acts of violence. It was in this role as public defender that he cemented his reputation as a petty tyrant. A military man at heart, Trepov never lost his love of order, discipline, and unconditional obedience. To these traits he added an almost paranoid suspicion of social activists of any stripe, seeing conspiracy and danger where none existed. He had a volatile personality and was never particularly concerned to rein in his temper. Stories circulated about his mistreatment of subordinates, city officials, and prisoners alike. Once, when an assistant prosecutor dared to confront Trepov about a prisoner held without charges, Trepov had the prosecutor arrested, detained, and exiled from the city. Later, when a minor newspaper published a short item vaguely critical of the police, an enraged Trepov sent his officers to ransack the editor's office. Over time, stories about Trepov reached mythic proportions. Rumor had it that he mercilessly tortured prisoners and manufactured evidence against innocent people. By comparison, Trepov's flogging of Bogoliubov began to look like a minor incident. Many thought that the governor somehow "had it coming."[11]

These abuses of power would have been notorious enough, but Trepov also had the reputation of being a grasping social climber. By all accounts he took bribes, obsequiously flattered those above him, and treated those beneath him with unrelenting contempt. Even the tsar himself supposedly disliked the man, and some believed Trepov was appointed to his prestigious post because of some dark secret, perhaps even because Trepov was the illegitimate half brother of the tsar himself.[12]

In the court of public opinion, Trepov was condemned. In direct allusion to the Bulgarian atrocities, people openly muttered that "Bashi-Bouzuks were nearer home than Bulgaria."[13] Soon after he was shot, Trepov began to receive packages containing miniature birch rods, used to flog prisoners, tied together with ribbons. "Your favorite emblem," the enclosed notes read.[14]

～

A dog's death to all dogs! Trepov, Palen, Mezentsev, Peters, etc.!

The dog Trepov deserves a dog's death! And you too, Palen, Mezentsev, Peters, Zhelkovskii, Judases!

There is a force that will stop at nothing: a dog's death to all dogs!

— Anonymous letters to Konstantin Palen, Fedor Trepov, and Nikolai Mezentsev, January 24, 1878[15]

Within a day after the attempt on Trepov's life, the tsar received incontrovertible evidence that the governor was the victim of a terrorist plot. After reading Vera's police report, which detailed her political radicalism and her years of imprisonment and exile, Alexander II wrote in the margin: "This perversity is entirely reminiscent of Karakozov." In subsequent days, more unnerving evidence was unearthed by the secret police. Informers who had infiltrated student groups heard rumors of a supposed meeting the night before the shooting, during which conspirators cast lots to determine who would shoot Trepov. There were reports of a list of officials to be executed. As if in confirmation, the postmaster in St. Petersburg turned over menacing letters addressed to various government officials. Composed on hastily torn pieces of paper, they contained anonymous death threats written in block letters.[16]

There could not have been a more propitious time for the Russian government to reveal evidence of a revolutionary terrorist plot. The regime could have exposed the radical background of this mysterious female assassin, and the public might have been convinced that this was no isolated blow against regime brutality. Vera's innocence might have been undermined. But Palen, who had been so eager to paint radicalism as brutal and amoral during the Trials of the Fifty and the 193, now hushed up all talk of terrorism. When Koni asked Lopukhin whether any evidence of a political motivation for the crime had been found, Lopukhin lied and said that there was none.[17]

To this day, the regime's suppression of evidence in the Zasulich case remains a mystery. Historians are baffled at Palen's decision, most likely approved by those above him, to treat Vera's assassination attempt as the isolated act of a woman bent on revenge. In the face of growing public hostility, the decision seemed an act of breathtaking incompetence. Indeed, Koni firmly believed that it was nothing more than a fatal carelessness on the part of the justice minister and Lopukhin.[18]

Most likely, the disastrous Monster Trials of 1877 weighed heavily on Palen's mind. If Vera had been accused of a political crime, her case would automatically be sent to a special session of the Senate, with its panel of judges and semisecret proceedings. Vera's act had attracted so much attention that sending her trial to a specially empowered tribunal would have whipped up public distrust and anger. It would seem as if the government were trying to hide something. A jury trial, on the other hand, would demonstrate that the Russian state was living up to its newly minted principles of openness and legality. Indeed, when the minister of the interior wrote to

Palen suggesting that press access to Vera's trial be limited, Palen bridled. It was inadvisable, he replied, because such measures would "lead public opinion in a mistaken direction" and allow people to suspect that Vera had been unjustly convicted.[19]

Perhaps Palen was also confident that this time he had the radicals where he wanted them. At last, one of them had committed an incontrovertible crime: attempting to kill a government official. The jury would assess the case and easily deliver a guilty verdict. It would be a delicious moment of triumph. A jury of Vera's peers would teach revolutionaries an invaluable lesson: "They will show the Russian and foreign admirers of Vera Zasulich's 'heroic exploit' that the Russian people bow before the Tsar, revere him, and are always ready to defend his faithful servants." Press reports would ensure that the crime and trial "elicit general indignation and full condemnation."[20]

Yet again, a good theory. Very soon, however, Palen began to suspect that he had made yet another mistake. Many in the general public were distinctly fond of Vera. A guilty verdict would make her into a martyr. Even Trepov, the villain of the hour, refused to help the government's case. To Palen's intense irritation, the general, citing the pain of his wounds and providing eloquent doctors' notes, refused to appear in court. But his health did not prevent him from wandering about town in his wheelchair, informing everyone he met that he held no grudge against Vera, even sincerely hoped for her acquittal.[21]

Palen's own concern about the case was only matched by his eternal lassitude. The trial was becoming complicated and confusing, and he increasingly wanted to wash his hands of the matter. He appealed to his old colleague Koni to assume control. Summoning Koni into his office, he asked whether he could guarantee a guilty verdict. Koni, horrified by the mere suggestion of any violation of liberal judicial principles, quickly professed his ignorance of what Palen was suggesting. How could he guarantee the verdict of the jury? Even if he were solely responsible for the verdict, he would refuse to render judgment without first considering all of the evidence! In despair, Palen lashed out against his former subordinate: "Why did you fail to tell me this before?"[22]

A few days before the trial, Palen made one final attempt to sway Koni. But the new judge had no intention of sullying his judicial principles. A judge, Koni lyrically declaimed, "carries in his hands a cup of the holy gifts. He cannot lean toward one side or the other, lest the gifts be spilled." These high-minded bromides merely elicited Palen's characteristic yawn. As Koni droned on, Palen began to nod off. Then, suddenly, he sat upright, jolted out of his stupor by an idea. Perhaps Koni could make a small mistake at the trial, Palen whispered. This would give the ministry an excuse to appeal the verdict. He winked at Koni slyly.

Outrage finally silenced Koni for good. He silently stood up and left.[23]

But it was not easy to cling to cherished principles in the partisan climate that pervaded Russia in the prelude to the trial. Koni sensed that, no matter the outcome, some faction would blame him. On the eve of the trial date, Koni entered the empty courtroom to make sure that everything was arranged properly for the next day. Standing in the large chamber, now growing dark as the sun set, he was filled with an ominous, undefined foreboding. "Who knows what awaits me tomorrow?" he thought, and reluctantly headed home.[24]

⌒

I am so morally destroyed, so oppressed by the rapid succession of strong emotions, which I had to experience in the course of a few hours of the trial, that I am not sure I have the strength to accomplish my task. I need to bring society into that courtroom; I must force them to experience, to suffer all the things which we, the audience, endured in that court. Only a few hours have passed, but it seems as if years have unfolded before you, as if a long repressed and gathering moral storm broke upon our heads, demanding that we evaluate everything that is good and bad within us, throwing open the doors of your soul and bringing it to an impartial, merciless court. Not one theater can provide you with this kind of drama.

—GRIGORII GRADOVSKII, *The Voice*, April 2, 1878[25]

On March 31, 1878, the crush outside the St. Petersburg courthouse was unprecedented. Though it was a raw, rainy day, and the roads were covered in ankle-deep slush, people from all walks of life had been milling around the courthouse since the early morning, warming their hands with their breath. By 10:00 A.M., it seemed that all of St. Petersburg had gathered on Liteinyi Prospekt: market women in their patterned kerchiefs, workers in dingy overalls, and a large contingent of students and radical activists muffled in distinctive plaid shawls. A cordon of policemen guarded the courthouse doors, to prevent anyone without tickets from entering. Though many on the street hoped to get in at the last minute, this was impossible. All tickets to the trial had been snatched up weeks in advance, mostly by those in St. Petersburg society with the proper connections. For Russia's aristocrats, government officials, and celebrity journalists, this was the event of the season.[26]

At 10:00 A.M., elegant carriages began to roll up to the main courthouse gate. Fur-clad merchants' wives and bejeweled countesses, generals and princes in gold-braided uniforms—all braved the mud and rain to push their way past the police and through the wrought-iron doors of the building. Both the upper and lower corridors of the entrance hall filled with a crush of people seeking seats. The courtroom itself held six hundred people, but even the most powerful aristocrats had to crush together in the packed galleries, and scores had to stand in the back. An experienced lawyer recalled that he had never before seen such excitement and nervous energy fill a single courtroom.[27]

Only the tsar's highest ranking officials—the ministers of war, foreign affairs, and finance—escaped the chaos and solemnly occupied the two rows of red armchairs at the head of the room, right behind the judges' bench. Sitting at the bench itself was Anatolii Koni, the president of the court, flanked by two subordinate judges. The prosecutor, Konstantin Kessel, and the clerk of the court were also seated at the bench, and all of the men were attired in the dark blue uniforms with gold braid that marked their status as state officials. To the left of the judges, a hastily gathered set of chairs was cordoned off by a rope to reserve it for the members of the press, including representatives of Russia's major newspapers, correspondents from German and French papers and from *The Times* of London, Britain's famous Russia expert, Donald MacKenzie Wallace, and the novelist recently turned political commentator, Fyodor Dostoyevsky.[28]

As the jurors processed in, it was observed that they seemed like an ordinary lot, a quotidian mix of clerks and public officials. Aware of the publicity that the trial would attract and the need to look respectable, the jurors wrote to Koni asking if formal tailcoats and white ties were appropriate for the event. Koni answered that this was not necessary. As a result, they all appeared in plain tailcoats and black ties.[29]

With surprising punctuality, the trial began at precisely 11:00 A.M., when the judge formally called the courtroom to order and asked for the accused to be led in. A sudden hush blanketed the galleries as Vera appeared, accompanied by two uniformed and helmeted gendarmes holding unsheathed swords upright at their sides. Her appearance was mesmerizing. Onlookers could not precisely say what they expected, but they certainly did not expect the woman who now entered the room. A worn black silk dress accentuated her thinness, and her hair, parted in the middle and hanging in two braids down her back, made her look much younger than her years. Some thought she looked no more than seventeen. Few found her beautiful, but many saw something vulnerable and inexplicably attractive in her sad, pale face and wide brown eyes. Clearly aware of the stares of the crowd, Vera fixed her own gaze on the floor. She was the picture of innocence, looking for all the world like someone waiting to be rescued from the swords of the gendarmes. As one witness wrote, "She looked almost saintly."[30]

"Was this really the villainess who, in broad daylight, in a crowd of people, raised her vengeful hand and pulled the trigger?" one witness remembered wondering. Indeed it was. A kind of pleasure filled the crowd in the courtroom. They settled in to watch what promised to be the drama of the century.[31]

As Konstatin Kessel watched the crowd pour into the courtroom, he must have been overtaken by a sense of foreboding. Soon, this godforsaken case would begin and all eyes would be on him. He was shrewd enough to recognize the perilous nature of his position: He was an inexperienced junior prosecutor taking on the most important trial in Russia since the 1864 reforms. He would have given anything to be relieved of the responsibility.[32]

Kessel knew that he was not Palen's first choice as prosecutor, nor even the second. The Ministry of Justice had originally pinned its hopes on the clever prosecutor Vladimir Zhukovskii, an orator to be reckoned with. He was said to look like a well-known statue of Mephistopheles and possessed an amazing talent for using sarcasm to great effect.[33] But Zhukovskii knew a bad case when he saw one. Giving a disingenuous excuse that fooled no one—that his prosecution of Zasulich would somehow put his radical brother in a difficult position—Zhukovskii declined. Sergei Andreevskii was approached next but also declined, frankly voicing his fear that he could not get a conviction.[34]

Thus the matter was unceremoniously thrust into Konstantin Kessel's lap. Even then, Palen had to order Kessel to take it. Kessel felt humiliated, forced to accept a case that his more prestigious colleagues easily rejected. Stricken, he went to Koni for help. Most likely, he knew his nervous demeanor and lack of rhetorical talent would damage the case. Anatolii Koni could not ease his fears: Kessel was indeed a colorless man with no sense of humor or of prosecutorial strategy. Koni appealed to Palen, but in vain. Palen did not wish to consider the matter any further. "After all," he told Koni in a resigned tone of voice, "that would accord the case too much significance . . . too much significance." Koni gently advised Kessel to do the best he could. If he calmly presented the evidence against Zasulich, he would fulfill his prose-cutorial duty. Now, looking at the expectant faces in the galleries of the courtroom, Kessel must have realized that in this case, simply doing his duty was not going to be nearly enough.[35]

In theory, of course, his case was open and shut. To prove murder in a Russian courtroom, the prosecutor had merely to show that Vera had in-tended to kill the governor. If she did not succeed, it was, in the words of the indictment, "only for very particular reasons, unforeseen by the defendant." Kessel's evidence was overwhelming. Vera admitted shooting the governor, dozens of witnesses saw her pull the trigger at close range, and the medical report proved that the wound was exceedingly dangerous. That Trepov sur-vived was certainly not due to anything Vera could control. A guilty verdict should have been certain.[36]

Perhaps lulled by the force of these facts, Kessel stuck closely to the ba-sic elements of the case. Colorlessly, heedless of the emotions generated by the assassination, Kessel called his witnesses: Major Fedor Kurneev, Trepov's assistant and the acting warden of the House of Preliminary Detention dur-ing the flogging of Bogoliubov; a few clerks and guards in Trepov's office; and the owner of the gun shop where Vera's gun was purchased. A duller collec-tion of people could not be found. As a bored public watched, Kessel sub-jected each man to the same insipid factual interrogation. Where was he standing when the shot was fired? Did he see the accused shoot Trepov? How far away was Zasulich when she pulled the trigger?

Often, the list of questions seemed almost haphazard, as if thought up on the spur of the moment. "What can you say of her state of mind after the shooting?" Kessel asked one of Trepov's guards. "Was she agitated?"

"It was not evident," came the reply.

"Did the governor speak with her at length?"

"No, he didn't."

"Were you standing far from the governor?"

"No, not far."

"When the shot was fired, did you see the revolver?"

"No."

"Was the tip of the revolver showing underneath her shawl?"

"No."

"Was the shawl wide and long?"

"Yes."

His final series of questions was asked of the owner of the gun shop, who testified that her gun was one of his most powerful. After finishing with his last witness, Kessel rested his case.[37]

Kessel merely hoped his questions made his point: Vera came armed with the intent to kill. He had established a few basic facts: She had concealed a revolver under her shawl, she had fired at close range, and her weapon had caused a serious wound. If Vera's had been an ordinary crime, this evidence might have sufficed.

In this case, however, the strategy seemed strikingly incompetent. There was little interest in the number of paces that separated Vera from her victim, the size of the gun, and the nature of the bullet wound. The public wanted to know about Vera, about Trepov, and about the entire drama that preceded the gunshot on that fateful day. It was as if Kessel were blind to the theatrical potential of trying a female assassin. He did nothing to demonize Vera or to humanize her victim. He might have thought that a sober account of the details of the crime would focus the attention of the jurors on the facts. But facts were far from their mind.

In essence, Kessel had followed Koni's advice. He did a competent job, made no major gaffes, and then rested his case. But no one paid the slightest attention. Everyone was waiting, breathless, for Peter Alexandrov to take the stage.

Peter Alexandrov, Vera's attorney, was an ugly man. He was small, and so thin that he looked emaciated. His tiny head had an odd shape that even a friend described as a "half-eaten herring." Though his voice was surprisingly resonant for his small frame, it was tainted by a nasal, snorting twang. Whenever he began a line of questioning or a summation, he feigned an offhand manner, as if he had come unprepared and was stating the first thoughts that came into his head. In the courtroom, Alexandrov rarely made a good first impression.[38]

Like every practiced performer, however, Alexandrov was able, almost magically, to transform himself into something he was not. Impeccably dressed in tie and tails, he looked taller than he was, duping at least one reporter into thinking that he was "long and lean." And after a few minutes of warming up, he made his listeners forget about his size, his voice, and his appearance. The pacing of his sentences, his ability to flip from biting sarcasm to poignant lyricism and then back again, mesmerized all who heard him.

Though his summations were sometimes hours long, his listeners devoured the last words as eagerly as they had the first.[39]

Alexandrov was already forty-two by the time of the Zasulich trial, and he moved around the courtroom with the ease of a trial veteran. In fact, Alexandrov was not an experienced defense attorney. He had spent most of his career on the other side of the law, as a highly positioned and well-regarded state prosecutor. A mere seven years after he graduated from the university with a law degree, he became one of Russia's youngest district attorneys, heading the district court of Pskov at the age of twenty-nine. In Palen's Justice Ministry, Alexandrov was viewed as firm and talented, a man of great promise. Those around him were certain he would fly high.[40]

There was only one obstacle to his success: Alexandrov himself. Though ambitious and driven, he was also a man of surprisingly inflexible idealism. Soon, his career would take several twists and turns, in order to maneuver around his firmly held principles.

His eccentricity was not long in betraying itself. In 1871, a mere five years after he was appointed district attorney, Alexandrov learned of a tragic case involving an ordinary soldier accused of a serious crime who was unable to afford a lawyer. Defying all precedent and his superiors, Alexandrov decided to volunteer his services pro bono. On the day of the soldier's trial, the jury was bewildered to see him appear in court, dressed in his civilian clothes and seated at the table for the defense. The soldier was eventually acquitted, and scandalous reports of the incident soon landed on Palen's desk. Palen, baffled, simply let the matter go, deciding to watch and wait.[41]

To Palen's relief, Alexandrov proved his reliability in that same year, when he was appointed as one of the prosecutors in the trial of the Nechaevites. Alexandrov did exactly what was expected of him and proved an incisive prosecutor. None of the blame for the unhappy outcome of the trial stuck to Alexandrov, and he continued to ascend the ladder. In no time, he was appointed as prosecutor in the appeals division of the Senate, the highest court in the land. He was at the pinnacle of his career.[42]

Once again, his principles tripped him up. In 1875, he was asked to rebut the appeals of two newspaper editors who had been convicted of libel for publishing articles critical of Russia's railway system. In his summation, Alexandrov caused a sensation by arguing in *defense* of the freedom of the press. Libel, Alexandrov argued, could only be prosecuted in cases where erroneous information was deliberately published by those in possession of the truth. This time, Palen was apoplectic. Nonetheless, Alexandrov's sole penalty was to be stricken from the Ministry of Justice's roll of honored state officials. It was a petulant but mostly symbolic punishment. Alexandrov was neither fired nor demoted, but he insisted that his integrity had been threatened. As a result, he could no longer in good conscience serve the state. He tendered his resignation.[43]

But Alexandrov loved the law, and so he entered the only path that remained open to him and became a defense attorney. In many ways, it was a decision that he should have taken long before. Soon, it was clear that the job suited both his hypersensitive conscience and his theatrical temperament. Alexandrov was now free to act as his sentiments dictated and select his clients according to his principles. In his own words, he became "a free man."[44]

By the time Alexandrov joined the Russian bar, the institution was a mere eight years old. Nonetheless, in the space of those eight years, the bar had made itself into one of the most independent and assertive guilds in Russia. Because of the reforms of 1864, Russian defense attorneys were meant to be entirely free of the control of the government. Answerable only to a council made up of senior attorneys, Russian defense lawyers did what they wished in the courtroom.[45] Most remarkable was their freedom of speech. They were permitted to make any argument in defense of the accused, even in political trials, even if this entailed open criticism of the regime. This alone made the defense attorneys some of the most free men in Russia; once in court, they could utter things that would subject them to arrest outside the courtroom.[46]

This comparative liberty attracted free-thinking men—both liberal and radical—into the legal profession. As time wore on, Russian defense attorneys began to see themselves as a class of social activists. Not a few of them openly sympathized with the revolutionary cause. Vladimir Spasovich, though a professed liberal by conviction, made his career defending revolutionaries in political trials. Dmitrii Stasov went even further, supporting Chernyshevskii financially and hanging up portraits of revolutionaries such as Vera Zasulich and Vera Figner on his office walls. Many attorneys saw themselves as the only line of defense against tyranny in the Russian state.[47]

Peter Alexandrov was by no means a revolutionary, but he made a name for himself in radical circles during the Trial of the 193. Although he was a junior lawyer among thirty-four other, well-known defense attorneys, his eloquent closing arguments nonetheless attracted much attention.[48] One of the defendants in the trial, Alexandra Kornilova, had been so impressed by his summation that she remembered his name in the days after Vera's assassination attempt. She was determined to have Alexandrov defend Vera, at any cost. Knowing that Vera had no money for a lawyer like Alexandrov, Kornilova organized a defense fund. After soliciting the students of St. Petersburg's institutions of higher learning, she had more than enough to pay for Vera's defense.[49]

Alexandrov needed very little convincing to take the case. His principles likely played an important role. Trepov's flogging of Bogoliubov was, for a man like Alexandrov, merely the latest in a series of arbitrary and brutal measures that the regime had undertaken with impunity. Alexandrov's sense of justice was aroused. But he also quickly understood the dramatic potential of the case. It was a fantastic challenge to defend a woman who had already confessed to committing a crime. But if he had the lawyerly virtuosity, he could make a name for himself not just among Russia's radicals but in Russia as a whole.[50]

Alexandrov prepared himself for the performance of a lifetime. Carefully, like a good director, he meticulously set the stage. He selected his witnesses carefully; he counseled Vera on her testimony and obsessively practiced his summation. He precisely choreographed the trial. Invited to a magnificent dinner party hosted by one of Russia's most powerful aristocratic families, Alexandrov availed himself of the opportunity to ask how the guests imagined Vera. Their answers were a trifle disappointing for the attorney, in that they corresponded little to reality. She was tall, thin, and beautiful, one woman suggested, dressed according to the latest fashion. She had elegant, ladylike mannerisms and spoke with a gentle voice. With this in mind, Alexandrov tried to remake Vera's appearance. One day, he appeared in Vera's cell, carrying a large package. To Vera's surprise, it contained a beautiful new cloak. Vera, who had not worn something so expensive since she attended church in Biakolovo, made an internal vow never to put it on. She did, however, agree not to bite her nails, since Russian juries considered it a sign of guilt.[51]

Though she had refused to wear the cloak, Vera eventually compromised something far more valuable: her political beliefs. Certainly at Alexandrov's insistence, she agreed to sanitize her biography, leaving her radicalism out of the story. Unlike her predecessors in the Trials of the Fifty and the 193, she decided, in the months before the trial, that she would not so much as mention her views on society, the state, and the future world. She was to take the stand and give only the barest outlines of her life, leaving her deepest beliefs and convictions out. It was a momentous decision, one that took from her hands the legacy of her act.

In return, Alexandrov must have reassured her that, in some indirect way, he would rewrite and repackage her ideas, to make them palatable to her jury. Injustice would be exposed, the state would be humiliated, and revolutionary violence would be justified. And no breath of socialist ideology would cross Alexandrov's lips. Vera was ultimately convinced that, in his own subtle way, Alexandrov would properly explain "the causes which prompted her deed."[52]

To the astonishment of his friends, Alexandrov boasted that he would easily win an acquittal for Vera. Even in the existing climate of swelling anger against Trepov and growing sympathy for Vera, it seemed like absurd overconfidence. Perhaps Vera's sentence might be mitigated. But there was little chance, in tsarist Russia, that a woman who shot a government official would remain unpunished.[53]

Unbeknownst to all, Alexandrov had even more ambitious plans, plans that he kept to himself. He was going to bring the courtroom to its feet.

When Alexandrov finally stood up and prepared to question his selected witnesses, the courtroom shook off its torpor. Aware of his reputation as a consummate defense attorney, those in the galleries watched him with eager curiosity, hoping he would inject some drama into the so far disappointing proceedings. As if reading the eager faces of the crowd, he immediately provided them with the drama they desired, no less than a kind of spectacle in three acts.

In the first act, Alexandrov introduced a fascinating cast of witnesses for the defense. All four were radicals and former political prisoners. Their appearance was appropriate for their parts: They were dressed simply, in obviously worn clothing. Many remembered them as having pale, thin faces etched with traces of their incarceration, and some were under the impression that they were still imprisoned and arrived directly from jail.[54]

They were not asked to testify about Vera. Indeed, most of them had never met her. Instead, they were called to perform a different role. They were to transform the victim, Fedor Trepov, into a ruthless and cunning villain.

The first witness, Nikolai Petropavlovskii, set the tone. Standing in the witness box, pale-faced and grim, he looked as if he were suffering under the weight of some terrible agitation. Alexandrov asked him a simple question:

Could he give an account of what took place on July 13, 1877, in the House of Preliminary Detention? Petropavlovskii obligingly told his tale. Through Petropavlovskii's eyes, the public relived every moment of the confrontation between Trepov and Bogoliubov, right up to the final climactic moment, when Trepov, shouting "Cap off!" swung at Bogoliubov. "The cap fell off his head," Petropavlovskii told the court in troubled tones. "He grabbed at it and just managed to put it back on, when the governor stepped toward him and took another swing at him. At that moment, I was in such an agitated state that I did not see whether he knocked the cap off his head again. Shortly thereafter, Bogoliubov was led away to the refractory cell."

"What caused the uproar among the prisoners?" asked Alexandrov gently.

"When they saw that last incident, when the governor knocked the cap off of Bogoliubov's head, then there was a collective cry of indignation."[55]

After Petropavlovskii stepped down, there was no doubt: Trepov was nothing more than a petty police tyrant, who could torment his victims on a whim.

The second witness, Sergei Goloushev, looked, if anything, more pale and sickly than the first. Arrested in 1874 when he was only nineteen, he had spent nearly four years imprisoned in the House of Preliminary Detention. As if in mockery, in the Trial of the 193 he was sentenced to five days in jail. His published memoirs later detailed his prison years with a kind of cheerful good humor. But his account on the witness stand was dramatic and painful. Like Petropavlovskii, Goloushev fixated on the moment when Trepov attacked Bogoliubov and on the general indignation that instantly swept through the prison. "When the shouting abated," he told the court, "Kurneev appeared in the courtyard and declared that Bogoliubov would be flogged." In an attempt at wry humor, he added, "Perhaps he wished to calm the prisoners." But his voice cracked under the strain of the remembered emotion, and he involuntarily let out a sob. Trying to regain control, he quietly apologized to the court. "Perhaps I am interjecting too much emotion into this tale."

Koni asked him to take some time to calm himself.

Finally, after a few breaths, Goloushev continued, with difficulty. "A general shriek of indignation rose up," he said, quickly wiping away tears, "the kind of indignation understood only by those who have experienced incarceration."

Goloushev concluded his tale by acknowledging that he did not personally hear Bogoliubov being flogged, since he had been thrust into one of the refractory cells. But other prisoners later told him terrible things about the punishment. "I heard that they planned to flog him in the courtyard, in full view of all the prisoners, but then for some reason changed their minds. Instead, they decided to do it in the corridor, so that the sound of the screams and the whistle of the birches could be heard by all."[56]

Gooushev's testimony caused a murmur among the spectators. Trepov, it seemed, was not the only villain in the story. The whole prison system seemed populated with sadistic officials who took perverse glee in abusing their helpless victims.

Anna Charushina, the final witness, confirmed this in her climactic testimony. Charushina had also spent four years in prison, only to be acquitted of all charges in the Trial of the 193. She spoke softly, in a trembling voice, and her entire demeanor was of a woman whose nerves were frayed by her years of suffering. Her wan face looked sad, and she spoke quietly, almost with effort. On July 13, 1877, Charushina had not witnessed the confrontation between Trepov and Bogoliubov. She had observed something far more terrible.

"In front of our windows," she told the court, "in the courtyard, stood two large sheds. All of a sudden, the shed doors were opened, and enormous bundles of birch rods were carried out and tied together. It was clear that they were getting ready. . . . They were preparing something awful, everyone started to guess—it was a punishment . . ."

She stopped. Though she tried to continue, she could not find her voice. Tears dripped from her eyes. Finally, she whispered, "I can't help but be upset at the memory . . ."

Koni urged calm. Charushina struggled for her voice. "As they were binding the rods," she said, "the guards turned to our windows and began making abusive gestures toward us and toward the men's section . . ."

Again she stopped, consumed by emotion. Koni turned to her and gently asked, "Did this give rise to unrest or clamor in the women's section?"

"Yes," Charushina replied, nodding. "The noise was extraordinary. Some demanded that the prison administration come and explain what it all meant, but no one came. In my opinion, the distress was natural, expressed in a manner that only a prisoner can express it."[57]

By the time Charushina left, a few women were seen surreptitiously dabbing at their eyes. *The Voice*'s editor and correspondent, Grigorii Gradovskii, recalled that the public in the courtroom experienced a kind of collective outrage that Russian officials and ordinary guards could so maliciously and brazenly participate in outright torture. He claimed that the sentiment was universal: Russia had rushed to save the Balkan Slavs from Turkish atrocities but had failed to see the mote in its own eye. Elizabeth Naryshkin, a noblewoman present in the galleries, admitted that the testimony "made me lower my eyes in shame."[58]

Konstantin Kessel, observing the reactions in the courtroom, felt his case spinning out of his control. To temper the damage, he asked the prison warden, Fedor Kurneev, to return to the witness stand. "You were questioned by judicial investigators regarding the riots in the House of Preliminary Detention?"

"Yes," Kurneev answered.

"In what capacity?"

"There was a complaint lodged against me."

"As a suspect?"

"Yes."[59]

It was a shrewd ploy. Kessel was trying to show that Trepov's brutalities, far from being condoned by the state, were being investigated. Vera's gunshot had interrupted the normal course of justice. For a moment, the public was collectively convinced that the trial had taken a sudden turn. "Everyone forgot," one observer declared, "about Alexandrov."[60]

Before these thoughts had a chance to settle, Alexandrov swiftly cross-examined the major. He asked him about the charges against him.

"The political prisoners complained that I ordered them to be beaten," Kurneev answered easily, almost carelessly.

"When was that?"

"After they were taken to the isolation chambers."

"So the investigation had nothing to do with the punishment of Bogoliubov?"

"No," Kurneev answered, "nothing at all," as if the idea were absurd.

Alexandrov allowed himself a caustic smile. "I have nothing further," he said sarcastically.[61] The first act was over.

～

But where is the accused? On the defendant's bench sits a young, pleasant-looking girl. She is a brunette, of average height, with a modest hairstyle, and a modest black dress. Her intelligent brown eyes glow with warmth, goodness. Her remarkable soul sparkles in that gaze. The pale, thin lines of her face bear the traces of spiritual travail and physical suffering. They say she is the accused. But a strange thing occurs. As the trial wears on, as the

drama in the court grows larger and more complicated, the face of the ac-
cused begins to disappear. I fall into some sort of hallucination. . . .

It appears to me, that she is not on trial, but rather I, all of us—society
is on trial. It seems to me that the witnesses expose who we are, that the
prosecutor's summation is a weak, polite attempt to defend us in this court-
room, and that the scalding summation of the defense, with blow upon blow,
like a hammer on an anvil, shatters our chances for acquittal.

— GRIGORII GRADOVSKII, *The Voice*, April 2, 1878[62]

In Alexandrov's second act, Vera herself took the stand. The courtroom, like a theater audience, prepared for her performance: Throats were cleared, people shifted in their seats, and, as one reporter put it, "everyone pricked up their ears." When she finally took the stand, the silence was so complete that Vera's thin, shy voice was clearly audible throughout the courthouse.

Alexandrov's effort to make Vera into a society lady had completely failed. She did not wear the elegant cloak he had purchased for her but rather a simple and worn black dress. Her hair was arranged in schoolgirl style. Nonetheless, in this respect, Vera's instincts were better than her lawyer's. The courtroom instantly took to the unpretentious, modest young woman whose mannerisms were those of a quiet nun. She was reluctant to speak and kept her eyes downcast, as if to avoid the stares of the public. She looked like someone inadvertently swept into a tale of brutality and violence—more victim than villain.[63]

In a hushed voice, in simple terms, she tried to explain her actions. She had read about the flogging of Bogoliubov in a newspaper and heard other stories about the incident, including details of the prison riot, the beatings, and the isolation chambers. "I know from personal experience," Vera told the jury, "how long years spent in isolation can lead to terrible nervous strain. . . . I could vividly imagine the hellish effects of the punishment on all of the prisoners, not to mention those who suffered flogging, beatings, and the refractory cells. What kind of cruelty was necessary to make all of them suffer these things, all on account of failing to doff a cap?"

Vera waited for the crime to receive its just punishment. But nothing happened. "Nothing would stop Trepov, or anyone equally powerful, from committing such violence again and again—since it is so easy to forget to doff one's hat, and so easy to find some other, similar weak excuse for a terrible reprisal."

Though she fought hard against them, Vera too succumbed to tears.

"Then, when I could not find any other way, I decided, at the cost of my own life, to prove that no one should be sure they are beyond punishment when they violate human dignity." She stopped, unable to continue. Someone brought her water, and then she finally was able to pronounce the words that were so often quoted after her trial: "I saw no other way. . . . It is terrible to raise one's hand against another human being, but I felt that I was obligated to do it."[64]

Vera was clearly upset and obviously deeply felt what she had spoken. There was no hint of staged emotion in her words or her demeanor. Her feelings were real; her thoughts, as she expressed them, were truly her thoughts. Hearts melted at the sight of her tear-stained face.[65]

But though she won public approbation, Vera must have felt a deep sting of conscience. The court saw her as someone she never wanted to be: an emotional, lonely young woman who killed a man out of quiet desperation born of personal tragedy. Her testimony had stripped her of all her years of self-education, all her deepest convictions about the injustice of the present world order and the promise of the world to come. Her attack on Trepov was meant to signal a new revolutionary movement, one that would terrorize the state and energize rebellion. And yet, in a crowded courtroom, Vera merely suggested that she was a confused girl who, in her hysteria, had identified with the suffering of a man she never met and decided to shoot an official who had never harmed her in any way.

Her doubts surfaced when she tried to narrate details about her own life. She often had to stop, confused. At one point she told the judge, "I related my biography to my attorney. Perhaps he should tell it to the court." In effect, she had trouble remembering what she was supposed to say. She had desired, all her life, to become a martyr for her deeply held beliefs. Her testimony was supposed to be, instead, that of a helpless victim pleading for mercy. As she stepped down from the witness stand, she heard the judge say: "Mr. Assistant Prosecutor, you have the floor." Finally, the trial was entirely out of her hands.[66]

Nearly 130 years later, the text of Kessel's closing statement reads like a crafted, well-reasoned, and entirely convincing account of Vera's guilt. In Kessel's summation, all of the theatrics of the case evaporated. Cold, deliberate logic remained, and it pointed, inexorably, to a murder conviction. Vera had planned her crime with malice aforethought. She had bought one of the most powerful revolvers available, a six-chamber English Bulldog, and loaded all six chambers. Knowing the power of the weapon she had chosen, she had nonetheless waited until she was standing mere steps away from her victim. Cleverly, she kept the revolver hidden underneath the shawl as she aimed and fired, so that Trepov's guards, standing quite close to her, would not have time to knock the gun out of her hand. Then she aimed one shot right into his abdomen. She might have testified that she had not cared whether she killed or merely wounded the old general, but it was impossible to imagine that she expected him to remain alive.[67]

As for Vera's motives for the crime, Kessel argued it was not his place to judge them. Trepov was not on trial in the courtroom, and the jury was not called upon to pronounce the victim guilty or innocent. Moreover, Kessel refused to challenge Vera's account of her own feelings. "I fully believe," he told the court, "that the facts that she presented as the motives of her actions really did appear to her in the light she has described. I also accept those emotions, which she described to us." Vera might have decided that Trepov deserved punishment, and she did what she thought was right. But her feelings were not at issue. A courtroom was not the place to adjudicate the legitimacy of emotions. A court had to judge actions. "Every person," Kessel explained, "is free to love or hate whomever they choose, but no one is free to violate another's rights."

Vera may have wished to "prevent acts which, in her mind, were harmful to society." And there was no doubt, Kessel affirmed, "that every person is obliged to help society to progress." But there was also no doubt that "not one person has the right to elevate their own personal conviction into a judicial sentence." Kessel's conclusion was powerful in its simplicity. Vigilante justice could not go unpunished. Society would not survive if every person with a grievance was allowed to resolve disputes with a gun. In a country governed by laws, judges and juries must decide guilt or innocence. In what should have been a memorable moment, Kessel stated powerfully that "I am fully convinced that you will agree that every person in society, whoever he is, has the right to a court of law, and not to the court of Zasulich."

With an involuntary prescience, Kessel warned the court: "I am convinced you will agree that social life and social organization is impossible in a place where social activists, administrators, judges, local officials, and publicists always have to keep in mind that, whatever they might do, they can expect a gun to be leveled at them." It was a plea for reason—a plea to recognize that one act of terror, if sanctioned or excused, could lead to more such acts down the line.

His pleas were ignored; no one was really listening. Kessel was a miserable orator: His voice was dry and cracked, and he could barely be heard in the galleries. Some thought that he looked unsure on his feet, as if he were about to faint.[68] In any case, the public had no interest in cold reason. They wanted emotion, passion, drama. And Alexandrov was about to give it to them, in spades. The time had come for his third and final act.

〜

We must pay attention to the particular characteristics of the moral nature of crimes against the state. The physiognomy of such crimes is often quite variable. That which yesterday was considered a crime against the state, today or tomorrow becomes a highly respected act of civic courage. State crimes are often just the untimely expressions of a doctrine of premature reform, the preaching of that which is not yet ripe and whose time has not yet come.

—PETER ALEXANDROV, summation, trial of Vera Zasulich[69]

Slowly, Alexandrov rose from his seat. Everyone expected some grand gesture, an oratorical pose. Instead, Alexandrov was calm, almost introspective. "Gentlemen of the jury!" he said gently. "I have heard the noble, moderate summation of the assistant prosecutor, and I am completely in agreement with much of what he said. We differ only in a few, small things." The remarks, as usual, seemed almost unpracticed. They created the impression that Alexandrov was about to begin some quiet, informal conversation about the case, strictly among friends.

The effect was, in time, mesmerizing. He held his audience in a rapt attention.[70]

It was true, Alexandrov argued, that the bare facts of the case weighed against his client. If one merely looked at the events of January 24, then the "matter was so simple, there would be almost no reason to discuss it." Vera's act would be one of "vigilante justice." But Alexandrov's purpose was to widen the perspective of the audience and fill in points left unspoken. Before the events of January 24, 1878, Alexandrov told the jurors, came the events of July 13, 1877, and the two dates were inextricably linked. If Bogoliubov had not been flogged, Trepov would not have been shot.

And before July 13, 1877, Vera's life was driving her, inexorably, into helplessness and despair. Kessel, Alexandrov explained, was fundamentally wrong about how to assess the nature of a crime. Some acts, he argued, could not be understood in a strictly legal sense. Some acts had to be judged on motives alone. Vera's state of mind was not some incidental detail but rather the essence of her innocence or guilt. She had to be judged, he explained, for who she was. And so the court had to hear the story of Vera's life.

On the surface, Alexandrov merely followed the prearranged blueprint. He did not even hint at Vera's radical beliefs and told a very simple story about her life, stripped of its most important elements. Nowhere in his biography of Vera did he mention the fervent teenage nihilist, the woman tempted by Nechaev's revolutionary passion, the angry prisoner tormented by the Russian regime, and finally the rebel and terrorist who had spent months at target practice preparing for the day of revolution. In their place appeared a naive, innocent victim, a woman whose whole life was mapped by others.

When she met Nechaev, Alexandrov stated, Vera was merely seventeen years old. She had no idea that the cunning revolutionary was anything other than a "simple student, who played some role in student protests." She agreed to do him a "very ordinary favor" and pass on a few letters to his friends. She never even knew the contents of the incriminating letters she received from him. To her terrible surprise, Nechaev turned out to be a criminal mastermind, and she was entangled in his plots. The regime took no pity on her age and her innocence. She was coldly thrust into prison.

Alexandrov, in hushed, lyrical tones, asked the public to imagine themselves in such a circumstance. "For a young woman, the years of her youth are the years of blossoming, of development," Alexandrov poetically explained. "No longer a child, but as yet free of the responsibilities of a wife and a mother, a young girl lives full of joy, with a full heart. This is the age of first love, free of care, of cheerful hopes, of unforgettable joys; the age of friendships." Quietly, ominously, Alexandrov's tone grew darker. "It is easy to imagine," he intoned, "how Zasulich spent these best years of her life, with what games, with what joys she spent that precious time, what sweet dreams troubled her behind the walls of the Lithuanian Castle and in the towers of the Peter and Paul Fortress." For two years, she saw no one, neither her mother nor family nor friends. The walls stared back at her, and she had nothing but "foul air, little exercise, terrible dreams, bad meals."

In those two years alone, Vera developed one strong, unshakeable sentiment: a profound sympathy for her fellow sufferers. "A political prisoner, whoever he was, became her best friend, a comrade of her youth, a comrade of her upbringing. The prison was her alma mater."

Even after her release from prison, Vera's suffering continued. She was relentlessly persecuted by the tsarist police; her life became a nightmare. She was taken suddenly, without warning, into exile, to the town of Kresttsy. Behold the cruelty of the authorities, Alexandrov said, with a gesture toward Vera: With nothing but a thin coat on her back, a ruble in her pocket, and a small box of chocolates, she was declared free to fend for herself. She might have starved to death, were it not for the generosity of a local family who agreed to take her in. After a few months, she was sent back to her own family, only to be snatched away once more and again sent into exile, this time to Soligalich. Only after six long years, in 1875, was she declared free to go.

She decided to live a quiet life with her sister's family on a Penza provincial estate. It was there, Alexandrov concluded in the first part of his speech, that Vera learned the story of Bogoliubov.[71]

In the courtroom, the story had the desired effect. It was an eloquent cautionary tale about the tyranny of the tsarist regime and the ease with which the government authorities could crush innocent and unsuspecting victims. It was a story perfectly pitched to elicit the sympathies of St. Petersburg's liberal society. Muffled sobs were heard in the galleries, and even some men were seen wiping tears from their eyes. Vera herself bowed her head, perhaps overcome by Alexandrov's retelling of her sad tale, or perhaps unwilling to watch as he forced her into a persona she had long rejected.[72]

After a sip of water, Alexandrov abruptly switched his tone from melancholic musing to biting irony. "Please allow me . . . ," he told the courtroom, in a tone of sharp sarcasm, "to make a small digression into the topic of flogging." Alexandrov reassured his audience that he did not wish to bore them with a long tale of the birch rod. Rather, he said lightly, he would turn to "the last days of its life."

There was a time, he explained, when the rod ruled Russia. Its "melodious bell" was heard everywhere, at least until that fateful day of April 17, 1863, when "the rod passed into the realm of history." Deftly, alliteration rolled off Alexandrov's tongue. "At that time there were many concerns about the full extinction of flogging. . . . It seemed somehow unnerving and unsafe to leave Russia without the rod. . . . Was it possible to be suddenly bereft of the cement of Russia's social foundation?"

Alexandrov's irony gradually subsided into pensiveness. With the abolition of corporal punishment, he said quietly, came a new Russian sense of human dignity. That which had been a sentence borne without complaint was now a shameful violation of an individual's honor. Especially the most educated, most civilized, and therefore most sensitive members of Russian society were now appalled by the very notion of a flogging.

Bogoliubov was such a man. He was no ordinary criminal and could not be classed along with "thieves and murderers." He was a political activist, a man of refined moral sensibilities. He was educated, cultured, and horrified by the very idea of violence. But the penal system made no distinctions. Bogoliubov was deprived of his civil rights and sentenced to exile, thus rendered eligible for corporal punishment. Such was the cold rationality of the law. But anyone with a spark of human feeling would realize that such a punishment, for such a person, was nothing more than a "violation of his moral dignity."

And Vera was a woman with more than just a spark of human feeling.

"Who was Bogoliubov to Vera?" Alexandrov asked. "He was neither her relative nor her friend. He was not her acquaintance; she never laid eyes on him and did not know him. But is it really necessary to be a sister, a wife, or a lover in order to be filled with anger at the sight of a morally crushed man, to be indignant because of the shameful mockery of a helpless person?"

Insistently, Alexandrov was building to the climax of his summation. The audience was tense with expectation as he told of how Vera read about the Bogoliubov incident in the paper, how she was overcome with "bitter memories of her own suffering," and how her excitable imagination overcame her. "In her feminine, exalted mind an image of Bogoliubov arose," Alexandrov declared, "of a man submitting to a degrading punishment."

In a rhetorical coup de theatre, Alexandrov described just how Vera imagined Bogoliubov's torturous punishment:

Behold him, brought to the place of execution and devastated by the knowledge of the shame that awaited him. Behold him, full of indignation, thinking that the strength of this indignation would give him the strength of Samson, to stand his ground in his battle with the lictors, the executors of his punishment. Behold him, crushed under the weight of human bodies that pinned his shoulders, spread out on the floor, shamefully stripped of his clothing, enchained by a few pairs of hands as if by iron, deprived of all ability to resist. And above him—the measured whistle of the birches, as the noble administrators of the punishment meted out the blows. Everything grew quiet in the anxious expectation of a cry; the cry was heard. It was not a cry of pain—they expected more—it was the tortured cry of a suffocated, humiliated, desecrated, and crushed man. The solemn rite was performed, the disgraceful sacrifice was accomplished![73]

Without warning, the public in the galleries erupted. All around the room wild applause, cheers, and shouts of "Bravo!" sounded. The audience was captivated. It was something no one had experienced at a Russian trial before. The crowd forgot they were in a courtroom.[74]

Anatolii Koni was incensed. He was deeply affronted by this transformation of the trial into a spectacle. "The behavior of the public should reflect a respect for the court!" he shouted over the din. "The court is not a theater, and expressions of approval or disapproval are forbidden here. One more time, and I will be forced to clear this room!"[75]

When everyone had quieted, Alexandrov continued as if nothing had happened. But he was by no means done with his theatrics. It was time to conclude the summation and return to Vera, the innocent victim of fate. Her heart was aflame; her mind reeled. She suffered for another, and suffered keenly. But from her pain was born a new determination, a new strength of character. The events of July 13, 1877, changed Vera forever.

In the months after she read the article, she tormented herself with thoughts of Bogoliubov's humiliation. An almost holy question arose: "Who will stand up for the tattered dignity of the helpless prisoner? Who would cleanse and redeem his shame?" Vera waited for someone to step forward to avenge Bogoliubov's honor. But no hero appeared. The press wrote nothing, public opinion grew quiet, and the law remained mute. The incident was fading from view, and Bogoliubov was fast becoming another anonymous victim of tsarist oppression.

"And suddenly," Alexandrov exclaimed, "an unexpected thought, like a lightning bolt, flashed through Zasulich's mind: 'And I? . . . A cry is needed, and I have breath in my lungs to let out such a cry. I will cry out and force everyone to hear!'"

Vera's gunshot was not a violent act—it was a shout against the silence, an exclamation of outrage. There was no premeditation, no real plan of action, merely the agitated thoughts of an "excitable, sentimental soul." Vera did not reason; she was like an artist or an "inspired" poet, who chooses words and rhythm but never allows cold reason to quell his exaltation.

The prosecutor had portrayed Vera as a coldblooded woman bent on revenge. "Revenge," however, was an ill-chosen word. Revenge was personal and petty. Vera acted nobly, for someone she did not know. She did not care what happened to Trepov, and cared still less what happened to her. Her gunshot was a highly symbolic act of protest against all of Russian society. She wanted to declare before Europe and all the world that even in Russia, people believed in "moral honor and dignity."

Once she fired her shot, Alexandrov concluded, she dropped the revolver. "Her song was sung, her idea incarnated, her act accomplished." And now, her fate was in the hands of the court.

Many women had come before this court: women who had killed their seducers, their unfaithful lovers, their luckier rivals. And many of them had been acquitted. The jury, in each of these cases, understood that it was but a pale imitation of that higher, divine court of law, where justice is always tempered with mercy. If such women had been granted ultimate clemency, why not Vera? If bitter shame and jealous rage were mitigating motives, why not a love for humanity?

Vera herself did not care whether she was acquitted or convicted. She was, in this respect, the perfect martyr. "When she stepped over the threshold of the governor's residence," Alexandrov assured his listeners, "she knew and understood that she would sacrifice everything—her freedom, the rest of her shattered life, everything fate had left to her." She was on trial not because she wished to be acquitted but to make a full confession and unburden herself before the jury, and thus make her sacrifice complete.

Alexandrov left the jurors with a parting thought: "Without reproach, without bitter complaint, without insult, she will accept your decision. . . . She might leave this place convicted but she will not leave defeated. We can only hope that similar incidents will never again occur, instigating similar crimes and inspiring similar criminals."[76]

After Alexandrov sat back down, a stunned silence reigned in the court. His final act had accomplished his purpose and turned the trial on its head. Vera, the accused, no longer appeared as the defendant in the trial. In her place, Trepov and the Russian state that employed him stood in the dock. In the world that Alexandrov had conjured for his listeners, the state regime stood defiant in its violations of human rights, and the public remained silent in the face of state crimes. In such a world, it was inevitable that sensitive souls, trembling with indignation, would take the law into their own hands, to ensure that evil was punished and innocence was redeemed. As Grigorii

Gradovskii of *The Voice* wildly told his readers: Society was to blame. Society was indifferent to Vera's youthful plight, and it was silent in the face of Bogoliubov's flogging. "We forced her to raise her hand against another," he concluded dramatically. "Do we now have the right to punish her?"[77]

Vera watched Alexandrov with wide eyes, entranced by his account of her mental state, her motives, and her actions. And with good reason. Masterfully, he had managed to transform her socialist vision into a set of simple, palatable ideas sweetened for popular consumption. He critiqued the state and its tyrannical behavior, he critiqued society and its indifference, and he declared, almost openly, that those who now preached crimes against the state would later become society's most cherished heroes. He had transformed an ordinary victim of circumstance into a determined martyr for human dignity—a woman who would sacrifice her life for the sake of a more just, more humane world.[78]

Perhaps her moment was finally at hand. Perhaps she could now end her life in the martyrdom of her dreams.

Anatolii Koni had the final word. Judges in the Russian courtroom were permitted, in their instructions to the jury, to give a kind of summation of their own, in which they weighed the arguments of the prosecutor and defense attorney and presented counter-arguments. It was an extraordinarily powerful tool and could easily sway the jurors' judgment. Koni did his best to calm the passions aroused by Alexandrov and inject a dose of reason into the proceedings.[79]

The first question the jury had to answer, Koni explained, was, "Do you find before you an individual who is responsible for his actions?" Koni decisively told the jury that this was not a debatable question. She was of age, she was mentally competent, and though the defense emphasized Vera's nervous agitation, it never proved that this nervousness "darkened her mind."

But a second question was far more difficult to answer and proved central to determining whether a crime had been committed. The jury had to determine "the goal and intention of the accused." The fact of the shot and the wound was not in question. But its significance was. Simply put, did Vera intend to kill Trepov? The defense declared that she did not, that her aim was merely to shoot at him "to raise the issue of restoring the honor of Bogoliubov and of investigating the true character of the events of July 13." But Koni rhetorically dismantled this explanation, asking very simply, "Is shooting someone with a revolver and at a distance from which it is difficult to miss the only, unavoidable means of doing so?" And if a social ill is diagnosed, is a "criminal act" the only available medicine?

The final question, Koni informed the jury, was of premeditation. Here too, the judge carefully undermined the arguments of the defense. A crime of passion, he explained, was not a crime committed in anger or agitation. It was a crime committed "in a sudden rage, which fully overwhelms a person." Whenever circumstances permitted "the possibility of reconsidering, turning back, or reflecting, there the law sees the conditions of premeditation." Clearly, Koni implied, Vera had plenty of time to plan and consider her actions.

Finally, Koni asked the jury to cast aside emotion and consider the "facts." Only the facts would lead to a reasonable outcome for the trial. "If the facts are thrown aside, then every conclusion appears arbitrary and deprived of meaning." It was a plea for reason and dispassionate analysis. Pity for the accused had its place, but it resided in the realm of mitigating circumstances. If the jury felt compelled to take into account Vera's difficult life, her emotional state, and the terrible actions perpetrated on an innocent prisoner, then they could recommend leniency.[80]

In the spirit of his summation, Koni handed the jury three questions composed with compromise in mind:

1). Is Captain's daughter Vera Zasulich, 29 years of age, guilty of deciding to revenge herself on the St. Petersburg Governor, General-Adjutant Trepov, for the punishment of the prisoner Bogoliubov, of acquiring a revolver to that end, and of causing serious injury to General-Adjutant Trepov by shooting him in the pelvis, with previously formulated intent, with a large caliber bullet from the revolver brought for that purpose?

2). If Zasulich committed the act described in the first question, did she, in that instance, intend to take the life of Gen. Adj. Trepov?

3). If the accused did intend to take the life of Gen. Adj. Trepov, did she do everything in her power to accomplish her aim, and was the death of Gen. Adj. Trepov prevented only by circumstances independent of Zasulich?[81]

Koni was pleased with these formulations. He thought they were carefully designed to guide the jury toward a moderate compromise. Ever the liberal centrist, he did not wish the case to result in an extreme outcome, either by sentencing Vera to exile and hard labor for life or by acquitting her and allowing a confessed criminal to go free. If the jurors said yes to the first question and found Vera guilty of intending to harm Trepov, then, in their answers to the next two questions, they could suggest either that she did not intend to kill him or that, if she did, she did not do everything possible to ensure his death resulted. And finally, even if they answered yes to all three questions, then they could suggest leniency, as Koni recommended. In any case, justice would be served. A would-be assassin would be convicted of some crime, sending the message that society did not tolerate vigilante justice and terrorism. But Vera would be lightly punished, and the state would be free from any charges of tyrannical behavior in her case. The Russian judicial system would seem reasonable and moderate, living up to its newly liberalized and European ideal.

Koni handed the questions to the foreman, who led the jurors out of the room for deliberations. Then he declared a recess, stepped down from the bench, and retired to his office. He was exhausted but satisfied. He had done his best.[82]

After Koni finished his instructions, the mood in the courtroom sobered. The exalted, electric atmosphere that followed Alexandrov's speech died down, and most of the faces in the galleries were gloomy. During the recess, as crowds mingled in the courtroom and in the corridors, experienced lawyers who had watched the trial shook their heads. The consensus suggested that Vera would be convicted. The only hope left, it seemed, was for leniency. The jurors might be willing to compromise and consider her "half-guilty." Gradovskii remembered how Dostoyevsky, who had carefully taken notes during the trial, was convinced of Vera's innocence. "She should not be convicted, and punishment is inappropriate, superfluous; but one wishes one could say to her 'go, and do not do that again.'" Presciently, he added, "It seems that we do not have such a judicial formula, and for all I know, she will now become a heroine."[83]

Though it seemed to some like an eternity, the jury only deliberated for thirty minutes. Then the bell rang from the deliberation room, signaling that the jurors had reached their verdict. A furious crush ensued as all the spectators rushed to return to their seats. Some did not make it and had to stand in the doorways or aisles. Without waiting for everyone to be seated, Koni entered and loudly called for order. The jury solemnly filed in and took their places, their expressions inscrutable.

The crowd suddenly grew absolutely quiet, as if all of the observers were holding their breath. The foreman slowly handed Koni the list of questions, with separate verdicts written on each page. As the juror resumed his place, Koni, with preternatural deliberation, looked at the first page of the list, then mechanically turned it over and looked at the second page.

Impassively, wordlessly, he handed the list back to the jury. The foreman, as was required by law, read out the first question in its entirety and at a maddeningly snail-like pace, lingering over every word: "Is Captain's daughter Vera Zasulich, 29 years of age, guilty of deciding to revenge herself on the St. Petersburg Governor, General-Adjutant Trepov, for the punishment of the prisoner Bogoliubov, of acquiring a revolver to that end, and of causing serious injury to General-Adjutant Trepov by shooting him in the pelvis, with previously formulated intent, with a large caliber bullet from the revolver brought for that purpose?"

Hearts were beating faster and faster. Anxious faces leaned forward to see the foreman's face, hoping to divine some early clue to the verdict.

Finally, in a clear voice that filled the whole room, he thundered: "No! Not—"

He did not get past the "Not." As if on cue, the entire courtroom exploded. The moment was later declared "indescribable"—as if an "electric current" had swept through the public. Every person was on his or her feet, clapping, laughing, cheering. Shouts were heard everywhere—"Bravo!" and "Long live the jury!" People who did not know each other embraced as if they were long-lost friends and shouted, "Congratulations!" Gradovskii remembered finding himself in the arms of an old general, who began to yell in his ear, though nothing could be heard over the din. Behind the judges' bench, the tsar's dignitaries broke with their usual decorum and joined in the jubilation. Koni was particularly surprised that the round, red-faced old Count Barantsov began to jump up and down in front of his chair. When he met Koni's eyes he sheepishly stopped, but resumed his excited dance after Koni's back was turned.

For a time, Koni quixotically rang his bell to restore order. Soon enough, he gave up. There was nothing to do but wait for the public to quiet down of their own accord. And so the three judges on the bench sat, as Koni wryly described it, "unmoving and silent, like Roman senators during the invasion of the Gauls."[84]

The only other person sitting quietly was Vera herself. She was stunned, unsure of what to do next. Dozens of people surrounded her, shouting their congratulations, but she acted as if she heard nothing. Koni looked at her in pity and gently said, through the bedlam, "You are acquitted." He instructed her to go back to the prison to collect her things, hoping to briefly spare her from the uncontrolled hysteria of the crowd surrounding her.

Silently, she followed the guards out through the underground passage-way and into the House of Preliminary Detention. In deference to the ver-dict, the swords of the gendarmes were now sheathed.[85]

CHAPTER 11

The Turn to Terror

~~~

By seven o'clock in the evening, the crowd in front of the courthouse had swelled to unheard-of proportions. By some estimates, more than a thousand people had massed along Liteinyi Prospekt, pressing against the gates of the courthouse and craning to see beyond the wall of police barring entry into the building. Many had stood there since the early morning, their agitation accumulating with each passing hour. Others had embarked on long journeys from the outskirts of the city, hoping to arrive in time for the announcement of the verdict.[1]

Finally, the acquittal came. The doors of the court building flew open, and ecstatic spectators poured out of the courthouse. Accosted by the agitated crowd, they answered happily: "She was acquitted. . . . No, not guilty!" The news quickly flowed through the throng. Caps sailed into the air, and spontaneous cheers erupted: "Hurray! Vera! Verochka!" Complete strangers embraced one another, shouting out random congratulations. When Alexandrov, serenely unaware of the mood of the crowd, calmly stepped out the doors of the building, he found himself suddenly lifted off his feet. Borne on the shoulders of the crowd, he was applauded and cheered. Hundreds pressed forward to shake his hand.[2]

Above the scene, from his office in the courthouse, Koni observed the celebrations with growing alarm.[3] As he watched, a paltry group of about thirty gendarmes vainly tried to form a cordon to block the crowd from turning onto Shpalernaia Street, where the entrance gates of the House of Preliminary Detention were located. But the masses would not be prevented—they wanted to greet the heroine of the day. Soon, the cordon broke, and in a rush, hundreds of people stampeded toward the gates of the prison.

Koni was seized with anxiety. He could predict what was about to happen. Vera would be set free and left to the mercy of her gathering well-wishers. She would be lifted up on the shoulders of her adoring fans, and the procession would degenerate into a wild demonstration. Overwhelmed by sheer numbers, the police would panic and overreact. Bloodshed could result.

In an instant, the solution flashed through Koni's mind. What if she were to be let out through the alternate exit on Zakharevskaia Street, through doors that were normally kept locked? She could be whisked away in a carriage; someone could announce that she had already left the building. The energy of the crowd would dissipate on its own, and the police would never need to step in.

Koni needed to find someone with authority over prison officials to give the order for this alternate plan of action—someone from the prosecutor's office. He began to run through the corridors, looking for help, but was told that everyone had left the building. In desperation, he sought out the St. Petersburg chief of police, Trepov's right-hand man, Adrian Dvorzhitskii. He met the handsome but blank-faced young chief in the corridor. Koni hurriedly explained the situation and then appealed to Dvorzhitskii's sense of duty: "It is your responsibility to prevent a riot, whose dimensions we cannot even predict." Dvorzhitskii smiled wanly and bowed, his expression inscrutable. "Rest assured, Your Honor," Dvorzhitskii said politely, "our duty is to avert disturbances."

Koni stared at Dvorzhitskii for a moment, unsure of his intentions. Then he shrugged—he had done his best. He gathered his hat and coat and finally left the building, pushing his way through the remaining bystanders. As he turned down Liteinyi Prospekt and headed toward Nevskii, a man in a medical coat, breathless with excitement, grabbed Koni and demanded, "Would you mind telling me, were you at the trial? Do you know how the matter ended?"

"The trial is over. Zasulich is acquitted," Koni answered tersely.

"Really? Acquitted? My God!" The man's face lit up. Unexpectedly, the stranger wrapped his arms tightly around Koni, planted his lips on Koni's cheek, and, just as suddenly, released him and ran off.

Shaking his head, Koni continued on his way. He hoped that he had seen the last of the Zasulich affair.

Koni did not know that the chief prosecutor, Alexander Lopukhin, was about to give the Prelim prison warden, Mikhail Fedorov, very different advice. Fedorov met Lopukhin in the courthouse after the trial and informed the prosecutor that Vera had returned to prison to collect her things. As if passing along an informal suggestion, Lopukhin quietly told Fedorov that he should delay Vera's release "until further written notice." As Fedorov slowly walked back toward the prison, contemplating this "advice," he was accosted by

Dvorzhitskii, who impassively conveyed Koni's "secret" plan. The confusion of the moment was almost comical.[4]

When he reached the prison, Fedorov offered Vera some tea. He needed time to think. Neither of the suggestions he had received seemed appropriate. Vera was an acquitted woman, and there was no reason to hold her any further. As for spiriting her away through a separate exit—this too seemed unsound. It violated protocol and might have unforeseen consequences. Angry rumors would spread that she was held against her will, hidden deep in the bowels of the prison.

As it turned out, the decision was made for Fedorov. While he was considering his options, some fifteen hundred people had gathered outside the gates of the prison. A full hour had passed since Vera's acquittal, and the crowd was getting impatient, even angry. Soon, shouts rose that made Fedorov's blood run cold: "Gentlemen! What are we waiting for! Can't we break through the gates and free Zasulich?" Deafening thumping and clanging could be heard. The crowd was attempting to force the gates open.[5]

Fedorov had no intention of facing the angry rabble. He ran to Vera's cell. "Vera Ivanovna," he practically shouted, "put your things together quickly and go. Don't you hear the clamor?" He led Vera to the gate, opened the enormous doors, and pushed her out.[6]

It must have been a terrifying moment, even for a heroine. There Vera stood, alone in front of the prison doors, clutching a small bag, facing a sea of anonymous well-wishers. There was no place to hide. Within seconds, a thunderous roar went up, and the crowd swarmed toward her, shouting congratulations. Hands hoisted her high above the masses, and from everywhere came shrieks of joy and cheers of "Long live Zasulich! Glory to Zasulich!"[7]

"Gentlemen! Put me down!" Vera shrieked in terror. "I'm falling! Let me go! Let me go!" Vera tried to brace herself, her hands landing on the heads of those who jostled around her. But those who carried Vera could not have let her go even if they tried. There was no space, and she easily might have been crushed underfoot.

Soon enough, a few sympathetic individuals took pity on her. Voices called out for a carriage. Sergei Goloushev, one of Alexandrov's witnesses, leaped to her aid. On Shpalernaia Street he saw a lone carriage idling, its driver improbably fast asleep at the reins. Goloushev jumped onto the box, grabbed the reins from the surprised driver, and drove the carriage right through the crowd, as onlookers dove out of the way. Invisible hands lifted

Vera into the carriage. Someone else grabbed the reins, and Goloushev jumped off, running alongside the carriage through the crowd.

Once in the carriage, Vera maintained a stunned silence. The driver, trying to escape the mob, turned the carriage down Voskresenskii Prospekt and headed toward Nevskii Prospekt. At that moment, an ordinary bystander was randomly chosen as Vera's companion, forcibly lifted into the carriage, and then thrown dozens of rubles to pay the cab fare. Abruptly, Vera's new companion found himself face-to-face with the dazed young woman, who looked almost as if she were about to faint. Quickly, the stranger did his best to fill his new role. "Where would you like to go?" he asked, hoping to direct the carriage.

"Perhaps you know best," came Vera's sole reply. The carriage continued its aimless, slow movement through the throngs, down Voskresenskii Prospekt.

Accounts of what happened next are conflicting. According to some witnesses, a line of policemen was seen heading toward the demonstrators. Some claimed that the police were on foot, wielding batons; others declared that they were on horseback, led by the handsome Dvorzhitskii, who, with his carefully trimmed hair and sideburns, apparently looked like Alexander II himself. Either way, police columns advanced, relentlessly, toward the masses.[8]

Dvorzhitskii himself later testified that his sole intention was to ensure Vera safe passage out of the violent crush. But Vera's well-wishers were seized with the suspicion that she was about to be rearrested. When Dvorzhitskii shouted for people to move away from the carriage, several men pulled in closer, to block the doors of the vehicle. As uniformed police waded through the crowd, violently thrusting people aside, many shoved back. Shouts and shrieks were heard as a melee broke out between the people and the police.

And then, out of nowhere, the crack of two gunshots resounded above the crowd.

A cry went up: "The police are shooting at us!" Pandemonium ensued as people ran to dodge the expected bullets. A policeman fell to the ground, a bullet lodged in the visor of his helmet. A woman shrieked and collapsed, clutching her chest. Eyewitnesses saw the police swinging their batons and a pregnant woman stumbling on a sidewalk, screaming, "They're trying to kill us!" Panicked, the crowd scattered down the side streets and alleyways.

In the chaos, the path cleared in front of Vera's carriage. The man in the driver's seat urged the horses on, and the vehicle dashed away, disappearing down a side street. Vera had finally escaped the police and the crowd. Within hours, Russia's celebrity of the day vanished without a trace.

One victim was left behind. A young man lay on the ground, the blood running from his left temple. His name was Grigorii Sidoratskii, and he was dead.

Many years later, St. Petersburg would become accustomed to such scenes. But in 1878, they were a shocking novelty. The demonstration after the trial, the battles with the police, and the death of Sidoratskii made for instant public scandal. News reports suggested horrifying police brutality. For those still reeling from the testimony in Vera's trial, the incident seemingly confirmed the lawlessness of the Russian regime. Rumors spread that a warrant had been issued for Vera's arrest and that the police were sleeplessly hunting her down. And sympathy went out to Sidoratskii, an apparently innocent victim of an enraged Russian gendarmerie.[9]

Only later, after eyewitness reports, medical examiner's notes, and the testimonies of the police were gathered, did the press report the definitive version of the events of March 31. The violence of the demonstrations was entirely due to a series of calamitous misadventures. Though an arrest warrant for Vera had been issued, it arrived long after the police had been dispatched to disperse the crowd. In fact, the police chief was tasked with restoring order and ensuring Vera's safety. None of the policemen had fired a weapon; all of the police guns on hand that day were found to be fully loaded. Experts revealed that the bullets extracted from the shoulder of the injured woman, the gendarme's helmet, and Sidoratskii's skull all came from a small-caliber six-chamber Smith & Wesson, which was not government issue. The only such weapon known to have been on the scene was Sidoratskii's own.

The remaining details of the story were so extraordinary that for years they were believed to be a police cover-up. But several eyewitnesses, including Vera herself, independently confirmed the facts. Sidoratskii, who was sitting on the box of Vera's carriage, became wildly agitated as the police began to surround her. He drew his gun and, in an attempt to defend her, fired two shots. One struck the policeman's helmet, but the other missed its target and hit the woman in the crowd. As the woman collapsed in pain, some feared that she was dead. Sidoratskii, by now hysterical, leaped from the carriage and fled down the street in the confusion.

Perhaps mortified that he had shot an innocent bystander, or perhaps simply overwhelmed by the agitation of the crowd, Sidoratskii stopped abruptly at a street corner. Standing calmly as others fled past him in panic, he slowly put the gun to his head and pulled the trigger.[10]

〜

Brutal tyranny and violence, in whatever form they appear, always trouble
the soul and unbearably oppress each and every one of us. He who lives by
the sword, dies by the sword. Whoever breaks the law places others outside
the law. This is especially true of those in power, and this served as the main
reason for the acquittal of Zasulich.

— ST. PETERSBURG REGISTER, April 1, 1878[11]

March 31, 1878, had all of the elements of a public sensation: a modest and gentle female assassin, rousing courtroom theatrics, a riot in the streets, a battle with the police, and a guiltless victim. The events of that day would arouse enormous public interest, fuel concern about police brutality and the Russian legal system, and aggravate Russian officialdom. The day would be seen, in future years, as a turning point in Russian history. And most important for Russia's newspapers, it would sell copy.

On the morning after the trial, the reading public was greeted with dozens of breathless articles reporting the events. Many newspapers devoted as much space to the riots after the trial as they did to the proceedings themselves. The coverage was sprinkled with superlatives. *The Week* declared: "In the chronicles of the Russian court there has not yet been a trial so important and so expressive, having such enormous significance and creating such a strong impression as the trial of Vera Zasulich." The *Telegraph* explained that public interest had reached such enormous proportions that it would serialize the entirety of the trial in four installments. But no one topped Grigorii Gradovskii of *The Voice*. To this day, his article on the Zasulich trial reads as if it were written in a state of delirious exaltation, feverishly dictated minutes after the events themselves. In Gradovskii's account, Vera was immortalized as the suffering victim of regime abuse, and in turn, the regime and society were placed in the dock as the accused. In Gradovskii's imagination, he and all the rest of Russia had been found guilty of the twin crimes of rampant injustice and inexcusable complacency.[12]

In the coming days, liberal newspapers followed Gradovskii's lead. Their verdict was, in Koni's succinct summary, *"caveant consules,"* or "the government beware." News editors proclaimed that Alexander II's regime would do well to hear the voice of an outraged public, which spoke through Vera's jury.

The disrespect for personal dignity and the habitual arbitrariness so characteristic of the Russian regime had to end. Abuse of power would no longer be casually tolerated. Vera's acquittal, the *St. Petersburg Register* declared, "was the verdict of all who were present. It was the voice of the people." "If we don't hear the voice of the society in such instances," *The Week* concurred, "then when will we hear it?"[13]

If the regime refused to hear what Russians were saying, then more such actions were inevitable. The *Northern Messenger* demanded not less dissent but more. The public needed legal outlets to express their dissatisfaction, more "valves" to relieve the pressure of popular opinion. Otherwise, the *Northern Messenger* implied, they would release their frustrations in other, more violent ways. Hope increased that the trial might be a "turning point" in Russian history. Gradovskii expressed it most poetically: Perhaps the trial was a crisis like those "so common in serious illnesses—a very difficult, but desired moment that signals the return to health."[14]

Soon enough, Vera herself quietly faded from the news accounts. To the editorialists at least, it appeared that the trial was not about her after all. Alexandrov's summation had transformed her into a mere instrument of public protest. Her life had been a cruel one, and her despair impelled her to act against her oppressors. She was the passive victim of circumstances beyond her control. The jury had not focused on Vera but on the "social facts" surrounding her case, the *Messenger of Europe* editorialized. *Notes of the Fatherland* added that "in our circumstances, a person who suffers, but knows that he is completely innocent, sometimes has no place to lodge a complaint, and no way to receive satisfaction."[15]

Eagerly devouring the news accounts, the reading public soon echoed and amplified this liberal interpretation of events. Throughout Russia, ordinary Russians expressed a quiet rage against the regime. The Third Section gathered letters that revealed the general joy attending Vera's acquittal. "The Asiatic order that prevails in our administration is beginning to agitate the public," wrote one friend to another. The trial, he added, "revealed all of the abuses of our regime." The tsar himself, wrote another correspondent, was surprised at what he learned from the affair. Others characterized the crisis in stark terms, rejoicing that the trial might well be Russia's "fall of the Bastille."

But the public never forgot Vera's role in the ordeal, and cast her as a heroine. She was dubbed, rather inconsistently, Russia's Charlotte Corday, Joan of Arc, and a modern version of the biblical Judith. Like the saints of old, she had followed the voice of her conscience, heedless of the consequences. "Then a girl, silently, without speaking, wove herself a laurel crown of immortality," wrote a man in Poltava to his friend in St. Petersburg. The Third Section, upon investigating the sender, was surprised to find that he was an ordinary employee of the Ministry of the Interior.[16]

Even in elite circles, sympathy for Vera prevailed. The day after the article appeared, friends and admirers came to Gradovskii's office to congratulate him on his article. Letters poured in from touched readers. One highly connected society lady invited Gradovskii to tea and then, in confidence, confessed that she had gathered sufficient sums to pay for Vera's flight abroad, should this become necessary. She refused to believe that Gradovskii had no knowledge of Vera's whereabouts.[17]

One conclusion was accepted without question: Vera posed no threat to society. Her biography was extraordinary, her situation unique. The confluence of events that triggered her assassination attempt was likely never to be repeated. Ugly rumors that she was "a dedicated revolutionary, a hothead," had been dispelled at the trial. Vera was nothing more than a fragile young woman, and her attempt to shoot Trepov was merely the natural response of an overly sensitive soul.[18] There was no chance that Vera's act would be imitated.

In just a few short months, this complacency proved entirely unfounded.

Russian officialdom, meanwhile, did everything in its power to confirm its reputation for irrationality and tyranny. Brazenly disregarding her acquittal and the demonstrations in her favor, Alexander II issued an order to arrest Vera Zasulich and hold her in the House of Preliminary Detention until further notice. When it was discovered that she had escaped arrest and remained in hiding, the acting governor of St. Petersburg ordered the police to take "the most energetic measures" to locate and apprehend her. In August, the Third Section received word that Vera had fled to Switzerland. For a time, the tsar insisted on petitioning the Swiss government for extradition. He only relented when his counselors advised against it, arguing that the regime could hardly wish for another trial of Vera Zasulich. By October 1878, the tsar had formally decided not to pursue her any further.[19]

In the court and the ministries, bureaucrats discussed the trial in somber tones. It was viewed as a humiliating defeat for the Russian regime. The tutor to the heir to the throne, Konstantin Pobedonostsev, set the tone by angrily denouncing the trial as nothing less than "a second Plevna," which was, if anything, "more terrible, more horrible than the first." Local governors from across Russia echoed the sentiment. Provincial society, it seems, was "confused" by the verdict, failing to understand how a potential assassin could go free. Above all, a very intimate fear swept through the corridors of power. A deadly precedent had been established: Assassins could become heroes. "If things continue this way," some bureaucrats whispered, "we will need to flee the country."[20]

Beside himself with fury, Alexander II went on the offensive and demanded a widespread purge of the legal system, the press, and any person who dared to voice sympathy for Vera. Impulsively, almost unthinkingly, he and his ministers took broad swipes at the reforms that they had once been so eager to implement. In no time, serious damage was done to newly liberalized Russian institutions.

Their first targets were those immediately involved in the Zasulich trial. Alexandrov, though considered a "scoundrel," was untouchable because of the independence of defense attorneys. Anatolii Koni, as a government representative, was not so fortunate. He was immediately and roundly denounced as the true "guilty party" in Vera's acquittal. Word spread that his instructions to the jury had encouraged a verdict of not guilty. Some called him a "red nihilist" in disguise. One general blamed him specifically for *asking* whether Vera was guilty. "She confessed that she shot him," the old general apparently said indignantly, "and then Koni asked the jury: 'Is she guilty?' What kind of a question is that: Is she guilty?"[21]

On April 5, Palen summoned Koni into his office. Koni immediately sensed that he and Palen were about to have their final confrontation. The minister was himself feeling the wrath of his superiors. As a man who had lived his life in the corridors of power and who enjoyed the perks of his office, Palen was in despair. He feared that he was about to lose it all. Frantically, he sought to scramble back into the tsar's favor, by expressing his anger at subordinates down the line.[22]

In a tone of anxious irritability, Palen accused Koni of doing everything to ensure Vera's acquittal. He warned Koni, in no uncertain terms, that the tsar was incensed at his summation. Koni once again launched into a long-winded justification, but Palen was in no mood. With a grim face, he insisted Koni immediately write a personal apology to the tsar and ask to resign. The tsar would not be angry for long, he added in softer tones. Koni was a young man; "it would merely be a temporary hiatus" in his career. Should Koni insist on his rights as judge, however, then he would lose the tsar's favor forever.

Koni, as ever, held fast to principles. According to the 1864 reforms, he insisted, judges were independent and served for life. "With the help of an imperial order, you can kill me in the professional sense," Koni said, "but your suggestion that I commit professional suicide is quite in vain." He would remain in his position not because he had any remaining pleasure in his duties but in order to vindicate the principle of judicial independence. Palen was angry but helpless. Koni would remain a judge.

In frustration, Palen took revenge on those he could control: the state prosecutors Andreevskii and Zhukovskii. Calling them into his office, he demoted them to provincial posts for refusing to undertake the prosecution of Vera Zasulich. Both men immediately resigned their positions and turned to the only career open to them: the bar. On the day of Zhukovskii's resignation, friends quietly gathered at his home to offer moral support. Among them was Koni himself, who after dinner proposed a toast to those who had been "thrown overboard" from the ship of justice. "We have gone through a storm," he intoned, "and we have lowered our flag to half mast for our fallen comrades."[23]

The warden of the House of Preliminary Detention was the next to go. For his refusal to heed the "advice" of Lopukhin to keep Vera incarcerated until further notice, the tsar personally ordered Fedorov to spend seven days under arrest. The interim governor of St. Petersburg, Alexander Kozlov, recognized the absurdity of this decision and tried to break the news to Fedorov as gently as possible. Nonetheless, Fedorov broke into tears at the news. He never crossed the threshold of the House of Preliminary Detention again.[24]

On May 5, in an almost quixotic final act, Palen succeeded in cajoling the still hapless Kessel into appealing Vera's acquittal in the Russian Senate, Russia's highest court. The grounds for appeal were entirely manufactured, but the Senate was under extreme pressure to invalidate Vera's verdict under any pretext. On May 20, in a split vote, the Senate brazenly declared a mistrial in the Zasulich case and sent it to the Novgorod district court for retrial. In the end, this proved an empty gesture. Vera would never be brought to trial again.[25]

Of all the measures Palen took in the wake of the trial, one proved most consequential for Russia's liberal judicial system. On April 2, immediately after the trial, he proposed to the State Council enacting a law that would try all assassination attempts and terrorist acts by military tribunal. At that particular moment, even the regime was as yet unprepared to take such extreme measures. The proposal was rejected as premature. It took several more terrorist attacks before the law on military tribunals was adopted on August 9, 1878. After that date, political trials were handed over to the tribunals in cases where there was "armed" action against the government. The regime explained that revolutionaries were "receiving sympathy" in civilian jury trials.[26]

By then, however, it was far too late for Palen. He was relieved of his duties as minister on May 30, 1878.[27]

Other departments in the administration played their role in seeking retribution for the outcome of Vera's trial. The minister of the interior did his best to support his comrade at Justice. After the trial, he was given a complete list of the newspapers that had published accounts of the trial favorable to Vera and had ostensibly rendered "murder a heroic act." The chilling suggestion was made that the editors of these newspapers be warned about publishing such material in the future. The minister himself gave a lengthy report to the tsar on Gradovskii's article in *The Voice*. Gradovskii, he claimed, was actually "aiding youths in their anti-government activities." Andrei Kraevskii, the editor of *The Voice*, was to receive his first official warning. Other newspapers were still less fortunate. In early April, the *New Times* and the *Northern Messenger* were forbidden to sell papers and charged with "dissemination of false news."[28] By January 1879, these sporadic efforts at censorship became official policy. After that date, newspaper coverage of political trials was restricted either to reprinting official stenographic accounts or to conveying the simple facts of the case.[29]

The Third Section tackled public opinion. Gathering evidence from posted letters, the secret police separated out all that conveyed sympathy with Vera or that applauded the results of the trial. The senders were investigated for evidence of prior political activity. Often, the secret police were surprised to find that the authors were ordinary individuals with no previously declared political opinions. On one of the reports, Alexander II's personal frustration at the breadth of Vera's popularity was revealed. In a furious scrawl, Alexander wrote in the margin of one letter, "Who are these people?"[30]

Ironically, the final casualty of the trial was Fedor Trepov himself. Though officials publicly considered him the victim of the affair, he was privately blamed for his impulsive decision to flog Bogoliubov. One week after the trial, perhaps regretting that he had failed to testify on his own behalf, Trepov wrote to the minister of the interior, asking that he be allowed to publish a short justification of his flogging of Bogoliubov in the regime journal, the *Government Messenger*. Trepov's request was referred to the Committee of Ministers. But the government had had enough of Trepov, and his request was denied with a simple explanation: "The publication of this explanation is *inopportune at the present time*."[31]

A more nimble regime would have responded with a propaganda campaign of its own. It would, at last, have released the evidence that proved who Vera really was: her history of radicalism, the death threats sent to different officials, the rumors of a wider, conspiratorial plot. Instead, the regime lashed out at its critics, which merely vindicated public suspicions.

The lone defender of the regime's case was the legendary reactionary publicist Mikhail Katkov, editor of the *Moscow Register*. Katkov was a newly minted conservative, a man whose original sympathies had been with Alexander Herzen and the "superfluous men" but whose opinions had veered dramatically to the right with the nihilism of the 1860s. By the late 1870s, Katkov was a staunch supporter of Russian assertion abroad and autocracy at home. His contacts with the Russian court, his powerful presence in the Russian journalistic world, and his often intemperate rhetoric resulted in his nickname: "Thunderer." He lived up to his reputation during the Russo-Turkish War, when he wrote a series of angry editorials demanding the most vigorous prosecution of the war and the most bellicose policy against Europe.[32]

In the aftermath of the Zasulich trial, Katkov used his powerful editorial voice to hurl scathing critiques at liberal society and its new predilection for assassination. He accused the liberal press of simply ignoring the facts of the case: that a woman had shot at a higher administration official. The jury might reasonably have mitigated her sentence, he angrily opined, but it did not have the right to flatly ignore the law.[33]

Katkov derided Zasulich's devotees as effete liberal intellectuals, lacking the common sense of ordinary Russians. It would not have occurred to an average man to acquit a confessed murderess, let alone venerate her as "an icon." On April 3, 1878, Katkov was overjoyed to find concrete evidence for his views. On that day, a radical student protest was set upon by Moscow merchants, doormen, and butchers, some wielding knives. Katkov wrote a gleeful editorial, declaring that the "Russian masses" had spoken out against "the traitors to the tsar." It was a "healthy" rebuff, he argued, to the contorted justifications for radicalism issued by the intelligentsia.[34]

But Katkov's voice was an isolated one. Especially after the April 3 melee, liberals and radicals joined to denounce Katkov's sudden enthusiasm for mass violence. In all seriousness, the liberals proclaimed themselves opposed to "mass vigilantism" and the "vigilante justice of the revolver." The irony of this debate was apparently lost on both sides. Russian liberals and radicals celebrated the elite demonstrations cheering on Vera and denounced the protests of ordinary workers as "mob violence." The reactionary Katkov, on the other hand, attacked Russian elites for supporting terrorism while celebrating the violent demonstrations of ordinary workers. The warfare among liberals, reactionaries, and the regime continued to rage in the press. The tone was often personal. When Katkov declared that thousands of "Vera's comrades" would "imitate her plans for assassination," the *Messenger of Europe* indignantly opined that even "conservatives" normally did not "reason in such an empty-headed fashion."[35]

Obsessed with these polemical exchanges, conservatives, liberals, and the government alike failed to perceive that surreptitiously, but insistently, the radical movement was learning an altogether different lesson from Vera's trial: Terrorism paid. Without delay, they began to act on what they learned.

⌇

We are socialists. Our goal is to destroy the existing economic system and to eradicate economic inequality, which are, in our opinion, the roots of all human suffering. . . .

Gentlemen of the gendarmes, and of the administration! You possess a million-man army, and a numerous police force; your spies flood all the cities and will soon flood the villages; your prisons are terrible and your punishments merciless. But know this: with all of your armies and your police, with your prisons and your punishments, you are still powerless and helpless before us! No punishments will frighten us! No force will protect you from our hand!

You were scared by our first blows and decided to turn to military tribunals, to terrify us with the threat of bloody retribution.

Woe, woe to you if you decide to follow this path to the end! You will not frighten us, you know this yourselves. You will only make us more merciless toward you. And know this: We have means more horrible than those you have already experienced, but have not used them until now, because they were too extreme. Beware lest you bring us to the extreme, and remember that we never make empty threats. . . .

Not by the day, but by the hour, our movement is growing.

Remember, we started down this path not long ago. It has been less than six months since the shot of Vera Zasulich.

— SERGEI KRAVCHINSKII, "A Death for a Death"[36]

Russian revolutionaries never forgot March 31, 1878. It was the day that the public issued an open, resounding slap in the face to the Russian autocracy. After years of enduring the mute indifference of ordinary Russians, radicals at last saw signs of awakening. Society had condemned the arbitrary rule of the Russian regime and had embraced Vera and her vigilante act. It was a glorious moment, a turning point that would lead to the inevitable collapse of the existing Russian system.

In the days following the trial, illegal pamphlets rained down on Russian cities. The pamphlets issued defiant proclamations of victory in the Zasulich case. The Land and Freedom group warned that Vera's trial was a mere prologue of coming events. Under the influence of the trial's theatrics, they predicted the public would soon take the stage in the "historical drama that is called the trial of the regime by the people."[37]

March 31, 1878, would be "a day forever remembered in Russian history." For centuries the Russian people had quietly tolerated injustice and tyranny. Frightened, they had allowed others to suffer on their behalf. They merely watched as the "best, most freethinking people" were condemned to languish in prisons and in the camps of Siberia. Vera's gunshot was, as she had hoped, a clarion call.[38]

Fear was finally banished from Russian hearts. Vera had stripped the regime of its omnipotent aura. A lawless administration was now powerless. Facing the demonstrators after Vera's trial, it vengefully attacked them, but only succeeded in murdering Sidoratskii. Even then, out of cowardice, they proclaimed his death a suicide.[39]

In the aftermath of the trial, two exemplars of human courage remained. Vera was the heroine, who declared it "difficult to raise one's hand against another" but who did so out of a love of human dignity. She was a "pure soul," an "incarnation of the Russian conscience." Sidoratskii was the martyr, who died so that Vera might live. A newly founded radical journal, aptly titled *The Beginning*, eloquently proclaimed that "from this youth's innocent blood will grow a beautiful plant . . . and our enemies, the enemies of the people, will not be able to root it out."[40]

"The enemies of the people." In that phrase, the darker undertones of the moment betrayed themselves. "Who is not with the government at the present time, must be against it," announced Land and Freedom. Other pamphlets spoke still more ominously: "A secret committee of public safety should be formed. And then woe to the insane ones, who block the path of history."

Vera might have been the first, the pamphlets seemed to say, but she would not be the last to take up arms against the state. "Out of the silence of these quiet streets," declared *The Beginning*, "terrible demons will appear, demanding an accounting for all of the spilt blood. Woe, woe to those murderers who live to see the day of judgment!"[41]

It should have been the happiest period of Vera's life. It should have been the vindication of the years of embattled striving that took her from her provincial noble backwater to the pinnacle of the revolutionary movement. After the sting of Nechaev's betrayal, after the loneliness of prison and exile, and after the disappointment of life among the Rebels, Vera had finally climbed to the pinnacle of the Russian revolutionary movement. She was the first in history: a noble terrorist, a female assassin, a radical heroine. Single-handedly, she had proven the worth of the Russian socialist movement, especially of its female contingent. She might have considered the adulation of the crowds and the adoration of the press as nothing more than just compensation for a life bravely led.

Instead, in the days after the verdict, Vera's mood spiraled downward into depression. Her acquittal, it seemed, was both unexpected and unwelcome. Radical comrades who encountered her after the events of March 31 were shocked to find her silent and morose, and almost angry at her admirers. "Everyone who comes here," she contemptuously told a friend who visited her, "considers it his duty to sing dithyrambs to me."[42]

In part, the trouble lay in Vera's intense shyness. This retiring young woman was completely unprepared for the glare of fame. Within hours of the verdict, comrades swarmed the tiny hideout that sheltered her for a few days. Curious eyes were trained on her, and she was expected to answer questions about every aspect of her ordeal, to reveal her innermost thoughts. Subject to this intense scrutiny, Vera found she could barely "keep herself together." Her lack of tact often landed her in uncomfortable scenes. Within one hour of the verdict, a young man Vera had never met before ran up to her and eagerly exclaimed: "You must be very happy now!" Without thinking, Vera answered honestly, "Not very." As she watched bitter disappointment cross the man's face, she immediately regretted her words. She quickly tried to explain that she was tired, but it was to no avail.

As the weeks wore on, matters worsened. Vera's comrades had learned of the new warrant for her arrest and insisted that she move from apartment to apartment to evade detection. She was thus continually thrust into new social situations and forced to meet new admirers as intrusive as the last. She later wrote that she felt "more lonely than I had ever felt in the House of Preliminary Detention."

In her memoirs, however, Vera struggled to explain the more serious aspect of the disconnect between the exultation that surrounded her and the internal despair that weighed her down. When deciding to shoot Trepov, Vera wrote, she had mentally relinquished her freedom: "I had said farewell to my free life and did not think of it anymore." But the jury unexpectedly rejected this noble offer of self-sacrifice. "They returned it to me, and I needed to decide what to do with it, and to decide this as soon as possible."[43] She had wanted, more than anything else, to become a martyr. Instead, she had become a celebrity.

This, to her mind, was not a fair exchange. Celebrity was the reward for self-seeking; martyrdom was the true gift of self-sacrifice. If she was to become known, she wanted it to be for what she was willing to suffer. Deep in her heart, Vera must have harbored a residue of anguish over her intent to assassinate Trepov. Though he was, in her eyes, the consummate villain, murder was still a crime. She did not want to be praised; she wanted to be punished, so that her suffering would expiate the sin. Many years later, Albert Camus, the French philosopher, best captured the mindset of Vera and other terrorists like her. He called them "fastidious assassins" for their self-proclaimed sense of ethics. "Necessary and inexcusable," he wrote, in part about Vera, "that is how murder appeared to them." To justify themselves, they "conceived the idea of offering themselves as a justification." Indeed, in their minds, "he who kills is guilty only if he consents to go on living." Denied martyrdom, Vera felt the sting of guilt. As she confessed later to her close friend Lev Deich, by mid-April she had made plans to turn herself in to the police.[44]

At the last moment she was rescued by a man who had never met her before but took great interest in her fate—Dmitrii Klements. He was renting an apartment from an orthopedist with ties to the radical movement. It was an excellent hiding place. The only entrance was through another inhabited apartment, occupied by an old woman who refused to allow visitors. Klements offered Vera a room in the apartment for free. For weeks, Vera never set foot outside this new home. But she was finally, paradoxically, happy. She had all that she required: a small burner for her tea, a few books, and food delivered daily by an earnest young student.

Klements proved the perfect companion. They were forced to share a tiny space for weeks on end, but Vera never felt crowded by Dmitrii's presence. Klements, like Vera, liked to sit in silence and was often considered taciturn. But his soft brown eyes just barely concealed an extraordinary intelligence and warm sense of humor.[45] Above all, Vera valued his sensitivity. He immediately understood Vera's spiritual anxiety and her desire to be left alone. At first, he graciously avoided speaking with her. The two would spend whole days in separate rooms, breaking the silence only to share a meal. Vera's other acquaintances eagerly besieged her, but Klements asked her nothing at all. Soon, however, they found that they had much in common. They spent hours in their memories of the "to the people" movement and exchanged their stories and experiences. Klements grew fond of his charge.

Knowing that the vise surrounding Vera was closing, and that her tiny hideaway could not remain safe for long, Klements urged her to flee abroad. He knew this would not be easy. Vera did not like the idea of fleeing the scene; it appeared particularly cowardly after her initial desire to turn herself in. It would look as if she were skulking away from her crime. Nor could she face abandoning her comrades in the movement—it seemed like a kind of betrayal. One of her close friends, Ekaterina Breshko-Breshkovskaia, had written her a letter urging her not to desert the Russian revolutionary cause. "Why would you want to play the role of a discharged hero?"

Klements did not attempt to refute these arguments. He merely made a tempting proposition. What if the two of them traveled to Switzerland and enjoyed some quiet time hiking in the Alps? "I am not asking you to 'play a role,'" he said, quietly mocking Breshko-Breshkovskaia, "but to hike through the mountains. There you won't be playing any 'roles.' As for 'heroism,' a very different kind is required: Whether it's steep or not, you'll have to climb." It would be a glorious experience, he urged. "What heights I could lead you to!"

Finally, Vera succumbed. She learned that her verdict was to be overturned in the Senate. Improbably, word spread that a highly placed military official, possibly even a member of the royal family, offered personally to conduct Vera across the border, passing her off as his wife. To Vera, Klements's company seemed far preferable to that of some "old general." In May 1878, Vera finally fled across the border, headed for the mountains of Switzerland. At that moment, she officially relinquished control of her legacy. She would never regain it.

The day before Vera emigrated, she briefly met the man who would become her lifelong admirer and fervent imitator, Sergei Kravchinskii. Kravchinskii was the darling of the revolutionary movement, a man who inspired affection in even the most peripheral acquaintances. With his round face, pink cheeks, and angelic golden curls, he looked, in Vera's words, like a "village beauty." He radiated an almost childlike innocence, which earned him the nickname "the Baby." He especially charmed women, who found him irresistible in his elegant, light-colored summer suits, which he wore well into the fall season to lend himself an aristocratic air. He flamboyantly encouraged female attention, even though he was rumored to be gay.[46]

Kravchinskii's entire revolutionary career was built on a combination of restless energy and mischievous pranksterism. In 1874, he was one of the first to don a peasant caftan and head to the villages to preach socialism. Later, he composed a series of moralizing socialist pseudo-folktales for radicals to take to the villages, with titles such as "The Tale of a Kopek." Years after the "to the people" movement was a mere memory, Kravchinskii confided to Vera that he was embarrassed by the naive, almost cloying plot lines of these tales, but Vera reassured him that she had witnessed more than one radical weeping while reading them. In 1875, the revolt in Bosnia-Herzegovina broke out, and Kravchinskii was seized by the desire to fight as a Balkan rebel. Grabbing his gun, he headed for the Balkan hills and spent days perched on barren rocks, shooting at the Ottoman army. Ultimately disappointed in the stubborn nationalism of his Bosnian comrades, he nonetheless emerged from this experience unscathed.[47]

He glided through the revolutionary years of the 1870s with astonishing ease. In part, he relied on his unnatural physical strength. While many of his "to the people" companions languished in the fields or in the factories, Kravchinskii took on field work, carpentry, even assembly-line labor with considerable stamina and skill. Peasants and workers admired him for his ability to keep up. Kravchinskii also possessed uncanny good luck. In 1877, he was imprisoned in Italy for trying to instigate an anarchist revolt, and the death penalty loomed. But suddenly, in January 1878, Italy's King Victor Emmanuel died, and his successor, King Humbert, gave amnesty to all political prisoners. Set free, Kravchinskii sauntered into Switzerland, ready to resume his revolutionary way of life as if nothing happened.[48]

He was in Zurich when he heard reports of the Zasulich trial and of Vera's acquittal. Intoxicated with glee, he rushed to St. Petersburg to meet his new heroine. When Vera first laid eyes on him, he was "all aglow, in a most exhilarated mood." Kravchinskii adored the role Vera played at the trial; for him, there was something beautiful and unearthly about a modest, young terrorist martyr. And the heartfelt, instant adoration of the public confirmed his view.[49]

In a flash, Kravchinskii grasped the new imperative for the Russian revolutionaries: to create more Veras—a battalion of terrorists, all able to kill their enemies without mercy, and all willing to suffer for their deeds.

Among his Russian comrades, he sketched his dream for the future. Revolutionaries would once again fan out into the countryside. This time, they would be united by direction from the center. They would become more dedicated, more ruthless, more conspiratorial. Their tactics would be tightly focused: carefully plotted assassinations of Russia's worst officials. After each assassination, underground presses would produce tracts declaring that each terrorist act was aimed at the tyrants and abusers that ruled Russia. The public would love them, just as they loved Vera. Terrorism would be seen as a noble, beautiful sacrifice for the people's good. This would be a magnificently effective terrorist organization—a true party of Land and Freedom.[50]

A few weeks after Kravchinskii laid out this blueprint, he decided to enlist as the first soldier in the new terrorist army. He chose a symbolic target, General Nikolai Mezentsev, the head of the Third Section during the Trials of the Fifty and 193 and the arch-enemy of Russia's revolutionaries, a man with a reputation for mercilessly persecuting prisoners.

Kravchinskii announced his intentions to his friends in July 1878, after he heard a secret report on the harsh treatment of those sentenced during the Trial of the 193. "Tomorrow," he said, almost offhandedly, "General Mezentsev will be killed in his reception room." Kravchinskii's comrades were, by turns, surprised and concerned, but Kravchinskii was deadly serious. For some time now, he had been yearning to follow in Vera's footsteps.[51]

Lev Deich insisted that the careless Kravchinskii have a detailed plan of action. Kravchinskii would slay Mezentsev on the street and then escape in a waiting cabriolet to a designated hiding place. At first, Kravchinskii dismissed the plan with a wave of his hand. He had no intention of escaping after his attack. He wished to die a martyr's death. But Kravchinskii's friends finally prevailed, convincing him that he was too valuable to the movement. Still, he refused to take the preparations seriously, acting as if he were planning nothing more interesting than a summer trip.[52]

The day arrived. On the morning of August 4, Mezentsev was taking his usual stroll through Mikhailovskii Square. Casually, an elegantly dressed Sergei Kravchinskii stepped toward him, as if toward an old friend. One can imagine Kravchinskii's mischievous smile as he drew a knife out of the newspaper he was holding and stabbed Mezentsev in the chest. Mezentsev's companion, a junior officer, began to beat Kravchinskii with an umbrella and tried to grab him. But Kravchinskii, with his uncanny luck, eluded capture. His accomplice shot at Mezentsev's companion, seriously wounding him. Kravchinskii skipped into the cabriolet, which dashed away to safety within minutes. He never even became a suspect in the case.[53]

That night, as Mezentsev slowly died of his wounds, Kravchinskii sat down to compose a public declaration justifying the murder. He entitled it, ominously, "A Death for a Death." In this short pamphlet, Kravchinskii eloquently defended the turn to terror. Socialists wanted nothing more than the good of the people, but they were forced to suffer for their beliefs at the hands of a reactionary clique. The government wielded the full power of the penal system against idealist radicals. Revolutionaries died slow, tortured deaths in prisons and in exile. The time had come for them to fight back.

The government had a mighty army and a police force to defend it, but the terrorists had means far more ruthless and terrifying. They were ready to do anything, and sacrifice anything, to defeat the enemies of the people. Every persecution of a socialist would be met with a terrorist act.[54]

The terrorist war had been declared.

"A Death for a Death" merely made an ideological virtue out of a trend that had begun immediately after Vera's attempt on Trepov's life and had intensified further after her trial. It all began days after Vera's assassination attempt, in February 1878. The instigator was a dapper nobleman named Valerian Osinskii, who, like Kravchinskii, was consumed with a passion for revolution. But Kravchinskii, despite his rhetoric, killed only one man. Osinskii, by contrast, thrived on murder.

Osinskii's first terrorist act, the assassination of an ordinary worker turned police informer, occurred on February 2, 1878. On February 23, he attempted to kill a Kiev prosecutor by firing upon him when he was walking with his wife. The prosecutor's life was spared only by the thickness of his overcoat. The next attack, though planned by Osinskii, was executed by a comrade. Gregory Popko, like Kravchinskii before him, plunged his knife into the chest of the Kiev chief of police in the middle of a crowded street.[55]

In a peculiarly flamboyant fashion, Osinskii added a dash of Nechaevism to his terrorist exploits. He tacked up posters throughout the city, advertising each attack as the work of a nonexistent Executive Committee of the Russian Socialist Revolutionary Party, whose seal looked suspiciously like that of

Nechaev's old Society of the People's Revenge. But Osinskii was no Nechaev. He was too impulsive to be effectively conspiratorial, and his theatrics inevitably led to his capture.[56]

Soon, the Nechaevite banner was again raised by a shadowy figure emerging out of the Land and Freedom movement: Alexander Mikhailov. Superficially, nothing about Mikhailov resembled Nechaev. Mikhailov possessed little personal charisma; he was taciturn, gentle, and withdrawn. He spoke languidly, if at all, and his appearance—with his wide eyes and serene gaze—lent him the air of a gentle ascetic. In the words of one historian, Mikhailov "was the kind of revolutionary Alyosha might have made," if Dostoyevsky had actually carried through on his intent to write "a sequel to *The Brothers Karamazov* on Alyosha as a terrorist."[57]

Appearances aside, Mikhailov lived Nechaevism. Deeply devoted to Nechaev's *Catechism,* he strove for a pure revolutionary asceticism. Conspiracy seemed in his blood. He lived furtively. He checked under beds when he entered unfamiliar rooms; he used intricate routes through back alleys in order to shake off potential tails. He learned to recognize police spies. He had no friends and no family. He lived as Nechaev would have wished, as "a doomed man."[58]

Mikhailov concealed these conspiratorial tendencies during the heady days of the "to the people" movement, when such Machiavellianism was out of favor. But Mikhailov had difficulty embracing the chaotic, freewheeling, emotional proselytizing of his comrades among the peasants. Even then, he knew that nothing would come from such decentralized and disorganized efforts.

Vera's gunshot came as a revelation to him as well. Instantly, he saw the potential of her act. On the evening of January 24, he overcame his usual reticence, interrupted the festivities at a student dance, and proposed a toast to Vera. Like Kravchinskii, he had a sudden vision of a terrorist army, conducting attacks on all levels of the Russian government. But unlike Kravchinskii, Mikhailov had both the inclination and the energy to oversee these complicated plans. From April 1878 forward, Mikhailov worked tirelessly to transform the loosely knit, disorganized Land and Freedom movement into a highly effective conspiratorial organization.[59]

Meticulously, he crafted a "constitution" for Land and Freedom that would guide its future endeavors. The document bore striking resemblance to Nechaev's old "General Rules of the Organization," with its hierarchically organized cellular system. The constitution also proclaimed "fundamental principles" of revolution, which distinctly echoed the *Catechism*. Real revolutionaries, Mikhailov wrote, were unquestioningly obedient, loyal, secretive, and ready to sacrifice everything for the cause. Point nine of the "fundamental principles" captured their essence: "The ends justify the means."[60]

After Kravchinskii's illegal printing of "A Death for a Death," the moment seemed ripe to unleash the new terrorist movement. The assassination of Mezentsev had triggered regime counter-attacks against the revolutionaries. The Third Section swept through Russian towns and cities, rooting out and arresting all suspicious activists. Mikhailov himself was briefly captured but managed to evade arrest by swinging his cuffed hands at a police officer and then making his escape.[61]

According to the threats issued in "A Death for a Death," such police reprisals would be answered with more terror. But Kravchinskii himself had no stomach for this escalation of violence. His flamboyant temperament, like Osinskii's, was entirely unsuited for sustained conspiracy. By 1878, the passionate revolutionary was becoming a liability for himself and the movement. He was sent abroad late that year, ostensibly to school himself in dynamite technology. He never returned to Russia again.[62]

It was now up to Mikhailov to make good on Kravchinskii's threats. He did so with devastating speed. In January 1879, Mikhailov infiltrated the Russian Third Section and gained access to secret police records. He could now identify police informers. To send a warning to other would-be traitors, Mikhailov planned the execution of Nikolai Reinshtein, a longtime police spy. In a scene that recalled the attacks on Ivanov and Gorinovich, Reinshtein was lured to a Moscow hotel room on the pretext of revolutionary business. There, an assassin stabbed him twice and left him in a pool of blood with a note attached to his body: "The traitor-spy, Nikolai Vasilevich Reinshtein, is condemned and executed by us, the Russian socialist revolutionaries. Death to Judas-traitors!"[63]

In February 1879, Mikhailov directed the murder of the governor of Kharkov, who was shot in his carriage by an assassin waiting in the dark doorway of his home. Alexander Drenteln, Mezentsev's successor, was next. The chosen assassin, a young Polish nobleman, planned to approach Drenteln's carriage on horseback and shoot through the window. Drenteln survived the attack only by chance: The shot went astray, and the assassin's horse bolted. A true Mikhailovite conspirator, the assassin never lost his cool. He dismounted on a street far from the scene, asked an unsuspecting policeman to watch his horse for a moment, and then quietly slipped away.[64]

Later that month, Mikhailov was offered the ultimate prize. A strange and potentially suicidal young man named Alexander Soloviev approached Mikhailov with a tantalizing proposition: the murder of Alexander II. Mikhailov was, at first, deeply tempted. But he feared that Land and Freedom was not yet ready for this ultimate step. At a hastily arranged meeting of the organization, members voiced concerns about instigating an episode of "white terror," like that which followed Karakozov's shot in 1866. The organization declined to assist Soloviev but agreed not to stand in his way.[65]

Soloviev reminded many of Karakozov, with his wild-eyed mental instability and his suicidal tendencies. Like Karakozov, he refused to be deflected from his purpose. On the morning of April 2, acting alone, he took his Smith & Wesson and a cyanide pill to the tsar's Winter Palace. He was prepared to join the ranks of the terror-martyrs.[66]

Soloviev had no real plan. As the tsar emerged from the palace, followed by his entourage, Soloviev merely walked up to the sovereign and began shooting. Alexander's guards were some distance away, so the tsar was left exposed. Long years of military training stood him in good stead. Alexander simply ran away from Soloviev, dashing from side to side. Not one of the five shots from Soloviev's gun hit their target. Finally, Soloviev was tackled and brought to the ground. His cyanide pill, hastily swallowed, failed. Soloviev would have to wait more than a month before his dreams of martyrdom would be fulfilled.[67]

On May 28, Soloviev was taken to the very spot, Semenevskii Square, where Dostoyevsky had prepared himself for what he believed to be his own certain death years earlier. Only this time, there was no last-minute reprieve. Soloviev curtly refused the priest's offer for final consolation, and then the noose was thrown over his head. He accepted death without any regrets. He had already told investigators that he had shot at the tsar in order to bring about a "radiant future."

Before the scaffold, Palen watched the proceedings, perhaps aware that the execution of Soloviev would be his last act as minister of justice.[68] He was not aware that Soloviev's death was but the escalation of the warfare between the revolutionaries and the regime. It was now an open struggle to the death.

～

He is noble, terrible, irresistibly fascinating, for he combines in himself the two sublimities of human grandeur: the martyr and the hero.

He is a martyr. From the day when he swears in the depths of his heart

to free the people and the country, he knows he is consecrated to Death. He
faces it at every step of his stormy life. . . .

The force of mind, the indomitable energy, and the spirit of sacrifice
which his predecessor attained in the beauty of his dreams, he attains in the
grandeur of his mission, in the strong passions which this marvelous, intox-
icating, vertiginous struggle arouses in his heart. . . .

He fights for himself. He has sworn to be free and he will be free, in de-
fiance of everything. . . .

Such is the Terrorist.

—SERGEI KRAVCHINSKII, *Underground Russia*[69]

By 1879, revolutionaries left the Russian villages and factories, abandoning what now seemed to be the passive inactivity of preaching socialism.
They ecstatically threw off years of disappointment and paralysis. Finally, a
new path had opened before them, a path of vigorous activism and invigor-
ating empowerment. A terrorist was a revolutionary who could no longer patiently wait for others to join him in violence. A terrorist took the initiative
and inflicted violence on his own terms.[70]

The numbers of the new terrorists were few, but numbers ultimately
meant little. The force of the idea they served was overpowering. The report
of a gun, the explosion of a bomb—these were not meant just to kill but to
proclaim. Each death thinned the ranks of the enemy. Each death brought
the state closer to its knees. But more important, each death spoke more effectively than any words of the inevitable triumph of socialism. Deeds were
the only propaganda that would waken the lulled masses and break the
chains that had held them captive for centuries. Aleksandra Iakimova recalled that terrorism had seemed the perfect antidote to fatalism. It "used
blows to awaken consciousness."[71] In the mind of the terrorist, death brought
liberation and life.

Thus, what would later become known as the "turn to terror" was not a
rational decision to change course but a fiercely embraced passion. Many
years later, those who witnessed the turn to terror described it as a form of
intoxication. In an instant, one person could paralyze a government, and one
explosion remake the world. In that instant, the terrorist strode onto the
stage as the incarnation of God-like power—invincible and glorious. Those
around him were forced to worship in adoration or tremble in fear. As
Kravchinskii wrote, with the benefit of hindsight, the terrorist was "proud as

Satan rebelling against God." Terrorism was a temptation, as some remembered, because it was "more alive, more belligerent."[72]

Russian terrorists of every stripe were happy to pay tribute to their patron saint, Vera Zasulich. Her single shot, fired point-blank at the enemy, was, as many recalled, a "spark," a "signal" to launch armed resistance against the state. Immediately after January 24, a slogan emerged: "To the weapons!" The power of Vera's act was confirmed by the electric effects of her trial. On the stand, her modest, plain-spoken defense of her deed achieved more than the decades of propaganda that preceded her. She appeared to have roused the normally docile Russians into action.[73]

Though she never became a martyr, her desire to pay the ultimate price was the most inspirational of her exemplary acts. Terrorists knew that the cost of killing for the cause would, most likely, be dying for the cause. But this was a cost gladly borne. Martyrdom itself lent extra nobility to an already noble act. It made murder into an act of supreme self-sacrifice. Though Vera never became the martyr she longed to be, for her comrades she was the purest example of the power of this impulse. "We thought her the happiest person on earth," one radical recalled, "and every one of us wished to follow in her footsteps." She was the emblem of "heroic self-sacrifice," a "holy relic." After Vera Zasulich, wrote the famous terrorist Vera Figner, radicals realized that "if there were no martyrs, then there would be no followers either." The "era of martyrs" had dawned. Lev Deich summed it up succinctly: "One is therefore completely justified in declaring Vera Zasulich the progenitor of the terrorist struggle in Russia."[74]

In June 1879, in the spa town of Lipetsk, Mikhailov had convened a gathering of the terrorist faction of Land and Freedom. There, on one sunny afternoon, aspiring terrorists found a perfect shade grove for a picnic, and incongruously, amid the plentiful food and bottles of vodka, they constructed a new organization. Two major decisions were made. First, the organization would officially become secret, conspiratorial, and hierarchical, run by an all-powerful "Executive Committee," which would subordinate all members to its will. Second, terror would have a new focus. The terrorists had voted to concentrate all of their resources on one single act: the murder of the tsar.[75]

A few months later, rumors spread that Vera Zasulich, the terrorist icon, had personally arrived in Russia to take part in the revolutionary debates. To the shock of many, this revolutionary heroine was said to be entirely opposed to the "turn to terror" and had specifically come back to Russia to dissuade the movement from embarking on this new and dangerous course. Few were actually able to meet with her; her mere presence in Russia was an act of recklessness, since the police would be overjoyed to get their hands on her. So her opinions remained obscure.[76]

In any case, her actions had already spoken far louder than any words she could subsequently utter. By the fall of 1879, Land and Freedom was no more. The fate of the revolutionary movement was now in the hands of Russia's first internationally infamous terrorist organization. It called itself "the People's Will."

～

2. Destructive and terroristic activity

Terrorist activity, consisting of the elimination of the most harmful members of the government for the purposes of defending the party from espionage, and punishing the most egregious acts of violence and tyranny by the state, etc., aims to explode the fascination with government forces, to give unceasing examples of the possibility of battling against the state, to arouse the revolutionary spirit of the people and give them faith in success and, finally, to form forces appropriate for battle. . . .

5. Organization and execution of a coup

In light of the oppression of the people, in light of the fact that the government through partial pacification can long delay a general revolutionary movement, the party is required to take upon itself the initiative of a coup, and not to wait until that time when the people are able to do without it. As to the means of achieving a coup . . . (this part of the 5th point is not appropriate for publication).

— Program of the Executive Committee
of the People's Will, 1879[77]

The party that assumed the grandiose name of the People's Will may never have had even a hundred members. Nonetheless, they adopted this name without a hint of irony. They believed that underneath the placid surface of the Russian peasant countryside, there was a smoldering desire for liberation from the tsarist yoke. It was fear, they argued, that silenced the impoverished Russian masses. But the hold of fear could be broken, if the supposedly invincible government was exposed as a mere "iron colossus with feet of clay."[78]

Terrorism would bring down a society built only upon oppression and economic exploitation. Then the voices of the people would be heard, and their will would be fully expressed. The evidence was incontrovertible. Who among the revolutionaries could forget the thousands massed outside the courthouse after Vera's acquittal? Who could ignore the sudden upwelling of public sympathy for a terrorist woman, proclaimed a hero for doing what others only dreamed?

Each terrorist attack would swell popular support for socialism, until it became a wave of revolution. To achieve this dream, no method was beyond the pale. Mikhailov once again triumphed in the new program of the People's Will: "The end justifies the means."[79]

The People's Will moved quickly to coalesce into a secretive, tightly run, and highly effective machine. Mikhailov's principles of caution and fanatical secrecy prevailed. The Executive Committee began to direct events from the center. It made its decisions clandestinely and was obeyed unquestioningly. Networks of secret cells were to extend, like tentacles, from this central committee.[80]

The People's Will itself, on the other hand, publicly proclaimed its purpose. Its illegally printed tracts did everything to enhance the mystique of terror. They narrated glorious tales of the lives of "martyrs" and listed the black deeds of "traitors." The leaflets and pamplets created the impression that terrorists were lurking everywhere, silently shadowing the government and its minions, ready to strike at a moment's notice.[81]

By 1880, all of the energies of the organization were directed at a single purpose. Their goal was described in military terms as "firing at the center." In legal terms, it was justified as "a death sentence." Either way, Alexander II was to die.[82]

On November 19, 1879, the first bomb exploded beneath the tsar's railway carriage as it traveled near Moscow. The bomb derailed the train, but the tsar was unhurt. By pure chance, he had gone ahead in another carriage. The second attempt was much more spectacular. The People's Will managed to get one of their own employed as a workman in the tsar's Winter Palace. Using dynamite he kept under his pillow at night, the workman constructed a bomb underneath the floorboards of the tsar's formal dining room. The bomb exploded during dinner on February 5, 1880. Again, Alexander was not in the room and was unhurt. The only victims were his guards.[83]

Alexander's luck enraged the People's Will. He seemed invincible. And terrorism appeared increasingly ineffective. In October 1880, Alexander Mikhailov himself was arrested, and the group was deprived of its leader. Members lapsed into despair.

Encouragement came from an entirely unexpected quarter.

In January 1881, a conspirator appeared in the central headquarters of the People's Will. In his pocket he bore a small pouch, which he tossed onto the table with a terse "From Nechaev, in the Fortress." It contained a packet of letters from Russia's first real terrorist conspirator. In these letters, Nechaev expressed his deep admiration for the work of the People's Will. He offered them his services. He needed only one small favor—he wished to be freed from the Peter and Paul Fortress.[84]

During his years of incarceration, Nechaev had not been idle. Slowly, carefully, he had been observing his prison guards and mentally noting their personal quirks, preferences, conversational styles, and psychological inclinations. Soon, he was able to gain their confidence and trust. In time, he had managed, against the odds, to create a kind of radical cult among them. Employing his newfound influence, Nechaev was able to smuggle correspondence out of the prison. He confidently asserted that these same guards were standing ready to assist in his escape.[85]

The effect of this news on the People's Will was electrifying. For so long, Nechaev's name had been a term of abuse, associated with Machiavellian ruthlessness. As if in a flash of inspiration, the People's Will recognized everything they owed his legacy. As Vera Figner remembered: "Everything that remained like a dark spot on Nechaev's personality vanished." It was unanimously decided that Nechaev should be freed.[86] Nonetheless, those plans had to wait. First, the final attempt on Alexander's life had to be accomplished.

The final plot was much more meticulously constructed. Several members of the People's Will purchased a small building on Malaia Sadovaia, near the route typically taken by Alexander II out of the palace every Sunday. The pretext for the purchase was the establishment of a cheese shop, but the real purpose of the building was to dig a tunnel from the basement to a place directly beneath the street. There, conspirators would lay a dynamite mine, timed to explode with the passing of Alexander's carriage. This time, however, the People's Will supplemented the primary plan with alternative arrangements. If the mine failed, four bomb throwers would be waiting along the same route to hurl their dynamite at the tsar's vehicle.[87]

On March 1, 1881, everything was finally ready. The mine was laid; the bomb throwers took positions. At first, Alexander's uncanny luck seemed to hold. The carriage turned away from the mined route, so the backup plan had to be put into action. On the Catherine Canal, the first terrorist threw his bomb. The explosion rocked Alexander's carriage, but he was able to get out, unhurt. With characteristic foolish bravado, he attended to his entourage, to ensure that no one was injured. According to legend, someone then asked whether he was wounded. He answered, "No, thank God." The second bomber then supposedly replied, "It is too early to thank God," and the second bomb flew. This one hit its mark. The tsar lay on the ground, mortally wounded. His assassin was stretched out next to him, also fatally injured.[88]

Thus the tsar-liberator had been slain, in the name of liberty. History provided one further irony. In January 1881, one of the tsar's closest advisors proposed to Alexander that he should create an elected, consultative body for Russia. On the day he was assassinated, in his usual agreeable fashion, Alexander verbally declared his readiness to implement this proposal. A myth was thus born, and persisted for centuries, that Alexander II died with Russia's first "constitution" clutched to his chest.[89] The terrorists had killed not only the tsar but also Russia's liberal hopes.

The trial of Alexander's assassins began on March 26. To the shock of the People's Will, the public mourned the passing of their tsar as if a martyr had died. There was no popular rejoicing; there was only shock and grief. Terrorism, tolerated for so long, was now openly rejected as an extremist evil.[90]

Departing from protocol, the Ministry of Justice opened the trial of the assassins to the public. The prosecutor utilized the example of Vera's trial to masterful effect. Playing from Alexandrov's score, he dramatized Alexander II's last moments, depicting them as a hero's death. "Thus he fell," the prosecutor lyrically intoned, "a warrior at his Imperial post of danger, fell in the battle for God, for Russia, and for Russia's peace, in mortal combat with the enemies of Justice, of Order, of Morality, of Family Life, and of all that is strong and holy in human society."[91]

The six accused were unperturbed. For members of the People's Will, next to the terrorist act itself, the trial was the most zealously awaited moment in their revolutionary careers. During the trial, like Vera before them, they could declare the reasons for their actions. They could expose their noble motives. In short, they could "confess their faith." One of the terrorists, Andrei Zheliabov, did precisely that. Asked about his religion, he emphatically proclaimed: "I admit the teaching of Christ to be the basis of my moral convictions. I believed in truth and justice. . . . I hold it to be the duty of a sincere Christian to fight on behalf of the weak and oppressed, and if need be, to suffer for them. That is my faith."[92]

On April 3, 1881, five of the six terrorists were led to the scaffold. All but one were composed, even radiant. They had long prepared for this moment of sacrifice. Sofia Perovskaia, the sole woman among them, realized that she would become a new symbol for the movement. She had taken part in the most minute plans of the People's Will. She had personally directed the bombers in their assault against the tsar. And now she would die, in direct imitation, as one comrade wrote, "of Christ." Perovskaia's name was now added beside Vera's in the pantheon of revolutionary saints—the first female martyr.[93]

It was of Sofia and Vera that Kravchinskii later wrote: "Women, it must be confessed, are much more richly endowed with the divine flame than men. This is why the almost religious fervour of the Russian revolutionary movement must in great part be attributed to them; and while they take part in it, it will be invincible."[94]

CHAPTER 12

Nihilists Abroad

~~~

In 1878, the charms of the Swiss village of Sion were unknown to the hordes of European tourists that inundated Switzerland every summer. Sheltered in the Rhône Valley, surrounded by breathtaking mountain peaks, Sion was not mentioned in the indispensable European travel guide, Baedeker's. For Dmitrii Klements, this was precisely what afforded Sion its charm. A good friend of his owned a chalet in the hills above the village. Klements and Vera chose it as a base from which they proposed to climb the innumerable mountains that surrounded it.[1]

Klements and Vera traveled without maps or guides, and Vera soon discovered that Klements was about to lead her off of the well-defined trails. All of the roads leading from Sion quickly dwindled into little more than footpaths through the brush, trodden by shepherds seeking new pastures. At times, even these disappeared, and Vera was required to scale sheer rock faces. To her surprise, though she was a novice, she possessed considerable agility and stamina.

Vera's indifference to personal comfort and appearance served her well during these months. At sunset, after eating whatever provisions they had, Vera and Dmitrii would simply curl up on the grass and sleep until dawn. Then, in the early morning, they would seek out one of the many shepherd's huts scattered throughout the remote terrain. Designed as temporary shelters, these were kept open for common use and often contained a small stove and kettle. Vera and Dmitrii would boil water for tea, devour a quick breakfast, and then set off again.

Aside from the occasional shepherd, who obligingly sold them cream and cheese, the pair met not a single human soul. In their characteristic mutual silence, they feasted on the visual spectacles that their tour afforded. They encountered dizzying vistas, hidden glaciers, and peaks of barren rock. Vera remembered that Dmitrii was quietly overjoyed at Vera's appreciation of "his" mountains. "You are so proud of them," she jested, "one might think that they are your own creation."

"And whose are they, in your opinion?" he replied. "Who invented them?"

Vera fondly recalled that indeed, for her, he had invented them, so vividly had he portrayed them while she was still concealed in the tiny apartment hideaway in St. Petersburg.

Vera never forgot her trip with Dmitrii. She would later spend much time in the mountains, trekking through forests and searching for sites earnestly recommended by Baedeker. But nothing could rival those weeks she spent alone with Dmitrii, who worked a kind of magic on her soul. He was able, for a brief time, to relieve all of Vera's anxiety about past events and her uncertainty about the future. In the mountains, she merely surrendered herself to a present bliss. Standing atop the hills, looking down on the world below, she often thought that it was as if she had "landed on the moon."

But soon enough, Vera had to come down from the mountains and confront the world that she, in part, had made.

～

For forty-eight hours, Europe entirely forgot the war, the peace, Mr. Bismarck, Lord Beaconsfield, Prince Gortchakof, in order to occupy itself with nothing but Vera Zassoulitch and the strange judicial adventure in which this unknown woman was the heroine.

— G. VALBERT, "Procès de Vera Zassoulitch,"
Revue des Deux Mondes, May 1, 1878[2]

For Europe, 1878 dawned as an anxious year. The tremors of the Russo-Turkish War of 1877 shook the European Great Powers out of their complacency. With Russian victories in the Balkans, the long-awaited "Great Eastern Crisis" had finally arrived. The "sick man of Europe," the Ottoman Empire, was finally in its death throes, and a newly aggressive Russia was threatening to occupy entire swaths of orphaned Balkan lands left behind. The careful balancing of political power and international influence, which had served Europe so well since the defeat of Napoleon in 1815, was about to be thrown into disarray.

Throughout 1878, newspapers thus filled their pages with news of the delicate diplomatic dance performed by Britain's clever prime minister, Disraeli, Germany's assertive chancellor, Bismarck, and the unfortunately sick and senile Russian foreign minister, Gorchakov. European diplomats agreed that Russia's triumph at San Stefano could not stand, and an isolated Russia could do little against a united European onslaught. Former Ottoman territory now had to be carefully carved up in order to restore European military and political balance. A "Congress" was scheduled to take place in Berlin in June. There, the leaders of the West's most powerful countries would meet in ornate conference rooms among elegantly laden buffet tables to slice up southeastern Europe. Readers of the European newspapers in the early days of 1878 could be forgiven for believing that the political scene belonged to those with written invitations to shape it.[3]

Then, in mid-April, politics received some uninvited guests. Vera Zasulich swept onto the European stage. For a moment, the celebrity of a young, mysterious Russian woman eclipsed that of all the European statesmen combined. Her name was splashed across the front pages of all the European papers; her portrait was prominently placed in the illustrated weeklies. For months on end, Europeans forgot about the powerful men of Europe and fixated on the tales of a hitherto unknown young assassin.

"What a strange country is Russia!" exclaimed the St. Petersburg correspondent to the French *Le Temps*, voicing openly what other European and American newspapers merely implied.[4] For the West, the trial of Vera Zasulich was both a dramatic tale of an unlikely terrorist and a brief glimpse into a Russia that loomed over the borders of Europe. Westerners eagerly devoured tales of the exotic and mysterious eastern country where sadistic government officials battled idealistic young assassins. It was a Romantic land, full of passionate extremes.

Only in Russia, it seemed, was tyranny so peculiarly arbitrary and cruel. Extraordinary stories were printed in Britain and France about the torture of dissidents and even the most innocent of Russian citizens. Vera, many journalists claimed, was by no means the only Russian to have spent her youth in a "vile dungeon." And Bogoliubov was not the only dissident to have fallen victim to a government official eager for blood. One French newspaper openly condemned the Russian state for its "terror" regime. In Russia, Trepovs were a dime a dozen—refined, elegant torturers. Rumors were reported that Trepov had "violated" Vera's female dignity in some manner, or that he had turned a blind eye while one of his subordinates did so. The willingness of reporters to believe even the most fanciful of stories about the Russian police was best captured in a *New York Times* article about a supposed Russian interrogation method known as the "cabinet bleu," in which a suspect was supposedly seated in a special chair that, at a moment's notice, could be dropped below the floor. "Unseen hands" would then subject the lower half of the victim's body to "a flagellation the severity of which was only equaled by its ignominy."[5]

With almost equal (and illogical) astonishment, European and American reporters marveled that only in Russia could a jury of ordinary citizens acquit an assassin "unanimously and without discussion" and "in the teeth of the evidence." The correspondent to *La Presse* scorned the mulish failure of the Russian jury to consider the perceptions of "the civilized world." Russia's police might be exceptionally cruel, but the Russian people were also exceptionally sensitive. How else to explain, one British reporter asked, that a Russian jury would consider it a crime to subject a prisoner to "a little patriarchal castigation with the birch"? Russians were not "singularly insensible to the distinction between right and wrong," he surmised. They were, rather, "a peculiar people, who never do anything by halves."[6]

And only in Russia, it seemed, could you find a woman like Vera. There was something irresistible about this young but heroic radical. The French reporters were especially quick to remark that she was not beautiful. But she was striking and attractive. "She had very lively black eyes," wrote one correspondent. She was "modest and unpretentious," added another. In every respect, her femininity was accentuated in order to sharpen the contrast with her coldly violent act. The British illustrated paper *The Graphic* chose to print an old portrait of Vera, drawn when she was nineteen. In *Le Monde Illustré*, an illustration portrayed her as a wilting heroine, sorrowfully greeting the demonstrations that followed her acquittal.[7]

Her story was written like a sketch for the most fanciful of romantic novels. In the papers, even the most casually mentioned details gave spice to the narrative: her "innocent" involvement in the Nechaev affair "as a schoolgirl of 17," her years spent "in a dungeon," her "continual persecution at the hands of police," and finally her mysterious membership in unnamed "secret societies." The romance of her biography was seen as peculiarly Russian; her "spirit was enveloped by the sad Russia that is the immensity and silence of the steppes."[8]

When facts seemed insufficient, gossip was added—gossip that also borrowed from the tropes of Romantic literature. A few articles implied that Vera was Bogoliubov's lover and her assassination attempt nothing more than an act of vengeance for her beloved. Others insisted that Vera was a member of a mysterious committee of assassins who had secretly ordered her to shoot Trepov and whom she obediently obliged. Still more fanciful were tales that that the tsar himself had arranged Vera's acquittal when he had heard of Trepov's abuses.[9]

But perhaps the most imaginative account was narrated in *The New York*

Times, under the headline THE TRUE STORY OF THE ST. PETERSBURG AF-FAIR. The newspaper's correspondent in St. Petersburg revealed that Vera had known Trepov far more intimately than the public had guessed. In 1875, when she was a governess in a noble family, Trepov had succumbed to her wiles and became her lover. When he abandoned her after a few months, Vera, ashamed, turned to her former lover, Bogoliubov, and asked him to avenge her honor. Bogoliubov journeyed to Poland and tracked down Trepov in Warsaw, where he horsewhipped the old general in a public square. For this, Bogoliubov was tried, flogged, and exiled to Siberia. Nihilism had nothing to do with it, the article asserted. Vera was merely a woman scorned.[10]

As 1878 wore on, Vera's fame reached extraordinary proportions. The French were particularly entranced by her story and followed detailed accounts, including long excerpts, from the trial. In Italy, a play about the trial was performed at Naples; as Anatolii Koni wryly noted, the presiding judge wore a glorious red cape. A drama entitled *Vera Zasulitch* was also performed at Lugano, Switzerland, wildly applauded by the audience and giving rise to near riots in the streets. By year's end, the French *Revue des Deux Mondes* declared her to be one of the most influential people of the year. At a Paris fair dedicated to the artistry of breadmaking, where bakers molded their dough into extraordinary shapes, a surprised Russian correspondent found Vera's face prominently displayed in bread form. "What a strange city is Paris!" he could not help exclaiming.[11]

Through Vera, a new word entered European imaginations: "nihilism." This foreign doctrine, with its enigmatic name, became a European fascination. After the Zasulich trial, nihilism seemed at once menacing and alluring, violent and noble. It was a "sect" or a "religion" of destruction. It was "the negation of nearly everything which ordinary communities hold dear," preached by "zealous apostles." Nihilists submitted to a "moral mutilation in order to gratify a savage instinct for destruction." They possessed a "cold fanaticism," tempered by a desire to "suffer for the oppressed." Above all, nihilist women absorbed these doctrines with a combination of "eagerness and frenzy."[12]

As the violence escalated in Russia, nihilists became more and more important in the eyes of foreign journalists. They seemed cunning, ubiquitous, and all powerful, directing a vast international network of secret societies, with adherents "in every grade of society." *The Times* breathlessly relayed the opinion of an anonymous Russian "secret police agent": "It is the Nihilists who are everywhere and nowhere. If you see ten persons together, you can never tell whether nine of them do not belong to them."[13]

In short, Vera and her trial confirmed for Europeans that Russia was an exotic, eastern "despotism tempered by assassination." And the worst was yet to come. "Russia has long been pointed out as the destined scene of a worse than French revolution," the British *Morning Post* pronounced. The French were particularly eager to draw revolutionary parallels. Vera was ceaselessly compared to Charlotte Corday, the daughter of an aristocrat who had stabbed the radical Jacobin Jean-Paul Marat in 1793. Vera's act, *Le Bien Public* declared in carefully chosen terms, inspired "terror in the souls of those who are on high, of those privileged with power and fortune." Gorchakov only confirmed this opinion in European minds when he somewhat unthinkingly pronounced: "There is something rotten in the state of Denmark."[14]

In some journalistic circles in Britain and France, there was more than a little quiet glee at the outcome of the trial. The Russia that so earnestly strove to liberate the Balkans and enter European power politics was exposed as a tyrannical "oriental" backwater. Russia had accused Europe of Machiavellian tactics for allowing the Balkan Christians to languish under Turkish domination. Now, it seemed that the Russian "liberators" were no better than the supposed Ottoman "oppressors."[15] Russia was, in fact, still the land of the Tatars.

The tone of the accounts suggested that Americans and Europeans felt safe from the Russian nihilist malady. In all of its romance, its cruelty, and its passion, the story of Vera and the nihilists appeared to be a peculiarly Russian drama. The "lesson" of the Vera Zasulich trial, according to the western newspapers, was for Russia alone—a "warning to absolutism."[16]

And then, in that very year of 1878, the age of assassinations began.

～

Isolated, the rebels are doomed to death, but their example is not lost, and other malcontents rise after them. They form a league and from defeat to defeat, they finally arrive at victory.

— ELISÉE RECLUS, *Le Révolté*, 1882[17]

Within weeks of Vera's trial, the terrorist infection crossed Russia's borders. As if on cue, on May 11, 1878, a handsome young loner named Max Hodel waited in a Berlin crowd for Kaiser Wilhelm I to pass by in his carriage. As the carriage drove by, Hodel fired repeatedly at the kaiser, eventually emptying his six-chamber revolver. The shots went astray, and the kaiser was unhurt. Hodel was arrested and interrogated at length, but the German police were convinced that Hodel's was the act of a solitary, deranged man.[18] Still, the German newspaper *Allgemeine Zeitung* could not ignore the connection between the celebration of Vera's acquittal and the actions of a man like Hodel.[19]

The kaiser, like his fellow sovereign Alexander II, was determined to show his unflinching bravery and continued to promenade in an open carriage, without any extra guard. This stubbornness nearly cost him his life. On June 2, 1878, a philosophy student turned radical, Karl Nobiling, aimed a double-barreled shotgun at the kaiser's carriage and managed to fire a series of shots into the kaiser's face, arms, and back. Though Wilhelm was by now eighty-one years old, and though the wounds bled profusely, he did not die. His helmet and thick coat spared him the worst.[20]

German society was shaken. Sympathy for the wounded regent was expressed in public forums, and prayers were said for his speedy recovery. Barely a murmur was heard when the government cracked down on seditious activity and arrested hundreds of suspects. No less than 521 people were convicted of offenses against the person of the kaiser and sentenced to punishments of varying severity. The German chancellor, Bismarck, found it an ideal moment for launching a long-desired political goal: a dissolution of the German parliament, the calling of new elections, and the passing of an antisocialist law. He achieved all of these by September 9, 1878. The German socialists were, after that date, prohibited from forming societies, publishing books or pamphlets, or even meeting in public places without government approval.[21]

German investigators were now convinced that both attempts on the life of the kaiser were somehow part of an international conspiracy. They enlisted the help of the Russian police in exploring any potential connection with the Russian terrorist movement. The tsar was eager to oblige this request. Soon, there was mutual cooperation between the two states in suppressing revolutionary activity.[22]

But the infection spread still further, and other European states succumbed. In October 1878, the anarchist Juan Oliva Monacasi tried to kill King Alfonso XII of Spain; one month later, Giovanni Passante stabbed the arch-reactionary King Humbert I of Italy. Surveying these international events from their Russian stronghold, Land and Freedom rejoiced in the Europe-wide consternation over these attacks. Their journal, *Land and Freedom*, denied all connection with international terrorism but expressed unmitigated approval. Assassinations were signs of a "coming storm," indeed, a "coming revolution." The year 1878 would be forever remembered in history, *Land*

and Freedom wrote. It was the beginning of a new age, and assassination was "the idea of the century."[23]

European anarchists were the first to seize upon the Russian example and transform it into an ideological stance. Peter Kropotkin, a Russian exile, was one of the first to advocate for a new path for anarchism. After he fled Russia in 1876 to escape Russian imprisonment, he lived for a time in Switzerland and quickly rose in the ranks of the anarchist party. Mild-mannered and soft-spoken, with soft eyes and a long, flowing beard, he bore no resemblance to his fiery anarchist predecessor, Bakunin. To many, he appeared to embody a temperate, humanitarian socialism.[24] Beneath his genteel surface, however, Kropotkin cherished a fascination with violent radical action.

Kropotkin met Vera in 1878, mere months after she had fled to Switzerland. He later remembered how the bravery of the "heroic girl" captivated him. Vera's courage, her modesty and self-effacement, and, above all, her sudden, vertiginous celebrity convinced Kropotkin that she was the model for other revolutionaries to follow. After 1878, Kropotkin occasionally felt deep misgivings about individual acts of violence. But time and again, glorious Russian terrorist acts aroused in him the temptation to celebrate assassination as the true path to revolution.[25]

Elisée Reclus, Kropotkin's close friend and anarchist comrade, found himself similarly enthralled by Russian terrorism in 1878. In the early 1870s, this French geographer turned anarchist exile had gained a reputation in Switzerland as a scholar of revolution. For many years, he had insisted on "education" and persistent propaganda in order to carefully lay the groundwork for the coming socialist order. But in 1878, Reclus tasted, for the first time, the intoxicating spirit of revolt. In July of that year, two wandering Russian exiles, Vera Zasulich and Dmitrii Klements, stopped at his home during their tour through the mountains. Reclus found himself utterly entranced by these "nihilists." He immediately wrote to his brother that he had discovered "the salt of the earth." For Reclus, "their devotion to duty, their contempt of death, their spirit of solidarity, their tranquillity of soul amaze me, and I turn red when I compare myself to them." Through Vera and Dmitrii, Reclus became convinced that a "new society of peace, joy and love," could only be born when young people "were not afraid to die."[26]

In August 1878, Kropotkin and Reclus together redefined and refurbished an older anarchist phrase: "propaganda by the deed." Originally, this term was meant to describe practical revolutionary action of all types: strikes, uprisings, rebellions. Now, these tactics were crowded out by a more narrow focus on pure terror—terrorism of the knife, the gun, and the bomb. Actions, after all, spoke far louder than words. In a society where force was the principle of government, spoken propaganda was of limited value. The only weapon against violence was violence itself. As Zasulich, Hodel, and Nobiling had all shown, even failed attacks against state agents shook the foundations of state power. The spirit of revolt was "contagious" and would quickly spread throughout an entire movement.[27]

Kropotkin and Reclus forcefully argued for adopting this new form of "propaganda" as official anarchist policy. In 1879, they launched a journal, *Le Révolté*, which included articles on the glories of individual acts of violence— "permanent revolt by word of mouth, in writing, by the dagger, the rifle, dynamite."[28] For three years, they had limited success. Then came the spectacular assassination of Alexander II in 1881.

In July 1881, as Europe was still reeling from the news of the bomb attack on St. Petersburg's Catherine Canal, the anarchist congress in London passed a formal resolution stating that a new era had dawned. "It is absolutely necessary," the resolution proclaimed, "to exert every effort towards propagating, by deeds, the revolutionary idea and to arouse the spirit of revolt in those sections of the popular masses who still harbor illusions about the effectiveness of legal methods." Ominously, "technical and chemical sciences" were singled out as means to that end.[29]

From 1881 on, anarchists were convinced that terror spoke more effectively than "thousands of publications and a flood of words." Like the People's Will before them, European anarchists believed that acts of destruction could create shock waves that would ripple through society and "shake the colossus" of government. Supposedly all-powerful states would be exposed as weak and cowardly. The fear of the powerful would, in turn, breathe hope to the oppressed. The toiling millions would recognize their champions. Bomb blasts and gunshots would sound the alarm, awaken the sleeping masses, and inspire the dispossessed to seize what was rightfully theirs.[30]

Above all, the inspiration of terrorism could be drawn not just from the deeds themselves but from the superior character of those who perpetrated them. Terrorists became, in Kropotkin's words, "intrepid souls who know that it is necessary to dare in order to succeed" and "lonely sentinels who enter the battle long before the masses are sufficiently aroused to raise openly the banner of insurrection."[31]

And in their calm embrace of arrest, imprisonment, and even death, they became saints. "These heads which pass proudly under the noose, proclaiming to the crowd, on high from the scaffold, the promise of a better future, will not fall in vain," Kropotkin wrote in 1879, after Soloviev's execution for his attempt on the life of the tsar. And again, in 1881, he urged the revolutionaries to follow Sofia Perovskaia and the other members of the People's Will, so that "the blood of the martyrs is not to be shed in vain." All socialists could learn from the examples set by these sacrificed heroes: "For what picture could be more gripping, more sublime, or more beautiful than that of the efforts made by the precursors of revolutions?"[32]

Kropotkin and Reclus had no compunction about venerating those who killed. For them, the aim of violence was not revenge, nor was the motive hatred. Anarchists did not embrace murder for its own sake; they did so out of love, out of hope, and, above all, out of an ideal of universal brotherhood. Terrorists were, in effect, condemned to act when others could not, forced to turn their hands against the oppressors of the many. Men like Soloviev, Kropotkin declared, had one sole aim: "to sacrifice themselves to help the people throw off the yoke, under which they have groaned for centuries."[33]

Reclus took up his pen to convince the skeptical. Anarchism appeared a violent, chaotic creed, he wrote, but the appearance was the opposite of the truth. The existing world was to blame for violence, misery, and chaos. The anarchist wished to replace this terrifying reality with the ideal of the centuries: the ideal of "brotherhood," as first described in the New Testament. Like the apostles of old, anarchists scorned the pleasures of life and lived "with the wretched and outcasts." In the name of those who suffered, anarchists warred against "the furies which are ever bringing people into hostile collision, and all of which arise from the bondage of the weak to the strong under the form of slavery, serfage, and service." The anarchist, then, despite his violence, was Christ-like in his "devotion and self-sacrifice."[34]

In France, the anarchist call for hero-martyrs was not ignored for long. In 1882, a young radical assassinated a wealthy industrialist in Roanne, and a series of bomb blasts rocked the Lyon region. One of the bombs detonated in an ordinary music hall during an afternoon concert. Leaflets printed by *Le Révolté* claimed the credit: "Yes, we are guilty of proceeding with the practice of our theories by all means, by the word, by the pen, BY THE DEED— that is to say, by revolutionary acts, whatever they may be."[35]

The French authorities found themselves following in the footsteps of their Russian and German counterparts. In 1883, to quell the anarchist violence, French police arrested any and all remotely connected with the anarchist movement. Sixty-five people were charged with promoting anarchism, Kropotkin among them. Forced to take the stand in court, Kropotkin calmly followed the example of his Russian predecessors. He denied nothing, and caused a sensation when he proclaimed that "when a party, like the nihilists of Russia, finds itself in a position where it must either disappear, subside, or answer violence with violence, then it has no cause to hesitate and must necessarily use violence."[36]

His accusers were in no position to protest, Kropotkin argued. After all, he reminded them, "This idea is so just and so humane that you yourselves, gentlemen, in France, applauded Vera Zasulich for firing at the oppressive magistrate, General Trepov."[37]

"Propaganda by the deed" spread through Europe and America in ever-widening circles. In the 1880s, one man above all others expanded the reach of radical violence across two continents. His enemies derided him as "General Boom-Boom," for his love of the bomb, but his name was Johann Most. Most was perhaps the most single-minded and ruthless of all anarchist agitators. For him, violence was neither the regrettable progeny of oppression nor a necessary evil to be used sparingly. It was, in fact, the essence of revolution.

Most's unquenchable anger at the existing world was born in the misery of his childhood in Germany. His family was poor, his stepmother tyrannical and abusive. His jaw was severely deformed, which made his face appallingly ugly until his later adulthood, when he grew a large beard to cover it. The fierce love of violence that marked his revolutionary career was, by his own admission, the product of an "embittered" youth.[38]

Most's first real feelings of true "joy" were found in socialism. Like Vera before him, Most was drawn to the camaraderie and friendship found in radical circles. In his memoirs, Most explained the transformation that overcame him during his first socialist meeting in Switzerland in the early 1860s: "I began to feel like a real human being. . . . I began to live in the realm of ideals. . . . The cause of humanity became my cause."[39]

Even in his early years in the movement, Most was an indomitable presence somehow out of step with the mostly temperate Swiss and German Social Democratic parties. A powerful orator, he had the charisma to inspire in his listeners a restless urge for action. In 1878, Most believed that his true purpose had been revealed. Without hesitation, Most called for more violence, more assassinations. The German Social Democrats, reeling from Bismarck's repression, distanced themselves from Most's extremist rhetoric. Most himself was expelled from Germany in December 1878 and fled to England.[40]

From the safety of London, Most founded *Freiheit*, a newspaper that tirelessly championed a turn to violence in the German socialist movement. In *Freiheit*, Most finally unleashed the savage rhetoric that would become his signature for the rest of his revolutionary career.

Freiheit soon became the premier European organ advocating propaganda by the deed. "Shoot, burn, stab, poison and bomb," Most wrote. "Revolutionaries with the courage of your convictions and the sense to assassinate: ready, aim, FIRE!" Like Nechaev many years before him, Most proclaimed openly: "All methods are justified to achieve the social revolution." "Comrades of *Freiheit*," he wrote, "we say murder the murderers. Rescue mankind through blood, iron, poison, and dynamite."[41]

The Nechaevite rhetoric was no accident. In 1880, Most published a translation of Nechaev's *Catechism* in *Freiheit*, and he was seemingly familiar with Nechaev's *General Rules of the Organization* as well. Throughout the early 1880s, Most tirelessly utilized Nechaev's conspiratorial tactics. When *Freiheit* was banned in Germany, he sent it through the mail using disguised return addresses. When the German police threatened to open all German mail in order to prevent the newspaper from reaching subscribers, Most used smugglers to carry thousands of copies across the German border. In 1879 and 1880, his close ally Wilhelm Hasselman went to Germany to radicalize the Social Democratic movement by creating a secret organization, based on a system of cells, to carry out agitation and propaganda. The cells adopted all of the paraphernalia of conspiracy and terror: invisible ink, secret passwords, revolvers, and dynamite.[42]

In 1881, Most finally went too far. On March 19 of that year, he gleefully celebrated the assassination of Alexander II on the front page of *Freiheit*. "AT LAST!" the headline screamed. "Sterling propaganda by the deed!" Most exultantly proclaimed. "Let more monarchs be killed!" In gruesome detail he described how the bomb "fell at the despot's feet, shattered his legs, ripped open his belly, and inflicted many wounds." Most even rejoiced in the tsar's slow death, "in the greatest of suffering." The tsar died, "as he deserved to die—like a dog."

This was too much, even for the proudly tolerant British government.

Most was arrested immediately and charged with libel and encouraging assassination under the "Offences Against the Person Act."[43]

His April 1881 trial, like Vera's three years earlier, proved the sensation of the year. Tickets to the trial sold out, and both sympathizers and detractors filled the courthouse, to get a glimpse of the émigré terrorist. Most's lawyer did his best to argue for acquittal based on the freedom of speech. But when he attempted to argue that the authorship of the anonymous article could not be technically proven, Most refused to cooperate, insisting, "I wrote those words. I meant them." The British jury did not hesitate to convict. Most was sentenced to sixteen months at hard labor.[44]

While Most was incarcerated in Clerkenwell prison, his cause received another blow. In 1882, the British were staggered by a terrorist attack all their own. Four radical Irish republicans, who called themselves "the Invincibles," stabbed Lord Frederick Cavendish, the secretary for Ireland, and Thomas Burke, the undersecretary, in Dublin's Phoenix Park. The murders were horrific—the victims were ripped apart by long-bladed surgical knives. *Freiheit,* even in Most's absence, celebrated the Phoenix Park assassins, who had so "splendidly annihilated the evil representatives of a malignant government." The British police now declared war on the newspaper. Numerous arrests were made; ink and typesetting machinery were confiscated. When Most was released from prison in 1882, he had no future in England. So he fled again, to the United States.[45]

The émigré radicals in the United States gave him an enthusiastic welcome. First in New York, and then in Chicago, he preached the "propaganda of the deed" to throngs of disgruntled anarchists. Most exhorted his listeners to take up every kind of armed action against the state—guns, bombs, knives, and even poisons. In 1885, he published his carefully researched *Revolutionary War Science: A Little Handbook of Instruction in the Use and Preparation of Nitroglicerine, Dynamite, Gun-Cotton, Fulminating Mercury, Bombs, Fuses, Poisons, Etc. Etc.* By now, his urge to destroy could not be satiated with targeted assassinations. He desired larger, more cataclysmic acts: "Set fire to the houses, put poison in all kinds of food . . . dig mines and fill them with explosives, whet your daggers, load your revolvers, cap them, fill bombs and have them ready!"[46]

As U.S. anarchists imbibed Most's propaganda, some found themselves inexorably drawn to the terrorist way. When a bomb exploded during a demonstration in Chicago's Haymarket on May 4, 1886, "propaganda by the deed" finally arrived in the United States. Like their European predecessors, the Chicago police wasted no time. Eight men were arrested and indicted for the outrage, though no concrete proof was found that any had hurled the bomb. The trial was a sensation, elevating anarchism into a national obsession. In almost a mirror image of Vera's trial, the Chicago jury convicted men who were likely innocent. Four were hanged, and instantly achieved the kind of "martyrdom" that Vera herself never attained.[47]

In the years following Haymarket, Johann Most's terror campaign continued to bear fruit. Alexander Berkman, a typesetter for *Freiheit*, was a Lithuanian-born émigré who converted to radicalism upon his arrival in the United States at the young age of seventeen. In 1892, Berkman longed to reenergize a waning anarchist movement with one spectacular act. He decided to assassinate Henry Clay Frick, the industrialist who, in that same year, violently broke up the Homestead steel strike in Pennsylvania, killing ten workers. Berkman boldly entered Frick's Pittsburgh office, shot him twice in the neck, and then stabbed him several times in the leg. Frick survived, and Berkman served fourteen years in prison.

Under interrogation, Berkman confessed that he took the false name Rakhmetov for the purposes of his act. The Pittsburgh police entirely missed the reference, but Berkman had chosen the name in honor of his favorite character in Chernyshevskii's *What Is to Be Done?*[48]

Such tributes to the Russian pioneers of radicalism were common. Legends of the Russian terrorists circulated widely among American anarchists. Most's translation of Nechaev's *Catechism* became staple reading, and some enterprising anarchists wrote and produced a drama about the assassins of Alexander II. Sofia Perovskaia was depicted as "a noble anarchist girl." The "nihilists" became the idols of the hour. Most himself once confessed to the famous anarchist Emma Goldman his contempt for women in general, and radical women in particular. He made an exception for only one nation—the Russians. Given the examples of Sofia Perovskaia, Vera Zasulich, and Goldman herself, Russian women obviously had the wherewithal to become true revolutionaries.[49]

It was little wonder that, by the end of the nineteenth century, terrorism became known throughout the world as "the Russian method." What had originally seemed so exotic in the distant Russian context now loomed as a threat terribly near. Especially in the West, the Russian nihilists were justified in authoritarian Russia, but an outrage in staunchly "liberal" Europe and America. William Gladstone, the great British prime minister, petulantly voiced this hypocrisy in 1893: "This form of Anarchy is the Russian Nihilism imparted by way of contagion to a few hopeless subjects in other countries. In Russia, the Nihilists have much to say, if not for themselves, yet against their opponents. In other countries, it is in the main a causeless, and therefore a degenerate Nihilism."[50]

～

Never has a novel by Alexander Dumas filled us with as much delight as these extraordinary adventures.

— *LE TEMPS,* April 24, 1878

Nihilism had arrived abroad. As violence became a brutal political fact for so many western countries, the imaginations of the literary and intellectual world were enflamed by visions of mysterious foreign radicals arriving on western soil, bringing a Pandora's box of violent rebellion with them.

The sources for this fascination were, of course, the endless stories of nihilists printed in western papers. Especially after the assassination of Alexander II, nihilists became an obsession. Articles with titles such as "The Secret of Nihilism," and "Talks with a Nihilist" appeared in newspapers. Nihilists were analyzed and interviewed. Their psychological makeup was scrutinized, and even their physical characteristics were typed. The women were of particular interest—they seemed to simultaneously possess the feminine trait of empathy for the oppressed and the masculine urge for violence. Though, in the words of *The New York Times,* they were labeled "destroying angels" that perpetrated "red terror in Russia," they remained an impenetrable, and therefore intriguing, mystery.[51]

Then, in 1883, Europe finally found a willing nihilist spokesman—one who freely offered to provide exclusive insight into the mind of Russian radicalism from the standpoint of personal experience. And nihilism could find no more eloquent or more dashing representative than Sergei Kravchinskii.

By 1880, Kravchinskii had resigned himself to a life of permanent exile in Europe. Especially after he married in 1879, Kravchinskii lived the Russian radical movement only vicariously. Barred from direct action, he developed his talents as a writer, speaker, and public intellectual. His innocent good looks and impeccable refinement eased his admission into European intellectual circles; Kravchinskii was just the kind of romantic, chic young radical with whom European leftists liked to associate.[52]

Immediately after 1881, with Europe still stunned by the assassination of Alexander II, Kravchinskii decided to write the book that would uncover Russian nihilism for the West and make his own name. Published in 1882 in

Italy as *La Russia Sotteranea,* it was quickly translated into English as *Underground Russia.* In time, its popular, overwrought style and exotic subject matter made it a European sensation.

In *Underground Russia,* Kravchinskii crafted an extraordinary paean to the heroes of Russian nihilism. The book confirmed Europe's most romantic impressions of Russian radicalism: that Russia was a land of unremitting tyranny and cruelty; that the spirit of resistance and revolt permeated all classes; and that there existed a particular cohort of self-abnegating, virtuous individuals prepared to suffer unto death for the sake of Russian freedom.

In Kravchinskii's Russia, soldiers patrolled the streets, rendering the cities virtual "military camps." Arrest, imprisonment, and exile occurred on the slightest of pretexts—a breath of gossip or a single pamphlet. Prisons themselves were mere torture chambers, where guards inflicted "vile and useless cruelty" to please their superiors. Under such conditions, ordinary Russians languished as little more than slaves "exhausted by hunger, broken down by toil," their lives "full of sorrow, of suffering, of outrage."[53]

In such a world, the desire for violent revolution was natural, the most "spontaneous" of impulses. In Russia, Kravchinskii explained, "a man must have been either blind or hypocritical to believe in the possibility of any improvement except by violent means." Fear paralyzed most, but a few noble individuals dared to fight. They were Romantic figures—bold, daring, self-sacrificing. Each revolutionary "takes in his heart a solemn oath to consecrate all his life, all his strength, all his thoughts, to the liberation of the population." Each revolutionary was consoled and inspired by a vision, a "sublime idea," which allowed him to endure suffering and "meet death with a glance of enthusiasm and a smile of happiness." Kravchinskii left himself out of the story, but traces of his flamboyant spirit mark every page.[54]

In *Underground Russia,* terrorists were heroes. Motivated by "grief and rage," they turned against the oppressors of the people. Defenders of "outraged humanity," they were also "proud as Satan," refusing to bow to the yoke of despotism. Kravchinskii understood his European audience: Terrorism appealed to many as "noble, terrible, and irresistibly fascinating."[55] He sprinkled *Underground Russia* with hagiographies of his friends and acquaintances. A variety of intriguing portraits emerges. Some radicals were dreamy idealists, others hardheaded Machiavellians; some were terrifying and powerful, others modest and saintly. But each and every one was a character worthy of adoration.

Kravchinskii lavished particular praise on two noblewomen turned terrorists he admired: Vera Zasulich and Sofia Perovskaia. In *Underground Russia,* they were sketched as striking contrasts. Vera was not beautiful, Sofia was. Vera was quiet and moody, Sofia lively and willful. Between them, however, a common portrait emerged of a modest, self-abnegating woman who disguised, beneath a simple exterior, an iron will, a passion for revolution, and a saintly drive for martyrdom.[56]

Kravchinskii's description, together with Alexandrov's summation at the trial, formed the image of Vera that forever endured in the West. It is a study in contradictions. Vera was "an angel of vengeance," who gave terrorism "its divine aureola, and gave to it the sanction of sacrifice and of public opinion." Her modesty concealed a brooding, almost wild internal life. When a certain mood moved her, Kravchinskii wrote, she sought consolation in nature, sometimes roaming alone throughout the night. She possessed, in his words, "a mind of the highest poetry."[57]

Vera's essential yearning was for a life of action. "Vera would like to shoot Trepoffs every day, or at least once a week. And, as this cannot be done, she frets." And when reminded that "we cannot sacrifice ourselves every Sunday, as our Lord is sacrificed," Vera struggled to submit to fate. She was, in sum, "a woman for great decisions and great occasions."[58]

Kravchinskii's book of idealized nihilists traveled to England in 1883, and Kravchinskii himself followed shortly thereafter. He was no less adept at charming Britons than Russians. Friedrich Engels characterized him as "dreamy, sensitive," and George Bernard Shaw found in him "the heart of an affectionate child." *Underground Russia* made a profound impression on many, and it was not long before fiction embraced a whole pantheon of nihilist characters. Nihilists began to appear even in the most unlikely literary endeavor. Nihilist women, in particular, were used to spice up otherwise conventional Romantic works of fiction.[59]

They appeared in the least likely places. They could be found in English drawing rooms, as in Mary Hawker's pseudonymous *Mademoiselle Ixe.* In this rather breathless novel, a nihilist becomes a governess and improbably shoots a Russian government official in her employers' home. The entire scene reads like an account of Vera's assassination attempt, transposed into an English country estate. As the victim falls to the ground with a crash, the nihilist-governess calmly allows herself to be disarmed, tersely explaining that her victim was "the enemy of my people, and of humanity too." In Vernon Lee's *Miss Brown,* a supposed ex-nihilist, Madame Elaguine, arrives from Russia to seduce the rather susceptible protagonist, Walter Hamlin.

Hamlin is especially tempted by the passionate exoticism of this young woman who tells a terrifying tale of a mysterious secret society determined to execute her as a traitor.[60]

Sometimes, readers had to be taken to Russia in order to experience the full flavor of the nihilist atmosphere. In the novel *On Peter's Island,* by Arthur and Mary Ropes, an American journeys into the heart of Russian radicalism and entangles himself in the conspiratorial world of a nihilist secret society, where members are known only by numbers and enemies are assassinated with cold, ruthless precision. The protagonist is particularly charmed by a short-haired, redheaded young woman, who is the quintessential Russian female radical: shy, reticent, and yet fearless enough to plot the assassination of the tsar.[61]

Some of the most well known European authors could not resist the temptation to write of Russian nihilism. One of the least likely happened to be one of the first: Oscar Wilde. Oddly, the man whose work would later be characterized as "aesthetic hedonism" chose Vera Zasulich as the subject of his first play. *Vera, or the Nihilists* contains none of the satire and cynicism for which Wilde would later become so well known. Instead, it is an earnest tragedy, a sincere attempt on the part of Wilde to enter into the world of the nihilists and expose what he called their essential "passion."[62]

Unfortunately, what resulted was nothing less than melodrama. *Vera* is full of secret societies with complicated oaths, passionate dreams of violent revolution, and noble acts of self-sacrifice. The backdrop is the Russia of the British news accounts—a monstrous tyranny, where martial law threatens at every turn and convicts are marched daily to their Siberian fates. The tsar of the play is an unrepentant tyrant, who thinks nothing of locking up scores of Russians, since, in his words, "there are too many people in Russia, too much money spent on them."

Vera is the centerpiece of the play, a nihilist woman par excellence. She is an ordinary peasant girl whose brother has been sent to Siberia and whose desire for revenge against the Russian state takes her into the tsar's throne room. Like Vera Zasulich of the newspaper accounts, Vera Sabouroff is a quintessential contradiction: a coldblooded assassin with the heart of a sensitive woman. She is "as hard to capture as a she-wolf is, and twice as dangerous." She does not flinch at the thought of killing.

But Wilde simply could not resist giving Vera a quintessentially feminine flaw: a capacity to fall passionately in love with the wrong man. In a Wildean flight of fancy, Vera finds herself smitten by a particularly dashing and noble co-conspirator, who turns out to be Alexis, the heir to the Russian throne. Though Alexis is sympathetic to the nihilists, he becomes their target once his father dies. And Vera is the chosen assassin. Her ruthless will and her woman's heart clash. There is only one solution: death. In the crowning melodramatic ending, Vera does not shoot the tsar, she shoots herself. Her last words are: "I have saved Russia!"

Wilde's first play was, not surprisingly, a dramatic failure. By sheer co-incidence, it was scheduled to open in late 1881, after the assassination of Alexander II, and Wilde agreed to put off production for a time. The first performance took place in New York in August 1883. The reaction of the critics was uniformly negative: "unreal," "fanciful," and "dramatic rot." But Wilde insisted that his intentions were entirely serious. He wanted, he said, to depict "modern Nihilistic Russia, with all the terror of its tyranny and the marvel of its martyrdoms."[63]

Just three years later, the American-born British novelist Henry James hoped to succeed where Wilde had failed. James's *The Princess Casamassima* is the most idiosyncratic of his novels, an earnest attempt to enter a distinctly un-Jamesian world of ruthless conspiracies and political assassinations. Hyacinth, the protagonist, is an illegitimate son of a nobleman, and thus a natural rebel against the upper classes. He is easily beguiled into a secret society consumed by revolutionary ideals. When he meets the Princess Casamassima, he inadvertently draws this elegant aristocrat into his subterranean radical life.

In the end, however, James, like Wilde, failed to capture the contradictory combination of self-abnegation and violence that was the signature of genuine Russian radicalism. His characters were true Jamesian figures, beset by interior contradictions and hesitations. Despite his humble background, Hyacinth is far too genteel and squeamish to be truly fanatic. And the princess, the noblewoman turned nihilist, never becomes more than an ethereal radical, dabbling in revolution to satisfy a thirst for extreme sensations. In sum, James was too much the artist of the tentative and elusive to tackle something as rough-edged and real as nihilist terrorism.[64]

In a less serious vein, even Sir Arthur Conan Doyle could not resist including a Russian nihilist in one of his Sherlock Holmes mysteries. In "The Adventure of the Golden Pince-nez," the murderer turns out to be none other than a homely, near-sighted nihilist woman. The story is a short one, but Doyle does not fail to include hints of assassinations, secret societies, and an undying love for a cause that evokes a passionate love of sacrifice. Above all, he includes a nihilist whom he describes as possessing "a certain nobility" and a "gallantry in the defiant chin and in the upraised head, which compelled something of respect and admiration."[65]

In every case, the nihilists were feared and admired, the products of an alien culture with its desperate bravery and cold cruelty. A deep ambivalence about them made them charming—it was hard to know whether to praise them for their idealism or condemn them for their extremism.

In the end, however, it was fated that the man who had given birth to nihilism on Russian soil was also the man who sent his nihilists abroad. The most popular European novel about Russian radicalism was written by none other than Ivan Turgenev himself.

Turgenev wrote the novel *Virgin Soil* in the 1870s, during the height of the "to the people" movement. As with *Fathers and Sons,* he sought to capture something of the spirit of radicalism, especially what he saw as its idealistic and noble populist impulses. Unlike his previous masterpiece on nihilism, however, *Virgin Soil* never managed to captivate audiences in Russia. His characters were seen as flat and lifeless, invented by a man who had spent too much of his time away from his native land.

Abroad, however, the book became a minor sensation. Translated into all of the major European languages, it was praised by leading literary figures such as Gustav Flaubert and Henry James. There is little doubt that James borrowed heavily from *Virgin Soil* when writing *Princess Casamassima.*[66]

After the trial of Vera Zasulich in 1878, *Virgin Soil* was elevated to the status of a prophecy, this time because of its depiction of a female revolutionary: Marianna. German and French critics were quick to notice the eerie similarities between Marianna and Vera, despite the fact that Turgenev had not heard of Vera before 1878. The parallels in physical appearance were particularly striking: gray eyes, chestnut hair, and a long aquiline nose. Like Vera, Marianna is a noble outcast taken in by wealthy relatives, and like Vera, she rebels against her subordinate status. To free herself, Marianna reads revolutionary literature, and thus overcomes her personal suffering with a determination to help those less fortunate. Most important is Marianna's impulse to martyr herself for the people. "It seems to me at moments," Marianna passionately declares, "that I suffer for all the oppressed—the disinherited people, in Russia; or rather, I don't suffer, I get indignant, for them. I revolt; I am ready to give my life for them." It was perhaps this very passage that led a journalist in *Revue des Deux Mondes* to explain that "like Marianne, Vera did not have pity for her own misfortune, she suffered for the oppressed, the disinherited. Or rather she did not suffer, she was indignant, and she revolted. She was inspired to act against her own powerlessness."

Perhaps inspired by his own prophecy, Turgenev did write about Vera herself in 1878. He composed a short poetic piece entitled "The Threshold," in which a "girl" is about to cross a threshold into a world of "suffering" and "sacrifice." As she takes the fateful step, an anonymous voice intones the final word of the poem: "Saint!"[67]

～

In the midst of universal enthusiasm and true adoration, Zassulic preserved all the simplicity of manner, all the purity of mind, which distinguished her before her name became surrounded by the aureole of an immortal glory. That glory, which would have turned the head of the strongest Stoic, left her so phlegmatic and indifferent, that the fact would be absolutely incredible, were it not attested by all who have approached her, if only for a moment.
　　—SERGEI KRAVCHINSKII, *Underground Russia*[68]

For the rest of her life, celebrity dogged Vera wherever she went. From the first moments of her escape to Switzerland, her movements were tracked. Repeated rumors of her return to Russia were printed in various papers, as were odd tales of her appearance at various functions and even of her seclusion in a few convents.[69] Her fame completely overtook the unlucky Trepov, who could not be mentioned in news accounts without a recounting of the Zasulich affair. When Trepov died in 1889, his obituaries dwelt on Vera's attempt to kill him eleven years earlier. In 1918, Trepov's nephew was afforded the same treatment: The news of Mikhail Trepov's death was accompanied by a story about his infamous uncle, shot by the legendary Vera Zasulich.[70]

Throughout the 1870s and 1880s, in both Russia and Europe, Vera was universally acknowledged as the woman who inspired Russian terrorism. In February 1880, when the bomb under the tsar's dining room exploded, European newspapers speculated that Vera was in St. Petersburg, involved in these murderous events. When the tsar was assassinated, Vera was declared the woman who had led the nihilists down the road to terror. It seemed that few reporters could resist linking the long chain of Russian terrorist attacks back to her. She had been instrumental in making "political assassination a recognized means of action" and was "regarded as a sort of ideal Jeanne d'Arc of the party." She was, without doubt, a "heroine of the revolution," one of the "Russian Destroying Angels."[71]

Various European socialist movements tried to acquire her as a symbol.

French anarchists wrote to her in Geneva, inviting her to receptions in Paris, where they promised to gather thousands of well-wishers. German anarchists asked her to write letters condemning German Social Democracy. The French socialist in exile Henri Rochefort, who helped secure Vera a secret apartment in Geneva immediately after her arrival, was determined to exploit the celebrity of his new charge. Within days of her arrival, the impeccable gentleman formally arrived at her apartment to invite her to a dinner with some of his French friends.

Vera, finding European fame no more tolerable than the Russian, at first steadfastly refused all invitations. She once made an exception, to her ever-lasting regret. Agreeing to appear at Rochefort's apartment for dinner, Vera arrived dressed in her usual disheveled nihilist fashion. His splendid resi-dence was filled with guests attired in tailcoats and dresses, representing the cream of the French and Swiss intelligentsia. Vera was seated at the head of a sumptuously laden banquet table and was feted as Russia's revolutionary heroine. Horrified and angry at this display of radical chic, Vera sat for a time in stunned silence. Finally, she urged Klements to take her home.[72]

Klements, who continued to live with her for some months after their mountain adventure, screened her from the flood of curious onlookers and eager devotees. She was particularly determined to avoid public participation in European left-wing disputes. As an émigré, she at first knew very little about German Social Democracy, and even less about European anarchism. Her spirit remained in Russia, where her friends and comrades continued the fight in her absence.[73]

At times, loneliness threatened to overwhelm her. She felt empty in the absence of the movement and wanted nothing more than to return to the days of happy activity when she lived in its bosom, as in Kiev or in the En-glish Commune in St. Petersburg. With the floodlight of fame upon her, peo-ple seemed to stare at her as a phenomenon. Few truly knew her as a person.

In August 1878, in despair, Vera wrote a distraught letter from Geneva to her old friend Masha. She sensed that Masha had grown cold toward her. So many misunderstandings had developed between the two women in the months after the assassination attempt, and Vera wanted to clear the air and revive their friendship. While the world lionized her, Vera privately con-fessed her dark regrets about that January day. One after the other, black consequences had followed from her deed. Her overnight celebrity had shown her the "nasty" side of human beings. Her criminal status in Russia had separated her from friends and family and isolated her from the revolutionary movement. Above all, her fame and exile had estranged her from the one friend whom she had cherished through all the years of struggle.

In the end, Vera was convinced that the events of January 24 had marred a wonderful friendship. Vera's fortuitous success and Masha's equally fortuitous failure had placed an insurmountable barrier between them. Vera was now known as Russia's first female terrorist, and Masha was forgotten. But Vera would have done anything to change history. When she thought of the vicissitudes of fate, she said that "tears came to my eyes." It was "the kind of revenge," she continued, that Trepov "himself could not invent, even if he possessed the imagination of a genius."[74]

Vera never received Masha's response. On the night of October 11, before Masha could post her reply, her apartment was raided by gendarmes seeking evidence relating to the murder of Mezentsev. Determined not to give the police what they were looking for, Masha shot at the gendarmes twice, but missed both times. Desperately, she tried to destroy her letter to Vera by tearing it apart and swallowing the pieces. But it was too late. The gendarmes tore the revolver out of her hands and pried the paper fragments from her mouth. Masha was tried and convicted for armed action against the state. She was sentenced to hard labor and exile.[75]

This fresh blow nearly splintered Vera's already fragile nerves. While Vera sat and did nothing in Switzerland, her closest friend slipped into a life of unremitting suffering. As Vera wrote to a former acquaintance, she had spent the entirety of 1878 trying to regain her balance and "make peace" with her fate. But then, she added in revolutionary code, she received the news of Masha's "illness." Now, she found, she "could not come to terms at all."[76]

Her friends in Geneva no longer saw a quiet and shy but ultimately good-humored woman, the woman Vera had been in Russia. Instead, they grew increasingly worried about Vera's persistent dark moods, which occasionally lapsed into painful depression. Toward the end of 1878, Vera decided to take an apartment on her own, unable to tolerate the presence of other people for any length of time. She returned to her beloved books and surrounded herself with stacks of reading materials. At times, she emerged from her monastic existence and spent long evenings with her friends Deich and Kravchinskii, her companions in exile. They would cheerfully debate the latest news, and Vera would even engage in pleasant repartee with those present. Too frequently, however, she would wrap herself in complete silence, and even refuse to emerge from her apartment for days. Kravchinskii, whose boisterous personality found Vera's moodiness somewhat irritating, often rebuked her for her tendency to "self-criticism." He attributed her gloominess to "the special malady of the Russians, that of probing her own mind, sounding its depths, pitilessly dissecting it, searching for defects, always imaginary, and always exaggerated."[77]

Vera believed she had good reason to be self-critical: She had inadvertently, and now regrettably, encouraged dozens of Russians to follow in her footsteps. She was personally responsible for the Russian "turn to terror." The weight of that responsibility sat heavily on her shoulders. Each fresh incident delivered a shock to her system; she felt accountable for both the lives of the victims and the fates of the assassins. Fully aware of how terrible it was to commit such a "crime," recognizing that even the fame that followed her act was tainted by the act itself, Vera found the parade of imitators impossible to endure.

Olga Liubatovich, who would later become yet another famous female terrorist, remembered how Vera reacted to the news of Alexander Soloviev's attempt to kill the tsar on April 4, 1879. While other radicals in Switzerland rejoiced, Vera retreated into funereal silence. She remained secluded in her room for several days, refusing to see anyone. A few weeks later, she wrote to her friend and now lover, Lev Deich. On the day she heard the news of Soloviev's assassination attempt, Vera told Deich, she took a long walk in the rain until she was thoroughly soaked. Terrorism filled her with anguish. She feared that it would be "the final phase of the movement." A vision of utter failure tormented her: revolutionaries crushed by the forces of reaction, rejected by society, and thus enduring a "spiritual collapse." In short, "everything would be lost." It was impossible to endure this turn of events, she wrote, "on which my act had so much influence."[78]

That very day, after her wild walk in the rain, Vera made a momentous decision. Despite the fact that she was one of the most wanted women in Russia, she would return. If she was so influential in motivating other to commit terrorist acts, surely she could be equally persuasive in convincing her comrades to abandon their dead-end obsession with terror.[79]

Others in Switzerland agreed with her: It was time to bring the Russian radicals back to the true spirit of socialism. By August 1879, Deich and Liubatovich declared that they would join Vera in the journey back. Complicated plans were made: The conspirators first rented a house in Montreux, so that they would arouse no suspicions among the police in Geneva. From Montreux they traveled by train, through Bern and Berlin. At the border, they dressed up as Jewish merchants and pretended to speak Russian poorly, in order to confuse the border guards. It was a nerve-racking, desperate trip, but Vera was overjoyed. She was finally going home.[80]

Though it is not clear what Vera expected to find when she arrived, it must have come as a shock to find that she came far too late. Terrorism had already embedded itself deep within the psyche of the Russian revolutionary movement, and even Russia's first female terrorist could not dampen the enthusiasm of her followers. Worse still, she was prevented from trying. Since the police saw her as a highly dangerous political criminal and would have done anything to get their hands on her, she was obliged to remain in hiding in St. Petersburg. Few of her former comrades even knew she had come back.

Lev Deich later claimed that many would-be terrorists later told him that, "if Vera Zasulich herself is against terror, then that means of struggle must be wrong." But few of them seemed to act on this sentiment. The party of the People's Will grew stronger and stronger, and many of the most active Russian radicals joined in the terror plots. Vera, Deich, and a few others tried to form a more peaceful, more peasant-centered alternative organization. Calling themselves "Black Repartition," in reference to the peasants' desire for the redistribution of all agricultural land, Vera and the others tried to reconnect with villages in the south, where they had preached revolution so many years before. But to no avail. No one wished to join them. Who wanted to return to an old, failed strategy of rebellion when the possibility of assassinating the tsar was so tantalizingly near?

Soon enough, after rumors spread that the Russian police were checking the validity of every single passport in St. Petersburg, Deich and Zasulich decided to flee abroad once more. In some sense, they were happy to go, finding the Russian revolutionary climate inhospitable to their ideas. But when they left Russia in January 1880, they were still naively convinced that, in Deich's words, "the infatuation of the most forward-thinking young people with terrorism would soon fade, and then it would once again be possible to return to Russia and work among the people."[81]

～

Now, if there are those who still want to resume terror, let them ask themselves: What will they do in the time of terror? And how will they, during that time, pay for it?

—VERA ZASULICH, "Apropos of Current Events"[82]

As the infatuation with terrorism in Russia failed to fade, Vera became ever more determined to stand against it. For the rest of her life, she repeatedly took up the challenge to condemn the political tactic that she had once so eagerly embraced. In several precisely reasoned articles, she explained her conversion. Though the intoxication with terror was forgivable, she wrote, and though terrorist acts appeared harbingers of inevitable revolution, they were always, in the long run, feeble gestures. In fact, Vera argued, terrorism only exhausted the strength of the revolutionaries and tested the forbearance of society. It could not create the conditions for revolution. Glorious acts of heroic individuals became like individual performances to be applauded, but could not inspire mass action. "Liberal individuals," she wrote, "could cry in sympathy with the heroism of the terrorists, but would not feel any greater desire to act and to risk." As a result, terrorist attacks dropped one by one into the vast silence of the masses.[83]

More remarkable, however, was this former terrorist's willingness to condemn terror on moral grounds. In 1901, she precisely formulated the ethical anguish that had tormented her since the day of her acquittal: Even if shooting an evil tsarist official was "necessary," how could it be morally justified? Oddly enough, she borrowed an argument from Russia's most conservative novelist, Dostoyevsky: Who could consent to creating a kingdom of peace and freedom at the price of torturing a child? Vera twisted this question around and declared that the only person who had the right to consent was, in fact, the person who agreed to be that child. Terrorists could kill for the sake of humanity only if they were willing to suffer and die for the sake of humanity as well. Would all future terrorists be willing to pay that price?

Despite all of her precise and eloquent argumentation, Vera was not entirely immune to the temptation of supporting terrorism, and she succumbed to its appeal every now and again. The most marked of her lapses occurred in 1880, on the eve of the planned silver jubilee for the reign of Alexander II. In that year, Vera drafted an article full of violent rhetoric calling for assassination. In this singular piece, all of her younger hopes for an imminent revolutionary apocalypse, all of her hatred of the tsar as the devil who crushed revolutionary dreams, came rushing back and spilled out into a cathartic screed. "Let the shameful old man, trembling with fear and hatred in his Winter Palace, celebrate the 25th anniversary of his atrocities!" she fumed. The ordinary Russians, like the subjects of all "Asiatic despotisms," eagerly awaited the day of his death.

"Oh, Karakozov," she wrote, with uncharacteristic devotion, "if the Russian people one day achieve a humane existence, if freedom and popular justice have not disappeared from Russian soil . . . then to you, to you above all, they will erect a monument in the forum of the new age." The terrifying deeds of the new generation had ushered in "the hope of a new salvation." "Let the tyrant celebrate his jubilee," she ominously prophesied, for it would be "the last triumph of the Russian Empire." The fireworks would become the symbol "of its demolition and destruction."[84]

In March 1881, she got her wish—the old "tyrant" was dead. Impatiently, Vera awaited news that the Russians had finally been liberated. If Russia seized the moment and demanded a constitution, a free press, and basic human rights, then she could return to Russia and resume her old work of preaching revolution to the people. Could this be the revolutionary apocalypse she had been waiting for all her life?

But new hopes were as quickly dashed as the old. As she had originally predicted, ordinary Russians remained silent as ever. The moment of salvation never arrived. Instead, a new tsar was enthroned, more reactionary and despotic than his father. The assassination of Alexander II turned out to be "a tempest in a teapot."[85]

After 1881, Vera's faith in terror vanished for good. She was now known as the Russian terrorist who had renounced terrorism. A new phase of her revolutionary career was about to begin.

Epilogue

~

In 1880, a remarkable proposal was presented to Vera Zasulich. A group of Russian radical émigrés decided to make Russian radicalism palatable to the European reading public. Perhaps buoyed by the intense fascination that Vera and the Russian nihilists had aroused in the European press, they wanted to launch a new journal, *The Nihilist*. The pages would be filled with readable articles on Russian socialism, written by leading lights such as Peter Lavrov and Peter Kropotkin. Vera would serve as the editor, and her fame would guarantee subscribers. The idea seemed so promising that none other than Karl Marx supported it, and suggested that Friedrich Engels might be tempted to fund it.[1]

The journal never materialized. But the very proposal signaled the turn that Vera's radicalism was about to take. Never again would Vera live on the front lines of revolution. She would never again plot a revolt or an assassination. Instead, in the 1880s, she would begin a new phase in her career, one that was perhaps better suited to her temperament and character: She would assume the more placid and intellectual role of a Marxist theoretician.

The life of the girl assassin was over.

Always an introspective person, with an intense love of theoretical reading and intellectual debate, for the next few decades Vera poured her energies into studying and writing. The result was a flood of articles on socialist philosophy and theory; translations of theoretical and literary works from German and French into Russian, including the "Communist Manifesto"; and book-length Marxist interpretations of Voltaire and Rousseau, which, even in their unfinished form, elicited admiration from Russian socialist contemporaries such as Anatolii Lunacharskii and Vladimir Lenin.[2]

Vera's productivity was no accident. She shunned society and became reclusive to the point of asceticism. Her routine was invariable: Each morning she arose, made herself a pot of dark, bitter coffee, and immediately set pen to paper. She stopped only to smoke or, occasionally, to purchase a few paltry groceries, most often nothing more than a strip of meat. At night, when tired of writing, she would lie down on her rumpled bed with another tome of socialist theory. It was, by her own admission, a painfully lonely life. Nonetheless, in another sense, she had found her calling.[3]

Despite her near misanthropic fear of social engagements, Vera never lost her status as a celebrity. Her untidy, disheveled hair and nihilist-inspired clothing, her aura of chain-smoking, philosophical seriousness, and, above all, her reticence enveloped her with an air of mystery. Though she did not seek company, devotees sought her. Russian radicals in exile traveled the length of Europe to find her, and Europeans often found themselves by turns charmed and bemused in her presence. The socialist Lydia Dan remembered her first meeting with Vera: "It was like an Orthodox believer seeing an icon leave the iconostasis and come toward him."[4]

For radicals in particular, whether European or Russian, she radiated a pure, untainted commitment to socialism. In all of her theoretical writings, editorial work, and organizational activities, her only thought was to encourage the oppressed to revolt and to gain their freedom. She could not be bothered with logical consistency on the finer points of theory. She avoided factionalism and infighting. Some blamed her for this, labeling it philosophical confusion. But she sought nothing more than the good of the revolutionary movement as a whole.[5]

Most of Vera's writings would later slip into oblivion, with a single, extraordinary exception: Vera's exchange of letters with Karl Marx himself. In 1881, a fierce debate about proper revolutionary strategy in Russia erupted among her émigré friends. Vera decided personally to write to Marx and ask him the question that plagued Russian socialists who read his work: Did Russia have to become capitalist before it could become revolutionary? Could the Russian peasant commune serve as the basis of a future Russian Communism, or did Russia need to undergo the painful process of the destruction of peasant life in order to develop a true, industrial working class?

This technical question masked a deeper, more anguished dilemma, as Vera poignantly revealed in her letter. Was it really true, she wondered, that the Russian rural peasants needed to first become landless workers "thrown onto the streets" of Russia's cities, at the mercy of the rising capitalist class, in order to become true revolutionaries? How many "decades," even "centuries," would Russian socialists have to wait for all of this to come to pass?

Vera thus boldly and concisely presented the ultimate obstacle to Marxism for Russian socialists. Marx seemed to condemn Russian revolutionaries to an interminable inactivity, waiting for a real Russian working class to appear. For those who had spent so much time in the villages and the factories, preaching their beliefs, such passivity was unthinkable.

Marx was perhaps charmed by the combination of Vera's celebrity status and her direct, almost naive question. In his reply, he sought to ease her fears. Perhaps, he told his "Dear Citizeness," Russians did not have to wait for the perfect capitalist conditions to arise. Perhaps rural, backward Russia was an exception to his rule. Marx, it turned out, had been carefully following Russian events and had been deeply impressed by the active, fervent radicalism of Vera and her comrades. He assured Vera that his theory of the "historical necessity" of capitalism was written with Europe in mind. Russians were, for Marx, advanced pupils, and could therefore be permitted to skip a step in their revolutionary education.[6]

It might have been this letter that facilitated Vera's eventual conversion to Marxism. Marx's response acknowledged the suffering Russian people and conceded that their needs trumped the iron laws of abstract theory. She continued to study the work of Marx and Engels, and here found a socialist doctrine eminently suited to her philosophical tastes. Marxism required an immense knowledge of economics, politics, and philosophy, and thus demanded what Vera always willingly embraced: reading and reflection. Together with George Plekhanov, the erstwhile populist who would soon become known as the father of Russian Marxism, she dedicated her time and energy to proselytizing for Marxism, especially among Russian émigrés and those with contacts in Russia.[7]

Vera and Plekhanov tried to convince the Russian radicals that the perpetual failures of Russian socialism, in its various Nechaevite, populist, and terrorist incarnations, was directly related to its "unscientific" qualities. In one of her more influential articles, written in 1890, she warned her Russian compatriots that they were at a turning point in revolutionary history. The disappointment in the work among "the people," and the spectacular failures of the terrorist attacks, required a complete reassessment of the goals and strategies of revolutionary socialism. It was time for the Russians to accept the "only possible revolutionary world view: scientific worker's socialism." Ironically, in almost direct contradiction to Marx's own letter to her, she told the Russians: "Only by awakening the workers can one call them to the struggle for political freedom. Without the workers, there is no struggle at all."[8]

Because of her articles and translations, Vera's prestige among Marxists rose. In the late 1890s, when she lived in London for three brief years, she befriended such well-known figures as Friedrich Engels and Marx's daughter, Eleanor Aveling. Her friendship with Engels became so affectionate that she nursed him while he was dying and was one of the most prominent figures at his funeral in 1895. In 1899, Vera was additionally accorded respect by another influential Marxist, Vladimir Lenin. He had read her work and was impressed by her intellectual abilities. He told his wife, "Wait until you see Zasulich, she is a crystal-clear human being."[9]

In 1900, Vera, Lenin, and a number of other prominent Russian Marxists gathered in Munich to found the Marxist journal entitled *Iskra* (the Spark). It seemed the perfect moment. Marxism was flourishing in Russia, in part because the seeds of industrialization were taking root. For the first time, socialists saw the prospects of a burgeoning Russian proletariat. In Munich, a heady atmosphere enveloped Vera and the others, much reminiscent of the days spent in Kiev in the 1870s. Vera even took to living in a communal apartment with a few of her colleagues. Revolutionary comrades found it a congenial place, where anyone could get a cup of tea or a place to stay. In 1902, after the whole enterprise moved to London, communal arrangements and all, Leon Trotsky paid a visit. He left an unsurprising description of what he found in Vera's apartment: "a state of rank disorder." Revolutionaries meandered in and out of the apartment's common room, which was filled with smoke and littered with dishes and coffee cups. Lenin was even more amazed by the number of people who passed through the place on any given day. It was "more than a house with open windows, it was a public thoroughfare." Lenin's wife, Nadezhda Krupskaia, confirmed that Vera lived like a "nihilist." Her room was a mess: The floor was covered in cigarette ash and the desk with books and papers. And Vera's cooking was growing even more appalling. "I remember her frying some meat on the oil stove," Krupskaia wrote, "and snipping off pieces with scissors, and putting them in her mouth."[10]

Vera put her heart into the journal, working diligently on her editorial tasks and contributing numerous articles. But her happiness was not to last. Tensions among the powerful personalities on the editorial board constantly smoldered. They exploded in 1903, during what became famous as the Second Congress of the Russian Social Democratic Labor Party, which gathered in Brussels. There, Lenin surprised his fellow comrades with the fervency of his insistence that Russian Marxists could not afford to run a mass movement. Instead, he persistently argued that they had to form a highly organized, tightly knit, entirely dedicated clique of revolutionaries, who would exercise a definitive role in determining the goals and strategies of the party. Vera must not have been alone in seeing the ghost of Nechaev behind these words.[11]

Like a typical Nechaevite, Lenin was immediately prepared to practice the Machiavellianism he preached. To the shock of those at the Congress, Lenin proposed to eliminate potential opponents by, among other things, removing them from the *Iskra* editorial board. Vera was, in his words, "unproductive." Vera's biographers have been perplexed at the silence that shrouded Vera during the Congress. Not once did she speak against Lenin. But for the rest of her life, Vera never forgot her first glimpse of Lenin's striking resemblance to Sergei Nechaev.[12]

After the Congress, Russian social democrats split into Bolsheviks and Mensheviks. Lenin and his new conspiratorial ideas formed the core of the Bolshevik faction. Vera sided with the Mensheviks. After the 1905 revolution swept Russia, and liberalization unchained Russian politics, Vera returned home. But by now, her activism had waned. She was fifty-seven years old, and perhaps finally felt she could play the role of the "discharged heroine" that she had so long rejected.

In 1906, she bought a small summer cottage and took up gardening. In her spare time, she began her memoirs. Though the outbreak of World War I briefly stirred her, and she forcefully argued for war against Germany, her voice counted for little in those times. Other radicals, full of more passionate energy, had overtaken and overshadowed her.[13]

After the October Revolution of 1917, Vera drank the cup of disillusionment to the dregs. The Bolsheviks and their tactics appalled her. They were the new "autocracy," with their "Red Guard" that was reminiscent of the tsarist gendarmerie. She called for the most progressive minds of Russian society to struggle against this new evil. "In your publications," she wrote, as if to her Bolshevik interlocutors, "you declare from time to time that of your kingdom there will be no end. I think that, to the contrary, it will not last long, though I will not add 'thank goodness,' because you will still have time to accomplish much ineradicable evil in your native land." Her view of Lenin was equally grim: "He was willing to lie . . . if that lie, in his mind, was useful to the working class." To her sister, she was more direct. "Everything that was dear to me for my entire, long life has crumbled and died."[14]

In 1919, Vera wrote her last thoughts: "The Russia that I knew and loved is gone." She died in May of that year. When she was finally taken from her apartment in the Writers' Home in St. Petersburg, her friends were dismayed, but not shocked, to find that her rooms were so dirty with cups, plates, ashtrays, and books that there was simply no place to sit.[15]

Her funeral was quiet, attended by a few former comrades, including her closest companion, Lev Deich. The woman who had once been the most famous revolutionary in all of Europe was now all but forgotten. Vera's fame clung briefly to the faint memory of the events of 1878. Her obituary in *The New York Times* came two years too late, and was a mere three sentences long. "Included in her crimes," the correspondent erroneously reported, "was the killing of General Trepoff, Prefect of Police of St. Petersburg, in 1878."[16] After all her years of revolutionary activism, it was ultimately the assassin that they remembered.

Her death returned her to the obscurity from whence she arose.

～

It seems to you that in my last novel, The Brothers Karamazov, *there was much that was prophetic. But wait for the continuation. In it Alyosha will leave the monastery and become an anarchist. And my pure Alyosha will kill the Tsar.*

— FYODOR DOSTOYEVSKY to
Aleksei Suvorin, February 1881[17]

There is only scattered evidence that Fyodor Dostoyevsky was influenced by Vera Zasulich and his attendance at her famous trial. Aside from his few brief words about her to Grigorii Gradovskii in 1878, we have little direct proof that he thought of her again. There are a few tantalizing hints, however, that the Zasulich case stayed with Dostoyevsky for the rest of his life. Most significant are the passages describing Dmitrii Karamazov's trial in *The Brothers Karamazov*. The setting of the fictional trial might well have been transplanted from St. Petersburg in 1878. "Every ticket of admission had been snatched up," the narrator of the novel explains, and every seat filled with "lawyers, ladies, and even several distinguished personages." The presiding judge, much like Anatolii Koni, is a "humane and cultured man" and "a man of advanced ideas." The lawyer is "celebrated," causing a buzz when he enters the courtroom. Dostoyevsky's description of the lawyer's summation perfectly evokes Alexandrov's speech of March 31, 1878, and the reaction of the crowd to his summation completes the picture: "The enthusiasm of the audience burst like an irresistible storm. It was out of the question to stop it: the women wept, many of the men wept too, even two important personages shed tears."[18]

More intriguing are Dostoyevsky's more general comments to a friend, in which he sketched a planned portrait of Vera's generation. Contemplating the sequel to *The Brothers Karamazov*, the novelist promised a book sure to shock his readers. He was planning to turn his gentle former monk, Alyosha Karamazov, into a terrorist.[19]

Alyosha the terrorist—readers of Dostoyevsky will find it difficult to imagine. In *The Brothers Karamazov*, Alyosha is the unassuming, pious inter-locutor of his more fiery brothers, especially Ivan. Indeed, it is Ivan, the sec-ular rebel, who seems far more likely to take up the cause of assassination. While Ivan, in a Bakunin-like rage, revolts against the injustice of God, it is Alyosha who seeks to soothe his passions with a brotherly, Christian kiss. Dostoyevsky even concludes the novel with Alyosha's final words at the fu-neral of the boy Ilyusha. His message is unerringly Christian, speaking of reconciliation, of love, and of the promise of resurrection and life eternal.[20]

How does such a man become an assassin? We do not know how Dos-toyevsky planned the transformation, but the idea evokes the image of Vera herself. On the stand at her trial, Vera was the very picture of a self-abnegating terrorist. She was modest and gentle, and yet took upon herself the momentous task of avenging injustice and redeeming the honor of a fel-low sufferer. She had said, "It is hard to raise one's hand against another." This statement elicited Dostoyevsky's only comment on her act after her trial: "Her vacillation was more moral than the shedding of blood could have been."[21] He may have decided that it was precisely Alyosha's love, and not Ivan's rebellion, that would lead down the path to terror.

To begin as a monk and end as a terrorist—it was not an unheared-of path for Vera's comrades. What began as a fervent desire to devote oneself to God and his love became a very human and very earthly yearning for material salva-tion. Faith in God was transposed into a faith in man—and the Kingdom of God thus dragged down to earth. The radical did not abandon the love that origi-nally consumed him as a believer. Perhaps such love burned even more brightly: love for the oppressed, love for comrades, love for a perfect future order; a love that empowered acts of bravery and aroused a yearning for martyrdom.

There was but one obstacle to a love like this: the principalities and pow-ers of the existing world. Rotten with the sins of inequality and injustice, the present could not be healed. The apocalypse had to come. Love thus dictated destruction—and became a love so intense that it joined with hatred. The state appeared as a hydra, its tentacles reaching ever deeper into the move-ment and martyring its most valued apostles. Death had to pay for death.

But death itself was not to be feared. Those who loved so much that they were willing to kill also loved to die. Death crowned each act of violence with a halo, elevating the murderer into a saint. It proved that blood was not an end in itself but a means, a willing sacrifice, for the kingdom of justice to come.

In that manner, love led to terror.

It took seventy-five years for this tantalizing idea of Dostoyevsky's to receive its indirect elaboration. Writing during the depths of the Cold War, the French existentialist Albert Camus sought to explain for himself, and for others, where his terrifying century had gone wrong. He found his explanations in the past, and he touched upon Russia, where the seeds of the totalitarian disasters of his own generation were planted. Camus believed that the Russian terrorists of the nineteenth century, so convinced of the beauty of their deeds, paved the way for the mass violence in the name of justice that, in Soviet Russia and elsewhere, became known as "the Terror."

Strikingly, Camus also began with Vera Zasulich, and her shot fired at Trepov. This act launched, in Camus's own words, the age of the "fastidious assassins." After Vera, self-proclaimed lovers of humanity dedicated themselves to murder and joined a "thirty years' apostolate of blood." Their terrorism, however brutal, was not motivated by hatred nor by vengeance. It was motivated by a perfect ideal, a perfect future, for which individual lives needed to be sacrificed. They attempted to assuage their own moral qualms through their "fastidiousness," their exacting will to prove, on the gallows if necessary, that anything worth killing for is worth dying for. For Vera and the Russian terrorists after her, assassination and martyrdom were entwined to create the perfect humanistic act of violence.

To kill and to die—the future world could only be born when men were willing to do both. "The terrorists no doubt wanted to destroy," Camus wrote, "to make absolutism totter under the shock of exploding bombs. But by their death, at any rate, they aimed at recreating a community founded on love and justice, and thus to resume a mission that the Church had betrayed." Thus from the tomb of the old God arose a new divinity, which promised to redeem both murder and martyrdom.[22]

Love and justice, born of terror. This was the ultimate temptation of the terrorist. It was the fierce, raging belief that, in Vera's own words, "everywhere, heroism, struggle, and revolt were always connected with suffering and death."[23]

Notes

1. *Assassin*

1. Stepniak [Sergei Kravchinskii], *Underground Russia: Revolutionary Profiles and Sketches from Life* (London: Smith, Elder, 1883), p. 38.

2. This account is taken from Evtikhii Karpov, "V. I. Zasulich—na kanune pokusheniia," *Vestnik literatury* 6 (1919), pp. 2–4.

3. *Sankt-Peterburgskie Vedomosti*, no. 27 (January 27, 1878), p. 3; A. F. Koni, *Vospominaniia o dele Very Zasulich* (Moscow: Academia, 1933), p. 119.

4. Katerina Breshkovskaia, *Hidden Springs of the Russian Revolution* (Stanford: Stanford University Press, 1931), pp. 155–156.

5. The following account is taken from Vera Zasulich, *Vospominaniia* (Moscow, 1931), pp. 65–70.

6. Contemporary descriptions of St. Petersburg are found in: J. M. Buckley, *The Midnight Sun, the Tsar, and the Nihilist* (Boston: D. Lothorp, 1886); Isabel F. Hapgood, *Russian Rambles* (New York: Houghton, Mifflin, 1895); John Geddie, *The Russian Empire: Its Rise and Progress* (London: T. Nelson and Sons, 1885); W. E. Curtis, *Russia: The Land of the Nihilist* (Chicago: Belford, Clarke, c. 1888); Wickham Hoffman, *Leisure Hours in Russia* (London: George Bell and Sons, 1883); Augustus J. C. Hare, *Studies in Russia* (New York: George Routledge and Sons, c. 1885); Donald Mackenzie Wallace, *Russia* (New York: Henry Holt, 1905); Theophile Gautier, *Russia*, trans. Florence MacIntyre Tyson (Philadelphia: International Press, 1905).

7. W. Bruce Lincoln, *Sunlight at Midnight: St. Petersburg and the Rise of Modern Russia* (New York: Basic Books, 2000), pp. 1, 7–8; James H. Bater, "Between Old and New: St. Petersburg and the Late Imperial Era," in Michael Hamm, ed., *The City in Late Imperial Russia* (Bloomington: Indiana University Press, 1986), pp. 43–78.

8. Lincoln, *Sunlight*, p. 125; Gautier, *Russia*, pp. 111, 113–117; Buckley, *Midnight Sun*, p. 165.

9. Lincoln, *Sunlight*, pp. 127–129; Gautier, *Russia*, pp. 118–123; Geddie, *Russian Empire*, p. 310.

10. Bater, "St. Petersburg," p. 65; Hapgood, *Russian Rambles*, pp. 41–42; Lincoln, *Sunlight*, p. 127; Gautier, *Russia*, pp. 160–164.

11. Hapgood, *Russian Rambles*, pp. 41–42; Gautier, *Russia*, pp. 139–140.

12. Lincoln, *Sunlight*, p. 131; Hapgood, *Russian Rambles*, pp. 54, 59.

[13] Zasulich, *Vospominaniia,* p. 66; Hapgood, *Russian Rambles,* pp. 7–9, 67–69.

[14] Literary descriptions of the plight of a petitioner include Fyodor Dostoevsky, *Notes from Underground* (New York: Penguin, 1991), p. 4; and Alexander Herzen, *My Past and Thoughts* (Berkeley: University of California Press, 1973), pp. 263–266.

[15] Koni, *Vospominaniia,* p. 118.

[16] Zasulich, *Vospominaniia,* p. 66.

[17] Description of Trepov's reception room in "Pokushenie na zhizn s-peterburgskogo gradonachalnika F. F. Trepova," *Sankt-Peterburgskie Vedomosti,* no. 2 (January 24, 1878), pp. 1–3. Portrait in I. Bozherianov, *Nevskii Prospekt, 1703–1903* (St. Petersburg: A. I. Vilborg, 1903); D. Gertsenshtein, "Tridtsat let tomu nazad," *Byloe* 6 (1907), p. 250.

[18] These and the following details of the shooting can be found in Zasulich, *Vospominaniia,* pp. 66–67; "Pokushenie na zhizn," pp. 1–3; and Koni, *Vospominaniia,* pp. 108–110, 114–118.

[19] Koni, *Vospominaniia,* pp. 62–63; Gosudarstvennyi arkhiv Rossiiskoi federatsii (hereafter GARF), fond (f.) 109, Sekretnyi arkhiv III-ego otdeleniia (hereafter Sekretnyi arkhiv), opis (op.) 11, delo (d.) 717, list (l.) 4; M. Popov, "Iz moego revoliutsionnogo proshlogo," *Byloe* 5 (1907), pp. 297–299.

[20] Koni, *Vospominaniia,* p. 62.

[21] Koni, *Vospominaniia,* p. 62.

[22] *Novoe Vremia,* no. 687 (January 26, 1878), p. 3; *Sankt-Peterburgskie Vedomosti,* no. 27 (January 27, 1878), p. 3; *Severnyi Vestnik,* no. 27 (January 27, 1878), p. 2; *Nedelia,* no. 5 (January 29, 1878), pp. 174–175.

[23] *Sankt-Peterburgskie Vedomosti,* no. 24 (January 24, 1878), p. 2; *New York Times,* February 6, 1878, p. 1; *Times* (London), February 6, 1878, p. 5; *Le Temps,* February 10, 1878, p. 2.

[24] *Nedelia,* no. 10 (March 5, 1878), p. 333; *Moskovskie Vedomosti,* no. 26 (January 27, 1878), p. 2; *Severnyi Vestnik,* no. 27 (January 27, 1878), p. 2, *Morning Post,* February 19, 1878, p. 4; *News of the World,* February 24, 1878, p. 2; *Le Temps,* February 10, 1878, p. 2.

[25] Koni, *Vospominaniia,* p. 69.

[26] GARF, f. 109, Sekretnyi arkhiv, op. 1, d. 717, l. 3.

[27] GARF, f. 109, Sekretnyi arkhiv, op. 1, d. 717, ll. 2, 3, 10, 19, 31, 37.

[28] Jay Bergman, *Vera Zasulich: A Biography* (Stanford: Stanford University Press, 1983), p. 35.

[29] Koni, *Vospominaniia,* p. 66.

[30] Lincoln, *Sunlight,* pp. 151–154.

[31] The reports on the discovery of the leaflets throughout Russia are found in GARF, f. 109, 3-ia ekspeditsiia (eksp.), op. 163 (1878), d. 68.1, ll. 36, 54–56. The text of the leaflets is published in V. I. Nevskii, ed., *Istoriko-revoliutsionnyi sbornik* (Leningrad: Gosudarstvennoe izdatelstvo, 1924), vol. 2, pp. 331–336.

[32] Breshkovskaia, *Hidden Springs,* pp. 155–156; A. Iakimova, "Pamiati Marii Aleksan-

drovny Kolenkinoi-Bogorodskoi," *Katorga i ssylka* 31 (1927), p. 180; Karpov, "V. I. Zasulich," p. 4.

2. *Dreams of Martyrdom*

[1] Stepniak, *Underground Russia,* p. 116.

[2] Descriptions of Vera are found in P. M. Plekhanova, "Stranitsa iz vospominanii o V. I. Zasulich," in L. G. Deich, ed., *Gruppa "Osvobozhdenie truda": Iz arkhivov G. V. Plekhanova, V. I. Zasulich, i L. G. Deicha* (Moscow-Leningrad, 1926), vol. 3, p. 85; L. S. Fedorchenko, "Vera Zasulich," *Katorga i ssylka* 23 (1927), p. 301; and Lev Deich, *Za polveka* (Newtonville, MA: Oriental Research Partners, 1975), vol. 1, pp. 257–263.

[3] Deich, *Za polveka,* vol. 1, p. 260.

[4] GARF, f. 109, 3-ia eksp. op. 163 (1878), d. 68.1, l. 40.

[5] Existing biographies of Vera are incomplete, and even erroneous, mostly because they depend on Vera's later trial testimony and the summation of her defense attorney. As will be shown in chapter 10, these sources are unreliable to varying degrees. The most accurate accounts of Vera's early life are found in Evelyn Meincke, *Vera Ivanovna Zasulich: A Political Life* (Ann Arbor, MI: University Microfilms International, 1984); Margaret Maxwell, *Narodniki Women: Russian Women Who Sacrificed Themselves for the Dream of Freedom* (New York: Pergamon Press, 1990), pp. 3–49; Bergman, *Zasulich;* Wolfgang Geheiros, *Vera Zasulich und die russische revolutionäre Bewegung* (Munich: R. Oldenbourg Verlag, 1977).

[6] M. Tsebrikov, *Materialy dlia geografii i statistiki Rossii, sobrannye ofitserami generalnogo shtaba: Smolenskaia guberniia* (St. Petersburg: Tipografiia departamenta generalnago shtaba, 1862), p. 65; V. S. Orlov, *Gzhatsk. Goroda Smolenshchiny; ocherki po istorii gorodov Smolenskoi oblasti s drevnikh vremen do nashikh dnei* (Smolensk: Smolenskoe knizhnoe izd-vo, 1957).

[7] Tsebrikov, *Materialy,* p. 49.

[8] Tsebrikov, *Materialy,* p. 93.

[9] Descriptions of a typical noble female upbringing are found in Priscilla Roosevelt, *Life on the Russian Country Estate: A Social and Cultural History* (New Haven: Yale University Press, 1995), p. 182; and Aleksandra Uspenskaia, "Vospominaniia shestidesiatnitsy," *Byloe* 22 (1918), p. 19.

[10] Uspenskaia, "Vospominaniia," p. 19.

[11] Roosevelt, *Life,* pp. 240–242; E. Vodovozova, *Na zare zhizni* (Moscow, 1964), vol. 1, pp. 150–152; Barbara Alpern Engel, "Mothers and Daughters: Family Patterns and the Female Intelligentsia," in David L. Ransel, ed., *The Family in Imperial Russia* (Urbana: University of Illinois Press, 1978), pp. 44–59, 48.

[12] Uspenskaia, "Vospominaniia," p. 19.

[13] Uspenskaia, "Vospominaniia," p. 19.

[14] Uspenskaia, "Vospominaniia," p. 20.

[15] Uspenskaia, "Vospominaniia," p. 20.

16. Bergman, *Zasulich,* p. 2.

17. Vera Zasulich, "Masha. S pometami Plekhanovoi P. M. i L. G. Deicha," Rossiiskaia natsionalnaia biblioteka, Otdel rukopisei (hereafter RNB, OR), Dom Plekhanova, f. 1098, op. 1, d. 95, l. 1.

18. Zasulich, "Masha," l. 1 ; Roosevelt, *Life,* pp. 171–174.

19. Leo Tolstoy, *Childhood, Boyhood, Youth* (New York: Penguin, 1964), p. 52. The thesis of the nineteenth-century happy childhood as a "myth" of the Russian nobility is eloquently argued in Andrew Baruch Wachtel, *The Battle for Childhood: Creation of a Russian Myth* (Stanford: Stanford University Press, 1990). See also M. Marina, "Golovino," *Russkii arkhiv* 3 (1915), p. 44.

20. Roosevelt, *Life,* pp. 172–173.

21. P. V. Pasevev, "Iz epokhi krepostnogo prava," *Istoricheskii vestnik* 96 (1904), p. 809.

22. Wachtel, *Battle,* pp. 125–126; Tolstoy, *Childhood,* pp. 34–35, 53.

23. Wachtel, *Battle,* pp. 129–130; V. Glinskii, "Iz letopisi sela Sergeevki," *Istoricheskii vestnik* 58 (1894), p. 61; Zasulich, "Masha," l. 9. Similar sentiments are found in Pasevev, "Iz epokhi," p. 810.

24. Roosevelt, *Life,* pp. 177–179.

25. Quoted in Roosevelt, *Life,* p. 160.

26. Zasulich, "Masha," ll. 4, 11.

27. Zasulich, "Masha," ll. 3–4; Zasulich, *Vospominaniia,* p. 10.

28. Zasulich, "Masha," l. 3; Zasulich, *Vospominaniia,* p. 15.

29. Zasulich, *Vospominaniia,* pp. 10, 11, 15; Zasulich, "Masha," ll. 3, 4, 7.

30. Wachtel, *Battle,* pp. 119–121; Uspenskaia, "Vospominaniia," p. 21; Vodovozova, *Na zare zhizni,* p. 134; Zasulich, *Vospominaniia,* p. 16.

31. Uspenskaia, "Vospominaniia," p. 21.

32. Zasulich, *Vospominaniia,* p. 16.

33. Quoted in Jane E. Good and David R. Jones, *Babushka: The Life of the Russian Revolutionary E. K. Breshko-Breshkovskaia* (Newtonville, MA: Oriental Research Partners, 1991), p. 7.

34. Good and Jones, *Babushka,* pp. 7–8.

35. Peter Kolchin, *Unfree Labor: American Slavery and Russian Serfdom* (Cambridge, MA: Belknap Press, 1987), pp. 52–53.

36. Kolchin, *Unfree Labor,* pp. 3, 63.

37. Roosevelt, *Life,* pp. 103–104, 262–263, 246–248.

38. Steven L. Hoch, *Serfdom and Social Control in Russia: Petrovskoe, a Village in Tambov* (Chicago: University of Chicago Press, 1986), pp. 51–52, 55, 59–62; Kolchin, *Unfree Labor,* pp. 106–107, 151.

39. Kolchin, *Unfree Labor,* p. 121; Hoch, *Serfdom,* pp. 163–164, 173–176.

40. L. Obolenskii, "Kartinki proshlogo," *Istoricheskii vestnik* 106 (1906), pp. 115–116.

41. V. A. Shompulev, "Mnimoumershii," *Russkaia starina* 194 (May 1898), pp. 347–349.

42. Roosevelt, *Life,* pp. 186–187; Kolchin, *Unfree Labor,* pp. 112–113.

43. Kolchin, *Unfree Labor*, pp. 261–263, 281–285.

44. V. Shompulev, "Provintsialnye tipy sorokovykh godov," *Russkaia starina* 95, no. 8 (August 1898), p. 326.

45. Kolchin, *Unfree Labor*, pp. 57, 117; Hoch, *Serfdom*, p. 119.

46. Aleksandr Nikitenko, *Up from Serfdom: My Childhood and Youth in Russia, 1804–1824,* trans. Helen Saltz Jacobson (New Haven: Yale University Press, 2001), p. 169.

47. In their autobiographies, nobles either simply left out their experiences of peasant life or openly spoke of their parents as "kind" to the peasants. This is evident in the following pages of their autobiographies: *Deiateli SSSR i revoliutsionnogo dvizheniia Rossii: Entsiklopedicheskii slovar Granat* (Moscow: Sovietskaia Entsiklopediia, 1989), pp. 28–29, 42–43, 72, 86–87, 164, 238, 305, 317–318, 515, 577–578. The two exceptions are on 105, 613–614. In this sense, they were like the rest of the Russian nobility and clung to a "myth of the contented peasant," derived from personal memories of friendships with peasants on their estates. See Wachtel, *Battle,* pp. 111–114.

48. Zasulich, *Vospominaniia*, p. 16.

49. Zasulich, *Vospominaniia*, p. 16.

50. By far the most detailed and complete biography of Bakunin's life and thought is found in Arthur P. Mendel, *Michael Bakunin: Roots of Apocalypse* (New York: Praeger Publishers, 1981). Letter quoted on p. 62.

51. Mendel, *Bakunin*, pp. 48, 62.

52. Paul Avrich, *Anarchist Portraits* (Princeton: Princeton University Press, 1988), pp. 5–6.

53. Mendel, *Bakunin*, pp. 14–15.

54. Mendel, *Bakunin*, pp. 15–16.

55. Mendel, *Bakunin*, p. 22, 24.

56. "Bukh, Nikolai Konstantinovich," and "Sidorenko, Evgenii Matveevich," in *Deiateli*, pp. 42, 414; Good and Jones, *Babushka*, p. 6. The religious roots of Russian nineteenth-century radicalism are discussed from a number of different angles in the literature, but a complete study has yet to be written. For an account of early religious narratives and their influence on female revolutionaries, see Hilde Hoogenboom, "Vera Figner and Revolutionary Autobiographies: The Influence of Gender on Genre," in Rosalind K. Marsh, ed., *Women in Russia and Ukraine* (Cambridge: Cambridge University Press, 1996), pp. 85–86.

57. "Moreinis-Muratova, Fanni Abramova," and "Dobruskina, Genrieta Nikolaevna," in *Deiateli,* pp. 291, 119.

58. Hilde Hoogenboom makes the argument that this was a phenomenon among female revolutionaries exclusively. See Hoogenboom, "Vera Figner," p. 85. A similar argument is made in Engel, "Mothers," p. 125. But it is clear that, in their autobiographies, men were about as likely to mention early religiosity and a drive to asceticism as women were. In addition to Bakunin, see "Pribilev, Aleksandr Vasilievich," "Chernavskii, Mikhail Mikhailovich," and "Chuiko, Vladimir Ivanovich," in *Deiateli,* pp. 344–346, 563–564,

581–582; Figner quote in Vera Figner, *Memoirs of a Revolutionist* (De Kalb: Northern Illinois University Press, 1991), p. 33, and *Deiateli,* p. 461; "Golovina (urozhd. Iurgenson), Nadezhda Aleksandrova," *Deiateli,* p. 72.

[59] "Pribilev, Aleksandr Vasilievich," "Chernavskii, Mikhail Mikhailovich," "Cherniavskaia-Bokhanovskaia, Galina Fedorovna," and "Chuiko, Vladimir Ivanovich," in *Deiateli,* pp. 344–346, 563–564, 581–582, 605.

[60] Zasulich, *Vospominaniia,* pp. 13–14.

[61] Anatole Mazour, *The First Russian Revolution, 1825: The Decembrist Movement* (Stanford: Stanford University Press, 1969), pp. 127, 164, poem quoted on p. 127; Gregory Frieden, "By the Walls of Church and State: Literature and Authority in Russia's Modern Tradition," *Russian Review* 52, no. 2 (April 1993), pp. 157–159.

[62] Zasulich, *Vospominaniia,* p. 15.

[63] RNB, OR, Dom Plekhanova, f. 1098, op. 1, d. 29, l. 1.

[64] Zasulich, "Masha," l. 23.

[65] Zasulich, *Vospominaniia,* pp. 16, 17.

[66] Zasulich, *Vospominaniia,* p. 16.

3. *Nihilists*

[1] Accounts of the following incident are found in Daniel R. Brower, *Training the Nihilists: Education and Radicalism in Tsarist Russia* (Ithaca: Cornell University Press, 1975), pp. 128–129; Franco Venturi, *Roots of Revolution: A History of the Populist and Socialist Movements in the 19th Century* (London: Phoenix Press, 2001), pp. 226–228; Abbot Gleason, *Young Russia: The Genesis of Russian Radicalism in the 1860s* (Chicago: University of Chicago Press, 1980), pp. 152–155; Edvard Radzinsky, *Alexander II: The Last Great Tsar,* trans. Antonina W. Bouis (New York: Free Press, 2005), pp. 135–138.

[2] Nicholas V. Riasanovsky, *Nicholas I and Official Nationality in Russia, 1825–1855* (Berkeley: University of California Press, 1969), p. 223n.

[3] The account of Alexander's education is found in Radzinsky, *Alexander II,* pp. 49–50, 52–53.

[4] Radzinsky, *Alexander II,* p. 49.

[5] David Saunders, *Russia in the Age of Reaction and Reform* (London: Longman, 1992), pp. 204–205; quote on p. 205.

[6] Bruce Lincoln, *The Great Reforms* (Dekalb: Northern Illinois University Press, 1990), pp. 37–38; Larissa Zakharova, "Autocracy and the Reforms of 1861–1874 in Russia," in Ben Eklof et al., eds., *Russia's Great Reforms, 1855–1881* (Bloomington: Indiana University Press, 1994), p. 21.

[7] Lincoln, *Great Reforms,* pp. 42–43; Zakharova, "Autocracy," p. 23.

[8] Retold in Lincoln, *Great Reforms,* p. 49; another version is found in Adam B. Ulam, *Prophets and Conspirators in Prerevolutionary Russia* (New Brunswick, NJ: Transaction Publishers, 1998), p. 30.

[9] Herzen, *My Past and Thoughts,* p. 533.

[10.] Kolchin, *Unfree Labor*, pp. 179–180.

[11.] Quoted in Hugh Seton Watson, "Preparation of the Reform," in Terence Emmons, ed., *Emancipation of the Russian Serfs* (New York: Holt, Rinehart, and Winston, 1970), p. 57.

[12.] Saunders, *Russia*, pp. 217–218, quote on p. 217; Lincoln, *Great Reforms*, p. 68; Zakharova, "Autocracy," p. 32.

[13.] Lincoln, *Great Reforms*, pp. 87–88; Zakharova, "Autocracy," p. 32.

[14.] Lincoln, *Great Reforms*, pp. 87–88.

[15.] Daniel Field, *Rebels in the Name of the Tsar* (Boston: Unwin Hyman, 1989), pp. 33–34.

[16.] Kolchin, *Unfree Labor*, p. 50.

[17.] Lincoln, *Great Reforms*, p. 164; quotes from Saunders, *Russia*, p. 241.

[18.] Susan K. Morrissey, *Heralds of Revolution: Russian Students and the Mythologies of Radicalism* (Oxford: Oxford University Press), p. 22; Gleason, *Young Russia*, pp. 118–119.

[19.] Morrissey, *Heralds*, pp. 22–23; Brower, *Training*, pp. 122–124. Vera Zasulich provides a firsthand account of the *skhodki* in Zasulich, *Vospominaniia*, p. 26.

[20.] Brower, *Training*, pp. 129–130; Lincoln, *Great Reforms*, p. 166.

[21.] Zasulich, "Masha," l. 35.

[22.] Brower, *Training*, pp. 102–103.

[23.] Brower, *Training*, pp. 42, 44, 103 (quoted), 114. On the myth of the effect of the lower classes on student radicalism, see Morrissey, *Heralds*, p. 23.

[24.] On the transition to school as a "trauma," see Wachtel, *Battle*, pp. 129–130.

[25.] Mendel, *Bakunin*, pp. 11–13.

[26.] Zasulich, "Masha," ll. 25–27; the details of the school's rules and curriculum are found in Uspenskaia, "Vospominaniia," pp. 22–23.

[27.] Zasulich, "Masha," ll. 26, 35–36.

[28.] See the memoirs of "Drei, Mikhail Ivanovich," "Ivanovskaia, Praskovia Semenovna," "Salova, Neonila Mikhailovna," and "Olovennikova, Elizaveta Nikolaevna" in *Deiateli*, pp. 131, 152, 318, 397.

[29.] See Brower, *Training*, pp. 147, 154–155, and the memoirs in *Deiateli*, pp. 131, 152, 318, 397.

[30.] Ivan Turgenev, *Fathers and Sons*, trans. Rosemary Edmonds (New York: Penguin, 1975), pp. 94–95.

[31.] Ivan Turgenev, "Apropos of Fathers and Sons," in *Fathers and Sons*, trans. and ed. Michael R. Katz (New York: W. W. Norton, 1996), p. 161.

[32.] Frank Friedeberg Seeley, *Turgenev: A Reading of His Fiction* (Cambridge: Cambridge University Press, 1991), pp. 7–8; Leonard Shapiro, *Turgenev: His Life and Times* (New York: Random House, 1978), pp. 2–6.

[33.] Seeley, *Turgenev*, pp. 9–10; Shapiro, *Turgenev*, pp. 19–22; Fyodor Dostoyevsky, *The Devils* (New York: Penguin, 1971), pp. 98–99, 368–381.

[34] Seeley, *Turgenev*, pp. 14–15; Shapiro, *Turgenev*, pp. 43–44, 68–69, 87–93.

[35] The best descriptions of the intellectual preoccupations of the forties generation are found in Isaiah Berlin, "A Remarkable Decade," in *Russian Thinkers* (New York: Penguin, 1979), pp. 115–135 (p. 132 quoted); and Andrzej Walicki, *The Slavophile Controversy* (Notre Dame: University of Notre Dame Press, 1989), pp. 336–393.

[36] E. H. Carr, *Romantic Exiles: A Nineteenth-Century Portrait Gallery* (London: Penguin, 1933), p. 13.

[37] Walicki, *Slavophile Controversy*, pp. 446–447; Berlin, *Russian Thinkers*, pp. 126–127.

[38] Walicki, *Slavophile Controversy*, pp. 359–361; Berlin, *Russian Thinkers*, pp. 134–135.

[39] Walicki, *Slavophile Controversy*, p. 349; Berlin, *Russian Thinkers*, p. 126.

[40] Martin Malia, *Alexander Herzen and the Birth of Russian Socialism, 1812–1855* (Cambridge: Harvard University Press, 1961), pp. 330–331; quoted excerpt from Venturi, *Roots*, pp. 32–33.

[41] Aleksandr Herzen, *From the Other Shore* (London: Weidenfeld and Nicolson, 1956), p. 3.

[42] Ulam, *Prophets*, pp. 38–39.

[43] Herzen, *Other Shore*, p. 141. Herzen's ambivalence is praised by Aileen Kelly as a desire to avoid the "doctrinaire determinism of Left and Right." Aileen Kelly, *Views from the Other Shore: Essays on Herzen, Chekhov, and Bakhtin* (New Haven: Yale University Press, 1999), p. 14. Martin Malia, on the other hand, sees it as the "political irresponsibility" of an "idle spectator," who had no stake in any practical reform efforts. See Malia, *Alexander Herzen*, pp. 384–385.

[44] Evgeny Lampert, *Sons Against Fathers* (Oxford: Oxford University Press, 1965), pp. 183–184.

[45] V. I. Zasulich, *Revoliutsionery iz burzhuaznoi sredy* (Peterburg: Gosudarstvennoe izdatel'stvo, 1921), pp. 40–41.

[46] Turgenev, *Fathers and Sons* (Edmonds), pp. 86, 93, 121–122.

[47] This ambivalence is best captured in Isaiah Berlin, *Fathers and Children: Turgenev and the Liberal Predicament* (Oxford: Oxford University Press, 1972).

[48] Bazarov's dialogue here and in the next two paragraphs is from Turgenev, *Fathers and Sons* (Edmonds), pp. 123–128.

[49] Quoted in Venturi, *Roots*, p. 35.

[50] Ludwig Büchner, *Force and Matter: Empirico-Philosophical Studies, Intelligibly Rendered,* trans. J. Frederick Collingwood (London: Trubner, 1870), pp. lxxvii, 392.

[51] Turgenev, *Fathers and Sons* (Edmonds), pp. 119–120. Büchner's incredible popularity, and the popularity of "scientism" in Russia in general, is discussed in James Allen Rogers, "Darwinism, Scientism, and Nihilism," *Russian Review* 19, no. 1 (January 1960), pp. 11–12.

[52] Büchner, *Force and Matter*, pp. 28–29, 34, 249–250.

53. Turgenev, *Fathers and Sons* (Edmonds), p. 116.

54. Büchner, *Force and Matter,* p. lxxxi.

55. Turgenev, *Fathers and Sons* (Edmonds), pp. 181–182, 289. The discussion of Bazarov's essentially Romantic character is found in William C. Brumfield, "Bazarov and Rjazanov: The Romantic Archetype in Russian Nihilism," *Slavic and East European Journal* 21, no. 4 (1977), p. 501.

56. Peter Kropotkin, *Memoirs of a Revolutionist* (Montreal: Black Rose Books, 1989), pp. 278–280.

57. A description of the fires is found in Gleason, *Young Russia,* pp. 166–170 (p. 167 quoted).

58. Quoted in *Fathers and Sons* (Katz), p. 162.

59. Berlin, *Fathers and Children,* pp. 29–30; Peter C. Pozefsky, "Smoke as 'Strange and Sinister Commentary on Fathers and Sons': Dostoevskii, Pisarev, and Turgenev on Nihilists and Their Representations," *Russian Review* 54 (October 1995), pp. 571–572.

60. Berlin, *Fathers and Children,* p. 30.

61. Quoted in *Fathers and Sons* (Katz), p. 173.

62. Pisarev's review is translated in *Fathers and Sons* (Katz), pp. 185–206 (pp. 190, 189 quoted).

63. Ronald Hingley, *Nihilists: Russian Radicals and Revolutionaries in the Reign of Alexander II, 1855–1881* (New York: Delacorte Press, 1969), p. 16; Kropotkin, *Memoirs,* pp. 278–271; see also Peter C. Pozefsky, *The Nihilist Imagination: Dmitrii Pisarev and the Cultural Origins of Russian Radicalism, 1860–1868* (New York: Peter Lang, 2003), pp. 172–174. Herzen quoted in Brumfield, "Bazarov," p. 495.

64. Zasulich, "Masha," l. 36.

65. Zasulich, *Revoliutsionery,* pp. 40–41.

4. *The New People*

1. Descriptions of the scene are found in Radzinsky, *Alexander II*, p. 161, and Gleason, *Young Russia,* pp. 226–228.

2. Peter Kropotkin, *Ideals and Realities in Russian Literature* (Westport, CT: Greenwood Press, 1970), p. 281.

3. All of the previous is found in Nikolai Valentinov (N. V. Volsky), *Encounters with Lenin,* trans. Paul Rosta and Brian Pearce (London: Oxford University Press, 1968), pp. 69–71, 65–66.

4. Joseph Frank, "Nikolai Chernyshevsky: A Russian Utopia," in Joseph Frank, *Through the Russian Prism: Essays on Literature and Culture* (Princeton: Princeton University Press, 1990), p. 187.

5. Discussions of the reactions to the novel are in Frank, "Chernyshevskii," pp. 187–188; Irina Paperno, *Chernyshevskii and the Age of Realism* (Stanford: Stanford University Press, 1988), pp. 26–29, 36; and Andrew M. Drozd, *Chernyshevskii's*

What Is to Be Done? A Reevaluation (Evanston: Northwestern University Press, 2001), pp. 9–10, quote on p. 9.

6. Francis B. Randall, *N. G. Chernyshevskii* (New York: Twayne, 1967), p. 24; Venturi, *Roots*, pp. 132–133. The relevance of Chernyshevskii's status as a priest's son for his salvific socialist ideology is discussed in Laurie Manchester, "The Secularization of the Search for Salvation: The Self-Fashioning of Orthodox Clergymen's Sons in Late Imperial Russia," *Slavic Review* 57, no. 1 (Spring 1998), pp. 50–76.

7. Randall, *N. G. Chernyshevskii*, p. 29; quote in Michael R. Katz, "Introduction," in Nikolai Chernyshevsky, *What Is to Be Done?* trans. Michael R. Katz (Ithaca: Cornell University Press, 1989), p. 8.

8. Paperno, *Chernyshevsky*, pp. 81–84.

9. N. G. O. Pereira, *The Thought and Teachings of N. G. Cernysevskij* (Paris: Mouton, 1975), p. 26.

10. Paperno, *Chernyshevsky,* pp. 41, 45–48.

11. Similar insights into Marxist socialism are found in Andrzej Walicki, *Marxism and the Leap to the Kingdom of Freedom: The Rise and Fall of the Communist Utopia* (Stanford: Stanford University Press, 1995); and Igal Halfin, *From Darkness to Light: Class, Consciousness, and Salvation in Revolutionary Russia* (Pittsburgh: University of Pittsburgh Press, 2000).

12. In Mendel, *Bakunin,* pp. 36–112, there is a complete account of Bakunin's embrace of Schelling, Fichte, and Hegel.

13. Mendel, *Bakunin,* pp. 156, 175.

14. See "Aptekman, Osip Vasilievich," "Ivanova-Boreisho, Sofia Andreevna," and "Drei, Mikhail Ivanovich," in *Deiateli,* pp. 4–5, 144, 131.

15. "Pribylev, Aleksandr Vasilievich," in *Deiateli,* p. 3.

16. Venturi, *Roots,* pp. 134–135; Ludwig Feuerbach, *Principles of the Philosophy of the Future,* trans. Manfred Vogel (Indianapolis: Hackett Publishing, 1986), p. 53. The importance of Feuerbach in Russia is discussed in Pereira, *Thought,* pp. 13–15.

17. Venturi, *Roots,* p. 134; Paperno, *Chernyshevsky,* pp. 54–55.

18. Peter C. Pozefsky, "Love, Science, and Politics in the Fiction of Shestidesiatnitsy N. P. Suslova and S. V. Kovalevskaia," *Russian Review* 58 (July 1999), p. 363; Feuerbach, *Principles,* pp. 54–55.

19. Chernyshevskii's attachment to Fourierism is discussed in Venturi, *Roots,* p. 137.

20. Charles Fourier, *Theory of the Four Movements,* ed. Gareth Stedman Jones and Ian Patterson (Cambridge: Cambridge University Press, 1996), pp. 88, 190.

21. Fourier, *Theory,* pp. xiv–xv, 4.

22. Fourier, *Theory,* pp. 13–14, 20–21, 46–47.

23. Fourier, *Theory,* pp. 72–75, 91, 109–115, 172–174. "Suitors" who lost out on their bids for their favorite "virgin" would be announced as "wounded" and would be "consoled" by a specially chosen group from the opposite sex.

24. Fourier, *Theory,* pp. 48–50, 159, 292–293.

25. Venturi, *Roots,* pp. 138, 156–157; Pereira, *Thought,* pp. 65–66; Paperno, *Chernyshevsky*, p. 77 (quoted).

26. His illiberal scorn for his enemies is recounted in N. G. O. Pereira, "N. G. Chernyshevskii as Architect of the Politics of Anti-Liberalism in Russia," *Russian Review* 32, no. 3 (July 1973), pp. 276–277.

27. Pereira, *Thought,* pp. 29–30.

28. Pereira, *Thought,* p. 76.

29. Vladimir Nabokov, *The Gift* (New York: Vintage, 1991), p. 276.

30. Chernyshevsky, *What Is to Be Done?* p. 48.

31. Chernyshevsky, *What Is to Be Done?* pp. 139–140.

32. Chernyshevsky, *What Is to Be Done?* pp. 93–94, 153–154.

33. Chernyshevsky, *What Is to Be Done?* p. 150.

34. Chernyshevsky, *What Is to Be Done?* pp. 170–172.

35. Katz, introduction, *What Is to Be Done?* pp. 26–27.

36. The philosophical aspects of rational egoism are discussed in N. G. Chernyshevsky, "The Anthropological Principle in Philosophy," in N. G. Chernyshevsky, *Selected Philosophical Essays* (Moscow: Foreign Languages Publishing House, 1953), pp. 124–132; Frederick C. Barghoorn, "The Philosophic Outlook of Chernyshevskii: Materialism and Utilitarianism," *American Slavic and East European Review* 11 (1947), pp. 42–56; and Chernyshevsky, *What Is to Be Done?* pp. 116–118.

37. Chernyshevsky, "Anthropological Principle," pp. 130–131. In the novel, the metaphor of disease is used on pp. 197–198. On Chernyshevskii's ideas of good and evil, see Randall, *Chernyshevskii,* pp. 78–79.

38. Chernyshevsky, *What Is to Be Done?* p. 121.

39. Chernyshevsky, *What Is to Be Done?* pp. 189–199.

40. Chernyshevsky, *What Is to Be Done?* p. 195.

41. Alexander Herzen, *Who Is to Blame? A Novel in Two Parts* (Ithaca: Cornell University Press, 1984). An excellent discussion of the novel is Svetlana Grenier, "Herzen's *Who Is to Blame?:* The Rhetoric of the New Morality," *Slavic and East European Journal* 39, no. 1 (Spring 1995), pp. 14–28.

42. The story is found in Edward Hallet Carr, *The Romantic Exiles* (New York: Penguin, 1933), pp. 53–134.

43. Pereira, *Thought,* p. 79; Paperno, *Chernyshevsky,* pp. 121–122.

44. Pereira, *Thought,* pp. 97–99; Paperno, *Chernyshevsky,* pp. 102–103, quote from p. 120.

45. Chernyshevsky, *What Is to Be Done?* pp. 264–266, 305–307.

46. Chernyshevsky, *What Is to Be Done?* p. 326.

47. Chernyshevsky, *What Is to Be Done?* p. 252.

48. Chernyshevsky, *What Is to Be Done?* pp. 365–371, 376–377. This section of the

chapter is heavily indebted to the analysis of Paperno, *Chernyshevsky,* pp. 195–222, and to the notes by William Wagner in the Katz translation of *What Is to Be Done?* pp. 364–379.

[49.] Chernyshevsky, *What Is to Be Done?* p. 370n.

[50.] Chernyshevsky, *What Is to Be Done?* pp. 370–371; Pereira, *Thought,* p. 82.

[51.] Chernyshevsky, *What Is to Be Done?* p. 378.

[52.] Chernyshevsky, *What Is to Be Done?* p. 367n; Paperno, *Chernyshevsky,* pp. 214–215.

[53.] Chernyshevsky, *What Is to Be Done?* pp. 372, 379; Paperno, *Chernyshevsky,* pp. 195, 210–212, 218.

[54.] Drozd, *Chernyshevskii's . . . Reevaluation,* pp. 11–13.

[55.] Paperno, *Chernyshevsky,* pp. 28–29.

[56.] Katz, introduction, *What Is to Be Done?* p. 32; Valentinov, *Encounters,* p. 67.

[57.] Richard Stites, *The Women's Liberation Movement in Russia: Feminism, Nihilism, and Bolshevism, 1860–1930* (Princeton: Princeton University Press, 1990), pp. 106–107.

[58.] Stites, *Women's Liberation,* pp. 109–111.

[59.] Stites, *Women's Liberation,* pp. 107–108; Mendel, *Bakunin,* p. 258; Valentinov, *Encounters,* pp. 61–62.

[60.] Stites, *Women's Liberation,* p. 108.

[61.] Zasulich, "Po povodu iubileia Aleksandra II," Rossiiskii gosudarstvennyi arkhiv sotsialno-politicheskoi istorii (hereafter RGASPI), f. 262, p. 1, d. 4, l. 4; Chernyshevsky, *What Is to Be Done?* p. 376n.

[62.] Quoted in Valentinov, *Encounters,* p. 63.

[63.] Zasulich, *Vospominaniia,* p. 18.

[64.] Zasulich, *Vospominaniia,* p. 15; Stites, *Women's Liberation,* p. 101.

[65.] Stites, *Women's Liberation,* pp. 94–96.

[66.] Paperno, *Chernyshevsky,* p. 214.

[67.] Stites, *Women's Liberation,* pp. 107–111.

[68.] R. A. Kovnator, "V. I. Zasulich (K istorii russkoi kritiki)," in V. I. Zasulich, *Stati o Russkoi literature* (Moscow: Khudozhestvennaia literatura, 1960), p. 5; Zasulich, *Vospominaniia,* p. 15.

[69.] Zasulich, "D. I. Pisarev i N. A. Dobroliubov," in Zasulich, *Stati,* pp. 199–201.

[70.] Zasulich, "Masha," ll. 39, 49–50; Zasulich, *Vospominaniia,* 114–115 (n. 15).

[71.] Zasulich, "Po povodu," l. 4.

[72.] Fyodor Dostoevsky, *Notes from Underground* and *The Grand Inquisitor* (New York: Penguin, 1991), p. 19.

[73.] The best discussion of Dostoyevsky's polemic against Chernyshevskii is found in Joseph Frank, *Dostoevsky: The Stir of Liberation* (Princeton: Princeton University Press, 1986), pp. 312–331.

[74.] Dostoevsky, *Notes,* pp. 34, 112–113.

[75.] Dostoevsky, *Notes,* p. 32.

[76.] Dostoevsky, *Notes,* p. 31.

5. *Devils*

[1] Accounts of the Karakozov assassination are found in Gleason, *Young Russia,* pp. 324–328; Ulam, *Prophets,* pp. 1–5 (p. 3 quoted); and Radzinsky, *Alexander II,* pp. 177–180.

[2] Chernyshevsky, *What Is to Be Done?* p. 288.

[3] Gleason, *Young Russia,* p. 299.

[4] Venturi, *Roots,* p. 331 (quoted); Ulam, *Prophets,* p. 156.

[5] Venturi, *Roots,* p. 332.

[6] Venturi, *Roots,* pp. 331–334; Gleason, *Young Russia,* pp. 302, 304–305.

[7] Chernyshevsky, *What Is to Be Done?* p. 369n.

[8] Chernyshevsky, *What Is to Be Done?* pp. 275, 277–279, 281–282; Paperno, *Chernyshevsky,* p. 208.

[9] Chernyshevsky, *What Is to Be Done?* p. 273n.

[10] The following text relies on Venturi, *Roots,* pp. 336–339 (p. 337 quoted); Gleason, *Young Russia,* pp. 316–317, 322–323, 330–331; Ulam, *Prophets,* pp. 158, 166–167.

[11] Nikolai Dobroliubov, "When Will the Real Day Come?" in Ralph E. Matlaw, ed., *Belinsky, Chernyshevsky, and Dobroliubov: Selected Criticism* (Bloomington: Indiana University Press, 1962), pp. 189, 193.

[12] The following discussion of their serving cooperative relies on Uspenskaia, "Vospominaniia," pp. 25–26.

[13] Zasulich, *Vospominaniia,* pp. 18–19.

[14] Zasulich, *Vospominaniia,* p. 20.

[15] Zasulich, *Vospominaniia,* pp. 19–20.

[16] Zasulich, *Vospominaniia,* p. 19.

[17] Zasulich, *Vospominaniia,* p. 58.

[18] Dobroliubov, "When Will the Real Day Come?" in Matlaw, *Belinsky, Chernyshevsky, and Dobroliubov,* pp. 177–226.

[19] Zasulich, "N. A. Dobroliubov," in Zasulich, *Stati,* pp. 260–269.

[20] Zasulich, *Vospominaniia,* p. 59. Nikolai Volsky reported that Lenin also found "When Will the Real Day Come?" a tremendously inspiring review. Valentinov, *Encounters,* p. 68.

[21] Here and throughout the book, I will use a version of Nechaev's *Catechism of a Revolutionary* that is based almost entirely on Alan Kimball's translation, with commentary, found online at http://www.uoregon.edu/~kimball/Nqv.catechism.thm.htm.

[22] As will become clear in this chapter and the next, I am indebted to three excellent books on Nechaev: Philip Pomper, *Sergei Nechaev* (New Brunswick: Rutgers University Press, 1979), here pp. 24–25; Stephen Cochrane, *The Collaboration of Nechaev, Ogarev, and Bakunin in 1869: Nechaev's Early Years* (Giessen: Wilhelm Schmitz Verlag, 1977), here pp. 26–27; and F. M. Lure, *Nechaev: Sozidatel razrusheniia* (Moscow: Molodaia Gvardia, 2001), here p. 47; I also used Vera's own account in V. I. Zasulich, "Nechaevskoe delo," in Deich, *Gruppa "Osvobozhdenie truda,"* vol. 2, pp. 22–72.

²³· Pomper, *Nechaev*, p. 1; Cochrane, *Collaboration*, p. 25; Lure, *Nechaev*, p. 48.

²⁴· Pomper, *Nechaev*, pp. 15–16.

²⁵· Pomper, *Nechaev*, pp. 4–5; Cochrane, *Collaboration*, p. 3; Lure, *Nechaev*, p. 28.

²⁶· Cochrane, *Collaboration*, p. 1; Pomper, *Nechaev*, p. 9.

²⁷· Cochrane, *Collaboration*, pp. 3–4; Pomper, *Nechaev*, pp. 5–6.

²⁸· Cochrane, *Collaboration*, pp. 4, 15.

²⁹· Cochrane, *Collaboration*, p. 3; Pomper, *Nechaev*, p. 11.

³⁰· Cochrane, *Collaboration*, p. 9.

³¹· Cochrane, *Collaboration*, p. 11; Pomper, *Nechaev*, p. 14.

³²· Cochrane, *Collaboration*, pp. 17, 21; Pomper, *Nechaev*, p. 22.

³³· Pomper, *Nechaev*, p. 22 (quoted).

³⁴· Cochrane, *Collaboration*, p. 25.

³⁵· Cochrane, *Collaboration*, pp. 45–47.

³⁶· Zasulich, "Nechaevskoe delo," p. 34; Lev Nikiforov, "Moi tiurmy," *Golos minuvshego* 5 (1914), p. 169. Quote from Pomper, *Nechaev*, p. 45.

³⁷· Zasulich, "Nechaevskoe delo," p. 28; Nikiforov, "Moi tiurmy," p. 170.

³⁸· Nechaev, *Catechism*.

³⁹· The following is described in Zasulich, *Vospominaniia*, pp. 58–60.

⁴⁰· Uspenskaia, "Vospominaniia," p. 28.

⁴¹· Lure, *Nechaev*, pp. 51–52; Cochrane, *Collaboration*, pp. 51–52; described fully in Zemfir Ralli Arbore, "Sergei Gennadievich Nechaev," *Byloe* 7 (1906), p. 142.

⁴²· Pomper, *Nechaev*, pp. 56–57; rpt. in Cochrane, *Collaboration*, pp. 52–55.

⁴³· Cochrane, *Collaboration*, pp. 56–59.

⁴⁴· Cochrane, *Collaboration*, p. 50; Pomper, *Nechaev*, p. 26; quote from the New Testament, King James Version, Luke 3:9, 17.

⁴⁵· Nechaev, *Catechism*.

⁴⁶· Zasulich, "Nechaevskoe delo," p. 28.

⁴⁷· Zasulich, "Nechaevskoe delo," pp. 29–30.

⁴⁸· Zasulich, "Nechaevskoe delo," p. 32; Nikiforov, "Moi tiurmy," p. 170; Ralli Arbore, "Sergei Gennadievich Nechaev," p. 238.

⁴⁹· Zasulich, "Nechaevskoe delo," p. 31.

⁵⁰· Zasulich, "Nechaevskoe delo," p. 31; Cochrane, *Collaboration*, pp. 59–62.

⁵¹· Zasulich, "Nechaevskoe delo," p. 31.

⁵²· Lure, *Nechaev*, pp. 67–68.

⁵³· Nechaev, *Catechism*.

⁵⁴· The following is from Zasulich, *Vospominaniia*, pp. 59–62.

⁵⁵· Zasulich, "Nechaevskoe delo," pp. 32, 34; Uspenskaia, "Vospominaniia," p. 30.

⁵⁶· Zasulich, "Nechaevskoe delo," pp. 34–35; Nikiforov, "Moi tiurmy," pp. 171–172.

⁵⁷· Quoted in Aileen Kelly, *Mikhail Bakunin: A Study in the Psychology and Politics of Utopianism* (Oxford: Clarendon Press, 1982), p. 270.

58. Kelly, *Bakunin,* pp. 123–150.

59. Mendel, *Bakunin,* pp. 224, 225–227.

60. Kelly, *Bakunin,* p. 112; Michael Bakunin, "The Reaction in Germany," in Arthur Lehning, ed., *Michael Bakunin: Selected Writings* (London: Jonathan Cape, 1973), pp. 55, 56, quote from p. 58.

61. Mendel, *Bakunin,* p. 373; Bakunin, "Reaction," p. 58.

62. Cochrane, *Collaboration,* p. 114.

63. Pomper, *Nechaev,* p. 69; Mendel, *Bakunin,* pp. 317–318.

64. Lur'e, *Nechaev,* p. 101; Pomper, *Nechaev,* p. 84.

65. Cochrane, *Collaboration,* pp. 147, 151.

66. Cochrane, *Collaboration,* p. 138.

67. Nechaev, *Catechism.*

68. Cochrane, *Collaboration,* p. 135.

69. Cochrane, *Collaboration,* p. 135.

70. Cochrane, *Collaboration,* p. 115.

71. GARF, f. 109, 3-ia eksp., op. 154 (1869), d. 112.1, p. 19.

6. *The Fortress*

1. The following is summarized from Anonymous, "Belyi Terror," *Kolokol,* January 1, 1867, pp. 1889–1895.

2. Ulam, *Prophets,* p. 8.

3. Ulam, *Prophets,* pp. 163–168.

4. Zasulich, "Po povodu," l. 4; Ralli Arbore, "Nechaev," p. 137.

5. Jonathan Daly, *Autocracy Under Siege: Security Police and Opposition in Russia, 1866–1905* (De Kalb: Northern Illinois University Press, 1998), pp. 12–13; Ronald Hingley, *The Russian Secret Police: Muscovite, Imperial Russian, and Soviet Political Security Operations, 1565–1970* (London: Hutchinson, 1970), p. 31; Charles A. Ruud and Sergei A. Stepanov, *Fontanka 16: The Tsar's Secret Police* (Montreal and Kingston: McGill–Queen's University Press, 1999), p. 25.

6. Daly, *Autocracy,* pp. 12–13; Hingley, *Police,* p. 32.

7. Hingley, *Police,* pp. 32–33, 39–40.

8. Daly, *Autocracy,* p. 15; Hingley, *Police,* p. 43.

9. Hingley, *Police,* pp. 44–46; Daly, *Autocracy,* p. 16.

10. Joseph Frank, *Dostoevsky: The Years of Ordeal, 1850–1859* (Princeton: Princeton University Press, 1983), pp. 55–58.

11. Hingley, *Police,* pp. 49, 51.

12. Daly, *Autocracy,* p. 16; Hingley, *Police,* p. 53.

13. Daly, *Autocracy,* p. 19.

14. Daly, *Autocracy,* p. 19; Ruud and Stepanov, *Fontanka 16,* pp. 32–33; Hingley, *Police,* pp. 55–56.

15. "Trepov," in F. A. Brokgauz and I. A. Efron, eds., *Entsiklopedicheskii slovar* (St. Petersburg: I. A. Efron, 1890–1907), vol. 34 (1902), pp. 175–176; Koni, *Vospominaniia,* pp. 64–66.

16. Daly, *Autocracy,* p. 19; Hingley, *Police,* p. 55.

17. Cochrane, *Collaboration,* p. 72.

18. Pomper, *Nechaev,* p. 70; Cochrane, *Collaboration,* p. 101; Lure, *Nechaev,* p. 114.

19. Cochrane, *Collaboration,* p. 313.

20. Lure, *Nechaev,* p. 114.

21. GARF, f. 109, 3-ia eksp., op. 54 (1869), d. 112.1, l. 19; Pomper, *Nechaev,* p. 72.

22. Examples are found in GARF, f. 109, 3-ia eksp., op. 54 (1869), d. 112.1, ll. 49, 57, 59.

23. GARF, f. 109, 3-ia eksp., op. 54 (1869), d. 112.1, ll. 170; and d. 112.4, l. 11.

24. GARF, f. 109, 3-ia eksp., op. 54 (1869), d. 112.1, ll. 49, 171.

25. Uspenskaia, "Vospominaniia," p. 31.

26. Uspenskaia, "Vospominaniia," pp. 30–31; GARF, f. 109, 3-ia eksp., op. 54 (1869), d. 112.1, l. 199.

27. GARF, f. 109, 3-ia eksp., op. 54 (1869), d. 112.1, l. 217; Rossiiskii gosudarstvennyi istoricheskii arkhiv (hereafter RGIA), f. 1280, op. 1, d. 346, l. 80.

28. Zasulich, "Masha," ll. 31–32.

29. David M. Skipton, "St. Petersburg's Jails," *Rossica Journal* 128–129 (October 1997), p. 54; Nikiforov, "Moi tiurmy," p. 179.

30. Peter Kropotkin, *In Russian and French Prisons* (New York: Schocken Books, 1971), pp. 59, 236.

31. Bruce F. Adams, *The Politics of Punishment: Prison Reform in Russia, 1863–1917* (De Kalb: Northern Illinois University Press, 1996), pp. 46–47.

32. GARF, f. 109, 3-ia eksp., op. 54 (1869), d. 112.4, ll. 19, 25.

33. Nikiforov, "Moi tiurmy," pp. 180–181.

34. Zasulich, "Masha," ll. 31–32.

35. A. I. Barabanova et al., *Tainy "Russkoi Bastilii"* (Spb: Beloe i Chernoe, 1996), pp. 88–89.

36. GARF, f. 124, op. 1, d. 13 (chast' xi), l. 96.

37. Kropotkin, *Memoirs,* p. 320.

38. A history of the Peter and Paul Fortress in the years 1870–1900 is found in M. N. Gernet, *Istoriia tsarskoi tiurmy* (Moscow: Gosudarstvennoe izdatelstvo iuridicheskoi literatury, 1961), vol. 3, pp. 141–215.

39. Kropotkin, *Memoirs,* pp. 321–322; M. N. Gernet, *Istoriia,* vol. 2, pp. 240–277, 425–431.

40. Ulam, *Prophets,* p. 239; Nikiforov, "Moi tiurmy," p. 182. For the similarities with the Bastille, see Simon Schama, *Citizens: A Chronicle of the French Revolution* (New York: Knopf, 1989), pp. 389–394.

41. Kropotkin, *Memoirs,* pp. 326–328; Nikiforov, "Moi tiurmy," p. 183.

42. RGIA, f. 1280, op. 1, d. 347, ll. 320, 373.

43. GARF, f. 109, 3-ia eksp., op. 54 (1869), d. 112.4, l. 19.

44. Nechaev, *Catechism.*

45. Cochrane, *Collaboration,* p. 222.

46. Uspenskaia, "Vospominaniia," p. 32.

47. Cochrane, *Collaboration,* p. 219.

48. See Nechaev, *Catechism,* for the subsequent analysis.

49. The entirety of the document is reprinted in Cochrane, *Collaboration,* pp. 223–226.

50. Nechaev, *Catechism.*

51. Uspenskaia, "Vospominaniia," p. 33.

52. Uspenskaia, "Vospominaniia," p. 35; Pomper, *Nechaev,* pp. 102–106.

53. Zasulich, "Nechaevskoe delo," p. 52.

54. Zasulich, "Nechaevskoe delo," p. 60.

55. Cochrane, *Collaboration,* pp. 168–169.

56. Zasulich, "Nechaevskoe delo," p. 62.

57. Zasulich, "Nechaevskoe delo," pp. 64–65.

58. Pomper, *Nechaev,* p. 113; Lure, *Nechaev,* p. 166.

59. Lure, *Nechaev,* p. 166; Pomper, *Nechaev,* pp. 114–115.

60. Pomper, *Nechaev,* p. 115.

61. Pomper, *Nechaev,* pp. 117–118.

62. Uspenskaia, "Vospominaniia," pp. 34–35.

63. Lure, *Nechaev,* p. 171.

64. Ruud and Stepanov, *Fontanka 16,* pp. 34–35; RGIA, f. 1280, op. 1, d. 346, l. 80.

65. RGIA, f. 1280, op. 1, d. 345, l. 80; GARF, f. 109, 3-ia eksp., op. 54 (1869), d. 112.4, ll. 6, 11.

66. Boris Kozmin, *Nechaev i nechaevtsy: Sbornik materialov* (Moscow, 1931), pp. 31–32.

67. A. Kunkl, "Melochi proshlogo," *Katorga i ssylka* 38 (1928), p. 80.

68. Kunkl, "Melochi," pp. 80–81.

69. GARF, f. 124, op. 1, d. 2, l. 2.

70. Kunkl, "Melochi," p. 81.

71. Ruud and Stepanov, *Fontanka 16,* pp. 34–35; Nikiforov, "Moi tiurmy," pp. 196–197.

72. Daly, *Autocracy,* pp. 20–21; Ruud and Stepanov, *Fontanka 16,* pp. 35–36.

73. GARF, f. 124, op. 1, d. 7 (chast v), l. 180; GARF, f. 124, op. 1, d. 1, l. 20.

74. Kozmin, *Nechaev,* p. 167.

75. Zasulich's testimony is found in *Pravitelstvennyi vestnik* 161 (1871), p. 2.

76. Kozmin, *Nechaev,* p. 167.

77. Kozmin, *Nechaev,* p. 168.

78. Pomper, *Nechaev,* p. 121.

79. Pomper, *Nechaev,* pp. 109–110; Michael Confino, *Daughter of a Revolutionary: Natalie Herzen and the Bakunin-Nechayev Circle* (LaSalle, IL: Library Press, 1974), p. 21.

80. Confino, *Daughter,* pp. 38–39.

[81.] "Natalie Herzen to Sergey Nechayev" and Natalie Herzen, "Diary," in Confino, *Daughter,* pp. 170, 216–219; Pomper, *Nechaev,* pp. 151–152.

[82.] Mendel, *Bakunin,* pp. 317, 351.

[83.] Pomper, *Nechaev,* pp. 167–186, 198–200.

[84.] Dostoyevsky, *Devils,* p. 404.

[85.] D. C. Offord, "*The Devils* in the Context of Contemporary Russian Thought and Politics," in W. J. Leatherbarrow, ed., *Dostoevsky's* The Devils: *A Critical Companion* (Evanston: Northwestern University Press, 1999), pp. 69–70. The best analysis of the "veracity" of *The Devils* is found in Joseph Frank, "*The Devils* and the Nechaev Affair," in Frank, *Through the Russian Prism,* pp. 137–152.

[86.] Dostoyevsky, *Devils,* pp. 405–410.

[87.] Albert Camus, *The Rebel: An Essay on Man in Revolt* (New York: Vintage, 1991), p. 165.

[88.] Zasulich, "Nechaevskoe delo," pp. 69–70.

[89.] Zasulich, "Nechaevskoe delo," p. 69.

7. *To the People*

[1.] The following anecdote is taken from Deich, *Za polveka,* vol. 1, pp. 179–189.

[2.] Stepniak, *Underground Russia,* p. 25.

[3.] General accounts of the "to the people" movement are found in Venturi, *Roots,* pp. 469–506; Ulam, *Prophets,* pp. 203–233; and Richard Stites, *The Russian Revolutionary Intelligentsia* (Arlington Heights, IL: Harlan Davidson, 1970), pp. 111–129. In these accounts, the movement is presented as "populist," that is, focused on the peasantry to the exclusion of the workers. Typically, the "working-class movement" is portrayed as a separate undertaking. Intense debates in the literature of the 1970s tried to determine whether the working-class movement spurred the movement among the peasants, or vice versa. See Reginald E. Zelnik, "Populists and Workers: The First Encounter Between Populist Students and Industrial Workers in St. Petersburg, 1871–74," *Soviet Studies* 24, no. 2 (October 1972), pp. 251–269; and Pamela Sears McKinsey, "From City Workers to Peasantry: The Beginning of the Russian Movement 'to the People,'" *Slavic Review* 38, no. 4 (December 1979), pp. 629–649. Richard Pipes has convincingly argued that "populism" was a term used much later by Russian Marxists to distinguish themselves from their Russian socialist predecessors. See Richard Pipes, "Narodnichestvo: A Semantic Inquiry," *Slavic Review* 23, no. 3 (September 1964), pp. 441–458. As will be seen below, the memoir accounts of the time demonstrate that those who participated in the "to the people" movement often traveled from city to countryside and then back again, preaching similar propaganda to peasants and workers, and most of them saw all of their activities as part of the same revolutionary impulse. In this chapter, the evangelistic qualities of the enterprise will be the focus.

[4.] Philip Pomper, *Peter Lavrov and the Russian Revolutionary Movement* (Chicago: University of Chicago Press, 1972), pp. 95–97.

[5] Ulam, *Prophets*, p. 208.

[6] Peter Lavrov, *Historical Letters*, trans. James P. Scanlan (Berkeley: University of California Press, 1967), p. 139.

[7] Lavrov, *Historical Letters*, pp. 139–140, 160, 307–309.

[8] Lavrov, *Historical Letters*, p. 172.

[9] Quoted in Venturi, *Roots*, p. 504.

[10] M. F. Frolenko, *Zapiski semidesiatnika* (Moscow: Vsesoiuznoe obshchestvo politicheskikh katorzhan i ssylno-poselentsev, 1927), p. 44; Breshkovskaia, *Hidden Springs*, p. 27; Kropotkin, *Memoirs*, pp. 300–302.

[11] Venturi, *Roots*, p. 501; Frolenko, *Zapiski*, p. 47; Breshkovskaia, *Hidden Springs*, pp. 40–41. For a particular account of the populist approach to religious sects, see Alexander Etkind, "Whirling with the Other: Russian Populism and Religious Sects," *Russian Review* 62, no. 4 (October 2003), pp. 565–588.

[12] "Praskovia Ivanovskaia," in Barbara Alpern Engel and Clifford N. Rosenthal, eds., *Five Sisters: Women Against the Tsar* (New York: Schocken Books, 1977), pp. 105–106; Kropotkin, *Memoirs*, p. 305; Deich, *Za polveka*, vol. 1, pp. 185–186; Vladimir Debagorii-Mokrievich, *Vospominaniia* (St. Petersburg, 1906), pp. 134–135, 139.

[13] Frolenko, *Zapiski*, p. 45; Breshkovskaia, *Hidden Springs*, p. 23; "Ivanovskaia," pp. 102–104.

[14] Kropotkin, *Memoirs*, pp. 222–223.

[15] Breshkovskaia, *Hidden Springs*, pp. 34–35.

[16] Figner, *Memoirs*, p. 50.

[17] "Ivanovskaia," p. 104; N. A. Golovina-Iurgenson, "Moi vospominaniia (Iz revoliutsionnoi deiatelnosti 70–80kh godov)," *Katorga i ssylka* 6 (1923), p. 30.

[18] Debagorii-Mokrievich, *Vospominaniia*, p. 63.

[19] Debagorii-Mokrievich, *Vospominaniia*, pp. 61–62.

[20] V. N. Figner, "Protsess 50-ti," *Katorga i ssylka* 33 (1927), p. 11; Golovina-Iurgenson, "Moi vospominaniia," p. 32; Ulam, *Prophets*, pp. 218–219, 227.

[21] A. A. Kunkl, *Dolgushintsy* (Moscow: Vsesoiuznoe obshchestvo politicheskikh katorzhan i ssylno-poselentsev, 1931), p. 212. For an alternate translation, see Venturi, *Roots*, p. 499.

[22] Kropotkin, *Memoirs*, p. 300; Breshkovskaia, *Hidden Springs*, p. 50.

[23] Kunkl, *Dolgushintsy*, p. 213.

[24] Ulam, *Prophets*, p. 11; Osip Aptekman, *Obshchestvo 'Zemlia i volia' 70-kh gg.* (Petrograd, 1924), pp. 15; Venturi, *Roots*, p. 502; F. Kon, "Khozhdenie v narod," *Katorga i ssylka* 11 (1924), p. 16.

[25] For the subsequent analysis I am indebted to Erich Haberer, *Jews and Revolution in Nineteenth-Century Russia* (Cambridge: Cambridge University Press, 1995), p. 94, 97–99.

[26] Haberer, *Jews*, pp. 81–82.

[27] Deich, *Za polveka*, vol. 1, p. 32.

28. Haberer, *Jews,* pp. 5, 10–11.

29. Haberer, *Jews,* pp. 15–16, 18–19.

30. Haberer, *Jews,* pp. 58–59.

31. Deich, *Za polveka,* vol. 1, p. 11; Haberer, *Jews,* p. 60; "Aptekman, Osip Vasilievich," in *Deiateli,* p. 7.

32. Haberer, *Jews,* p. 68. More on Axelrod's approach to the Jewish question is found in Abraham Ascher, "Pavel Axelrod: A Conflict Between Jewish Loyalty and Revolutionary Dedication," *Russian Review* 24, no. 3 (July 1965), pp. 249–265.

33. Aptekman, *Obshchestvo,* pp. 164–168.

34. Aptekman, *Obshchestvo,* p. 89.

35. Kropotkin, *Memoirs,* p. 299.

36. "Ivanovskaia," pp. 108–109; Deich, *Za polveka,* vol. 1, pp. 172–173; Golovina-Iurgenson, "Moi vospominaniia," p. 30.

37. Deich, *Za polveka,* vol. 1, pp. 188–189; "Ivanovskaia," pp. 107–108.

38. Popov, "Iz moego," p. 279; Deich, *Za polveka,* vol. 1, pp. 199–200; Debagorii-Mokrievich, *Vospominaniia,* pp. 148–149.

39. Deich, *Za polveka,* vol. 1, p. 193; Aptekman, *Obshchestvo,* p. 163.

40. Debagorii-Mokrievich, *Vospominaniia,* pp. 173–174; Aptekman, *Obshchestvo,* p. 145. For an analysis of the peasant faith in the tsar, see Field, *Rebels*.

41. "Ivanovskaia," p. 105; Golovina-Iurgenson, "Moi vospominaniia," p. 30.

42. Deich, *Za polveka,* vol. 1, pp. 207–208.

43. Kovnator, "Zasulich," in Zasulich, *Stati,* p. 5.

44. GARF, f. 109, 3-ia eksp, op. 163 (1878), ll. 40, 42.

45. Zasulich, "Masha," ll. 30–31.

46. B. K.,"Nechaevets v ssylke (Pismo E. I. i L. P. Nikiforovykh k V. I. Zasulich)," *Katorga i ssylka* 10 (1924), p. 159.

47. B. K., "Nechaevets," p. 159; I. D. Pariiskii, "V. I. Zasulich v Soligaliche," in L. Belorussov et al., *Istoricheskii sbornik. Trudy Soligalichskogo Otdela Kostromskogo Nauchnogo Obshchestva,* vol. 3 (Soligalich, 1924), pp. 19–20.

48. Pariiskii, "Zasulich," pp. 17–18; GARF, f. 109, 3-ia eksp., op. 163 (1878), l. 42.

49. Pariiskii, "Zasulich," p. 21; L. S. Fedorchenko (N. Charov), *Vera Ivanovna Zasulich: Zhizn i deiatelnost* (Moscow: Novaia Moskva, 1926), p. 28.

50. Fedorchenko, *Zasulich,* p. 33.

51. Marshall Shatz, "Introduction," in Michael Bakunin, *Statism and Anarchy,* trans. Marshall Shatz (Cambridge: Cambridge University Press, 1990), pp. xxix, xxxi, xxxv, xxxvi; Bakunin, *Statism and Anarchy,* p. 197.

52. Bakunin, *Statism and Anarchy,* pp. 203, 212, 214, 216.

53. Pariiskii, "Zasulich," p. 22.

54. L. Deich, "Vera Ivanovna Zasulich," in Zasulich, *Revoliutsionery,* p. 6; Bakunin, *Statism and Anarchy*, pp. 61–62; Vera Zasulich, "Otkrovennye rechi. Vospominaniia o

1870-kh gg., rassuzhdenie o kharaktere svoego uma," in RNB, OR, Dom Plekhanova, f. 1098, op. 1, d. 29, l. 1.

55. Fedorchenko, *Zasulich*, p. 33. Russian socialists at the time called themselves "Bakuninists," to distinguish themselves from "Lavrovists," or the followers of Peter Lavrov. "Anarchism," as a term, was rarely used. Indeed, in memoirs published long after the 1917 revolution, 1870s radicals persisted in the use of the term "Bakuninism" to refer to their earlier ideology.

56. Fedorchenko, *Zasulich*, pp. 33–34.

57. The turn to Bakuninism is described in Venturi, *Roots*, pp. 570–572; A. Iakimova, "Bolshoi protsess, ili 'protsess 193-kh': O revoliutsionnoi propagande v imperii," *Katorga i ssylka* 37 (1927), pp. 12–13; and Aptekman, *Obshchestvo*, p. 180.

58. Breshkovskaia, *Hidden Springs*, p. 8; Deich, *Za polveka*, vol. 1, p. 263.

59. Iakimova, "Pamiati," pp. 12–13; Breshkovskaia, *Hidden Springs*, p. 31.

60. Iakimova, "Pamiati," pp. 178–179; Frolenko, *Zapiski*, p. 93; GARF, f. 109, 3-ia eksp., op. 163 (1878), d. 68.1, l. 42.

61. Debagorii-Mokrievich, *Vospominaniia*, p. 302.

62. Deich, *Za polveka*, vol. 1, pp. 234–235, 237–238, 256.

63. Deich, *Za polveka*, vol. 1, p. 259; Kravchinskii, *Underground Russia*, pp. 123–124.

64. Deich, *Za polveka*, vol. 1, pp. 239–240.

65. Venturi, *Roots*, pp. 560–562 (p. 561 quoted); "Pribyleva-Korba, Anna Pavlovna," and "Cherniavskaia-Bokhanovskaia, Galina Fedorovna," in *Deiateli*, pp. 377, 586.

66. Frolenko, *Zapiski*, pp. 59–60.

67. Frolenko, *Zapiski*, pp. 97–99; Debagorii-Mokrievich, *Vospominaniia*, pp. 301–303.

68. Debagorii-Mokrievich, *Vospominaniia*, p. 304.

69. The following account is taken from M. Frolenko, "Iz vospominanii o Vere Ivanovne Zasulich," *Katorga i ssylka* 10 (1924), pp. 241–247; and Frolenko, *Zapiski*, pp. 60–62.

70. Deich, *Za polveka*, vol. 2, pp. 80–82.

71. Golovina-Iurgenson, "Moi vospominaniia," p. 33; Frolenko, *Zapiski*, pp. 99–100.

72. Debagorii-Mokrievich, *Vospominaniia*, pp. 160–161.

73. The following is recounted in Deich, *Za polveka*, vol. 2, pp. 80–82.

74. Accounts of the Chigirin affair are found in Field, *Rebels*, pp. 113–202; Venturi, *Roots*, pp. 581–584; and Ulam, *Prophets*, pp. 257–261.

75. Field, *Rebels*, pp. 122–123; Debagorii-Mokrievich, *Vospominaniia*, p. 216.

76. Debagorii-Mokrievich, *Vospominaniia*, p. 206. Debates over the "ethics" of the Chigirin affair continued long after it was over. See Field, *Rebels*, pp. 163–169; and Zasulich, *Vospominaniia*, p. 76.

77. Debagorii-Mokrievich, *Vospominaniia*, pp. 267–268; Deich, *Za polveka*, vol. 2, pp. 122–123.

78. Deich, *Za polveka*, vol. 2, pp. 131–132.

79. Deich, *Za polveka*, vol. 2, pp. 120–121, 131; Frolenko, *Zapiski*, p. 100.

80. Debagorii-Mokrievich, *Vospominaniia,* p. 269; Frolenko, *Zapiski,* p. 100.

81. Debagorii-Mokrievich, *Vospominaniia,* pp. 240–241. The full text of the charter is printed in Field, *Rebels,* pp. 172–174.

82. Field, *Rebels,* pp. 175–180; Debagorii-Mokrievich, *Vospominaniia,* p. 239; Deich, *Za polveka,* vol. 2, pp. 13–14.

83. Field, *Rebels,* pp. 185–186, 193–194; Frolenko, *Zapiski,* p. 101.

84. Deich, *Za polveka,* vol. 2, pp. 90–91. Lev Deich, "Valerian Osinskii (K 50-letiu ego kazni)," *Katorga i ssylka* 54 (1929), p. 14. In this article, Deich contradicts what he stated in *Za polveka* and claims he sent Vera and Masha to St. Petersburg. But numerous other accounts confirm that Vera spent the summer of 1877 in Penza.

8. The European Prison

1. Popov, "Iz moego," pp. 272–273; Iakov Emelianov, "Vospominaniia o brate A. S. Emelianove (Bogoliubove)," *Katorga i ssylka* 11 (1930), p. 179.

2. A full account of the Kazan Square demonstration is found in Pamela Sears McKinsey, "The Kazan Square Demonstration and the Conflict Between Russian Workers and *Intelligenty,*" *Slavic Review* 44, no. 1 (Spring 1985), pp. 83–103. See also Aptekman, *Obshchestvo,* p. 189; Venturi, *Roots,* p. 544; Ulam, *Prophets,* pp. 253–254.

3. McKinsey suggests that Bakuninists and Lavrovists were evenly split over the demonstration. See McKinsey, "Kazan," pp. 84–90. Other sources emphasize that Bakuninism had become the prevailing doctrine in the cities. See Aptekman, *Obshchestvo,* p. 189; and Ulam, *Prophets,* pp. 253–254.

4. Koni, *Vospominaniia,* p. 4; Ulam, *Prophets,* p. 254; Venturi, *Roots,* p. 544; McKinsey, "Kazan," p. 95. A foreign eyewitness account is found in "Russian Students," *Times* (London), January 2, 1877, p. 6.

5. McKinsey, "Kazan," p. 95; Koni, *Vospominaniia,* p. 4; "Russian Students," p. 6.

6. McKinsey argues that some workers believed that the protesters were "Poles" ("Kazan," p. 95). This was an argument later spread by disappointed radicals trying to justify the attacks by the workers. Koni, *Vospominaniia,* pp. 7–8.

7. "Russian Students," p. 6; Plekhanov quoted in Aptekman, *Obshchestvo,* p. 190. Despite this patent failure, some later Soviet historians persisted in calling it "Russia's first labor demonstration." See E. A. Korolchuk, ed., *Pervaia rabochaia demonstratsiia v Rossii* (Moscow, 1927). Even Venturi calls it a "significant" moment in the working-class movement, in *Roots,* p. 545.

8. Quoted in Aptekman, *Obshchestvo,* p. 190.

9. Popov, "Iz moego," p. 288.

10. Koni, *Vospominaniia,* pp. 4–5; a characterization of Palen is also found in Wortman, *Development,* pp. 277–278.

11. Koni, *Vospominaniia,* pp. 5, 19; Daly, *Autocracy,* p. 22.

12. *Zapiska Ministra Iustitsii Grafa Palena: Uspekhi revoliutsionnoi propagandy v*

Rossii (Geneva: Tipografiia gazety Rabotnik, 1875), pp. 8, 10. See also Ruud and Stepanov, *Fontanka 16,* pp. 39–40.

[13.] Daly, *Autocracy,* p. 21; *Zapiska,* p. 11.

[14.] *Zapiska,* pp. 23, 24.

[15.] Letter from Evreinov, Prosecutor of the Odessa Higher Court, to Palen, found in appendix 2 of Koni, *Vospominaniia,* pp. 343–344.

[16.] Koni, *Vospominaniia,* p. 5.

[17.] "Russian Students," p. 6.

[18.] S. S. Tatishchev, *Imperator Alexander II: Ego zhizn i tsarstvovanie* (St. Petersburg: A. S. Suvorin, 1911), vol. 2, p. 549; Koni, *Vospominaniia,* p. 6.

[19.] Henry Mayhew and John Binney, *The Criminal Prisons of London* (London: Griffin, Bohn, 1862), p. 120.

[20.] B. M. Kirikov, ed., *Arkhitektory-stroiteli Sankt Peterburga serediny XIX–nachala XX veka* (Sankt Peterburg: Piligrim, 1996), p. 203; Gertsenshtein, "Tridtsat let." For a brief history of the St. Petersburg House of Preliminary Detention, see Mikhail N. Gernet, *Istoriia tsarskoi tiurmy,* vol. 3 (Moscow, 1952), pp. 361–367 (photo on p. 357). A fuller history is found in Viktor N. Nikitin, *Tiurma i ssylka, 1560–1880* (St. Petersburg, 1880), pp. 499–519. There is no article or book-length treatment of the history of the prison.

[21.] Adams, *The Politics of Punishment,* pp. 65–67.

[22.] Adams, *Politics of Punishment,* p. 70.

[23.] Mayhew and Binney, *Criminal Prisons,* p. 120.

[24.] Naturally, the literature on imprisonment and reforming prisoners is vast. Most well known are Michel Foucault, *Discipline and Punish: The Birth of the Prison* (New York: Vintage, 1979), and Michael Ignatieff, *A Just Measure of Pain: The Penitentiary in the Industrial Revolution* (New York: Pantheon, 1978). The history of imprisonment in France is found in Patricia O'Brien, *The Promise of Punishment: Prisons in Nineteenth-Century France* (Princeton: Princeton University Press, 1981), and the history in the United States in Michael Meranze, *Laboratories of Virtue: Punishment, Revolution, and Authority in Philadelphia, 1760–1835* (Chapel Hill: University of North Carolina Press, 1996). For this case, most relevant is Robin Evans, *The Fabrication of Virtue: English Prison Architecture, 1750–1840* (Cambridge: Cambridge University Press, 1982), pp. 349, 354, 357–358.

[25.] Evans, *Fabrication,* pp. 115–116; Mayhew and Binney, *Criminal Prisons,* p. 119.

[26.] Evans, *Fabrication,* pp. 115–116, 333.

[27.] Evans, *Fabrication,* p. 326. This concept of solitude as a path to reformation was debated earlier in the United States. See Meranze, *Laboratories,* pp. 227–228, 257–265; and Frederick Howard Wines, *Punishment and Reformation: A Study of the Penitentiary System* (New York: Thomas Y. Crowell, 1919), pp. 157–167.

[28.] Mayhew and Binney, *Criminal Prisons,* pp. 122–123.

[29.] Evans, *Fabrication,* p. 346; Norman Johnston, *The Human Cage: A Brief History of Prison Architecture* (Philadelphia: American Foundation, 1973), pp. 34–37.

30. Nikitin, *Tiurma*, p. 516.

31. *Golos*, no. 212 (August 2, 1875), p. 12; *Sankt-Peterburgskie Vedomosti*, no. 217 (August 17, 1875), p. 1.

32. Gernet, *Istoriia*, p. 361.

33. *Polnoe sobranie zakonov Rossiiskoi Imperii* (St. Petersburg, 1877), coll. 2, vol. 50, part 1, 1875, p. 268.

34. *Polnoe sobranie zakonov*, coll. 2, vol. 50, part 1, 1875, pp. 268–269.

35. *Polnoe sobranie zakonov*, coll. 2, vol. 50, part 1, 1875, pp. 268–269.

36. Adams, *Politics of Punishment*, pp. 52–53.

37. I. Dzhabadari, "V nevole," *Byloe* 5 (1906), pp. 45–46.

38. Sergei Glagol, "Protsess pervoi russkoi terroristki," *Golos minuvshego* 7/9 (September 1918), p. 147; S. Sinegub, "Vospominaniia chaikovtsa," *Byloe* 10 (1906), p. 49.

39. See M. Fedorov, "Iz vospominanii po upravleniiu S. Peterburgskim domom predvaritelnogo zakliucheniia," *Russkaia starina* 121 (January–March 1905), p. 71; Glagol, "Protsess," p. 147.

40. Glagol, "Protsess," p. 147; Gertsenshtein, "Tridtsat let," p. 240.

41. Kropotkin, *In Russian and French Prisons*, pp. 60–61; Fedorov, "Iz vospominanii," p. 63; Ignatiev, *Just Measure*, p. 9; Mayhew and Binney, *Criminal Prisons*, p. 168.

42. Sinegub, "Vospominaniia," p. 49; Glagol, "Protsess," p. 148. This form of communication has been referred to in various sources as an "international tapping code" or "prisoner's electric telegraph." Frederick Wines argued that this tapping code was actually invented in Russia. See Mayhew and Binney, *Criminal Prisons*, p. 163; Wines, *Punishment*, p. 165.

43. Sinegub, "Vospominaniia," p. 50; Breshkovskaia, *Hidden Springs*, pp. 137–138.

44. Sinegub, "Vospominaniia," p. 51.

45. Gertsenshtein, "Tridtsat let," pp. 239–240.

46. Glagol, "Protsess," pp. 147–148.

47. Sinegub, "Vospominaniia," pp. 51–52; Glagol, "Protsess," pp. 147–148; Breshkovskaia, *Hidden Springs*, p. 138.

48. Sinegub, "Vospominaniia," p. 50; for the flag, see Ulam, *Prophets*, p. 239.

49. Glagol, "Protsess," pp. 149–150.

50. Glagol, "Protsess," p. 148.

51. This and all of the following account of what took place between Bogoliubov and Trepov are taken from the memoirs of the incident found in Sinegub, "Vospominaniia," pp. 52–53, and Glagol, "Protsess," pp. 148–149.

52. Glagol, "Protsess," p. 149–150.

53. The doctor's account of the riot is found in Gertsenshtein, "Tridtsat let," pp. 243–246.

54. Fyodor Dostoyevsky, *The House of the Dead* (New York: Penguin, 1985), pp. 239–240.

55. The best history of the subject is Abby Schrader, *Languages of the Lash: Corporal Punishment and Identity in Imperial Russia* (De Kalb: Northern Illinois University Press, 2002).

[56.] Quoted in Adams, *Politics of Punishment,* p. 24.

[57.] The history of the abolition of most forms of corploral punishment and the transition to incarceration is documented in Adams, *Politics of Punishment,* pp. 12–39.

[58.] Adams, *Politics of Punishment,* p. 38.

[59.] Koni, *Vospominaniia,* p. 39.

[60.] Koni, *Vospominaniia,* pp. 10–11.

[61.] Koni, *Vospominaniia,* pp. 39, 42–43.

[62.] Report of Fuks, prosecutor of the St. Petersburg Higher Court, to the minister of justice, July 29, 1877, in appendix 5 of Koni, *Vospominaniia,* pp. 366–370. The investigation ended on July 18.

[63.] Nikitin, *Tiurma,* p. 507.

[64.] Fuks report, pp. 370–372; Gertsenshtein, "Tridtsat let," pp. 246–248.

[65.] The account of the doctor's visit to the isolation chamber is found in Gertsenshtein, "Tridtsat let," pp. 246–248.

[66.] Fuks report, p. 373.

[67.] Mayhew and Binney, *Criminal Prisons,* pp. 135–136; Gertsenshtein, "Tridtsat let," p. 247.

[68.] Gertstenshtein, "Tridtsat let," p. 248.

[69.] "O besporiadkakh v Spb Dome predvaritelnogo zakliucheniia," in GARF, f. 1405, op. 75 (1877), d. 7191, ll. 1–4.

[70.] Quoted in Iu. S. Karpilenko, *"Delo" Very Zasulich: Rossiiskoe obshchestvo, samoderzhavie, i sud prisiazhnykh v 1878 godu* (Briansk: Izdatelstvo brianskogo gosudarstvennogo pedagogicheskogo instituta, 1994), p. 14.

[71.] The foregoing discussion of Vera's situation relies on Lev Deich, "Vera Ivanovna Zasulich," in Zasulich, *Revoliutsionery,* pp. 7–8.

[72.] Though Aptekman argued that Vera Zasulich was one of the founding members of Land and Freedom, she declared she was unaffiliated during this time. See Aptekman, *Obshchestvo,* p. 199; and Zasulich, *Vospominaniia,* p. 74.

[73.] Breshkovskaia, *Hidden Springs,* p. 156. This turn from focusing on the people to focusing on the state is described in a number of memoirs. See, for example, Stepniak, *Underground Russia,* pp. 34–35; Figner, *Memoirs,* 60–61; Vladimir Debagorii-Mokrievich, *Ot buntarstva k terrorismu* (Moscow, 1930), pp. 379–380; and Aptekman, *Obshchestvo,* pp. 193–194.

[74.] Deich, *Za polveka,* vol. 2, pp. 301–303; Debagorii-Mokrievich, *Ot buntarstva,* p. 378.

9. *Justice*

[1.] The characterization of Palen is mostly taken from Koni, *Vospominaniia,* pp. 18–19, 26–27, 30, 39–40.

[2.] Koni, *Vospominaniia,* pp. 40–41.

[3.] V. I. Smoliarchuk, *A. F. Koni i ego okruzhenie* (Moscow: Iuridicheskaia literatura, 1990), frontispiece and p. 5.

4. Smoliarchuk, *Koni*, p. 6 (and portrait on frontispiece).

5. Smoliarchuk, *Koni*, pp. 5–6.

6. Koni, *Vospominaniia*, pp. 38–39.

7. Mark G. Pomar, "Anatolii Fedorovich Koni: Liberal Jurist as Moralist," *Carl Beck Papers in Russian and East European Studies*, no. 1202 (March 1996), p. 54.

8. The encounter with Trepov is found in Koni, *Vospominaniia*, pp. 35–41.

9. Quoted in Samuel Kucherov, *Courts, Lawyers, and Trials Under the Last Three Tsars* (New York: Praeger, 1953), p. 26.

10. Lincoln, *Great Reforms*, p. 115.

11. Lincoln, *Great Reforms*, p. 106.

12. Kucherov, *Courts*, pp. 38–39; N. A. Troitskii, "Russkaia advokatura na politicheskikh protsessakh narodnikov (1871–1890 gg.)," in *Iz istorii obshchestvennogo dvizheniia i obshchestvennoi mysli v Rossii* (Saratov: Izdatel'stvo Saratovskogo Universiteta, 1968), p. 95; Richard Wortman, *The Development of a Russian Legal Consciousness* (Chicago: University of Chicago Press, 1976), p. 259.

13. G. Dzhanshiev, *Osnovy sudebnoi reformy: Istoriko-iuridicheskie etiudy* (Moscow, 1891), p. 126ff.

14. Kucherov, *Courts*, pp. 59–60, 62, 65–67.

15. On the educational role of the judicial reforms, see Wortman, *Development*, pp. 245, 260. Joan Neuberger, "Popular Legal Cultures: The St. Petersburg Mirovoi Sud," in Ben Eklof, John Bushnell, and Larissa Zakharova, eds., *Russia's Great Reforms, 1855–1881* (Bloomington: Indiana University Press, 1994), pp. 231–232.

16. Wortman, *Development*, p. 259.

17. Wortman, *Development*, pp. 270–276.

18. N. A. Troitskii, *Tsarskie sudy protiv revoliutsionnoi Rossii* (Saratov: Izdatelstvo Saratovskogo Universiteta, 1976), pp. 118–119; P. I. Negretov, "K sporam vokrug protsessa Very Zasulich," *Voprosy istorii* 12 (1971), pp. 183–189.

19. Laura Engelstein, "Revolution and the Theater of Public Life in Imperial Russia," in Isser Woloch, ed., *Revolution and the Meanings of Freedom in the Nineteenth Century* (Stanford: Stanford University Press, 1996), pp. 340–341.

20. Complete citation found in Tatishchev, *Aleksandr II*, pp. 549–551; partial citation, and different translation, found in Venturi, *Roots*, p. 585.

21. "Iz vospominaniia Chudnovskogo o protsesse 193-kh," in M. Kovalenskii, *Russkaia revoliutsiia v sudebnykh protsessakh i memuarakh*, vol. 1: *Protsessy Nechaeva, 50-ti i 193-kh* (Moscow: Izdanie "Mir," 1923), pp. 196–197; Iakimova, "Bolshoi protsess," pp. 24–25.

22. Tatishchev, *Aleksandr II*, pp. 548–549.

23. Tatishchev, *Aleksandr II*, pp. 549–550.

24. Tatishchev, *Aleksandr II*, pp. 550–551.

25. Tatsichchev, *Aleksandr II*, pp. 549–551; Troitskii, *Tsarskie sudy*, pp. 158–160, 171.

26. Troitskii, *Tsarskie sudy*, pp. 101–104, 149; Wortman, *Development*, p. 281.

[27] Troitskii, *Tsarskie sudy,* pp. 101–104, 149.

[28] Wortman, *Development,* p. 280; Negretov, "K sporam," p. 185.

[29] Stepniak, *Underground Russia,* pp. 30–31.

[30] Troitskii, *Tsarskie sudy,* p. 116.

[31] Troitskii, *Tsarskie sudy,* pp. 118–119.

[32] V. N. Figner, "Protsess 50-ti," *Katorga i ssylka* 33 (1927), pp. 17–18.

[33] "Rech Bardinoi," in Kovalenskii, *Russkaia,* vol. 1, pp. 142–144; Figner, "Protsess 50-ti," p. 16.

[34] "Rech Petra Alekseevicha Alekseeva," in Kovalenskii, *Russkaia,* vol. 1, pp. 145–148; Figner, "Protsess 50-ti," p. 17.

[35] "Rech Petra Alekseevicha Alekseeva," in Kovalenskii, *Russkaia,* vol. 1, p. 148.

[36] Figner, "Protsess 50-ti," p. 17.

[37] Figner, "Protsess 50-ti," p. 18.

[38] "Iz vospominanii Stepniak Kravchinskogo o dele 50-ti," in Kovalenskii, *Russkaia,* vol. 1, p. 157.

[39] Fyodor Dostoevsky, *Diary of a Writer*, trans. Kenneth Lantz (Evanston: Northwestern University Press, 1994), vol. 1, p. 1002.

[40] B. H. Sumner, *Russia and the Balkans* (Oxford: Clarendon Press, 1937), p. 137.

[41] William Fuller, *Strategy and Power in Russia, 1600–1917* (New York: Free Press, 1992), p. 311–317; Dietrich Geyer, *Russian Imperialism* (New Haven: Yale University Press, 1987), pp. 46–47 (p. 47 quoted).

[42] Louise McReynolds, *The News Under Russia's Old Regime: The Development of a Mass-Circulation Press* (Princeton: Princeton University Press, 1991), p. 81.

[43] Edward Thaden, *Conservative Nationalism in Nineteenth-Century Russia* (Seattle: University of Washington Press, 1964); Richard Pipes, "Russian Conservatism in the Second Half of the Nineteenth Century," *Slavic Review* 30, no. 1 (1971), pp. 120–128; David MacKenzie, *The Serbs and Russian Pan-Slavism, 1875–1878* (Ithaca: Cornell University Press, 1967).

[44] Michael Boro Petrovich, *The Emergence of Russian Panslavism, 1856–1870* (Westport, CT: Greenwood Press, 1956), pp. 67–68; Nikolai Danilevskii, "Voina za Bolgariu," in N. Strakhov, ed., *Sbornik politicheskikh i ekonomicheskikh statei* (St. Petersburg: Tipografia Panteleevykh, 1890), p. 44; "Rossiia i Evropa na vostoke," *Russkii Vestnik,* no. 129 (May 1877), p. 146.

[45] Konstantin Leontev, *Against the Current,* trans. George Ivask (New York: Weybright and Talley, 1969), pp. 180–181, 205; Dostoevsky, *Diary of a Writer,* vol. 2, p. 833.

[46] Dostoevsky, *Diary of a Writer,* vol. 2, pp. 931–932; Leontev, *Against the Current,* p. 208.

[47] Quoted in Karel Durman, *The Time of the Thunderer* (Boulder, CO: East European Monographs; New York: Columbia University Press, 1988), p. 200.

[48] McReynolds, *News,* p. 83.

[49] McReynolds, *News,* p. 84.

50. David MacKenzie, "Russian Views of the Eastern Crisis," *East European Quarterly* 13, no. 1 (Spring 1979), p. 1; Durman, *Time,* pp. 187–189; K. Golovin, *Moi vospominaniia,* vol. 1 (St. Petersburg: Tipografia Kolokol, 1908), pp. 304–305; Elizabeth Narishkin-Kurakin, *Under Three Tsars,* trans. Julia Loesser (New York: E. P. Dutton, 1931), pp. 46–47.

51. Richard G. Weeks Jr., "Russia's Decision for War with Turkey, May 1876–April 1877," *East European Quarterly* 24, no. 3 (September 1990), pp. 327–328; David MacKenzie, "Panslavism in Practice: Chernaiev in Serbia (1876)," *Journal of Modern History* 36 (September 1964), p. 290; Sidney Harcave, ed., *Memoirs of Count Witte* (New York: M. E. Sharpe, 1990), pp. 45–46; P. A. Valuev, *Dnevnik, 1877–1884,* ed. V. A. Iakovlev-Bogucharskii and P. E. Shchegolev (Petrograd: Byloe, 1919), p. 8; Dimitrii A. Miliutin, *Dnevnik,* 4 vols. (Moscow: 1950), vol. 2, p. 148.

52. Radzinsky, *Alexander II,* p. 261; "Vnutrennee obozrenie," *Vestnik Evropy* 4 (May 1877), p. 375.

53. Dostoevsky, *Diary of a Writer,* vol. 2, p. 934; Radzinsky, *Alexander II,* p. 262.

54. Radzinsky, *Alexander II,* pp. 263–265.

55. MacKenzie, "Russian Views," p. 8; Valuev, *Dnevnik,* p. 10; Miliutin, *Dnevnik,* vol. 3, p. 80; Radzinsky, *Alexander II,* p. 262.

56. Karpilenko, *"Delo" Very Zasulich,* p. 15; Koni, *Vospominaniia,* pp. 50–51.

57. Koni, *Vospominaniia,* pp. 51–52.

58. "Rech Myshkina," in Kovalenskii, *Russkaia,* vol. 1, p. 194.

59. Wortman, *Development,* p. 280; Iakimova, "Bolshoi protsess," p. 24.

60. Iakimova, "Bolshoi protsess," p. 25; "Iz vospominanii Chudnovskogo," p. 197; "Rech Myshkina: Iz vospominanii E. Breshkovskoi," in Kovalenskii, *Russkaia,* vol. 1, p. 204; Breshkovskaia, *Hidden Springs,* p. 149.

61. "Iz obvinitelnogo akta," in Kovalenskii, *Russkaia,* vol. 1, pp. 163–169; "Iz vosp. E. Breshkovskoi," p. 205.

62. Iakimova, "Bolshoi protsess," p. 25; "Iz vospominanii Chudnovskogo," p. 198.

63. Iakimova, "Bolshoi protsess," p. 26; "Iz vospominanii Chudnovskogo," pp. 198–199; "O dele 193-kh: Iz vospominanii Sineguba," in Kovalenskii, *Russkaia,* vol. 1, p. 217.

64. "Protest podsudimykh i advokatov," in Kovalenskii, *Russkaia,* vol. 1, pp. 178–180; "Iz vosp. E. Breshkovskoi," pp. 208–209.

65. Breshkovskaia, *Hidden Springs,* p. 157.

66. "Iz vosp. E. Breshkovskoi," pp. 202–203; Iakimova, "Bolshoi protsess," p. 27.

67. "Rech Myshkina," pp. 181–182.

68. "Rech Myshkina," pp. 193–194.

69. "Rech Myshkina," pp. 195–196; Iakimova, "Bolshoi protsess," pp. 27–28.

70. Troitskii, *Tsarskie sudy,* pp. 188–189; Iakimova, "Bolshoi protsess," pp. 27–28; N. S. Tagantsev, "Iz perezhitogo," *Byloe* 9 (1918), pp. 137, 145; Breshkovskaia, *Hidden Springs,* p. 159.

71. Iakimova, "Bolshoi protsess," p. 29; Troitskii, *Tsarskie sudy,* pp. 196–197.

72. Troitskii, *Tsarskie sudy*, pp. 196–197.

73. Stepniak, *Underground Russia*, p. 31.

74. Karpov, "V. I. Zasulich," pp. 2–3.

75. Stepniak, *Underground Russia*, pp. 34–35; Iakimova, "Pamiati," p. 184.

76. Karpov, "V. I. Zasulich," p. 3.

77. Debagorii-Mokrievich, *Ot buntarstva*, pp. 376, 381; Zasulich, *Revoliutsionery*, p. 49.

78. Iakimova, "Pamiati," pp. 179–180; Debagorii-Mokrievich, *Ot buntarstva*, p. 375.

79. Iakimova, "Pamiati," pp. 183–184.

80. Iakimova, "Pamiati," p. 184. A discussion of the role of women in revolutionary movements in general and terrorist activities in particular can be found in Sally A. Boneice, "The Spiridonova Case, 1906: Terror, Myth, and Martyrdom," *Kritika* 4, no. 3 (Summer 2003), pp. 583–585.

81. Frolenko, *Zapiski*, p. 102; Popov, "Iz moego," p. 297; Frolenko, "Iz vospominaniia," p. 245.

82. Iakimova, "Pamiati," p. 184; Breshkovskaia, *Hidden Springs*, pp. 154–155.

83. RNB, OR, Dom Plekhanova, f. 1098, op. 1, d. 29, l. 1; RGASPI, f. 262 (Vera Zasulich), op. 1, d. 4, l. 4; Karpov, "V. I. Zasulich," p. 96; Stepniak, *Underground Russia*, pp. 42–43.

84. RGASPI, f. 262 (Vera Zasulich), op. 1, d. 4, l. 4.

85. M. R. Popov, *Zapiski Zemlevoltsa* (Moscow: Izdatel'stvo Politkatorzhan, 1933), pp. 92–94.

10. *The Trial*

1. The following is from Koni, *Vospominaniia*, pp. 59–60.

2. Olga Liubatovich, "Dalekoe i nedavnee," *Byloe* 5 (1906), p. 210, cited in Karpilenko, *Delo*, p. 21.

3. McReynolds, *News*, p. 93; Karpilenko, *Delo*, p. 20.

4. McReynolds, *News*, pp. 85–86; Weeks Jr., "Russia's Decision for War," pp. 308–309, 312.

5. MacKenzie, "Russian Views," pp. 9, 11; Valuev, *Dnevnik*, pp. 19, 22; Koni, *Vospominaniia*, pp. 74–76.

6. Koni, *Vospominaniia*, p. 76.

7. "Pokushenie na zhizn S-Peterburgskogo gradonachalnika F. F. Trepova," *Sankt-Peterburgskie Vedomosti*, no. 25 (January 25, 1878), p. 1; *Golos*, no. 25 (January 25, 1878), p. 3; *Severnyi Vestnik*, no. 27 (January 27, 1878), p. 2; *Moskovskie Vedomosti*, no. 26 (January 27, 1878), p. 2; *Novoe Vremia*, no. 686 (January 25, 1878), p. 2, and no. 687 (January 26, 1878), p. 3; *Nedelia*, no. 5 (January 29, 1878), pp. 174–175.

8. *Severnyi Vestnik*, no. 27, p. 2; "Vystrel v peterburgskogo gradonachalnika," *Nedelia*, no. 5 (January 29, 1878), pp. 174–175; "Khronika," *Novoe Vremia*, no. 687 (January 26, 1878), p. 3; *Sankt-Peterburgskie Vedomosti*, no. 24 (January 24, 1878), p. 1; Koni, *Vospominaniia*, pp. 64–66.

9. GARF, f. 109, Sekretnyi arkhiv, op. 1, d. 718, ll. 2, 3, 10, 19. 31, 33, 37.

¹⁰· "Izvlechenie iz meditsinskogo akta o rane, nanesennoi F. F. Trepovu," *Sankt-Peterburgskie Vedomosti,* nos. 25 (January 25, 1878), 27 (January 27), 28 (January 28); *Severnyi Vestnik,* no. 27 (January 27, 1878), p. 2; *Golos,* nos. 25 (January 25, 1878), 26 (January 26), 27 (January 27).

¹¹· Daly, *Autocracy,* p. 19; Koni, *Vospominaniia,* pp. 64–66; Gertsenshtein, "Tridtsat let," pp. 250–251; GARF, f. 109, Sekretnyi arkhiv, op. 1, d. 718, ll. 19, 37.

¹²· Koni, *Vospominaniia,* p. 64; Gertsenshtein, "Tridtsat let," pp. 237–238; GARF, f. 109, op. 1, d. 718, l. 37.

¹³· Koni, *Vospominaniia,* pp. 76–77; Gertsenshtein, "Tridtsat let," p. 237; "A Semi-Political Trial," *Times* (London), April 22, 1878, p. 8.

¹⁴· Breshkovskaia, *Hidden Springs,* p. 165.

¹⁵· GARF, f. 109, 3-ia eksp., op. 163 (1878), d. 68.1, ll. 27–30.

¹⁶· GARF, f. 109, 3-ia eksp., op. 163 (1878), d. 68.1, l. 1; GARF, f. 109, Sekretnyi arkhiv, op. 1, d. 718, ll. 1–33; GARF, f. 109, 3-ia eksp., op. 163 (1878), d. 68.1, ll. 27–30.

¹⁷· Koni, *Vospominaniia,* pp. 62–63.

¹⁸· Negretov, "K sporam," pp. 183–185.

¹⁹· Quote in Negretov, "K sporam," p. 184.

²⁰· Quote in Negretov, "K sporam," p. 184.

²¹· Koni, *Vospominaniia,* pp. 66–67.

²²· Koni, *Vospominaniia,* pp. 69–71.

²³· Koni, *Vospominaniia,* pp. 89–93.

²⁴· Koni, *Vospominaniia,* p. 96.

²⁵· G. K. Gradovskii in *Golos,* no. 92 (April 2, 1878), p. 2.

²⁶· Descriptions of the crowds are found in G. K. Gradovskii, "Sud po delu Zasulich," in Kovalenskii, *Russkaia,* vol. 2, p. 133; Maxwell, *Narodniki Women,* p. 4; *Moskovskie Vedomosti,* no. 85 (April 2, 1878), p. 3; "Sudebnaia khronika," *Telegraf,* no. 73 (April 1, 1878), p. 1.

²⁷· Gradovskii in *Golos,* p. 2; Karabchevskii, "Delo Very Zasulich," in Kovalenskii, *Russkaia,* vol. 2, p. 128.

²⁸· Gradovskii, "Sud," p. 132; Glagol, "Protsess," pp. 150–151; "Zasedanie 1-ogo otde-leniia peterburgskogo okruzhnogo suda po delu Very Zasulich," *Moskovskie Vedomosti,* no. 86 (April 3, 1878), p. 2; "Sudebnaia khronika," *Telegraf,* no. 73 (April 1, 1878), p. 1.

²⁹· Koni, *Vospominaniia,* p. 96.

³⁰· Descriptions of Vera are found in Gradovskii in *Golos,* p. 2; Naryshkin-Kurakin, *Under Three Tsars,* p. 54; Glagol, "Protsess," p. 151; Gertsenshtein, "Tridtsat let," p. 251; Gradovskii, "Sud," p. 133; and "Delo Very Zasulich," *Nedelia,* no. 15 (April 9, 1878), p. 496.

³¹· Quote in Karabchevskii, "Delo," p. 128; Maxwell, *Narodniki Women,* pp. 3–4.

³²· Koni, *Vospominaniia,* pp. 87–88.

³³· Koni, *Vospominaniia,* pp. 83–84; N. P. Karabchevskii, *Okolo pravosudiia* (Tula: Avtograf, 2001), p. 656.

34. RGIA, f. 1405, op. 534, d. 1141, ll. 4–6; R. Kantor, "K protsessu V. I. Zasulich," *Byloe* 21 (1923), pp. 89, 91.

35. Koni, *Vospominaniia,* pp. 88, 93.

36. Koni, *Vospominaniia,* p. 106.

37. The transcript of the trial is found in Koni, *Vospominaniia,* pp. 97–210. Kessel's case is transcribed on pp. 106–120.

38. N. A. Troitskii, *Advokatura v Rossii i politicheskie protsessy, 1866–1904* (Tula: Avtograf, 2000), p. 71; Glagol, "Protsess," 152.

39. Troitskii, *Advokatura,* p. 71; Gertsenshtein, "Tridtsat let," pp. 252–253; Glagol, "Protsess," p. 152.

40. Ia. G. Zviagintsev and Iu. G. Orlov, *Samye znamenitye iuristy Rossii* (Moscow: Veche, 2003), pp. 12–13.

41. Zviagintsev and Orlov, *Samye,* p. 13

42. Zviagintsev and Orlov, *Samye,* pp. 13–14.

43. Zviagintsev and Orlov, *Samye,* p. 15; "Literaturno-zhiteiskie zametki," *Nedelia,* no. 15 (April 9, 1878), pp. 509–510.

44. Karabchevskii, *Okolo pravosudiia,* p. 658.

45. Troitskii, "Russkaia advokatura," p. 95.

46. Kucherov, *Courts,* p. 214.

47. Troitskii, "Russkaia advokatura," pp. 98–101; Kucherov, *Courts,* p. 213.

48. Troitskii, *Tsarskie sudy,* pp. 102–103; Zviagintsev and Orlov, *Samye,* p. 16.

49. GARF, f. 109, Sekretnyi arkhiv, op. 1, d. 717, ll. 16, 19.

50. Troitskii, *Advokatura,* pp. 71–72; Breshkovskaia, *Hidden Springs,* p. 166.

51. N. Kuliabko-Koretskii, "Moi vstrechi s V. I. Zasulich," in L. Deich, *Gruppa "Osvobozhdenie truda,"* vol. 3, pp. 75–76.

52. Breshkovskaia, *Hidden Springs,* p. 160.

53. "Literaturno-zhiteiskie zametki," *Nedelia,* no. 15 (April 9, 1878), p. 509.

54. Naryshkin-Kurakin, *Under Three Tsars,* p. 55; Gradovskii, "Sud," p. 133.

55. Transcript, in Koni, *Vospominaniia,* pp. 124–126.

56. Transcript, in Koni, *Vospominaniia,* pp. 130–133.

57. Transcript, in Koni, *Vospominaniia,* pp. 135–137.

58. Gradovskii, "Sud," p. 133; Naryshkin-Kurakin, *Under Three Tsars,* p. 55.

59. Transcript, in Koni, *Vospominaniia,* p. 137.

60. Gertsenshtein, "Tridtsat let," p. 253.

61. Transcript in Koni, *Vospominaniia,* pp. 137–138; Gertsenshtein, "Tridtsat let," pp. 252–253.

62. Gradovskii in *Golos,* p. 2.

63. Glagol, "Protsess," p. 151.

64. Transcript, in Koni, *Vospominaniia,* pp. 138–139; Glagol, "Protsess," p. 151.

65. Glagol, "Protsess," p. 151.

66. Transcript, in Koni, *Vospominaniia,* p. 144.

[67] The following is from transcript, in Koni, *Vospominaniia,* pp. 144–160.

[68] Glagol, "Protsess," p. 151; Gertsenshtein, "Tridtsat let," p. 253; Naryshkin-Kurakin, *Under Three Tsars,* p. 55.

[69] Transcript, in Koni, *Vospominaniia,* p. 173.

[70] Glagol, "Protsess," p. 152.

[71] Transcript, in Koni, *Vospominaniia,* pp. 160–169.

[72] Gradovskii, "Sud," p. 134; Gertsenshtein, "Tridtsat let," p. 253.

[73] Transcript, in Koni, *Vospominaniia,* pp. 168–180.

[74] Gradovskii, "Sud," p. 134; Gertsenshtein, "Tridtsat let," pp. 253–254.

[75] Transcript, in Koni, *Vospominaniia,* p. 180.

[76] Transcript, in Koni, *Vospominaniia,* pp. 180–193.

[77] Gradovskii in *Golos,* p. 2; the same sentiments were voiced by Naryshkin-Kurakin in *Under Three Tsars,* p. 55.

[78] Glagol, "Protsess," p. 153.

[79] On the role of judges in the Russian jury trial, see Kucherov, *Courts,* p. 60.

[80] Transcript, in Koni, *Vospominaniia,* pp. 194–210.

[81] RGIA, f. 1405, op. 534, d. 1141, l. 12.

[82] Koni, *Vospominaniia,* pp. 211–214.

[83] This and the following description of the delivery of the verdict rely on Gradovskii, "Sud," pp. 134–135; Gertsenshtein, "Tridtsat let," p. 255; Glagol, "Protsess," pp. 154–155; Koni, *Vospominaniia,* pp. 215–216; and Naryshkin-Kurakin, *Under Three Tsars,* p. 55.

[84] Koni, *Vospominaniia,* p. 216.

[85] Koni, *Vospominaiia,* pp. 216–217.

11. *The Turn to Terror*

[1] *Severnyi Vestnik,* no. 89 (April 1, 1878), cited in Kovalenskii, *Russkaia,* vol. 2, p. 70; Gertsenshtein, "Tridtsat let," p. 255; Gradovskii's memoirs in Kovalenskii, *Russkaia,* vol. 2, pp. 133, 135.

[2] Kovalenskii, *Russkaia,* vol. 2, p. 70; Gertsenshtein, "Tridtsat let," p. 255.

[3] The following is from Koni, *Vospominaniia,* pp. 216–220.

[4] Fedorov, "Iz vospominanii," pp. 90–91.

[5] Fedorov, "Iz vospominanii," p. 91; Breshkovskaia, *Hidden Springs,* p. 166.

[6] Breshkovskaia, *Hidden Springs,* p. 166.

[7] Accounts of what happened to Vera during the demonstrations are found in Kovalenskii, *Russkaia,* vol. 2, pp. 136–137; Glagol, "Protsess," pp. 155–157; and Gertsenshtein, "Tridtsat let," pp. 255–257.

[8] Accounts of the riots and the death of Sidoratskii are found in Gertsenshtein, "Tridtsat let," pp. 255–256; Glagol, "Protsess," pp. 157–158; Kovalenskii, *Russkaia,* p. 137; *Telegraf,* no. 74 (April 2, 1878), p. 4; "Khronika," *Sankt-Peterburgskie Vedomosti,* no. 91 (April 2, 1878), p. 2; "Vnutrennie novosti," *Golos,* no. 93 (April 3, 1878), p. 1; and "Telegrammy," *Moskovskie Vedomosti,* no. 85 (April 2, 1878), p. 3.

9. *Telegraf,* no. 74 (April 2, 1878), p. 4; Tagantsev, "Iz perezhitogo," p. 255; Glagol, "Protsess," pp. 157–158.

10. "Pravitelstvennoe soobshchenie," *Telegraf,* no. 77 (April 6, 1878), p. 4; "Telegrammy," *Sankt-Peterburgskie Vedomosti,* no. 86 (April 3, 1878), p. 1; Gertsenshtein, "Tridtsat let," pp. 256–257.

11. *Sankt-Peterburgskie Vedomosti,* no. 90 (April 1, 1878), p. 1.

12. "Demonstratsiia 31-ogo marta okolo zdaniia suda," *Severnyi Vestnik,* no. 89 (April 1, 1878), p. 1; "Sudebnaia khronika," *Telegraf,* no. 73 (April 1, 1878), p. 1; *Nedelia,* no. 15 (April 9, 1878), p. 476; "Khronika," *Sankt-Peterburgskie Vedomosti,* no. 91 (April 2, 1878), p. 2; "Sudebnaia khronika," *Golos,* no. 92 (April 1, 1878), p. 2.

13. Koni, *Vospominaniia,* p. 228; *Sankt-Peterburgskie Vedomosti,* no. 90 (April 1, 1878), p. 1; *Nedelia,* no. 15 (April 9, 1878), p. 476.

14. *Nedelia,* no. 15 (April 9, 1878), p. 477; *Severnyi Vestnik* quoted in Karpilenko, *Delo,* p. 44; "Sudebnaia khronika," *Golos,* no. 92 (April 1, 1878), p. 2.

15. "Khronika," *Vestnik Evropy* 13, no. 5 (May 1878), pp. 346–347; "Vnutrennee obozrenie," *Otechestvennyie zapiski* 4 (April 1878), p. 314.

16. GARF, f. 109, Sekretnyi arkhiv, op. 1, d. 718, ll. 39, 40, 48, 50, 55.

17. Kovalenskii, *Russkaia,* vol. 2, p. 138.

18. *Nedelia,* no. 15 (April 9, 1878), p. 474.

19. RGIA, f. 1405, op. 535, d. 41, l. 1; Karpilenko, *Delo,* p. 53.

20. Koni, *Vospominaniia,* p. 231.

21. Koni, *Vospominaniia,* p. 231.

22. The following account is from Koni, *Vospominaniia,* pp. 247–261.

23. Naryshkin-Kurakin, *Under Three Tsars,* p. 56; Kantor, "K protsessu," p. 91; Troitskii, *Tsarskie sudy,* p. 218; Koni, *Vospominaniia,* p. 547.

24. Fedorov, "Iz vospominanii," pp. 92–93.

25. Koni, *Vospominaniia,* p. 277

26. Troitskii, *Tsarskie sudy,* p. 105; Koni, *Vospominaniia,* pp. 536n., 537n.

27. Naryshkin-Kurakin, *Under Three Tsars,* p. 56; Kantor, "K protsessu," p. 91; Troitskii, *Tsarskie sudy,* p. 218.

28. RGIA, f. 776, op. 1, d. 14, l. 1; RGIA, f. 776, op. 1, d. 18, l. 22.

29. "K istorii ogranicheniia glasnosti sudoproizvodstva," *Byloe* 4 (1907), p. 23.

30. "Vypiski iz pisem," l. 74.

31. Kantor, "K protsessu," pp. 92–93; GARF f. 109, 3-ia eksp., op. 163 (1878), d. 68.1, ll. 209–211.

32. Durman, *Time of the Thunderer,* p. 8ff; Michael Katkov, *Sobranie peredovykh statei Moskovskikh Vedomostei, 1863–1887* (Moscow: V. Chicherin, 1897–98), for year 1877, pp. 163, 229.

33. Karpilenko, *Delo,* p. 47

34. "Stolichnyie novosti," *Telegraf,* no. 77 (April 6, 1878), p. 3; Karpilenko, *Delo,* p. 48.

[35] Karpilenko, *Delo,* p. 49.

[36] S. M. Stepniak-Kravchinskii, "Smert za smert," in *Grozovaia tucha rossii* (Moscow: Novyi Kliuch, 2001), pp. 13, 14, 17, 20, 21.

[37] "K russkomu obshchestvu," in S. S. Volk, ed., *Revoliutsionnnoe narodnichestvo 70-kh godov XIX veka* (Moscow: Nauka, 1965), vol. 2, p. 53.

[38] "K russkomu" and "Letuchii listok," in Volk, *Revoliutsionnoe,* pp. 53–54, 56.

[39] "Letuchii listok," p. 56; "Boinia 31-ogo marta 1878 goda," *Nachalo,* no. 1, in Kovalenskii, *Russkaia,* vol. 2, p. 142.

[40] "Letuchii listok," p. 56; "Boinia," pp. 140, 142.

[41] "K russkomu," p. 55; "Letuchii listok," p. 57; "Boinia," p. 142.

[42] Zasulich, *Vospominaniia,* pp. 72–73; quote in Meincke, *Zasulich,* p. 335.

[43] Zasulich, *Vospominaniia,* pp. 72–73.

[44] Camus, *The Rebel* (New York: Vintage, 1991), pp. 169–170.

[45] Stepniak, *Underground Russia,* pp. 65–66; the subsequent story continues in Zasulich, *Vospominaniia,* pp. 73–75.

[46] Zasulich, *Vospominaniia,* p. 85; Lev Deich, *S. M. Kravchinskii* (Petrograd: Gosudarstvennoe izdatelstvo, 1919), p. 9.

[47] Zasulich, *Vospominaniia,* pp. 85–86; Deich, *Kravchinskii,* p. 7.

[48] Zasulich, *Vospominaniia,* p. 86; Deich, *Kravchinskii,* p. 7.

[49] Zasulich, *Vospominaniia,* p. 82.

[50] Deich, *Kravchinskii,* pp. 24–25.

[51] Deich, *Kravchinskii,* p. 10.

[52] Deich, *Kravchinskii,* pp. 19–20.

[53] Deich, *Kravchinskii,* pp. 26–27.

[54] Stepniak, "Smert," in *Grozovaia,* pp. 17–18.

[55] Ulam, *Prophets,* pp. 281, 283; Deborah Hardy, *Land and Freedom: The Origins of Russian Terrorism, 1876–1879* (New York: Greenwood Press, 1987), p. 62.

[56] Ulam, *Prophets,* p. 280.

[57] Hardy, *Land,* pp. 80–81; Ulam, *Prophets,* p. 291 (quoted).

[58] Hardy, *Land,* pp. 82–83.

[59] "Mikhailov, A. F.," in *Deiateli,* p. 267.

[60] "Ustav organizatsii," in Volk, *Revoliutsionnoe,* p. 35.

[61] Hardy, *Land,* pp. 84–85.

[62] Deich, *Kravchinskii,* p. 28.

[63] Ulam, *Prophets,* pp. 307, 311; "Ubiistvo shpiona Reinshteina," in *Listok Zemli i Voli* (March 12, 1879), in B. Bazilevskii, *Revoliutsionnaia zhurnalistika semidesiatykh godov* (Rostov na Donu: Donskaia Rech, n.d.), p. 278.

[64] Ulam, *Prophets,* p. 313; Hardy, *Land,* p. 84.

[65] Hardy, *Land,* pp. 91–92, 94.

[66] Hardy, *Land,* pp. 88–89.

[67] Radzinsky, *Alexander II,* pp. 292–293; Hardy, *Land,* p. 95.

[68.] Radzinsky, *Alexander II*, pp. 295–296 (p. 295 quoted).

[69.] Stepniak, *Underground Russia*, pp. 42–45.

[70.] Stepniak, *Underground Russia*, pp. 42–43.

[71.] "Iakimova, Anna Vasilievna," in *Deiateli*, p. 638.

[72.] Stepniak, *Underground Russia*, p. 53; "Pribylev, Aleksandr Vasilievich," in *Deiateli*, p. 356.

[73.] M. F. Frolenko, "Lipetskii i Voronezhskii s'ezdy," in V. N. Ginev et al., *"Narodnaia Volia" i "Chernyi Peredel": Vospominaniia uchastnikov revoliutsionnogo dvizheniia v Peterburge v 1879–1882 gg.* (Leningrad: Lenizdat, 1989), p. 68; "Kornilova-Moroz, Aleksandra Ivanovna," "Figner, Vera Nikolaevna," and "Pribylev, Aleksandr Vasilievich," in *Deiateli*, pp. 222, 467, 356.

[74.] R. M. Plekhanova, "Stranitsa iz vospominanii o V. I. Zasulich," *Gruppa "Osvobozhdenie truda,"* p. 83; Fedorchenko, "Vera Zasulich," p. 198; "Salova, Neonila Mikhailovna," in *Deiateli*, p. 401; *Literatura sotsialno-revoliutsionnoi partii "Narodnoi voli"* (Tipografia partii Sotsialistov-Revoliutsionerov, 1905), p. 99; "Figner, Vera Nikolaevna," in *Deiateli*, p. 535; Deich, "Osinskii," p. 27.

[75.] Frolenko, "Lipetskii," pp. 58–60.

[76.] Meincke, *Zasulich*, p. 346.

[77.] *Literatura . . . "Narodnoi voli,"* pp. 162–166.

[78.] *Literatura . . . "Narodnoi voli,"* p. 9.

[79.] *Literatura . . . "Narodnoi voli,"* p. 166.

[80.] Vera Figner, *Zapechatlennyi trud* (Moscow: Mysl, 1964), vol. 1, pp. 206–207.

[81.] *Literatura . . . "Narodnoi voli,"* p. 287.

[82.] Figner, *Zapechatlennyi*, vol. 1, p. 179.

[83.] Ulam, *Prophets*, p. 340; Radzinsky, *Alexander II*, pp. 333–334.

[84.] Figner, *Zapechatlennyi*, pp. 248–252.

[85.] Figner, *Zapechatlennyi*, pp. 253–254; Pomper, *Nechaev*, pp. 198–199.

[86.] E. A. Serebriakov, "Revoliutsionery vo flote," in Ginev et al., *"Narodnaia Volia,"* p. 207; Figner, *Zapechatlennyi*, vol. 1, p. 252.

[87.] David Footman, *Red Prelude: The Life of the Russian Terrorist Zhelyabov* (New Haven: Yale University Press, 1945), pp. 193–194; Figner, *Zapechatlennyi*, vol. 1, pp. 262–266.

[88.] Footman, *Red Prelude*, pp. 197–198.

[89.] Footman, *Red Prelude*, pp. 182–183.

[90.] Radzinsky, *Alexander II*, p. 423.

[91.] Footman, *Red Prelude*, p. 224.

[92.] Figner, *Zapechatlennyi*, vol. 1, pp. 379–382; "Rech Ovchinnikova," *Literatura . . . "Narodnoi voli,"* p. 14; Footman, *Red Prelude*, p. 219; "Vittenberg," *Literatura . . . "Narodnoi voli,"* p. 11.

[93.] *Literatura . . . "Narodnoi voli,"* p. 534.

[94.] Stepniak, *Underground Russia*, p. 139.

12. Nihilists Abroad

1. The following is taken from Zasulich, *Vospominaniia*, pp. 78–80.

2. G. Valbert (Victor Cherbuliz), "Procès de Vera Zassoulitch," *Revue des Deux Mondes*, May 1, 1878.

3. A description of the events leading up to the Congress is found in Misha Glenny, *The Balkans: Nationalism, War and the Great Powers, 1804–1999* (New York: Penguin, 2001), pp. 132–143.

4. "Acquittement de Vera Sassoulitch," *Le Temps*, April 18, 1878, p. 2.

5. "The Trial and Acquittal of the Girl Who Shot General Trepov," *Chicago Daily Tribune*, May 8, 1878, p. 1; *Standard*, April 15, 1878, p. 4; *Morning Post*, May 23, 1878, p. 3; "A Propos de Vera Zassoulitch," *La Presse*, April 24, 1878, p. 1; "A Political Murder in Russia," *New York Times*, July 7, 1878, p. 8.

6. "Vera Sassulitch," *Chicago Daily Tribune*, May 12, 1878, p. 4; "Acquittement de Vera Sassoulitch," *La Presse*, April 20, 1878, p. 2; "Revolution in Russia," *Graphic*, April 27, 1878, p. 406; *Standard*, April 15, 1878, p. 5; "A Semi-Political Trial," *Times*, (London), April 22, 1878, p. 8.

7. "Trial and Acquittal," *Chicago Daily Tribune*, p. 1; *Graphic*, May 4, 1878, p. 440; *Le Monde Illustré*, May 9, 1878, p. 292.

8. "Vera Sassulitch," *Chicago Daily Tribune*, p. 4; "Nihilism in the Russian Empire," *New York Times*, April 19, 1878, p. 1; "Acquittement de Vera Sassoulitch," *La Presse*, p. 2; Valbert, "Procès," p. 220.

9. *Times* (London), April 15, 1878, p. 5; "Seeds of War in Europe," *New York Times*, August 31, 1878, p. 10; "L'acquittement de Véra Zassoulitch," *Le Monde Illustré*, May 9, 1878, p. 287.

10. "A Russian Chief of Police: The True Story of the St. Petersburg Affair," *New York Times*, May 11, 1878, p. 5.

11. "L'affaire Vera Zassoulitch," *La Presse*, April 24, 1878, p. 3; "L'acquittement de Véra Zassoulitch," *Le Monde Illustré*, p. 286; Kropotkin, *Memoirs*, p. 388; "Parizhskaia zhizn," *Sankt-Peterburgskie Vedomosti*, no. 109 (April 22, 1878), p. 1.

12. *Morning Post*, April 25, 1878, p. 4; "Vera Sassulitch," *Chicago Daily Tribune*, p. 4; *Nation*, May 9, 1878, p. 301; "Vera Zassoulitch," *Le Bien Public*, April 20, 1878, p. 1.

13. *Morning Post*, April 25, 1878, p. 4; "Nihilism in Russia," *Times* (London), April 24, 1878, p. 3.

14. "Vera Zassoulitch," *Le Bien Public*, p. 1; "Nihilism in Russia," *Times* (London), p. 3; *Morning Post*, April 26, 1878, p. 4; "Nihilism in the Russian Empire," *New York Times*, p. 1; "A Warning to Absolutism," *Washington Post*, April 19, 1878, p. 1; "Vera Sassulitch," *Chicago Daily Tribune*, p. 4; "Acquittement de Vera Sassoulitch," *La Presse*, p. 2; *Allgemeine Zeitung*, April 17, 1878, p. 1584.

15. "Vera Zassoulitch," *Le Bien Public*, p. 1; "A Propos de Vera Zassoulitch," *La Presse*, p. 1; *Morning Post*, April 25, 1878, p. 4; Valbert, "Procès," p. 226.

[16.] "Nihilism in the Russian Empire," *New York Times*, p. 1; "A Warning to Absolutism," *Washington Post*, p. 1; *Standard,* April 15, 1878, p. 4.

[17.] Quote in Marie Fleming, *The Anarchist Way to Socialism: Elisée Reclus and Nineteenth-Century European Anarchism* (London: Croom Helm, 1979), p. 176.

[18.] Andrew R. Carlson, *Anarchism in Germany* (Metuchen, NJ: Scarecrow Press, 1972), vol. 1, p. 115.

[19.] *Allgemeine Zeitung,* May 16, 1878, p. 1996.

[20.] Carlson, *Anarchism,* p. 139–140.

[21.] Carlson, *Anarchism,* p. 158.

[22.] Carlson, *Anarchism,* p. 144; "Politicians and Players," *New York Times,* June 10, 1878, p. 1.

[23.] Article in *Zemlia i Volia* (December 15, 1878), reported in Bazilevskii, *Revoliutsionnaia,* pp. 103, 107.

[24.] Martin Miller, "Introduction," in P. A. Kropotkin, *Selected Writings on Anarchism and Revolution,* Martin A. Miller, ed. (Cambridge: MIT Press, 1970), pp. 6–7, 22–23; Steven G. Marks, *How Russia Shaped the Modern World: From Art to Anti-Semitism, Ballet to Bolshevism* (Princeton: Princeton University Press, 2003), pp. 38–57.

[25.] Kropotkin, *Memoirs,* pp. 387–388; Caroline Cahm, *Kropotkin and the Rise of Revolutionary Anarchism, 1872–1886* (Cambridge: Cambridge University Press, 1989), p. 109.

[26.] Vera's visit to Reclus is mentioned in her letter to A. N. Malinovska in E. Korolchuk, "Iz perepiski V. I. Zasulich," in Nevskii, *Istoriko-revoliutsionnyi sbornik,* p. 340; quote from Fleming, *Anarchist,* p. 171.

[27.] Fleming, *Anarchist,* p. 172; Carlson, *Anarchism,* p. 250; Kropotkin, "The Spirit of Revolt," in Peter Kropotkin, *Words of a Rebel,* trans. George Woodcock (Montreal: Black Rose Books, 1992), p. 186.

[28.] Fleming, *Anarchist,* pp. 171–172; Carslon, *Anarchism,* pp. 249–250; quote from Miller, "Introduction," in Kropotkin, *Selected Writings,* p. 20n.

[29.] Carlson, *Anarchism,* pp. 251–252.

[30.] Quote from Miller, "Introduction," in Kropotkin, *Selected Writings,* p. 20; Kropotkin, "Spirit of Revolt," p. 188.

[31.] Marie Fleming, "Propaganda by the Deed," in Yonah Alexander and Kenneth Myers, eds., *Terrorism in Europe* (London: Croom Helm, 1982), pp. 13–14.

[32.] Cahm, *Kropotkin,* pp. 123, 142; Kropotkin, "Spirit," p. 191.

[33.] Cahm, *Kropotkin,* p. 123.

[34.] Elisée Reclus, *An Anarchist on Anarchy* (Boston: Tucker, 1884), pp. 1–3, 22.

[35.] Fleming, *Anarchist,* p. 174.

[36.] Fleming, *Anarchist,* p. 174; "The Trial of Socialists," *Times* (London), January 10, 1883, p. 5.

[37.] Quoted in Miller, *Kropotkin,* p. 161; "The Trial of Socialists," *Times* (London), p. 5.

[38.] Frederic Trautmann, *The Voice of Terror: A Biography of Johann Most* (Westport, CT: Greenwood Press, 1980), pp. 4–6.

[39] Trautmann, *Voice*, pp. 4–8; quote from Paul Avrich, *The Haymarket Tragedy* (Princeton: Princeton University Press, 1984), p. 63.

[40] Carlson, *Anarchism*, pp. 181–182.

[41] Trautmann, *Voice*, p. 4; Carlson, *Anarchism*, p. 254.

[42] Avrich, *Haymarket*, p. 171; Trautmann, *Voice*, pp. 41, 44; Carlson, *Anarchism*, p. 192.

[43] Trautmann, *Voice*, pp. 52–53.

[44] Trautmann, *Voice*, pp. 54–55.

[45] Trautmann, *Voice*, pp. 68–69, 72.

[46] Avrich, *Haymarket*, p. 164.

[47] The classic accounts of the case are Avrich, *Haymarket*, and James Green, *Death in the Haymarket* (New York: Pantheon, 2006).

[48] Trautmann, *Voice*, pp. 138–139; Marks, *How Russia*, p. 15.

[49] Avrich, *Haymarket*, pp. 135, 138, 171; Trautmann, *Voice*, p. 92.

[50] Marks, *How Russia*, p. 17; H. C. G. Matthew, ed., *The Gladstone Diaries*, vol. 3, *1892–1896* (Oxford: Oxford University Press, 1994), p. 336.

[51] "The Secret of Nihilism," *Nation*, no. 767 (March 11, 1880), p. 189; "The Head-Quarters of Nihilism," *Times* (London), March 22, 1881, p. 8; "Russian Destroying Angels," *New York Times*, June 27, 1881, p. 3.

[52] Deich, *Kravchinskii*, pp. 38–39; James W. Hulse, *Revolutionists in London: A Study of Five Unorthodox Socialists* (Oxford: Clarendon Press, 1970), pp. 30, 33, 34.

[53] Stepniak, *Underground Russia*, pp. 11, 35–37.

[54] Stepniak, *Underground Russia*, pp. 18, 26, 12–13.

[55] Stepniak, *Underground Russia*, pp. 41–44.

[56] Stepniak, *Underground Russia*, pp. 116–117, 126–127.

[57] Stepniak, *Underground Russia*, pp. 118–119.

[58] Stepniak, *Underground Russia*, pp. 120–121, 122.

[59] Hulse, *Revolutionists*, pp. 29–30.

[60] Lanoe Falconer (Mary Hawker), *Mademoiselle Ixe* (New York: Mershon, 1891), pp. 7–8, 17, 36–37, 152–154, 161; Vernon Lee, *Miss Brown: A Novel* (London: William Blackwood and Sons, 1884), pp. 293–299. These and the other novels discussed here are treated in Barbara Arnett Melchiori, *Terrorism in the Late Victorian Novel* (London: Croom Helm, 1985). Unfortunately, Melchiori did not seem to be aware of the case of Vera Zasulich or its potential impact on the novels.

[61] Arthur Ropes and Mary Ropes, *On Peter's Island* (New York: C. Scribner's Sons, 1901), pp. 82–94, 160, 323–324.

[62] Norbert Kohl, *Oscar Wilde: The Works of a Conformist Rebel*, trans. David Henry Wilson (Cambridge: Cambridge University Press, 1980), pp. 21, 34–35. The subsequent analysis is based on Oscar Wilde, *Vera or the Nihilists* (London: Methuen, 1927), pp. 9–14, 21, 35–36, 72, 135–136.

[63] Kohl, *Wilde*, pp. 35–36.

64. Henry James, *Novels, 1886–1890* (New York: Literary Classics of the United States, 1989), pp. 143–158, 284–306. See also Taylor Stoehr, "Words and Deeds in *The Princess Casamassima*," *ELH* 37, no. 1 (March 1970), pp. 95–135, especially pp. 117–135; and W. H. Tilley, "The Background of *The Princess Casamassima*," University of Florida Monographs, no. 5 (Fall 1960).

65. See Marks, *How Russia*, p. 22; Sir Arthur Conan Doyle, *The Complete Sherlock Holmes* (New York: Garden City Publishing, 1930), pp. 607–621.

66. Schapiro, *Turgenev*, pp. 263–273; Tilley, "Background," pp. 3–5.

67. The similarities between Vera and Marianna are discussed in Bergman, *Zasulich*, p. 55fn; "Lettres de Russie," *Le Temps*, April 27, 1878, p. 2; and Valbert, "Procès," quote on p. 220. Descriptions of Marianna in Ivan Turgenieff, *Virgin Soil* (London: Ward, Lock, n.d.), pp. 37–38, quote on pp. 94–95. "The Threshold" is published in Ivan Turgenev, *Poems in Prose* (London: Drummond, 1995), pp. 64–65.

68. Stepniak, *Underground Russia*, p. 122.

69. "Civil Plots in Russia," *New York Times*, May 5, 1878, p. 1; "Current Foreign Topics," *New York Times*, June 10, 1878, p. 1; "Miscellaneous Foreign Notes," *New York Times*, July 9, 1878, p. 1; *Le Temps*, July 27, 1878, p. 3; *Le Temps*, August 30, 1878, p. 4; "Les Arrestations en Russie," *Le Bien Public*, May 7, 1878, p. 1; *Le Bien Public*, April 30, 1878, p. 1.

70. "Trepoff the Terrible," *New York Times*, December 26, 1889, p. 4; "Obituary," *Times* (London), December 14, 1889, p. 6; "M. Trepoff Shot. A Friend of the Allies," *Times* (London), October 10, 1918, p. 5.

71. "The Liberator Tsar," *New York Times*, March 14, 1881, p. 1; "Alexander II," *Times* (London), March 14, 1881, p. 10; "The Cause of Colonel Soudaikin's Murder," *Times* (London), January 29, 1884, p. 5; "Russian Destroying Angels," *New York Times*, June 27, 1881, p. 3.

72. Koretskii, "Moi vstrechi," pp. 70–71; "Vera Zasulich: Iz vospominanii Anri Roshfora," in Kovalenskii, *Russkaia*, vol. 2, pp. 148–150.

73. Zasulich, *Vospominaniia*, p. 77–78.

74. Korolchuk, "Iz perepiski," p. 342.

75. Korolchuk, "Iz perepiski," p. 338.

76. Korolchuk, "Iz perepiski," p. 346.

77. Liubatovich, "Dalekoe," p. 235; Stepniak, *Underground Russia*, p. 119.

78. Liubatovich, "Dalekoe," p. 241; Korolchuk, "Iz perepiski," p. 348.

79. Korolchuk, "Iz perepiski," p. 349.

80. Liubatovich, "Dalekoe," pp. 241–245.

81. Lev Deich, "Vera Ivanovna Zasulich," in Zasulich, *Revoliutsionery*, pp. 10–11.

82. Quoted in Maxwell, *Narodniki*, p. 42.

83. Zasulich, *Revoliutsionery*, pp. 48–49; "Vera Zasulich o terrore (1901g)," in Kovalenskii, *Russkaia*, vol. 2, pp. 151, 153.

84. RGASPI, f. 262, op. 1, d. 4, ll. 1, 4, 5.

85. Zasulich, *Revoliutsionery*, p. 48; Bergman, *Zasulich*, p. 78.

Epilogue

1. Meinecke, *Zasulich*, pp. 355–356. For this particular chapter I am indebted to the works of three of Zasulich's biographers, Evelyn Meinecke, Jay Bergman, and Margaret Maxwell. Meinecke's work contains the most detailed information on Vera's later life.

2. A. Brailovskii, "V. I. Zasulich," *Zaria*, no. 1 (April 15, 1922), p. 13; Fedorchenko, "Vera Zasulich," p. 198; Bergman, *Zasulich*, p. 164.

3. V. Zasulich, "Pisma k L. Deichu," in Deich, *Gruppa "Osvobozhdenie truda,"* vol. 4, p. 241.

4. Fedorchenko, "Zasulich," p. 200; V. Veresaev, *Vospominaniia* (Moscow: Gosudarstvennoe izdatelstvo, 1938), pp. 391–392; Deich, "Vera Ivanovna Zasulich," in Zasulich, *Revoliutsionery*, p. 12; quote from Leopold Haimson, *The Making of Three Russian Revolutionaries: Voices from the Menshevik Past* (Cambridge: Cambridge University Press, 1987), p. 110.

5. Bergman, *Zasulich*, pp. 116–117, 150–151.

6. V. I. Zasulich and K. Marks, "Pismo k Marksu i ego otvet," in Deich, *Gruppa "Osvobozhdenie truda,"* vol. 2, pp. 221–224; Meinecke, *Zasulich*, pp. 368–369; Bergman, *Zasulich*, p. 78.

7. Bergman, *Zasulich*, pp. 88–89.

8. Zasulich, *Revoliutsionery*, pp. 49, 59; Bergman, *Zasulich*, p. 99.

9. Meinecke, *Zasulich*, pp. 507–508, 536 (quoted).

10. Bergman, *Zasulich*, pp. 180–181; Valentinov, *Encounters*, p. 43; Meinecke, *Zasulich*, pp. 536–538.

11. Bergman, *Zasulich*, pp. 190–191.

12. Meinecke, *Zasulich*, pp. 562–567, 573; Bergman, *Zasulich*, pp. 191–192.

13. Bergman, *Zasulich*, pp. 210–211; Meinecke, *Zasulich*, pp. 587–591, 599–600.

14. RNB, OR, f. 1098, op. 1, d. 87, l. 1; RNB, OR, f. 1097, op. 1, d. 654, l. 18.

15. RNB, OR, f. 1097, op. 1, d. 637, l. 1; RNB, OR, f. 1098, op. 1, d. 213, ll. 1–3.

16. "Vera Sassulitch, Nihilist," *New York Times*, July 20, 1921, p. 12.

17. Quoted in Joseph Frank, *Dostoevsky: The Mantle of the Prophet, 1871–1881* (Princeton: Princeton University Press, 2002), p. 727.

18. Fyodor Dostoevsky, *The Brothers Karamazov* (New York: Modern Library, 1996), pp. 749–750, 751, 824, 849; see also Frank, *Dostoevsky: Mantle*, p. 695.

19. Frank, *Dostoevsky: Mantle*, pp. 726–727.

20. Dostoevsky, *Brothers,* pp. 292, 879–880.

21. Frank, *Dostoevsky: Mantle*, p. 712. An alternative scenario, mostly hypothesizing a kind of psychological breakdown, is found in J. L. Rice, "Dostoevsky's Endgame: The Projected Sequel to *The Brothers Karamazov,*" *Russian History* 33, no. 1 (2006), pp. 45–62.

22. Camus, *Rebel*, pp. 170–174, 164, 169–170, 166.

23. Zasulich, *Vospominaniia*, p. 15.

Index